TERROR IN BLACK SEPTEMBER

The First Eyewitness Account of the Infamous
1970 Hijackings

David Raab

palgrave
macmillan

TERROR IN BLACK SEPTEMBER

First published in 2007 by
PALGRAVE MACMILLAN™
175 Fifth Avenue, New York, N.Y. 10010 and
Houndmills, Basingstoke, Hampshire, England RG21 6XS
Companies and representatives throughout the world.

PALGRAVE MACMILLAN is the global academic imprint of the Palgrave Macmillan division of St. Martin's Press, LLC and of Palgrave Macmillan Ltd. Macmillan® is a registered trademark in the United States, United Kingdom and other countries. Palgrave is a registered trademark in the European Union and other countries.

ISBN-13: 978–1–4039–8420–3
ISBN-10: 1–4039–8420–4

Library of Congress Cataloging-in-Publication Data is available from the Library of Congress.

A catalogue record for this book is available from the British Library.

Design by Newgen Imaging Systems (P) Ltd., Chennai, India.

First edition: September 2007

10 9 8 7 6 5 4 3 2 1

Printed in the United States of America.

CONTENTS

Photosection appears between pages 130 and 131.

Acknowledgments vi
Author's Note viii

Aboard a Plane in the Jordanian Desert 1
September 11, 1970

"We Are All *Fedayeen*" 3
Summer 1970

"This Is Your New Captain Speaking." 9
Sunday, September 6

"Am I Leaving One Orphan or Two?" 28
Monday, September 7

"We May Have to Face a Tragedy" 48
Tuesday, September 8

Misery Loves Company 63
Wednesday, September 9

"They Forced Me into the Grave" 78
Thursday, September 10

Chaos, Confusion, and "Fantastic Tension" 91
Friday, September 11

Explosions in the Desert 104
Saturday, September 12

My Family Is Freed 116
Sunday, September 13

Negotiations at a Standstill 125
Monday, September 14

"I Just Want to Be Near My Daughter" 131
Tuesday, September 15

The Eve of War 142
Wednesday, September 16

"A Little Excitement" 149
Thursday, September 17

An Extremely Close Call 161
Friday, September 18

Hussein's Momentary Edge 168
Saturday, September 19

Our Fate in the Balance 174
Sunday, September 20

A Desperate Situation 184
Monday, September 21

Poised to Intervene 191
Tuesday, September 22

Switzerland and Germany Cave 198
Wednesday, September 23

What About the Hostages? 203
Thursday, September 24

European Hostages Rescued 207
Friday, September 25

Our Perilous Walk to Freedom 212
Saturday, September 26

Six Missing Hostages 218
Sunday, September 27

Nixon and Home 222
Monday, September 28

Last Six Finally Free 227
Tuesday, September 29

European Capitulation and Culmination 230
Wednesday, September 30

Epilogue 233

Notes 235

Bibliography and Sources 260

Index 266

To Leah:
Always at my side,
Even when I am far away.

For David: The Lord is my light and my salvation; whom shall I fear?
The Lord is my life's fortress; of whom shall I be afraid?
When evil-doers came upon me to eat my flesh, they—my adversaries and foes—stumbled and fell.
Though a host should encamp against me, my heart shall not fear;
Though war should rise up against me, in my faith I trust.
(Psalm 27)

ACKNOWLEDGMENTS

Without three dear, heaven-sent friends, this book would simply not have been written. Marilyn Henry encouraged me to first embark on this emotional yet fascinating journey and has been my personal fan club and literary adviser. Dr. Josh Teitelbaum was my informal academic adviser, introducing me to both research resources and academicians who further facilitated my way. Joe Mark renewed my self-confidence and provided the framework for me to live my dream and write this book. To each, I owe a debt of gratitude that I doubt I will ever be able to repay.

So many other people helped me along the way, and I wish to thank some of them here, if ever so briefly. First, my thanks to Professor Barry Rubin for helping me find the right home for this book. My thanks also go to Dr. Michael Oren and Dr. Baker al-Majali for helping me invaluably with my research in Jordan, and to the Jordanian Arab Army for its escort, information, and hospitality while I was there. Richard Amdur, Knesset member Colette Avital, Kate Carter, Dr. Leonard Cole, Dr. Moshe Fried, Rabbi Menachem Genack, Rabbi Meir Goldwicht, Martin J. Gross, Michael Hunter, Eli Jacobs, Yoram Katan, Dr. Mordechai Kedar, Christopher Little, Sylvia McKean, Dr. Musa Keilani, Martin Mensch, Fouad al-Nimer, my father, Rabbi Menachem Raab, Rebecca Raab, Dr. Yaron Raab, Abraham Rabinovich, Avi Raz, Dr. Robert Satloff, Dominic Sutherland, Yohanan Tzoreff, and Knesset member Abu Vilan and his aide, Paz Cohen—each helped me at critical junctures in this juggernaut. And, of course, my thanks to so many other friends and relatives who helped and continue to help me in so many ways. You know who you are (if you don't, ask me and I will tell you), and I thank you so very much for your friendship.

I want to thank my interviewees who shared their time and memories and those who shared their written accounts—their recollections were invaluable in helping me complete the picture. Special thanks to my mother, Sara Raab, Jim Majer, and Sarah (Malka) Bliner who, in addition, encouraged and trusted me to tell our story. I am grateful to the Jordanians I met with, all of whom showed me warmth and hospitality. Their personal pangs of shame, anger, and sorrow over my prior bitter experience in their country were palpable and appreciated.

Numerous archivists and historians helped me get at the material I needed for this book: Sally Kuisel, U.S. State Department Archives; Pat Anderson and Sam Rushay, Nixon Presidential Materials Library; Michal Saft, Israel State Archives; Dorit Paret and Marion Gliksberg, Moshe Dayan Center Library, Tel Aviv University; Helen Glass, Foreign and Commonwealth Office Information Management Department; Charlotte Berry, Exeter University; Lt. Col. Ali Nazzal al-Sirhan, Jordan Army Military Archives; Zana Allen, TWA historian. The richness of this story owes much to the material that they helped me locate.

I cannot thank enough my sister, Tikva, and Larry Yudkowitz and their family—at whose dining room table much of this book was written—for their welcoming and unstinting hospitality through my frequent and often extended stays, and my brother, Dr. Moshe Raab, for his always-cheerful, always-available technological support.

I am grateful also to my editor Alessandra Bastagli and her colleagues at Palgrave Macmillan for believing in me and this story and for making this book a reality.

A belated thank you to the millions of people in the United States, Israel, and around the world who prayed for our safe release. Your prayers made the difference.

Finally and most importantly, my gratitude to my dear wife, Leah, who nurtures me and encourages me in all my avocational endeavors, regardless of the emotional energy and time away from her that they demand. To her I dedicate this book.

I wish to pay tribute to all of the victims of Palestinian terror the week of September 6, 1970, and to their families for the ordeal that each endured; in particular, to my mother and my siblings—all hijacked with me—and to my father, who suffered alone at home; and, to the thirty-one men and women—Frank Allen, Miriam (Mimi) Beeber, William Burmeister, Thomas Burnett, Lennett Cain, Fran (Foozie) Chesler, Bruriah David, Rabbi Jonathan David, Rabbi Yaakov Drillman, George Falldine, Ben Feinstein, George Freda, Meir Fund, Ken Hubler, Rabbi Isaac Hutner, Dr. Pradash Kadaba, Al Kiburis, William Koster, Jim Majer, Sarah Malka, Mitchell Meltzer, Barbara Mensch, David Miller, Russell Morris, Richard Morse, Jeffrey Newton, Robert Palagonia, Walter Ridenhour, Mark Shain, Derrell Suttles, and Carroll D. Woods—with whom I sat through the harrowing Jordanian civil war in a three-room apartment in Amman. What we survived can now be understood and remembered.

AUTHOR'S NOTE

Shortly after my release as a seventeen-year-old hostage, I recorded my recollections of the ordeal. The italicized segments throughout this book are excerpts from my records, mildly edited for readability. Oral testimonies of others are similarly edited.

This book is fully documented, relying on recently opened archives in Washington, London, and Jerusalem, published material, contemporaneous accounts, and selected recent interviews. Due to space considerations, much additional research material has been omitted but can be easily accessed at www.terrorinblackseptember.com. The entire narrative of our hostage story is consistent with my recollections; I have thus not cited my own recollections as a source.

American spelling is adopted throughout, even when quoting British sources. Translations from Hebrew sources are my own. For simplicity, "German" is used instead of "West German."

ABOARD A PLANE IN THE JORDANIAN DESERT

SEPTEMBER 11, 1970

Two-thirty AM. Nearly a hundred people were asleep: some upright in their seats, some sprawled out over a few chairs, and some laid out on the floor between two rows. It was dark all around except up front and in back, where two gas lamps were making a constant hiss and giving off a bright but sinister light. It was deathly still inside the plane except for an occasional sigh of anguish, subconsciously made by a sleeping person after almost a week of constant tension.

Suddenly, a flashlight was shining in my face. I looked up and saw the copilot, Jim Majer, standing over me. His eyes were elongated from lack of sleep. The beginnings of a blond beard could be seen on his tanned face. His hair was a mess because he had run his fingers through it many times over the past few days. He had a sad look about him. He had had to bear much more than the rest of the passengers because he was a member of the crew and had to look out not only for his own good, but also for the good of all the other people on board. Now he was forced to be the bearer of bad news.

"David, they want you up front . . . for questioning."

Petrified, I quickly came to my senses, even though I had just been awakened in the middle of my first decent night's sleep in a week. Immediately, I smelled the foul odors emanating from the hundred human beings who had been living unwashed in these confines for five days, odors that were intensified daily by the heat of the desert and the increasing stench of the plugged-up toilets.

What was a plane doing in the middle of a desert, and what were a hundred people, including me, doing living there? Arab guerrillas had decided to bring this about by hijacking the plane I was on. And now some of these guerrillas wanted me . . . for "questioning."

I looked pleadingly at Jim, wanting to ignore what he had just said, but knowing that I had no choice but to obey. His answer to me was a look of sympathy that said that he didn't want to have to tell me to go and he didn't want me to go, but that he, too, had to do what he was told.

I got up and put on my shirt, socks, and shoes, for I had been sleeping in just a pair of short pants and an undershirt.

I thought to myself that it would be better not to think of what might be in store for me. But I knew I would be taken off the plane in a few minutes, never to see it again. What about my mother, three brothers, and sister who were also on the plane, my father at home nervously wondering and waiting? When would I see them all again? I tried to force these thoughts out of my mind.

My mother, who was sitting a few rows in back of me, saw me while I was shuffling around, looking for my shoes under the seats, and instinctively knew what was going on. She came over to me. Her face showed the surprise, sorrow, uncertainty, and fear that she was feeling—when would she see her son again? Though this was probably the saddest moment of our lives, we shed no tears. Crying would only make us feel worse and would probably wake up someone, robbing him of some well-deserved sleep. There was a mutual understanding between us—thank you for being so close to me for seventeen years, be brave, do the best you can, and try to survive. Hopefully, we'll be together again.

I started walking up the aisle with my mother close behind. I began to shake. I had lost control over my muscles and was twitching violently all over. But I continued walking. The Arabs would not take this as an excuse for my not getting off the plane. One of the men who had been summoned, and who felt equally as bad as I, saw my condition and put his arm around my shoulder, bringing me close to him and thereby stopping my shaking.

We were then told to get off the plane. I turned around and looked at my mother with pleading eyes, and she looked at me with sympathetic ones. We condensed into a short moment the lifetime that we deserved to have as mother and child.

Unable to hold back the tears much longer, I left the plane, slowly descending the ladder from the door of the plane, onto a jeep, and then onto the desert floor. I had a feeling of emptiness—I was being taken away from my family to a place that I didn't know anything about. I had no one to console me except nine other men who felt the same as I did.

"WE ARE ALL *FEDAYEEN*"

SUMMER 1970

By the time the hijackings occurred in September 1970, Jordan was a seething cauldron, superheated by friction between the Palestinian resistance movement and the regime of King Hussein.

1967: The Ingredients Are Mixed

In 1967 King Hussein made a disastrous decision. Jordan was moderate, Western-leaning, and, quietly, even on good terms with Israel. But in June 1967, at the behest and duplicity of Egypt and Syria, Jordan entered the Six-Day War and promptly lost its West Bank. During the fighting, about 200,000 Palestinian Arabs fled to the East Bank, planning to return once Jordan won. It did not, and these refugees instead joined over half a million others who had fled during Israel's 1948 War of Independence and whose descendants lived there too. By 1970 Palestinians made up over half the population of Jordan's East Bank, mostly unabsorbed into society, concentrated in refugee camps, awaiting their "return."

The Palestinian resistance movement, established to destroy Israel long before the war, also shifted its operations to Jordan's East Bank—what is now simply Jordan. The dynamics of the movement and its relationship with Hussein are integral to our story.

After the humiliating Arab defeat in 1967, Palestinians felt abandoned by Egypt, Jordan, and Syria, who now focused on regaining their lost territory rather than destroying Israel. Many Palestinian leaders concluded as well that Arab regimes could not destroy Israel even if their desire to do so resurfaced. They resolved to retake control over their own fate and to promote guerrilla warfare. Guerrilla groups created before the war grew, and new entrepreneurial groups began to proliferate. Some formed around individual leaders or philosophies; others were created by Arab states who wanted to have a hand in the guerrilla movement. Over time, certain groups began to stand out.

Fatah became the largest and most important of the *fedayeen* organizations. ("Fedayeen," meaning "those who sacrifice themselves," is how the Arab world referred to the guerrillas. "Fatah," meaning "conquest," is the reverse acronym of the organization's Arabic name.) Founded in the late 1950s by Yasser Arafat, Salakh Khalaf (Abu Iyad), and a few colleagues, its message was simple and appealing: Only Palestinians could be entrusted to destroy Israel. In spring 1968, Cairo-born, 37-year-old Yasser Arafat was named Fatah's spokesman.

Probably the second largest organization and certainly the key to our story was the Popular Front for the Liberation of Palestine (PFLP). Unlike Fatah, it was highly ideological, calling not only for the liberation of Palestine but for the creation of a Marxist-Leninist Arab society. Formed in January 1968 by 41-year-old Dr. George Habash and his second in command, 43-year-old Dr. Wadia (Wadi) Haddad, the PFLP was fiercely independent, although it did receive extensive funding from Iraq and had close ties with Red China. The group was militant and radical. "If [it] is the only way to destroy Israel, Zionism, and Arab reaction," Habash asserted in a 1970 interview, "then we want World War III to come." In another he warned, "America is our enemy," and the PFLP was about to "teach the United States a lesson." And, unlike Fatah, which at least officially vowed not to interfere in intra-Arab affairs, the PFLP never hid its intent to replace King Hussein as a first step in liberating Palestine. The group was also fractious, ravaged by intense disputes. Only months after its founding, two important fighters departed to form their own groups. Such disagreements would play an important part in our story too.[1]

1968: The Fire Is Lit

The year 1968 marked an important turning point for the Palestinian resistance movement when Arafat took credit for a limited battlefield success, with the Jordanian army's help, against a major Israeli retaliatory incursion. In a public relations coup, Arafat ignited the imagination of the Palestinians in Jordan and elsewhere in Arab world. His reputation soared, and thousands of young Palestinians swarmed to join Fatah and other guerrilla organizations.

Heady times ensued. As Bassam Abu-Sharif, a PFLP spokesman, later recalled, "People who had lost faith completely in Arab nationalism turned to these groups in huge numbers. Volunteers queued up to join, to become *fedayeen*. . . . In 1968 a Palestinian *fedayi* could travel right across the Arab world with nothing more than his organization card and be welcome everywhere. No passport—just the card. Nobody, nobody, in the Arab world then, dared raise a voice against a *fedayi*. . . . [T]he *fedayi* was god."

Building on the momentum, Yasser Arafat and Fatah gradually seized control of the Palestine Liberation Organization (PLO)—ironically, it had been created in 1964 by the Arab states to rein in uncoordinated terror activity—and transformed it into an umbrella guerrilla organization. Arafat was elected chairman in February 1969. By June 1970, the PLO's Central Committee, now headquartered in Amman, included twenty-seven commando groups. Despite the numerous factions, on one thing the PLO was unified: It wanted Israel eliminated and it opposed all diplomacy.[2]

1970: The Concoction Is Aboil

By 1970 the resistance movement in Jordan had swelled to about 20,000 full-time commandos, another 20,000 in popular militias, and perhaps another 20,000 to 30,000 active supporters. Fatah had between 5,000 and 10,000 armed men; the PFLP, 2,000 to 3,000. Despite the movement's swollen ranks, only a few hundred people were actually battling Israel. The rest, pushed back from the borders by Israeli retaliatory strikes and by Jordanians unhappy at being caught in those retaliations, now infested Jordan's cities, controlled refugee camps, flouted Jordan's laws, directed ever-increasing violence at the Jordanian regime and army, and essentially created a state within a state. Fatah began to see itself as King Hussein's equal, or his better. "We were sovereigns, masters of the situation," asserted Abu Iyad. Hussein's prestige at home and abroad began to erode, as did his control over the affairs of his country.

Adding to the charged mix, between 17,000 and 20,000 Iraqi troops, including tank and mechanized brigades, were permanently stationed northeast of Amman. These troops had come to fight in the 1967 war but now refused to leave or to answer to Hussein's command. Ominously, these forces were sympathetic to the *fedayeen,* and Iraq warned that it would not remain impartial if fighting were to break out.

With highly conflicted feelings, young King Hussein essentially stood by as the guerrillas steadily took control of his country, despite the growing frustration of his army of 65,000 soldiers—professional, well trained, and composed largely of fiercely loyal Bedouins. The *fedayeen* were a source of pride to Jordan's large Palestinian populace as the one force still daring to fight Israel. Plus, the *fedayeen* served Hussein's purposes: They diverted the public's attention from domestic issues and could perhaps help him one day regain the West Bank. When East Bankers and army leaders demanded that he crack down, King Hussein replied: "What should I do to a people who have lost everything—who were driven out of their country? Shoot them? I think we have come to a point where we are all *fedayeen*."

By summer 1970, however, the pervasive, disruptive, armed *fedayeen* had wrought anarchy throughout the kingdom. They set up roadblocks around the country not only to protect themselves from the government but to shake down civilians. They extorted shopkeepers, businessmen, foreigners, and civilians at gunpoint; they impounded cars and threatened judges. Fatah's "cowboys" swaggered around, heavily armed, recorded Arafat biographer Alan Hart, "as though they owned the place and could do what they liked."

Even more serious was the *fedayeen*'s hostile attitude toward the Jordanian army. Horror stories abound, evincing painful memories even today. The *fedayeen* took to sniping randomly at Jordanian soldiers, killing many. They accosted, kidnapped, disarmed, and abused soldiers to such an extent that soldiers were afraid to enter Amman. Many did not go home or visit their families for weeks at a time out of fear of being attacked. The *fedayeen* also terrorized soldiers' families; the son of the deputy chief of staff was assassinated in his house.

Gun, rocket, and mortar fire exchanges between the guerrillas and government troops echoed regularly in Jordan's cities, including Amman. King Hussein himself later described the situation: "No one—adult or child—could be sure on leaving his house whether his family would see him again. Amman became a virtual battlefield." To ensure his safety, the king was forced to lower his own profile to such an extent that people wondered whether he was still around. A bogus royal motorcade, including the king's double, had to be arranged to traverse Amman's streets just to reassure the people.

On June 9, the *fedayeen* opened fire on Jordanian Intelligence headquarters in Amman. When King Hussein went to see what was going on, his entourage was ambushed. One royal guardsman was killed, four were wounded. An infuriated army vented with firefights against the *fedayeen*. A cease-fire was agreed to the next day but collapsed the day after. On that same day Major Bob Perry, the U.S. assistant military attaché, was assassinated in front of his family by terrorists when he answered his door. Hume Horan, an American Embassy official in Amman at the time, recalls: "The police didn't dare to intervene. They were of no consequence and, besides, many were also Palestinians."

In an attempt to placate the Palestinians, on June 11 Hussein offered Arafat the premiership. Arafat declined. Instead, Hussein was forced to replace his uncle as army commander in chief with Major General Mashhur Haditha, who was on closer terms with the PLO. Hussein also appointed a new moderate prime minister, Abdul Moneim Rifai.

Despite these conciliatory moves, an agreement with the Palestinians was not reached until a month later. But even that cease-fire proved weak and was consistently violated. World capitals believed that Hussein was on his way out. "All the indicators were downward," recalls Horan. "The PLO factions were the darling of Arab intellectuals and the Arab street. Half of Jordan's population was Palestinian. A hostile Syria was to the north. An Iraqi tank division was encamped in [Zarqa]. And every Arab under 20 thought Hussein a stooge for Zionism and Western imperialism. King Hussein was extraordinarily isolated."[3]

Late Summer: The Cauldron Seethes

King Hussein then made a decision that sent the guerrillas over the edge. Concerned that an escalating war of attrition between Israel and Egypt along the Suez Canal might spiral out of control, U.S. secretary of state William Rogers in June asked Egypt, Jordan, and Israel to agree to a cease-fire and to hold peace talks. They consented, and on August 7 the cease-fire went into effect. The acceptance of the "Rogers Plan" infuriated the guerrillas, who remained committed to Israel's destruction and saw diplomatic efforts as a plot to "liquidate" the Palestinian issue. Habash warned: "If a settlement with Israel is applied, we will turn the Middle East into hell."

The brunt of Palestinian anger was leveled at Hussein. By late August several *fedayeen* organizations concluded that the time had come to attack the regime. Open calls for Hussein's overthrow could be heard. Even the PLO mainstream broached the need for a new national authority. At an emergency session on August 27 and 28, the Palestinian movement decided to stage a coup during September. The PLO declared, "If the Government wants a showdown . . . our armed revolutionary masses will determine the result—inevitable victory," and it alluded to overthrowing the "agent authorities in Amman." "Our masses . . . will cast out the advocates of defeatism and all their liquidationist plans."

The Jordanian army became increasingly angry and frustrated. Many officers requested the king's permission to crush the *fedayeen.* At one point, a Jordanian regiment decided to act on its own and made its way to Amman. When Hussein arrived to dissuade it, he was treated almost contemptuously. A brassiere fluttered from the antenna of one of the tanks. The king pointed to it inquiringly, surely expecting a bawdy tale. Instead, he was told that it was there because their king was a woman who was afraid to take action against the country's enemies. Hussein argued with the troops for nearly three hours before they reluctantly backed off.

By summer's end, the situation was reaching a climax. On September 1, King Hussein once again came close to being shot to death. The noise of the shooting was deafening, reinforcements to his guard detail arrived shortly afterward, and the king escaped. Twenty minutes later, the Jordanian army began shelling *fedayeen* positions in and around Amman. Ten people died and forty were wounded. The following morning Amman was tense. Traffic was light, and most shops, schools, and government offices were closed, as was the airport. Newspapers did not appear and telephone communications with the outside world were intermittent. The downtown area was completely under *fedayeen* control; not a single Jordanian Arab Army (JAA) soldier was to be seen. The *fedayeen* set up a roadblock near the railroad station, and the JAA established one on the Amman-Suwaylih Road on the western outskirts of Amman and searched all incoming cars.

On September 3 the *fedayeen* tightened their noose around other sections of the capital. In the afternoon clashes resumed, and by evening they had spread to Zarqa to the northeast and Suwaylih to the west. The *fedayeen* claimed that army shelling had killed 33 and wounded 160. The king felt compelled to broadcast a radio address to reassure his people and to ask the PLO to "exercise control" over its groups. Yet, Arafat did little to discipline the various factions or even his own men. "Distrust between government and *fedayeen* sharpened and [the] issue[s] themselves have become more intractable," wrote the U.S. chargé in Amman. "It is now more difficult for either side to satisfy [the] minimal demands of [the] other."

On September 5 the PLO's Central Committee and the Jordanian government reached yet another agreement under which the guerrillas would leave Amman, remove their roadblocks, and end their patrols. The Jordanian commander in chief in turn ordered his troops to withdraw from the outskirts of Amman "in order to end the military presence near the capital." Despite the agreement, sporadic firing rang out in downtown Amman the next day, Sunday, September 6. One round hit the U.S. embassy, passing through its reception room, shattering two windows. That evening King Hussein made yet another impassioned, almost desperate, radio address to his people. "I can no longer remain silent in the face of a painful flow of doubts and accusations, disorder and incitement, and ruin and destruction directed at the people [and] at the army," he lamented and urged his people to rally round him. He acknowledged that the government had neglected its duties and promised to rectify the situation.[4]

But the chaos was mounting and Hussein's grip on Jordan was fast eroding.

Into this maelstrom I and almost 800 other men, women, and children were suddenly thrust.

"THIS IS YOUR NEW CAPTAIN SPEAKING."

SUNDAY, SEPTEMBER 6

Lod Airport, 6 AM

I was a seventeen-year-old American kid from Trenton, New Jersey, who had just graduated high school. I had spent the summer in Israel—my first time there—touring. The rest of my family had been there too, but my father had returned home two weeks earlier. On Sunday of the Labor Day weekend my mother, my four younger siblings, and I headed back to the United States.

> *We came to Lod [Ben Gurion] Airport and boarded our TWA plane at 6:00 in the morning. It was a very bright, clear day. The sun was shining, and we thought it was going to be a regular flight home. We were scheduled to stop in Athens and Frankfurt, and then Kennedy Airport. But we made a wrong turn along the way.*

Frankfurt, 11 AM

Bettie McCarthy knew almost as soon as she boarded the plane that she and the rest of the cabin crew were not going to enjoy the flight. It had been a late night at the Mainz Weinfest, and they were still a bit groggy. They hadn't even had time for breakfast. And now they had a full load to take care of. With a crew of 10 and 143 passengers—14 in First Class and 129 in coach—plus 6 children on laps, the plane was packed. There was also going to be a lot of extra work with about fifty kosher, ten special kosher, and ten vegetarian special meals. Most of the passengers had boarded before Frankfurt (81 in

Lod alone), and they were already restless. McCarthy was amazed at the large number of children, some of whom were behaving badly. Rudi Swinkels, the purser, was upset that an upgraded woman insisted on changing her baby in the middle of the first class section. An older woman was gnawing on chicken bones in the first row of coach. And there was a commotion as some passengers argued over their seats.

Finally, TWA Flight 741 took off as scheduled at 11:45 AM and leveled off. The cabin crew set about their duties. Stewardess Rosemarie Metzner and trainee Frank Allen had finished serving cocktails in first class; Metzner was taking meal orders at row 3; McCarthy was in the first class galley; Swinkels was in coach working his way down the aisle selling headphones. The movie was going to be *Paint Your Wagon*, with Lee Marvin. Swinkels was standing at row 17.

> *I don't remember exactly what time it was. We were just a few minutes out of Frankfurt, and the captain had just announced that we were passing over Brussels.*

Suddenly, a man and woman, in their late twenties or early thirties, started running up the aisle in coach. "Imshi! Imshi!" they yelled in Arabic. "Move it! Move it!" Someone screamed and people started to point. Rudi Swinkels immediately turned around and saw a well-built man in a gray suit, with black hair and a thin, black mustache rushing up the aisle with long strides. At first Swinkels thought the man was fighting with another passenger, so he ran after him. The woman was ahead of him. She was wearing a whitish dress and white shoes with brass buckles. Passenger Dick Morse thought that the man was angry with his wife and was chasing her. A domestic dispute. But in his right hand the man brandished a shiny, nickel-plated revolver and in his left, a hand grenade; the woman was holding two hand grenades.

Hearing the commotion, Bettie McCarthy stepped slightly out of the galley and met them head on. The man pointed his gun at her and ordered her to let him into the cockpit. Anxiously, she rapped on the cockpit door. Swinkels was now standing between coach and first class. The hijacker turned around and, pointing his pistol at him, shouted very agitatedly, "Get back! Get back!" Swinkels quickly dove behind the bulkhead.

For the cockpit crew, this was supposed to be the final leg of their thirteen-day round-the-world assignment. Captain Carroll D. Woods, 51, a stocky, gentle Kansan and a veteran World War II pilot who had flown for TWA for many years, was in the pilot's seat on the left. Copilot Jim Majer, 37, tall, thin, blond, handsome, and even tempered, had been flying for fifteen years since his days in the Navy and with TWA for about five-and-a-half years. He was sitting on the right. Flight engineer Al Kiburis, 45, a resourceful, matter-of-fact person, sat behind Majer facing the instrument panel on the right side of the cockpit. He was closest to the door. The three had met only a few weeks before. Having flown in the previous day from Tel Aviv and slept overnight in Frankfurt, they were happy to be flying home. But there was this banging at their door.

Al Kiburis opened the door. "It's a hijacking!" Bettie McCarthy blurted and quickly ducked out of the way. The man and woman both entered. The man immediately pointed his .38 caliber pistol at Jim Majer. (He would keep the pistol trained at Majer on and off throughout the flight.) Then he said simply, "I want you to turn the plane around."

Majer's first thought was: "Keep him calm, keep him calm. Live to fight another day." The other two crew members had the same idea. There was no way to subdue the hijackers since they were armed, so the crew put their hands up. The captain calmly told the hijacker, "We can't do that. We're at the wrong altitude and have to advise Brussels air traffic control (ATC) what we're going to do." The hijacker consented, and the crew contacted ATC, changing the plane's call sign at the hijacker's insistence from TWA 741 to "Gaza Strip." Soon the plane made a wide arc and headed south.

The female hijacker sat down in the observer seat behind Captain Woods. The male hijacker sat in the second observer seat behind the first one.

The first feeling—at least on my part—was one of excitement. I had been reading about hijackings for the past couple of years, and I figured it always happened to the other guy. It never happened to you. And here I was, sitting in the middle of one of those hijackings. So—not knowing who had hijacked us or for what purpose—I just had a feeling of excitement at first. You know, "Here I am, one of those making history being hijacked."

A few minutes later, the female guerrilla announced over the loudspeaker: "This is your new captain speaking. We are taking you to a friendly country." Sure, friendly countries where they only have civil wars every once in a while. Anyway, we still didn't know where we were going, but Cuba seemed a little out of the question. First of all, we were too far away from it and it just didn't seem to make sense that somebody would come all the way to West Germany to hijack a plane to Cuba. It didn't seem to fit. But we could tell by the sun that we were headed south.

Later on, we heard another announcement that this was the doing of the Popular Front for the Liberation of Palestine (PFLP). And again we didn't know exactly where we were going, but thoughts and theories started coming into our minds. We knew we were going to an Arab country. Obviously, we had to think of a reason why; why would anyone want to take us to an Arab country? Immediately, the thought of the two Algerian diplomats being held in Israel came to mind. We figured that since we were headed south we would be going to Algeria, and within a couple of days we would be coming back after a trade for these two Algerian diplomats. But for most of the flight, we didn't know where we were headed.

When the female hijacker had first gotten on the PA system, she had added: "We will not harm anybody. Please stay calm." She instructed the first class passengers to move back to coach and ordered everyone to fasten their seat belts and put their hands behind their heads, which everyone did of course. Since coach was full, the crew had to squeeze four passengers into some rows, taking out the armrests. My eleven-year-old sister, Tikva, who had been in the rear lavatory this entire time, wandered innocently back to our seats toward the front of coach, wondering why everybody was sitting so strangely.

Shortly afterward, the cabin crew received permission to continue its routine.

> *The crew handed out free whiskey to everybody and gave everybody earphones so they could listen to the music. They wanted to show the movie, but I guess the guerrillas were afraid that when the screens were down something would happen. So they didn't show it. Except for the fact that we were headed in the wrong direction, it was a regular flight. Most of the people were not afraid at first. They were of course a little excited, but nobody expected any harm to come to us.*

The cabin crew tried to serve lunch, but people weren't particularly hungry. The plane was fairly quiet. There was fear, but no hysteria. "Where are we going? What's going to happen to us?" people kept asking the crew. The crew members, who knew no more than the passengers, tried to reassure and calm everyone.

As Bettie McCarthy was serving near the front of coach, the hijacker pointed his pistol through the curtain and ordered her into first class. He wanted her to make sandwiches and coffee for the hijackers and crew. She made chicken sandwiches with lettuce and mayonnaise. Of the crew, only Al Kiburis ate. Jim Majer looked at him with astonishment, wondering how he could eat at a time like this. Al responded, "Jim, you don't know when you'll get the next one."

After lunch, as the initial shock of the hijacking wore off somewhat, the passengers started to brave trips to the rear lavatories, going one at a time. The front lavatories were off-limits. Some anxiety-ridden people made several trips; one six-year-old boy went nonstop. A group of Jewish passengers also went to the rear of plane to pray.

The two hijackers had boarded in Frankfurt as Mr. A. Lapez and Miss Vasquez using forged Latin American passports. At first they sat in the second row in coach on the left side, but Susie Hirsch, 14, insisted that they move. Susie was traveling from Israel with her two younger brothers. The three youngsters had gotten off the plane in Frankfurt while the plane was refueling. When they reboarded, the two darker-complexioned people were in their seats. Susie argued with the poachers, not wanting to be separated from her siblings for whom she was responsible. She stood her ground, and they took seats further back.

The hijackers were very well prepared on all aspects of the flight. They had brought detailed flight path information, reams of pages. Plus, they had relatively complete and up-to-date Jeppesen air navigation maps—with VORs (long-range navigational aids that provide pilots with a course to or from a location) and ATC radio frequencies. They even had fuel calculation information and knew the plane's exact fuel status. When the captain wondered aloud whether there would be enough fuel for the trip, the hijackers assured him that there would. It became evident to the crew that the hijackers could not be bluffed. The PFLP had done some serious homework. The man, who was the lead, didn't tell the crew where we were headed. He divulged only two VORs in advance. The female hijacker sat rather passively throughout the flight, poring over the maps while holding her unpinned grenade. Periodically, she would take hold of the communications system and give a political spiel to the local ATC. Other than that, the hijackers were not in contact with anyone on the ground while we were airborne.

Through much of the flight, the male hijacker paced back and forth in first class, chain-smoking the Dunhill cigarettes that he had picked up at the Frankfurt airport dutyfree. At one point, he "asked" Bettie McCarthy to sit down with him. They talked about languages, he demonstrated the hand grenade to her, and they smoked. She told Rudi Swinkels later in the flight that the man was friendly and polite and wanted to teach her Arabic. But to Swinkels, she appeared shaken and pale.

The U.S. State Department got word of the hijacking from TWA at 10:50 AM in Washington, with an assessment that the plane was heading toward Amman. About half an hour later, our plane flew over Damascus. The department presumed that it would be taken to some Arab capital. But contrary to all speculation, the plane was not headed to any known airport in the Middle East. It was heading the entire time directly for the desert floor in Jordan.

At last the seat belt sign came on and the plane descended slowly. When it crossed the Syrian border into Jordan, the female voice came on the PA again: "You are now in a country with friendly people, Jordan. We want to reassure you again that we will not harm anybody." But this didn't help Susie Hirsch who suddenly became very scared. "Who are these people? What do they want from us? Will we survive?"

During the flight we knew we were headed toward an Arab country and we really weren't that afraid. But now, the thought that we were about to land in an Arab country, an unfriendly country—especially since we had just come from Israel—wasn't the greatest feeling we could have experienced. In fact, we were quite terrified.

Finally, around 6 PM, we started circling. At first, neither the crew nor the hijackers could find the desert landing strip. The crew brought the plane down to about 8,000 feet, and after a while the female hijacker spotted the strip. The crew was alarmed at what it saw. Only about a thousand feet of runway were marked off. Normally, a Boeing 707 requires at least five thousand feet to land. It can be done in four if one is prepared to blow the plane's tires and damage the plane in other ways too. But a thousand feet? The crew decided to gain altitude and jettison fuel in order to land in as short a stretch as possible. They determined, however, to retain 30,000 pounds of fuel so that if by some chance the plane would be permitted to take off again, it could do so and make it to somewhere, such as Tel Aviv or Cyprus.

Between finding the site and dumping the fuel, the plane circled for about thirty-five minutes. A hushed silence fell over the plane as the passengers sat in apprehensive anticipation of the landing and what might await them afterward. Some became nauseated by the plane's seemingly endless turns. Finally, the plane made a "low drag" of the field so that the captain could get a sense of what he was about to land on. The crew illuminated the no-smoking signs and set about lowering the landing gear. But today, of all days, the nose landing gear would not go down! In his fifteen years of flying, this had never before happened to Jim Majer, nor would it recur in his next twenty-two years. Flight engineer Al Kiburis, using the mechanism in the cockpit, cranked the wheels down by hand. Fortunately, the wheels descended. But, as it turns out, the "safe" indicator does not illuminate on the cockpit display when wheels are lowered manually. Kiburis would need to descend into the wheel well to visually confirm that the gear locking pin had inserted properly. If it hadn't, the wheel mechanism would collapse on contact.

The problem was that the hatch to the wheel well was directly under the two observer seats. Kiburis had to convince the suspicious hijackers to move aside so that he could go down. The female hijacker became edgy. When he came back up after establishing that the pin had in fact locked in place, she refused to sit down and strap herself in. She nervously ordered the crew to "Do it! Do it!" and land already. Still having no idea what kind of surface they'd be landing on and whether hitting some bump might dislodge the unpinned grenade from her hand, the cockpit crew worried. They had in fact already instructed the cabin crew to prepare for a crash landing; all passengers were now seated in the impact position with their heads in their folded arms.

By the time we landed at 6:41—and I noted the time well—it was dark. It wasn't really a runway, the place where we landed—we saw it because the guerrillas had put torches down the stretch and it illuminated the runway. I am sure the captain was very afraid because he didn't know the elevation of the place we were supposed to land—he didn't know if it was level or exactly how much of a runway he had, if he would sink as soon as he landed, or if the plane would blow up. But under the circumstances he made one of the best landings possible. In fact, many people said afterward that they couldn't even tell that we weren't on a runway, and I agree with that. He made a beautiful landing, and the crew praised him for it.

The landing had been particularly difficult for Woods because of the darkness. The thousand feet of runway had been illuminated by makeshift lighting that included torches—kerosene-drenched cotton stuck on poles in large biscuit tins—and car and truck headlights. It wasn't until the next morning that the crew realized they had brought down the plane on a 30,000-foot long, 100-foot wide, baked-solid dirt strip, and that there was all the room in the world for a safe landing. It had once served as an RAF airfield; RAF pilots had dubbed it Dawson Field after their commander, Sir Walter Dawson.

Actually, at the time we landed, we weren't concerned so much about how good the landing was as we were with the fact that we had landed and that we were now in Arab hands—a thought which every Jew, I think, has feared immensely: that thought of falling into the hands of guerrillas, into the hands of the Arabs. People think, What would happen if the Arabs win a war—God forbid—against Israel, what they would do to the Jews? And this is what we were worried about at the time of landing.

Immediately after the plane came to a stop, the forward passenger door was opened. Our arrival was greeted outside by an extraordinary assortment of trucks and people cheering wildly, euphoric at the feat that they had pulled off. A wooden ladder was leaned up against the plane. The hijackers said good-by to the crew and descended to the applause, adulation, and embraces of their comrades below. A middle-aged man then quietly made his way up the aisle and, to the amazement of Jim Majer and Al Kiburis, got off the plane to the cheers of the crowd and joined in the festivities. It may never be known whether he was part of the plot, but a Mr. Franz Zauner (traveling on an Austrian passport) was recorded as a passenger who boarded in Frankfurt but was unaccounted for in any list of released passengers that I have uncovered.

We waited. They turned off all the electricity in the plane, and the lights went out, of course, and the air conditioning went off. And we waited. We sat and we waited, wondering what was going to happen. The cabin was quiet and spooky, lit only by the emergency lights that came on once the engines were shut down.

I looked outside and saw guerrillas with machine guns, fifty of them surrounding the plane, and I thought, "Well, here we go, we're going to be shot up now." Because I knew that the PFLP had been blamed for blowing up a plane from Zurich a few years ago and for shooting up a plane in Athens, I figured that they were capable of doing something like shooting us right now. It was one of the moments that I was very scared and very much afraid for our lives.

Fortunately, one of the guerrillas got on the plane. As soon as the guerrilla got on the plane, I knew they weren't going to shoot us up because we had one of their own. Unless they wanted to get rid of her also. I say "her" because the fact is that they sent up a lady guerrilla—a woman commando—to start the operation. Now, I feel that it was a very good move—that they wanted to try to treat us well—because, although I'm not a psychologist, I'm sure that seeing a woman carrying guns and arms is not as frightening as seeing a man carrying guns. The guerrillas knew this and, not wanting to create any type of panic on the plane, they sent up a lady. I think that was very good psychology. But soon after, other armed guerrillas with loaded guns and bayonets also boarded the plane.

Anyway, the woman started asking for passports. She said, "Everybody take out your passports." And she started handing out small pink cards, asking for your name, address, passport number, and nationality. I thought I was registering at a hotel. Far from it. They collected these slips of paper and our passports. We've seen neither since. So just in case you see somebody walking around with an American passport having a picture of David Raab on it and it doesn't look too much like them, please tell them to return the passport to me.

The outwardly calm approach toward the passengers belied the true danger of the situation. As soon as the plane landed, the commandos rigged it with explosives, both in the cockpit and under the fuel tanks, wired for remote detonation. Jim Majer, who had left his passport in his jacket pocket in the cockpit, was not allowed to retrieve it because the cockpit was now wired.

Roughly forty minutes after landing, the emergency batteries ran out and the plane was shrouded in complete darkness except for the lights of the trucks outside, which kept coming and going.

An hour or hour and a half after we landed, we heard a huge, huge noise behind us. We all turned around, looked outside our windows, and saw a fireball coming right at us. We had no idea what it was. It was coming full speed at us, and it looked like it was going to hit us. Again, scared—what's going to be?[1]

Over Dijon, France, 1:15 PM

Up in the skies over Dijon, France, Swissair Flight 100, a McDonnell Douglas DC-8 from Zurich to New York with 143 passengers and 12 crew members aboard was hijacked. The hijackers were a female and male who had arrived in Zurich from Stuttgart and were traveling on forged Costa Rican passports under the names of Miss Fernandez and Mr. M. Fuentes. The male hijacker carried a silver revolver.

Only one announcement was made over the public address system to the effect that the plane had been taken over by the PFLP. Though at one point the male hijacker came through the passenger compartment with a black stocking over his face, the passengers did not panic throughout the flight. The pilot managed to press a panic button that alerted Zurich tower that a hijacking had occurred, but he was unable to provide it with any additional information. There were reports that the plane had requested permission to land in Amman and that authorities had denied it. There is no question, however, that this plane too was headed to Dawson.

> *Upon landing, the captain of the Swissair plane also didn't know what type of runway he had but knew that there was already a plane sitting down there, so as soon as he hit the ground, he put his engines in full reverse. In doing so, he brought all kinds of sand and dust into his engines, and the friction created fireballs. He damaged his airplane such that had the order been given, "Okay, these planes can take off," he would not have been able to do so. (Our crew said that we were able to take off: "Once we get the word, we can take off in ten minutes." We never got that word.)*

The Swissair plane had hit the ground very hard, and the reversed engines and the fireballs brought dust and smoke into the cabin. Some passengers thought the plane had caught fire, opened the emergency hatches once the plane stopped, and slid down. One passenger, Louise Fehse of Rochester, New York, panicked and jumped to the ground. She fractured her left wrist and was taken to the Italian Hospital in Amman.

The plane had come to a stop a mere seventy-five feet or so behind the TWA jet, very narrowly avoiding an on-the-ground collision. Later in the week, a correspondent described the landing of the two planes in the desert as "a miracle."

That this hijacking succeeded is puzzling, especially since a month earlier Swiss police had already begun preparing for such an eventuality. In July, the PFLP had hijacked an Olympic Airways jet to exchange for seven Palestinians jailed in Greece for various attacks against El Al in Athens. Switzerland, also holding some Palestinian terrorists, worried that a Swissair plane would be hijacked for similar purposes. On August 14, Swiss authorities had actually received credible intelligence that a Palestinian group might be planning to hijack a Swissair plane. What's more, the Swiss had even turned to Israel for advice on how to negotiate with hijackers so as not to cave in to their demands. It is all the more ironic that the Swiss would capitulate the next morning, only a few short hours after the hijackings, to PFLP demands that had not even been presented formally.[2]

Off the coast of England, 1:50 PM

Jumping up from their seats, she with two unpinned hand grenades and he with a handgun and a grenade, Leila Khaled and Patrick Joseph Arguello ran forward from the second row in coach through the drawn curtain to the first class section and toward the cockpit, knocking over a food cart. El Al Flight 219, a Boeing 707 with 140 passengers and 10 crew, was 21 minutes into its flight from Amsterdam to New York. Still in its climb, it was 2,000 feet shy of its cruising altitude of 31,000 feet. It was about thirteen miles off the coast where the English Channel meets the North Sea, set to enter British airspace as it struck a westerly course over England, Ireland, and the North Atlantic. Khaled and her colleague were about to hijack a third plane that day to bring to Dawson Field. Or so they thought.

The next few moments became a frenetic blur of hyperaction that different eyewitnesses would recall differently. But early in the sequence of events, a cabin crew member pressed one of the panic buttons that had recently been installed, and a hijack alert went off in the cockpit. Most of the cockpit crew discounted the signal since cabin crew, still unused to the new protrusions, often bumped against them accidentally, setting off false alarms. Captain Uri Bar-Lev, a 39-year-old veteran of the Israeli Air Force, sensed that this was the real thing. "Gentlemen, this is a hijacking," he said. They looked at him as if he had lost his nerve. So he repeated emphatically, "This is a hijacking."

Back in the cabin, upon hearing the commotion and seeing the shocked expression on the other cabin crew members' faces, Shlomo Vider, a steward who was sitting in a jump seat near the cockpit door, thought that someone had suffered a heart attack. "But immediately afterward I saw a man and a woman, armed with hand grenades and a gun, shouting wildly." The purser, Avraham Eisenberg, sitting next to Vider, told the pilot through the door that two hijackers wanted the captain to open the door. The two hijackers tried to force open the door, but it didn't budge.

The cockpit crew heard banging at the door and a threat that a stewardess would be killed if the captain didn't open up. In that instant, Bar-Lev came to the awesome realization that he had to play God: a life threat to one of his crew versus the fate of the entire plane and its 150 travelers. Instinctively, he decided that surrender meant losing control over everyone's destiny. He also recalled how Syria had mutilated Israeli air force pilots that it had captured in the past and, not knowing where his plane might be taken, he boomed, "*I* am not going to be hijacked!"

The banging became louder, and flight engineer Uri Zach looked out of the peephole. He saw the male hijacker holding a gun to stewardess Janet Demerjian's head and the female hijacker with two grenades. Vider then tried to move toward the passengers, but the male hijacker saw him and shot him in the leg, grazing the dress of the stewardess. The hijackers then tried and failed again to jar open the door. Vider noticed that the hijackers were taken aback that the pilot had still not opened the door and were hesitating, unsure what to do. Vider went at the male hijacker, grabbed his hand, and, as he recounted, bashed his head against the cockpit door. Vider fell and realized that he was groaning. He lost consciousness shortly afterward; the hijacker had shot him five times.

Meanwhile, a crew member alerted El Al sky marshal Motti Bar-Levav, who was sitting toward the rear of the plane and must not have seen the two terrorists streak forward through the drawn curtain of first class. He ran up and managed to get off some shots at the male hijacker.

After informing both El Al in Israel and London ATC of the situation—even before satellite communications, El Al had installed a radio system for worldwide voice communications with its aircraft for precisely this eventuality—Captain Bar-Lev was still unsure what to do. But he decided to take the helm, directing the copilot, who had been piloting the plane since takeoff, to give him the controls. Then, in an inspired move, Bar-Lev threw the plane into a steep, negative-G dive, a downward arc that creates momentary zero gravity. Bar-Lev knew that this move would cause the terrorists to lose their footing but would not harm the passengers and crew who were still strapped in. He also knew that the male hijacker would not be able to get a shot off at the stewardess. Bar-Lev continued his emergency dive at 8,000 to 10,000 thousand feet per minute down to 3,000 feet because he was afraid that the grenades that the terrorists were carrying might explode. Descending would decrease the pressure differential between the cabin and the atmosphere so that, if the grenades did go off, the plane's shell would not disintegrate. The descent was so rapid that it neared the maximum speed before the plane's structural integrity was jeopardized.

Sitting in the cockpit (against regulations) and alerted to the plan, the second sky marshal, Avihu Kol, held on tight. As soon as gravity returned, though still during the steep descent, he burst out of the cockpit. Both Khaled and Arguello had indeed lost their balance and fallen to the floor. All three grenades had fallen from their hands, but none exploded. (They had no detonating mechanisms, it turned out.) In short order, Bar-Levav finished emptying his seven-bullet clip into Arguello and Kol karate-chopped the back of Arguello's neck, apparently breaking it. A heavyset American man sitting in first class jumped on Khaled, then he and some crew members bound her tightly with neckties and scarves.

El Al Operations in Tel Aviv, on orders from the Shin Bet, Israel's General Security Service, instructed Bar-Lev to turn around and fly directly to Tel Aviv. Finding Vider "pale and barely conscious," however, the captain determined that he needed immediate hospitalization. When Tel Aviv remained adamant that he fly straight back, Bar-Lev, unaware of the larger conspiracy in progress, decided nonetheless to head for London's Heathrow airport believing that he would drop off Vider and then take off immediately for Israel.

As Bar-Lev began preparations for an emergency landing, Demerjian, who was Armenian and not Jewish, incredulously began to lead the passengers in singing Israeli folk songs. The air marshals picked up the loose grenades and repinned them. They strip-searched Khaled to see if she was carrying any explosives or other weapons and found her instructions hidden in her underwear. They pulled off her blond wig and recognized that she was the Leila Khaled who had hijacked a TWA Boeing 707 to Damascus the previous year. They also saw that she wore an oddly structured bra, which may have been how she got her nonferrous grenades on board.

But Bar-Lev was concerned about his sky marshals. In an attack on an El Al plane in Switzerland two years earlier, an El Al sky marshal, Mordechai Rahamim, had been arrested and charged with manslaughter for killing one of the terrorists who had just murdered one of the pilots in the cockpit. Rahamim had sat in a Swiss jail for several months, and it was only after intense diplomatic efforts that he was released. Bar-Lev did not want the same fate for Kol and Bar-Levav, but didn't know what to do.

Then, as he describes it, by pure chance, he heard his colleague, Captain Shimon Asch, on the ground at Heathrow requesting permission to taxi his El Al plane for takeoff to Tel Aviv. In an instant, Bar-Lev was speaking to him in Hebrew. He briefed him on what had happened and that he needed to offload the two sky marshals. "Listen, Shimon," he said, "taxi to the takeoff position on the runway and then make some excuse as to why you can't take off. Wait for me there. I'll land, taxi slowly by your plane, and we'll do our 'transaction.'" The two security guards would exit through an access hatch in the belly of the plane and enter through the same opening in Asch's plane. Overhearing the conversation, El Al's security chief in London, Nachum Degani, quickly got tickets printed for Bar-Levav and Kol on Asch's flight. As Bar-Lev's plane landed at 2:05 PM, Degani followed in a security van, picked up the two sky marshals, who did in fact drop out of the belly of the 707, gave them their tickets, and drove them over to Asch's plane, which they swiftly entered. They took their new seats, seemingly innocent, ticketed passengers on their way to Tel Aviv. They had taken all of the guns and grenades with them, but offloaded them, presumably to Degani.

While this was going on, the plane continued to taxi with the copilot back in control and with the fire engines close at hand—the plane had not had time to dump its fuel. Bar-Lev told the copilot to taxi slowly. He then called the crew together and instructed them that, should they be questioned, they should claim to speak only Hebrew and play dumb about any sky marshals.

As the plane rolled to a stop, the captain stood at the passenger door. Members of the Airports Authority Fire Brigade were the first to board the plane. They quickly removed Vider, in a state of profound shock with an unrecordable blood pressure, to a waiting ambulance. As Captain Bar-Lev began to close the door for takeoff to Tel Aviv, a British officer with the Criminal Investigations Division (CID) stepped in and stopped him. A dispute ensued until a police officer pointed a gun at Bar-Lev, ordered "Move! You are now on Great Britain's soil!" and forced him off the plane. The entire crew was then taken to a CID office at the airport. Through four hours of questioning and even when left alone in a room with a two-way mirror, none of the crew let on that they knew anything about any sky marshals.

A diplomatic tug of war that would linger for three months began to take shape. Israel wanted Khaled flown back to Israel at once. It claimed that the hijack attempt had taken place over international waters. That being the case, Israel, where the plane was registered and as the owner of the airlines, had the right to bring the hijackers to justice in Israel. But the British authorities took Arguello and Khaled off the plane, sending them away in another ambulance. Arguello was dead on arrival. Khaled, who had only a few light bruises, was subsequently taken to the Ealing police station in West London. The authorities were in no rush to let the plane go either, wanting to "first make a full enquiry of the incident." After all, there had been a hijack attempt, gunshots, and now a dead body, and the police wanted to determine whether a crime had been committed under British jurisdiction. (In fact, with the plane traveling five hundred miles per hour, or over eight miles a minute, it is safe to assume that some portion of the episode took place over British territory, even if it had started thirteen miles out.)

Over the next few hours, officers and representatives of various British security forces, the chief inspector from the Special Branch, and uniformed police officers all showed up. In particular, they wanted to know where the two security guards were.

As clever and exciting as it may have been, the sky marshal ruse, which took place in broad daylight with airport personnel swarming about and probably under someone's binoculared surveillance, did not fool anyone. But El Al officials denied that the two had boarded the other plane and claimed that the two had somehow disappeared. The police, who boarded the second plane, couldn't identify the two men, who were now holding tickets. Israel's ambassador to the United Kingdom, Michael Comay, who had arrived at the scene, quickly realized that "this game" would not only further delay both planes' departures, but would lead to a stalemate and possibly serious consequences for El Al. After some serious wrangling, the two marshals were identified, gave only the vaguest oral statements, and were released on their word to provide written testimony through the police as soon as they returned to Israel. With that, the second plane was released.

Meanwhile, the passengers had disembarked from the first plane. As soon as they arrived in Terminal 3, Mr. and Mrs. Hirsch rushed over to the TWA counter. Their three children, Susie, 14, Howie, 13, and Robert, 10, had spent the summer in Israel on tour. The parents had joined them for Howie's bar mitzvah but had had to travel separately for their return to the United States. The parents took the El Al flight, with only one scheduled stopover; the children were on a TWA flight with two. The parents had fully expected to greet their children at Kennedy Airport when they arrived. However, having just seen their lives pass before their eyes, Mr. and Mrs. Hirsch were thankful that their children had been spared this horrific experience. And now, they explained to the TWA representative, they needed to notify family in the United States that, since they were delayed, someone would have to meet the kids when they arrived in New York. The TWA representative took the Hirschs gently aside, put his arms around them, and walked them to the nearby lounge. With the greatest of difficulty, he told them that it was not known at this time exactly where TWA Flight 741 and their children were.

Patrick Arguello, it turned out, was an American citizen. He was born in California to a Nicaraguan father, Oscar, and an American mother named Kathleen Ryan. He was known to the FBI as an "agitator in South American politics," had traveled extensively to Latin and South America, but had no known connections with the PFLP. He was traveling on a forged Honduran passport under the name of Diaz but was also carrying a U.S. passport and a California driver's license. He was a mercenary who had taken on the job after an advance of £5,000.

Twenty-four-year-old Leila Khaled, on the other hand, was known to practically every Israeli because of her successful hijacking the year before. She had since undergone extensive plastic surgery by a top German surgeon, however, and was able to elude El Al security. She was traveling as Luna Maria Chaves, also on a forged Honduran passport. She and Arguello, whom she had met only a few days earlier, had boarded as a newly married couple. By detaining Khaled rather than letting El Al fly her back to Israel, Britain had just unwittingly enmeshed itself in an unfolding international imbroglio.[3]

Amsterdam, 3 PM

Peter Burton, a British citizen, had boarded Pan Am Flight 93 in Brussels and was sitting in the first row in coach. Dubbed Clipper Fortune, this spanking new Boeing 747 jumbo jet, built earlier that year, had logged only 1,125 flight hours. Now, at a stopover in Amsterdam, Burton noticed two well-dressed men board the plane and take their seats across the aisle from him. Ready for departure to New York were 19 crew members and 152 passengers, including 85 Americans.

As they were about to taxi, Captain Jack Priddy called the flight director, John Ferruggio, to the cockpit and asked him to search the two men. The tower had radioed El Al's suspicions about the two. "Look, Captain," said Ferruggio, "I suggest we take the plane back to the gate. I'm no cop." The pilot nixed the idea and summoned the two men on the PA to the flight director. When the two went forward, some stewardesses searched their seats and hand luggage, but found nothing. Captain Priddy searched the men himself and also found nothing. Informing the tower that he had no objection to flying them, he received permission to take off. Half an hour later, at about 4 PM over London, the two were in the cockpit. One had pulled a .25-caliber pistol from his crotch and held it to the side of the pilot's head. The other was holding a gun and a hand grenade. They announced that they were members of the PFLP and were taking over the plane.

Of the four hijackings attempted that day, this one was unplanned. In fact, the PFLP in Amman was at first unaware of it, initially claiming responsibility only for the other three.

Samir Abdul Majid Ibrahim and Ali As-Sayed Ali, Palestinians with black complexions and traveling on Senegalese diplomatic passports, were supposed to have been aboard the El Al plane, supporting Khaled and Arguello. According to El Al's Captain Bar-Lev, about an hour before his plane was scheduled to take off, the Israeli security chief at Schiphol Airport came into the cockpit to discuss four suspicious travelers. These were the early years of El Al's stringent security measures, instituted only after the first El Al hijacking in 1968. Its now-vaunted procedures were still in their formative stages, and the head of security, who was also relatively new at his position, needed Bar-Lev's advice. Two of the suspicious characters were Khaled and Arguello; Bar-Lev ordered thorough body checks, and, if found clean, they could fly. (In her recounting, Khaled does not mention an intense search.) But the captain sensed something fishy about the other two. They had bought their tickets that morning, paid in cash, and held sequentially numbered passports. So Bar-Lev refused to take them on his flight, and El Al helped them get onto a Pan Am flight scheduled to leave for New York a bit later. The two, undeterred, decided to hijack their new transport.

But where to take it? These two backups certainly did not know how to navigate to Jordan, assuming they knew at all that Jordan was the El Al plane's destination. Plus, they had no way to contact the PFLP for further instructions as they flew over Europe. So, they ordered Priddy to take the plane to where they, like Khaled, had probably received their marching orders—Beirut.

Ferruggio got on the loudspeaker and announced: "Ladies and gentlemen. . . . We have a gentleman who wants to go to Beirut today. The drinks are going to be on us."

The men cleared the upper lounge, except for one stewardess. One hijacker stayed upstairs, while the other stayed below and warned the passengers that, if they did not follow his instructions, the stewardess would be harmed.

When the plane reached Lebanese airspace at around 8:30 PM, the hijackers refused at first to allow it to land, since, they said, only the PFLP's representative in Beirut, Abu-Khalid, could authorize them to do so. So, they circled for about two hours while Abu-Khalid was summoned from a mountain resort town thirty minutes from Beirut. During the wait, contact was made with the PFLP to determine what to do with the plane. Not knowing if the huge plane could land on the desert floor, the PFLP decided that it should land in Beirut and that the two hijackers should demand the plane be flown to Egypt, "wire it up with explosives, [and] then explode it on the ground at Cairo airport. It would tell Nasser what we thought about his decision to start negotiating with the Israelis."

At last, Abu-Khalid arrived, accompanied by three or four armed *fedayeen.* At about 10 PM, Beirut agreed to let the plane land for "refueling" provided that only two local PFLP representatives would go aboard. Before landing, one of the hijackers threatened to blow up the plane with its passengers if anyone approached or interfered with it. The pilot repeatedly reiterated to the tower that he was convinced that the threat was deadly serious. At the hijackers' insistence, the Lebanese Army withdrew its vehicles from around the runways.

At 10:37 PM, the plane finally made the first 747 landing at Beirut airport, which was not built for such big planes. Between six and nine guerrillas then boarded the plane with a suitcase full of grenades and explosives. One terrorist, Mazen Abu-Mehanna, stayed aboard after the others deplaned. A Lebanese cabinet minister who came to the control tower implored the hijackers to release the passengers, or at least the women and children. The hijackers bluntly refused. Their instructions were clear: All passengers must remain on the plane. U.S. Ambassador Dwight Porter and Lebanese President Charles Helou tried to figure out how to keep the plane in Beirut even by force, by shooting out the tires or damaging the fuselage or wings. But, as Porter summed up: "It was clear that [the] hijackers were fanatically determined to carry out their mission, and we deemed we were in no position to test their resolve."

At about 1:30 AM, the plane took off, officially headed for Amman. Shortly after departure, however, the hijackers, having received handwritten instructions just prior to takeoff, ordered the Pan Am skipper to request a route to Cairo International airport. The hijackers had also been instructed "to blow themselves up along with the plane and passengers" if they were to arrive at an unfriendly airport.

Abu-Mehanna spent the flight wiring detonators and explosives inside the cabin. About a hundred feet above the runway in Cairo, he asked a stewardess for a match and lit the fuse. The passengers were told they had eight minutes to get off the plane. Ferruggio had already instructed the entire flight staff to evacuate the plane immediately. "Don't wait for me," he said. "Don't wait for the captain. Don't wait for Jesus Christ. Just get off this plane!" The huge jet landed at 4:07 AM and rolled to a stop at the far end of the runway, away from any terminal building. As soon as the plane came to a halt, the doors were opened and the passengers slid down the inflated ramps. One passenger who tape-recorded the drama reported: "The stewardess is right behind me waving her flashlight. She's gonna push me right out the door the first chance she gets."

It took only two minutes for passengers to clear out. Some managed to jump behind sand barriers as airport guards exchanged gunfire with the hijackers. Less than a minute after the passengers got out, the aircraft exploded. "The last crew member had just run clear of the wing as the huge 747 split open in a searing orange fireball of flame and smoke," reported Walter Cronkite. The aircraft was completely demolished; only its tail stood partially intact. Almost miraculously, the crew and passengers suffered only minor injuries and fractures, except for an American woman who sustained a more serious back injury and a Belgian woman who suffered a fractured wrist. The three hijackers were detained for questioning but were never brought to justice.

Four hijacking attempts in one day was a spectacular feat, a record that would last thirty-one years almost to the day. What made it all the more remarkable was that just a few days before, Interpol had issued a secret alert to airport security forces throughout Europe that numerous terrorists had arrived from Beirut with plans to hijack planes.[4]

Dawson Field, 9 PM

About an hour and a half after landing, a guy from the Red Crescent came on board and said we'd be sleeping on the plane. He said not to worry, not to be concerned, not to be afraid—he didn't know too many words—so he said not to be angry, not to be confused. He would go to the city and try to be back and clear the whole matter up within two days. People were moaning and groaning, "How can we stay in the plane for two days? This is ridiculous." Little did we know how long we would be staying in that plane.

The Palestinian Red Crescent Society (PRCS) was not a recognized chapter of the International Committee of the Red Cross (ICRC); it was a Fatah entity. The individual who came aboard was Ghazi al-Saudi, a PRCS vice president. Guy Winteler and Vassil Yanco, ICRC delegates in Amman, also came to see the hijacked planes. Winteler reported that we had enough food and drink for the moment and that he and Yanco would return the next morning to address "all humanitarian questions."

Outside, meanwhile, once the celebrations had died down, tensions began to mount. The PFLP commandos around the plane became increasingly jittery, fearing that the Jordanian army was about to attack. The JAA had in fact begun sending troops to the airstrip to "assist."

Major Shafic Ajeilat had been sitting and talking with other officers in Zarqa, about twenty miles southwest of us, when he spotted a plane circling over Amman. The plane disappeared, and he knew something was awry. Shortly afterward, he received orders to send units to our position. Ajeilat rolled out with fire brigades and two mechanized companies with over 150 troops. En route, they were accosted by Iraqi soldiers, and, when they arrived at Dawson, *fedayeen* and Iraqi units barred the forces from approaching the planes. So they formed a semicircular cordon a few hundred feet away (to the right of the planes was an impassable field of large basalt rocks). Ajeilat's orders were to let no one in or out but not to kill any *fedayeen,* even if an opportunity presented itself, so as not to endanger the passengers. At about 2 AM, the JAA reinforced its barrier. A tank company would join in the morning.

As if PFLP fears of a Jordanian attack were not enough, rumors began swirling, confirmed even by Jordan's assistant chief of staff, that Israeli helicopters had flown in and were near the planes. The Israel Defense Forces and Jordanian Army both later denied the reports. But fearing attack, the guerrillas announced that they would blow themselves and the aircraft up if there were any attempt to "checkmate" the situation. Inside our wired cocoons, we passengers had no clue as to the military developments around us. Nor did we have any inkling, sitting in a darkened plane on the desert floor in Jordan, that we were now pawns in a complex and grave PFLP conspiracy.

> *Before we went to sleep, I was looking out the window and I became very scared because the guerrillas had some cars outside and the lights were flashing on and off, on and off, on and off. It seemed that they were sending some type of message somewhere. It was a very, very scary feeling. Now, back in the United States, every time I see car lights flashing on and off, I become very frightened—I jump, in fact. I get a very big sensation up and down my spine because it reminds me of this time.*

Thirty-four years later I learned what those flashing lights were. Ajeilat had sent out an officer to reconnoiter the area and locate the planes. Two other

Jordanian officers had also come with scout car platoons. When Ajeilat later entered the area with his units, he raised the officers on the wireless and asked that the army vehicles flash their lights so that he could find them.

> *We were there for the night and we figured, well, we'll go to sleep. We sat and slept in our chairs. We had a full load of 156 people on board, sitting in their chairs trying to fall asleep.*[5]

"AM I LEAVING ONE ORPHAN OR TWO?"

MONDAY, SEPTEMBER 7

Dawson Field, 4:45 AM

Night was over very soon, as dawn arrived at about 4:45 AM. The sun rose on an incredible scene: In a vast, silent void, on a stretch of parched, yellow-brown sand with an occasional pack of camels meandering by, sat two giant airplanes. They had landed on the desert floor in the Zarqa province, about thirty-five miles northeast of Amman. The landing strip—mud flats, actually, that harden and crack under the searing summer sun—was known to the local Arabs as *Ga Khanna*. The PFLP now called it *Ath-Thawra,* Revolution Airport.

By 5:30 AM, everyone was moving about. Over 150 people had slept aboard a TWA Boeing 707-331B and were now beginning their day on it. Only 11.5 feet wide, 110 feet long from cockpit door to rear lavatories, and 7.5 feet high in the center of the aisle, its narrow confines were definitely not designed for this. First class, where the crew and some passengers had slept, had four rows, with two seats per row on either side of the aisle. Ahead of the seats on the left, set apart by a half-height divider, was a little lounge area with a table and facing benches. The passenger door was forward of the lounge on the left. On the right, parallel to the lounge, were a galley, a service door, and two lavatories. In coach, the twenty-four rows—five through twenty-eight—had three seats on either side of the aisle. In the back left was a passenger door, beyond which were three lavatories. On the right were a service door and galley. The plane was full, and it was cramped.

The implications of our surreal situation had not yet fully registered. It was inconceivable that we would not be on our way home soon. After all, between the two planes there were about three hundred people sitting in the desert. Our governments would surely sort this mess out quickly. So, the passengers remained passengers and the cabin crew, well, cabin crew.

Rudi Swinkels, the purser, immediately set out to clean the toilets. They were a mess since all night there had been neither light nor water for flushing. At around 6:30 AM, the flight attendants passed out the leftover rolls, first to the children and women. They also poured water from coffee pots that they had filled in the first class lavatory, where water was available even with the power off. The crew moved about rather cautiously, but the night's tension and uncertainty as well as the nervousness and intensity of the plane's new keepers had dissipated somewhat with daylight.

At around 9 AM, the commandos brought a large container of hot sweetened tea, and later they brought pitas filled with egg salad, jam, and cheese, wrapped in plastic. These would be the standard fare for meals that week. The guerrillas also provided biscuits in tins from England and hard-boiled eggs stamped that they were from Albania. The stewardesses told the passengers who kept kosher to take the nonkosher food and not to make a fuss and aggravate the guerrillas. Many did. Our family just ate the pitas.

Halla Joseph was the PFLP commando in charge of our plane. Wearing a khaki outfit like her male counterparts, it was she who had boarded first the prior evening. Though older-looking and somewhat weather-beaten, Joseph was thirty-one years old and pretty. She had dark curly hair and was quiet and understated; one crew member called her sweet. (The crew would later award her a TWA Wings pin.) She told the crew that she was to have been married the day the Six-Day War broke out, that her fiancé had been killed in that war, and that she would marry once the Palestinian-Israel conflict subsided. She said that she had a sister with children in Cincinnati and relatives imprisoned in Israel because they were affiliated with the PFLP. Joseph posted round-the-clock armed commando guards at each door. Our captors very soon began to show off their booty, putting us on display.

> *The whole week, guerrillas and Iraqi and Jordanian soldiers paraded back and forth down the aisles of the plane, back and forth, carrying guns, looking. First of all, they had probably never seen a plane like this before. Second, they probably hadn't seen so many Jews in their lives before. Third, they probably hadn't seen as many people in their lives before—I mean so many scared people sitting in a plane. The guerrillas were trying to impress people by showing them what they had done. They were bringing in all types of people showing them what they had captured. It became very annoying.*

Traipsing aboard, dusty and smelly from the desert, with bullet-laden bandoliers crisscrossing their bodies and many of their teeth missing or gold-capped, these nonstop tourists, in addition to being annoying, were repugnant, demeaning, and frightening. "The kaffiyeh-wrapped Arabs paraded through the plane, staring at us intently and commenting to themselves," remembers Susie Hirsch. "I felt like an animal in the zoo, trapped and stared at by curious passers-by. . . . [T]heir eyes bore into me, examining me, as if I was not a person, but some freak in the circus that they had come from afar to see." The show went on aboard the Swissair plane too, keeping the passengers "in a state of controlled fear and uncontrolled anxiety," according to Dr. Julius Besner, a psychiatrist who was a captive on that plane.

> *After a while, we asked Jim Majer, the copilot, to ask the guerrillas to please ask these people to leave their guns outside when they were walking through the plane. It became very upsetting to us and eventually they did, except for this one lady commando who constantly came in with a gun. It looked like she was going to shoot everyone down. But otherwise everybody, except for the guards at night, didn't carry guns when they were in the plane.*

In the meantime, outside, there was a flurry of activity. The guerrillas had put up two tents. A big one between the planes served as their field headquarters. Over it, hanging limply in the heat, flew a giant red, green, white, and black Palestinian banner. A camouflaged water truck was parked nearby; on it was a sign in Arabic that read: "The Popular Front at your service." The PFLP also draped its banners over the front doors of the planes and a map of "Palestine" (including Israel) with the PFLP's trademark arrow (indicating its intent to return) on the TWA's side.

Preparing for a possible military intervention, the commandos also began digging about thirty trenches around the planes and emplacing antiaircraft guns and about a dozen machine gun nests. The area bristled with Russian Kalashnikov submachine guns. Jeeps with mounted heavy-caliber machine guns and camouflaged trucks and other vehicles manned by heavily armed guerrillas swarmed the area.

About 250 yards away stood a "second ring of sun-heated steel"—the Jordanian army had deployed tanks, armored personnel carriers, antiaircraft guns, communication jeeps, ambulances, and fire trucks—"every vehicle pointing like the spokes of a wheel toward the planes." The passengers on the planes anxiously and morosely looked out of their windows at the comings and goings, and began having a sinking feeling that we were going to be stuck there for a while.[1]

Amman, 8 AM

The PFLP had immediately claimed responsibility for the spectacular hijackings, and this morning it basked in the afterglow. Hijackings were not new. By the 1960s, hijackings from the United States and Latin America to Cuba had become commonplace; by 1970, there had been 184 recorded successful hijackings. World governments had not yet come to grips with the phenomenon, however. Fewer than thirty nations had ratified the 1963 Tokyo International Convention that delineated governmental responsibilities in hijacking incidents. (The United States, United Kingdom, Germany, and Israel had ratified; Switzerland had signed but not ratified; Jordan had not yet signed.) Plus, the agreement lacked teeth, not mandating extradition, a critical deterrent to would-be hijackers.

In 1968 the PFLP adopted hijackings as a weapon against Israel. "We cannot fight [Israel] plane for plane, tank for tank, soldier for soldier," argued the strategy's mastermind, Wadi Haddad. "We have to hit the Israelis at the weak joints . . . spectacular, one-off operations [that] will focus the world's attention on the problem of Palestine." Rationalized PFLP head George Habash, "Israel's only link with its friends is by air and sea. It therefore becomes inevitable for us to blockade these routes . . . El Al planes are straightforward military targets."

Haddad put hijacker-candidates through rigorous training that went beyond weapons and explosives proficiency. They were taught the routines of pilots of the largest and most modern airliners so that they couldn't be bluffed. They were taught to land the planes in case the pilots were killed. Trainees practiced exchanging gunfire in the confined spaces of an aircraft's cabin and cockpit, were tutored on how to outsmart airport security, and studied the laws that could be applied to them in various countries if captured. An intelligence staff tracked airline routes, schedules, passengers, and airport security measures.

The string of Palestinian hijack attempts and deadly attacks against civil aviation targets over the ensuing two years is chilling. So is the fact that few perpetrators were punished. On July 23, 1968, PFLP guerrillas seized their first plane—an El Al flight from Rome to Lod—and forced it to land in Algiers. After holding the plane, eleven crew, and twenty-one Israeli passengers for five weeks, they succeeded in gaining the release, as a "goodwill gesture," of sixteen Palestinian prisoners from Israeli jails. The hijackers got off scot-free. Five months later, on December 26, two PFLP terrorists attacked an El Al plane with grenades and machine guns in Athens, killing an Israeli passenger and wounding a stewardess. They were sentenced to fourteen and seventeen years respectively but, as you will see, did not serve out their terms.

On February 18, 1969, four Palestinian terrorists with machine guns attacked an El Al plane at Zurich's Kloten airport, killing the pilot and wounding the copilot. One terrorist was killed by El Al security guard Mordechai Rahamim; the other three were each sentenced to twelve years of hard labor. They would become part of our story and would not serve out their terms. On August 29, Leila Khaled and a PFLP colleague hijacked TWA flight 840 from Rome to Tel Aviv, forcing it to land in Damascus, where they blew up its cockpit and nose. Two Israeli passengers were held hostage until December 5. Khaled and her associate were held briefly, then released. On December 21, an attempt to hijack a TWA plane in Athens was foiled. The three Palestinian gunmen were captured and sentenced to two years each. They did not serve out even these short terms.

On February 10, 1970, three members of the Action Group for the Liberation of Palestine executed a grenade assault on an airport bus headed for an El Al plane at Munich Airport, killing one and wounding eleven. The three were detained in Germany, awaiting trial. They too would become part of our story and never be tried. Less than two weeks later, on February 21, a Swissair plane was blown up after takeoff from Zurich for Tel Aviv. Forty-seven passengers died, including fifteen Israelis. That same day, a bomb exploded aboard an Austrian airliner carrying mail to Israel, but the plane landed safely.

Then, on July 22, 1970, the PFLP hijacked an Olympic Airways jet en route from Beirut to Athens, diverting it to Cairo. Through the intervention of the International Red Cross and André Rochat (who substituted himself as a hostage for the passengers on the plane) but against Israel's urgings, Greece agreed to release its seven Palestinian terrorist prisoners (the five above plus two others jailed for an attack on the El Al office in Athens on November 27, 1969, in which a Greek boy was killed) in return for the hijacked plane and passengers.

Now, for the first time in history, hundreds of innocent passengers on multiple planes were being held as human bargaining chips. The PFLP would reveal its asking price later in the day.[2]

Amman, 8 AM

The Jordanian government was powerless and humiliated. Other than condemning the hijackings "in principle," ringing the site with troops, and providing food and first aid, it was helpless. It controlled neither the planes nor the passengers. A band of outlaws was blatantly violating its sovereignty and using Jordan's territory to stow 300 captives in a major international spectacle. A military assault to free the hostages was out of the question. Although the army had "surrounded the whole lot," lamented the king, the presence of so many innocent people was like "a gun at our heads."

Unbeknown to anyone, however, the hijackings were the last straw for Jordan's King Hussein. "That's it," he said to himself that day.[3]

Dawson Field, 10:30 AM

Like the other mothers aboard the plane, my mother, Sara, would spend the coming week not only fearing for her own life, but fretting over her children's safety and well-being. It would not be easy to keep the younger ones occupied, to make sure they had enough to eat and drink, and to allay their concerns day and night. That she, like some other passengers, would be particularly harassed by the guerrillas over the next few days only intensified her anxiety.

"Toward the latter part of the morning," recounted my mother, "they were making a great to-do about the passports. They were looking for Israeli passports and they kept coming over to me. My children wear skullcaps and the guerrillas kept coming to me and saying that I was an Israeli and I was hiding Israeli passports. I told them that I was an American and now had no passports at all. I would satisfy one person and a few minutes later another would come. They would point their guns at me and accuse me of lying and of hiding Israeli passports. It was quite terrifying." One of my mother's accusers was a woman who spoke English and claimed to be a University of Chicago graduate. She came over with her machine gun and, recalled my mother, "almost jabbed me with it." But this would not be the end of it, either for my mother or for other Jewish passengers.[4]

Amman, 11 AM

Fighting broke out again in Amman between guerrillas and government troops. Chaos reigned, despite the two-day-old agreement. In the morning, the *fedayeen* conducted a mass search of houses in one neighborhood, kidnapped several Jordanian soldiers, and seized military and civilian vehicles. Telephone lines from Amman to Beirut were down yet again. In the early afternoon, shooting erupted around the U.S. embassy, and the embassy took a hit. Later in the afternoon, *fedayeen* directed machine gun and rocket fire at government radio and television buildings, an army position, and a police station. The car of a member of the royal family was fired upon in Amman's suburbs. Most shops were closed, and most parts of the city were near anarchy.[5]

Bern, 11 AM

In a move that would prove embarrassing and from which it would have to quickly back-pedal, the Swiss government capitulated to the PFLP—even before the PFLP had formally presented its demands. The two International Committee of the Red Cross (ICRC) delegates who had come out to Dawson the previous evening conveyed an oral message from the PFLP giving Switzerland seventy-two hours to release the three Palestinian *fedayeen* serving time for the Kloten attack a year earlier. After receiving the message Sunday evening, both the Swiss Federal Council and the Zurich Canton Grand Council—which had jurisdiction over the three in Regensburg prison—went into emergency session. Though expressing "shock" at the ultimatum and declaring that "such practices are contrary to all rules of law," both agreed to release the men in exchange for the Swiss plane, passengers, and crew. They were highly concerned that the Palestinians might blow up the aircraft with the passengers. The ICRC was asked to arrange the swap.

But the Federal Council did not have constitutional authority to release the three. And the Grand Council was not empowered to grant clemency until the prisoners had exhausted their legal rights, which they had not. Nonetheless, "[t]he law must yield to *raison d'état*," explained one senior official. Another rationalized: "while it is true that the decision impinges on the foundation of Swiss justice, 280 [*sic*] lives carry a lot of weight."

Although it later would claim that the deal had been for *both* aircraft and *all* citizens, Switzerland had in fact agreed to a swap for just its *own* citizens and plane. It was only after the interrelated demands on the other parties became known that the Swiss realized that they could no longer conclude a bilateral bargain. And, according to Jacques Freymond, a senior Red Cross official, the ICRC had refused to deal with the Swissair passengers alone because it was not prepared to discriminate among passengers based on nationality, religion, or any other consideration.

In any case, the Swiss decision was quickly and almost universally decried as setting "a dangerous precedent" that "condoned Arab blackmail."[6]

Dawson Field, noon

"As the morning wore on," reported *Newsweek*'s Loren Jenkins, "the 100-degree heat radiating up from the desert floor distorted the two planes into a shimmering mirage." Inside the planes, the heat became oppressive as temperatures rose to 120 degrees Fahrenheit with no electricity and no air conditioning. We kept the window shades down to keep the blazing sun out, and the crew opened the over-the-wing emergency exits to let some air in. Fortunately for me, my family was sitting near one of them. Unfortunately, the openings did not provide much ventilation to areas further away, like the middle rows of coach, which remained stifling. Plus, the desert breeze was hot and brought with it sand, particularly when twisters kicked up.

With the oppressive heat and the lack of diversions, babies and children became uncomfortable and restless. Some started screaming and running up and down the aisle. This upset the guards until, at one point, they ordered all of us to remain in our seats. This punishment would be reimposed periodically during the week. When it was, we would fearfully return to our places. Those who needed the lavatories would have to wave their hands to get the attention of the guard at the rear and obsequiously ask his permission to use the toilet. Gradually, people would start getting up and wandering around again, and life would return to "normal." This day, the guards eventually permitted the children to get off the plane to stretch their legs on the ground, but many parents did not let their kids go, fearing they might be snatched away.

Throughout the day, Rudi Swinkels made several announcements by megaphone exhorting everyone to keep the lavatories clean. His efforts were futile, though, because, with no electricity, no running water, and 150 people on board, the situation was impossible. The only result of his announcements was that the commandos took a liking to the megaphone and promptly took the second one off the plane.

Despite it all, morale aboard our plane was reasonably good so far. The full severity of our situation had not yet registered, and there was still hope that it might be resolved imminently. Outside, however, "the menacing presence of King Hussein's army" began to make the commandos edgy, and they threatened to blow up the planes unless the troops retreated.[7]

Amman, 1 PM

The start of the affair—the hijackings—was meticulously planned. The end game was not, and the PFLP's demands would evolve over time. This was due in part to changing circumstances, such as Khaled's failure to bring an El Al plane to Dawson and her unexpected capture. But it was also due to the PFLP's internal dissension that would make it increasingly difficult to find anyone to speak authoritatively and decisively for the organization.

Early this afternoon, a PFLP spokesperson, Abu-Omar, laid out the PFLP's demands in a "quiet and unemotional" manner to David Eugene Zweifel, a U.S. Embassy official in Amman. These were that Swiss nationals would be released upon release of the three Swiss prisoners; German nationals upon release of the three German prisoners; British nationals upon Leila Khaled's release; Israeli nationals and "dual nationals" (about fifty according to Abu-Omar) upon the release of *fedayeen* in Israeli prisons; and, nondual American citizens when all demands were met (that is, there were no specific demands for their release). Once Israel agreed in principle to a "prisoner exchange," the PFLP would reveal the names of those it wished released from among the three to four thousand Israel was holding. A dual citizen, added Abu-Omar, was anyone holding two passports or only one passport if the PFLP suspected that the person had been born in Israel.

Abu-Omar set a seventy-two hour deadline that began at 6 AM that morning. If the demands were not met by the deadline, he threatened, the planes and passengers would be blown up. He told Zweifel to make the demands known to the "highest levels of all governments concerned." He also warned that the PFLP would destroy the aircraft if Jordan or Israel attempted military intervention and urged Zweifel to impress upon the governments the seriousness of his threat.

Abu-Omar refused Zweifel's request to visit the planes, blaming the Jordanian army's cordon. The army was indeed adamantly refusing diplomatic access to Dawson. But the PFLP would probably have refused in any case, not wanting embassies to find out how many of their citizens were aboard. Throughout the entire three weeks, the PFLP would deny access by government representatives to their citizens and would not even provide a list of hostages.

The PFLP's demands clearly indicated its intent to isolate and then conduct protracted negotiations with Israel. In fact, the PFLP advised the United States, it was not expecting any Israeli prisoners to be released by the deadline. Rather, it wanted only Israel's agreement in principle to such an exchange. Negotiations could then drag on endlessly while the PFLP hung on to the Israelis and the "dual" citizens.

The PFLP demand for the prisoners in Germany was likely an afterthought once it learned that it held German hostages. The guerrillas in Germany were not PFLP members, and the PFLP had not hijacked a German plane. The PFLP demand of the British was not only an afterthought—Britain became a player only after insisting on detaining Khaled—but a bluff. As the British ambassador in Amman, John Phillips, cabled his Foreign Office that evening: "[T]he *fedayeen* have been trying to create the impression that they were holding British subjects when they were not in fact doing so." (Automated reservation systems were still some years off.)

The PFLP also bluffed about how many Israelis it held. It was holding nowhere near the fifty asserted by Abu-Omar and reported in that morning's leading Palestinian newspaper. In fact, the PFLP was probably quite taken aback at its paltry catch. Rather than holding a full El Al planeload of Israelis, as originally intended, it had netted only three "pure" Israelis—Mrs. Nava Goren and her two young children—and only fourteen or so dual nationals of whom only two were adult males. The PFLP would try desperately but in vain throughout the week to find more Israeli citizens—by interrogating Jewish TWA passengers, searching their luggage for "incriminating" documents and photographs, and trying to draw convoluted inferences. The PFLP's misinformation effort did succeed at first, however, and the number fifty was disseminated widely.

At 4 PM, the PFLP publicized its demands at a press conference at its headquarters in a small building behind the Philadelphia Hotel in downtown Amman. It also upped the ante, now insisting that Israel release two Algerian diplomats. The two had been taken off a BOAC plane that landed in Israel in transit in mid-August. They held senior positions and "special tasks" in the Algerian government, a country at war with Israel; one was reportedly the head of the Algerian security forces. Israel claimed to be merely exercising its "recognized rights" of detaining them on security grounds "for questioning."

The clock was now ticking toward the deadline set for Thursday morning, September 10, at 6 AM local time. If the PFLP's demands were not met by then, the planes would be blown up with us aboard.[8]

Dawson Field, 3 PM

Throughout the day we had a radio on board and we were trying to listen to it through an open window . . . trying to find out what had happened to us. We thought it was very amusing when we heard on the radio broadcast on Monday afternoon that we had landed in Amman, Jordan. It was very cute. We had been sitting there for a day, and they finally realized, and we were now hearing news broadcasts that we had landed.

The first break in the situation came when Jordanian Army commander in chief Haditha, who had been negotiating with the guerrillas since first light, emerged from the command tent and announced wearily: "We have managed to free the women and children. The rest are being held until the commandos' conditions are met." In return, he had reluctantly agreed to pull the army back about three kilometers. "As the vehicles turned to take up new positions about two miles away, the desert was turned into a scene . . . with half-tracks and tanks churning up 200-foot-long plumes of sand and dust," reported *Newsweek*'s Jenkins. Haditha had tried but failed to obtain the release of all hostages. But the Jordanian government now believed that at least all women and children from both planes would be brought into Amman.

They started taking passengers off the plane to take them to the hotels in Amman. At first, they started by nationality. They said that anybody from France and Pakistan and India and some other countries should get off the plane; they were going to hotels.

At one point, Klaus Jeschke, a German citizen, stood up and insisted that he be taken off as well. "I am German, not Jewish! Ich bin nicht kein Jude!" he yelled. Later in the week, after he in fact was taken away, his wife asked the terrorists why they were keeping her and her children since they were not Jewish and not a part of this conflict. A Holocaust survivor who heard this exchange turned to the woman and, in fluent German, said to her: "This time we're going to die together, Germans and Jews."

> *Then they came to America. They said all American women and children could get off the plane. So they all did. And I sneaked through also, even though by the guerrillas' standards I was a little too old to be considered a child. I put on a pleading, downcast face—as if I was about to cry—and they let me through.*

Two commandos sat in the first class lounge, and the debarking passengers had to state their name, nationality, and religion. My mother told them that we were Jewish. Fearing discrimination, however, some of the other Jewish passengers did not reveal their faith.

> *I was getting off the plane with my family. We were six people and we had, I think, fifteen pieces of hand luggage. So we walked down the aisle, schlepping all our stuff, and we had to get down from the plane. There weren't the usual steps, but there was a ladder; we had to climb down the ladder and then hand our stuff down. It was a very difficult operation, carrying out all our little packages.*

As the passengers descended the wooden ladder to the desert floor, some guerrillas took advantage of the opportunity to look up the women's skirts as they struggled down. Some of the women were even groped under the pretext of being helped down. My mother recalled, "Every time I would go up and down, they would hold me full bosom or look up my dress and cause me a great deal of embarrassment. . . . I had no one to complain to." No Arab women were present at the time.

> *Finally we got into the little buses they had for us. We squeezed into this little bus, the six of us, and then they brought in some more people, and all our packages and bundles. We're all settled down, and then after ten minutes they tell us, "Everybody out!"*

I still recall that when we sat in the little bus, my mother started to say something to me in Hebrew, which we spoke at home, and I tried frantically to get her to switch to English before anyone heard. Fortunately, no one did.

My mother recounts: "As soon as we were loaded, the Red Cross truck drove away and waved. They said 'We will see you at the hotel.'" As soon as the Red Cross truck had driven off, the guerrillas got on each bus and told us there had been a mistake and that we would have to get off the bus. They would call our names and, when we heard our names called, we were to get back on the bus.

So we schlepped all our luggage out again, out into a little area on the desert floor and we stood around. Then they started reading off names. That moment felt a little bit like a concentration camp—I don't know since I was never there, thank God—but, it seemed to me this is what it must have been like, because surrounding us were guerrillas with machine guns pointing down in our direction, and they were reading off names. Fortunately, it was nothing like a concentration camp, but what they were doing was taking all non-Jews to hotels; not one single Jew was taken to a hotel.

We stood in a circle hoping to hear our names called off the pink slips that we had filled out the previous evening. Some women became distraught. Mrs. Erna Jankelovitz, an Auschwitz survivor traveling with two young sons, saw history repeating itself. When the guerrillas said that was it, we realized that all the Jewish women and children were left standing with some non-Jewish women who had chosen to stay with their husbands. The buses drove off with the others. Millie Leser, 15 at the time, recalls, "And so it was—the convoy of vans drove away with most of the non-Jews, leaving all the Jews behind. There we were, Jews from all walks of life . . . standing in a large circle, surrounded by Arabs pointing their weapons at us. There was silence except for the occasional whimper of a baby. I carry this picture in my mind always. The sun was setting in the desert and there was nothing to see for miles except for the sky and the sand. . . . We Jews felt so isolated and alone and knew that only God could help us at this point."

The guerrillas then ordered us back on the planes. Dejectedly, we climbed the ladder, the guerrillas once again standing at its foot. Susie Hirsch tugged self-consciously at the hem of her miniskirt, knowing that she was being ogled.

So we had to schlep all our bundles back onto the plane. As soon as we got back on, I took off the Israeli army shirt I had been wearing when I had boarded the plane. In fact, I had been wearing a full uniform when I got onto the plane, and somebody had remarked to her husband how nice it was to see an Israeli soldier with a yarmulke. When I heard this remark, I was very happy. As soon as we had left Athens, I had taken off my army pants and put on some short pants, but I was still wearing my shirt. I hadn't taken it off while we were in Jordan, and I was pretty much afraid it would get me into some type of trouble, that they would think I was an Israeli soldier. I had noticed someone pointing me out, wearing this uniform, and, when we got off the plane into the cars, everybody who passed by looked at me, looked at my shirt, and pointed at me and stared. So I didn't feel too safe in it. I took it off, stuck it in our laundry bag, and took out a smelly shirt from the bag and put it on instead.

While this was happening on our TWA plane, the *fedayeen* took all the Swissair plane's women and children, including Jews, to Amman. By evening, 127 men, women, and children of various nationalities had been moved (37 in the TWA group, the rest, Swissair). The PFLP professed to the media that they had been taken off because they "were not in a condition to endure another night in the open desert." But it had nothing to do with endurance. Not one of the approximately eighty Jews who had boarded the TWA flight in Israel was taken to Amman. Thirty-three children were kept on board the TWA plane, almost all Jews. In total about 185 Israeli, American, German, and Swiss citizens, including several elderly Jews, remained in the desert.[9]

Bonn, 3 PM

During the afternoon, German officials met to decide whether to release the three *fedayeen* jailed in a Munich prison, as the PFLP had demanded. Unlike the Swiss situation, since the three had not yet been tried German law permitted the release if they were expelled from the country.

By 6 PM, haunted by the looming deadline and maintaining that "the security of the West Germans in both planes is of the first priority," both the federal and Bavarian state governments decided to yield. Learning from the Swiss mistake, however, they resolved to coordinate with the other governments. (They did not see Israel as one of "all the governments involved.") Their initial announcement, too, was vague, stating only that the government had "taken measures" to help free the German nationals. But news agencies reported that night that Germany had in fact agreed to surrender its prisoners.[10]

Bern, 4 PM

"Feeling sheepish" about how they had rushed into accepting PFLP demands "without consulting others concerned, particularly the Americans," the Swiss Federal Council now decided to release its prisoners only if all of the hostages would be released. It too decided to coordinate with the United States, Britain, and Germany, but not with Israel, "one of the combatants." Both Germany and Switzerland had now revealed their hands. They had awarded the PFLP concessions that would complicate matters for the other countries and undermine attempts to present a united front. For the next three weeks, the United States and Israel would work unceasingly to keep the Swiss and Germans from implementing their deal-in-principle until all passengers were released, while the PFLP would try nonstop to drive a wedge between the European countries and the other two.[11]

London, 4 PM

As no British citizens or planes seemed to be involved, Britain's only stake in the standoff for the moment was Leila Khaled. Nonetheless, Her Majesty's

Government, after urgent talks all day, was split between those who refused to yield to blackmail and those who sought a way out. The Foreign and Commonwealth Office (FCO) felt strongly about "some form of consultation among the governments immediately concerned . . . i.e., US, UK, FRG, and Swiss." Again, not Israel, whose presence at coordinating meetings "would be inhibiting." As to Khaled, the United Kingdom could prosecute her under British law, Attorney General Peter Rawlinson informed the Cabinet, if a crime was committed over British territory. Alternatively, he could keep her available, uncharged, as a bargaining chip. Or, he could extradite her to Israel. Under Britain's extradition treaty with Israel and the Tokyo Convention, the United Kingdom was obliged, upon Israel's request, to hold her either for trial in Britain or for extradition. Israeli Transportation Minister Shimon Peres had in fact already announced that Israel would ask for Khaled because her crime was committed on an Israeli plane, Israeli territory. Unsure what to do, the Cabinet directed that the criminal investigation be continued, for the moment.[12]

Jerusalem, 5 PM

Israel had a relatively small human stake in the drama since there were only three pure Israelis among the hostages. The fourteen or so other Israelis were also U.S. citizens, thus a U.S. responsibility. Nonetheless, Israel was extremely concerned that the PFLP would segregate its citizens (as it had done the prior year in Damascus) and the Jewish passengers, whom they would treat more harshly, and try to hold longer. It urgently sought the United States' help in preventing the other governments from striking separate deals that would leave Israeli citizens and Jews stranded in the hands of the PFLP.[13]

Dawson Field, 5:30 PM

By the time the women and children had climbed back on the plane and gotten themselves settled, it was getting dark. One woman recalled, "It was a very dejected group because we had experienced a terrible letdown. There was more lethargy, and we were just sitting and waiting for the next thing to happen."

> *Our family had rows eight and nine on the left side when we first got on board, but when we left the plane, we lost our seats. So we had one row, nine, and another row way back somewhere—twenty-four or twenty-five, I don't remember exactly. So, Monday I was sitting in row nine, right next to the emergency window, and outside there were guerrillas walking around all the time. Every once in a while they would point up to me, and call me and say "hey you, hey you." Some would even try speaking in Hebrew, trying to get us to "prove" that we were Israelis. It became very annoying at times, having them looking up at you.*

In the late afternoon, the commandos brought a hot dinner that had been provided by the Jordanian army. There was chicken, roast beef with gravy, beans, salad, potatoes, bananas, grapes, and tea, all of which the crew promptly distributed. The kosher passengers were particularly happy to get the grapes and bananas. So much so, that by the time the stewardesses were only halfway through the cabin, no fruit was left.[14]

Washington, 1 PM

Though unaware of how many of its citizens were immediately involved, the United States was painfully aware of its big stake in the events. It also recognized that the PFLP intended to use it as a lever against Israel. Since the United States did not yet have a plan, it realized that it needed the "closest possible consultation" with the other governments. Secretary of State William Rogers met with British ambassador John Freeman, Israeli ambassador Yitzhak Rabin, and the Swiss and German chargés in Washington.

Rogers began by framing the dilemma: "[T]o give in to *fedayeen* blackmail and save lives, or to take a very stiff stand and run the risk of losing lives." U.S. policy had been to never yield to such blackmail, believing that to do so would only encourage terrorism and make it impossible to hold a terrorist captive. Additionally, the United States would not countenance any hierarchies that the PFLP might try to establish among its citizens, such as singling out Jews or dual citizens. (Dual citizenship is permitted under U.S. law, and dual citizens are subject to the identical U.S. protection and efforts as nondual citizens.) Nor did it want the fate of its citizens tied to that of the Israelis or to have either Americans or Israelis detained after other hostages were released.

Rabin took the toughest line. Unlike the other four governments, Israel had been in this situation before, with its citizens held hostage by Palestinian terrorists. It believed that its experience taught it how best to negotiate: you don't, at least not ostensibly. Rabin asserted that Israel would not release the prisoners it held. "No one," he said, "should submit to blackmail," and he encouraged the others to work for the release of *all* passengers.

It quickly became obvious that the European countries, worried that the terrorists might kill the hostages, would not adopt Israel's tack. The U.S. administration, however, was less worried. The terrorists were not completely irrational, it held, and would not act rashly or spitefully as long as they still hoped to achieve their ends. They would want to negotiate. Rogers proposed that the five countries coordinate their positions, perhaps negotiating as a group. Rabin objected. He did not want to condone, even implicitly, the European inclination to accede to PFLP demands. He was probably also reluctant to subordinate Israel's policy to a group that might come back and pressure Israel. But the five agreed to continue "exchanging views" and to use the ICRC as their channel to the PFLP.

All five countries recognized that a united front was the humane and correct response. The Europeans knew that it was also, frankly, good for their relations with the United States. But they would vacillate over the next several weeks with shifts in their respective stakes, in their reading of the situation in Jordan, and in their domestic public opinions. These as well as their fundamental attitudes toward dealing with terrorist demands and the sanctity of their own laws and international commitments would color their actions and their grasp of, tolerance for, and ultimately patience with Israel's hard-nosed position and the American receptivity of it.

It didn't take long for Germany to back away from its commitment to a unified front. "Pressure to act unilaterally will grow irresistible as hours pass by without concrete results," it soon advised the United States. Germany believed that its deadline was some seven hours before the one communicated to the United States. The British also began quickly feeling out options. FCO Permanent Undersecretary Denis Greenhill cabled Freeman that he now thought that the PFLP might be "prepared to do a series of bilateral deals with governments concerned and that not all these [demands] are necessarily linked to one another."

European wavering notwithstanding, toward the end of the day in Washington, a proposal for a collective response to the PFLP began to take shape. The United States would ask the ICRC on behalf of itself, Germany, Switzerland, and Britain to insist that all passengers, crew, and aircraft be released for the prisoners in Germany, Switzerland, and the United Kingdom. Jordan would be asked to assure safe passage for the *fedayeen* at the airstrip, and Israel would be "notified" of the plan. Alexander Haig, deputy assistant to the president for national security affairs, saw this response as a way to buy time. But he believed that the PFLP would reject the offer and that the prospects of keeping the European countries in line were "rather dim."[15]

Intercontinental Hotel, Amman, 8 PM

The passengers taken off the planes arrived in Amman toward evening. Most were put up in the Jordan Intercontinental Hotel in a tony section of town, between the Second and Third Circles on Jabal Amman. When that hotel was filled, some TWA hostages were moved downtown to the older Philadelphia Hotel, a fifteen-minute drive away.

Despite their release, their status was ambiguous and would remain so for the duration. Had they been freed or just moved to a more comfortable location? Could they fly out at will? A PFLP spokesman said that they "were free to leave." The Jordanian government and U.S. embassy in Amman also believed that they were. But in fact, they were not. The Swiss were told flatly that these passengers were still under PFLP control and not free to go. None had passports. Legalities aside, traveling to the airport amid the fighting in and around Amman was risky. Plus, later in the week, the Red Cross itself would advise the countries to keep their citizens in Amman as negotiating leverage. So, these passengers were not going anywhere soon.

Although the hostages now in Amman were more comfortable, they were not much safer. In the evening, sporadic shooting was heard in several quarters of Amman, including the hotel area. At midnight, a mortar shell hit the Intercontinental itself.

The German embassy staff was pessimistic. They believed that there was little hope for a Jordanian-*fedayeen* cease-fire and not much more for the release of all hostages. Yusuf Sayigh, chairman of the PLO Planning Council, was also pessimistic. He saw little chance of settling differences with the government. The resistance movement was becoming increasingly unified, he believed. Further clashes with the government would only prompt Palestinian leaders to bury minor differences in order to achieve the "important goals of the resistance," presumably including King Hussein's overthrow.[16]

Bern, 9 PM

Bern, the countries agreed, would be the best place to coordinate action. It was closer to Jordan than Washington, and the ICRC was headquartered about an hour away in Geneva.

Meanwhile, in Geneva, the ICRC was being drawn somewhat ambiguously and reluctantly into this affair. It now faced a complex negotiating challenge, no longer the mere logistical arrangement originally requested by the Swiss. The ICRC would have to insert itself between Israel and the PFLP, problematic both because of its role in resolving July's Olympic Airways hijacking and because the PFLP was not a government. After serious deliberation, however, the Red Cross agreed to "offer its good offices" and serve as intermediary. Now, even before being officially approached by the four (or five) governments, one of its planes was being readied to leave before dawn with doctors, including a Dr. Roland Marti, Red Cross delegate Louis Jacquinet, and medicines and food for the hostages. Two Swissair technical staff would also secretly be aboard, as well as André Rochat.

With a large dose of haziness that would persist throughout the next three weeks as to its actual composition, role, and policy, the Bern Group, as it would be known, came into being. The ICRC too, unclear about its mandate or even whom it spoke for, became the intermediary with the Palestinians. On this rickety structure rested our fate.[17]

Dawson Field, 10:30 PM

As darkness descended this second night, the guards brought aboard two kerosene lamps, placing one at either end of the plane. The window exits were kept open for ventilation. Some passengers seated nearby complained that they were cold and wanted the windows shut. After some calm negotiation by the crew suggesting that they trade seats with passengers who were too warm, they quieted down.

People found different ways to cope with the stress and comfort themselves as they tried to fall asleep. Some fantasized about heroic rescues. I believed that the Israeli Air Force was overhead and would swoop in to save us. Susie Hirsch imagined that her cousin, Tommy, a pilot, would fly his boss's private jet the few short miles from Israel and rescue her and her brothers. But Susie also helped some of the mothers on the plane care for their little ones sitting near her. She played with them, held them, comforted them, and sang them to sleep. This was a tremendous comfort to her, too.

Just as Bettie McCarthy was preparing to sleep, a commando stopped her and directed her to help him find six passengers "for questioning." He had their names written in Arabic, which he read off to her, and instructed her to bring them forward. Although she tried to do so quietly, people realized that something was amiss. Many became frightened. McCarthy tried, unsuccessfully for the most part, to calm them.

> *Monday night before falling asleep around ten-thirty, eleven, twelve, the guerrillas came in and started calling off names. They called six people out. And of course anybody who was up when they called out those names didn't go to sleep the rest of the night. They took these six people off the plane and we didn't hear anything about them until they got back to the United States, which was after I did. I figured I would be called out that night also because they had seen my Israeli uniform. Fortunately, I wasn't. But I still didn't sleep that night.*

Neither did many of the other passengers. The stark, dire reality of our situation had hit home.

Jerry Berkowitz was the first one called. Fearful of being mistaken for an Israeli, he had earlier taken off his knitted *kippah.* A U.S. citizen, born and bred in Philadelphia, Berkowitz lived in the Bronx and taught chemistry at Bronx Community College. He and his wife, Rivke, were seated in the right bulkhead row with their two-year-old daughter, Talia, lying in front of them on the floor. They suspected that Rivke was pregnant (which she was). Jerry had fallen asleep without his shoes; Rivke was still awake. When his name was called, as somehow Rivke knew it would be, she told him to put on his shoes and jacket because she intuited that he would be taken off the plane.

At the forward exit, it wasn't easy for Berkowitz to get off the plane. The wooden ladder didn't quite reach the plane's door. Not able to see, because there was no light, Berkowitz probed with his foot until eventually it found the top rung. He climbed down and was directed toward the rear of the plane where he sat down on the desert floor under the tail. He had nothing with him but the clothes on his back. He sat there alone in the dark, shivering from cold and fear, without a clue as to what was happening to him or why.

A few minutes later, John Hollingsworth joined him, leaving his wife behind too. An American diplomat who had just completed his posting in Algeria, he had boarded with his wife in Frankfurt for home leave prior to taking on his next assignment in Luxembourg. He walked over to Berkowitz and matter-of-factly said: "John Hollingsworth, State Department. When they start the Gestapo tactics, ask for the International Red Cross."

The next two to come off were the Harari-Raful brothers. Both Abraham and Joseph were rabbis who taught at Flatbush Yeshiva High School in Brooklyn. Abraham was traveling with his wife and their two children; Joseph was traveling with his wife and three children. Their 75-year-old mother was on board too. Both brothers were citizens of the United States and Israel.

The last two men to be taken off the plane were Robert Schwartz and James Woods, Defense Department employees. Schwartz was director of the Research and Development Center in Thailand, a unit of the Advanced Research Plans Agency (ARPA); Woods, the defense chief at the center. Both were involved in counterinsurgency in Thailand as the Vietnam War raged. They had boarded in Bangkok carrying classified documents, making their way back to Washington to testify to Congress. Learning of their hijacking, the State Department would instruct the Bangkok embassy to respond "no comment" or "cannot confirm at this time" if questioned by the press about their internment. Otherwise, the State Department believed, "confirmation would risk leading to a prolonged retention, possibly even exploitation [of] the situation given [the] sensitive nature of many ARPA activities and concerns in Thailand." What the State Department had no way of knowing was that as soon as our plane was hijacked, the two had set about cutting passages out of their documents. They were sitting across the aisle from me, and I vividly recall the scene. They got rid of the clippings by eating some and flushing the rest down the toilet.

The six men were herded into a Land Rover and blindfolded. There were only five blindfolds, however, and Berkowitz was spared. Only one or two guards escorted them. As the car pulled away from the plane, Berkowitz had the distinct feeling that they were being taken away to be shot. Driving with their lights off, they would occasionally pass a sand dune, and Berkowitz would say to himself, "OK, this is it. They're going to shoot us and dump us behind one of these dunes. No one will ever find us."

Eventually, they hit a main road and then a checkpoint manned by Iraqi soldiers near Zarqa. The soldiers let the car through, and it traveled up the road past Ramtha toward Irbid, a city of 150,000 at the northern tip of Jordan. Riding through the night, Berkowitz wondered, as he would for the next three weeks, "Am I leaving behind one orphan or two?"[18]

"WE MAY HAVE TO FACE A TRAGEDY"

TUESDAY, SEPTEMBER 8

Dawson Field, 6 AM

Susie Hirsch awoke in a fright, realizing that the fathers of the children she had sung to sleep the evening before had been taken off the plane during the night. For the rest of the week, each approaching nightfall would bring fear and anxiety. Who would be taken off tonight? Where might they be taken? What might happen to them? Would the guerrillas consider her thirteen-year-old brother, Howie, a man, and take him away one night too?[1]

Dawson Field, 9 AM

> *Tuesday, they came up around 9:00 in the morning. They came and they said, "Today we have exercises. . . . Everybody* must *go outside for exercises." When I heard that everybody* must *go outside, I figured they were going to check the hand luggage. Again I became very frightened because I had not just the army shirt and pants I had been wearing but another uniform—a full Israeli army uniform with stripes and pins and buttons. I was even higher than Six-Day War hero, General Moshe Dayan himself, and I was very frightened that they would find this.*

Susie Hirsch was terrified too that they would find the picture she had taken with a handsome young kibbutznik whom she had met. She tore it up and wanted to "flush it" down the toilet, but the guerrilla guard would not let her in. Everyone had to get off the plane, including babies and children. Some of the older Jewish passengers didn't want to deplane, but the commandos insisted. Getting down the rickety ladder was again not a simple matter and the commandos again helped the people climb down. Once we were all off, the ladder was removed.

Despite the early hour, it was already hot, and we congregated in the shade of the plane's wings. The crew gave everyone a fresh TWA cup, half-filled with soda. We were told to hold on to them since the supply was running low. The cups became our all-purpose utensil. My mother remembers, "When the fruit cocktail came we had it in this cup. We had water in this cup, tea in this cup, and everything in this cup. We just wiped it around in order to clean it when we had water to spare." We milled about aimlessly. The guards stood around us with guns, and if we wandered too far they would raise their weapons. They pointed their guns at my mother: "I was walking, and we walked a little too far. They lifted the guns and pointed at us and threatened us to get back where we belong."

While we were outside, one of the guerrillas pointed a gun toward Jeffrey Newton. They had pointed to him before with their fingers and they told him to take off his yarmulke. At first he didn't want to but then the guerrilla pointed his gun at him and he decided to take it off. Now that I think of it, it was probably because he had a Jewish star on it; it was a white yarmulke with a blue Jewish star on it. So they told him to take it off and he did. After a while, I decided it would be the best policy for me too.

Before we got back on the plane, a female commando said, "Your governments have not responded to our demands and therefore your lives and property are not our responsibility." Of course, this frightened many of us.

It was getting very hot, and we were tired, hungry, and thirsty. There was no place to sit except on the hot sand. After about an hour and a half, the guerrillas finally leaned the ladder against the plane again, and everyone was ordered back on board. It was immediately obvious that the commandos had searched the hand luggage. They seemed very angry as they informed us that they had come upon documents, souvenirs, an Israeli passport, pictures of passengers with Israeli soldiers, and receipts for donations to organizations to Israel. Some of this they found in the hand luggage, some torn up in the garbage. The picture of Sarah Malka aiming a rifle amidst some Israeli soldiers really set them off.

Fortunately, they touched only one of our pieces of hand luggage and didn't find my uniform. But they took my mother's wallet out of her pocketbook.

They had also confiscated everything they found made in Israel. They took one of our prayer books, some Hebrew books, bottles of Israeli perfume, and several toys that my brothers had been playing with. They confiscated

Susie Hirsch's little prayer book. They would eventually expose all film of pictures taken in Israel.

Abu-Nidal had come on board to oversee the operation. A short man with big brown eyes, he was very upset. He and Halla Joseph ordered everyone to sit down and commanded crew members to go through the plane and tell us to turn in anything, except religious articles, made in Israel.

> *They said, "Everything made in Israel must come up front and don't try to fool us because we will spot-check the luggage again," which they did. So again I became very excited. I didn't know what to do. I quickly called over Al Kiburis. I told him "Listen, Al, I have a uniform with me with all the stuff. What am I going to do?" He said, "Give it to me, I'll get rid of it." As soon as I gave it to him, the first thing he did was get rid of a Six-Day War pin on it—and the rest of the uniform he gave to the guerrillas. I don't know what he said to them, but he got rid of it, and I didn't get into any trouble because of it.*

The crew collected quite a pile of items, which the guerrillas carefully examined. Discovering things like a bullet on a necklace or medals with Moshe Dayan's portrait sent them into a tizzy. The guerrillas suspected passengers of being Israeli soldiers and angrily accused TWA of transporting them. Then, for several hours, Abu-Nidal brought forward and interrogated various passengers, some intensely, about their connections to Israel. Mimi Beeber had a khaki bag that the guerrillas claimed was Israeli army issue. "They threatened very often to kill me," even cocking their guns at her at one point.[2]

Amman, 10 AM

André Rochat, the Red Cross's general delegate to the Middle East, arrived in Amman to pursue, until his unceremonious departure five days later, the release of the plane and passengers. Rochat, who stood out in his white hat and light summer suit, was well known and welcome to both Jordanians and Palestinians. Fluent in Arabic, he had organized an evacuation of foreign nationals from Amman in June and the Olympic Airways passenger-prisoner swap a month later. The Swiss felt that Rochat "knew what he was about." The United States too had great confidence in him.

But Israel was wary. It was unhappy about how quickly he had accommodated the PFLP in the Olympic Airways incident and how he had "poorly handled" a Red Cross attempt to free captured and wounded Israeli pilots shot down over Syria. Israel felt that his years in Arab countries and his fluency in Arabic made him sympathetic to the commandos. And, finally, it was concerned that he would be a free-wheeler, unbeholden to the countries involved.

Israel's concern was surely not assuaged when it later learned that Rochat had specifically asked that his mandate be "a brief oral commission," not written, loathe to be "imprisoned by the written word."[3]

Dawson Field, 11:30 AM

Even as the interrogations were going on, two ICRC representatives came on board, probably Dr. Roland Marti and Louis Jacquinet, who had arrived with Rochat and came directly to the planes. One of them "made a little speech of little significance," recalls Swinkels. (Rochat himself was in Amman and did not make it out to the planes that day.)

> *The Red Cross showed up on Tuesday. One of the doctors came in and gave out tranquilizers with a smile. The first thing he said when he came on the plane was, "We're glad to see you here." And we said, "Thanks a lot, man!" Of course, he didn't mean it that way. He said, "It's good that you haven't been blown up." He knew that we were charged up and ready to be blown up, so he was serious when he said it's good to see you here.*

People shouted, "We want to go home!" and "Are you doing anything about it?" All he responded, repeatedly, was, "We are doing everything we can. We are doing everything we can." He then smiled and gave out all kinds of tranquilizers.

> *The Red Cross had brought box lunches from Lebanon, which we were very happy for. Well, we hardly saw them after that. They came on once in a while, but we more or less didn't see them too often. They did have with them, however, a doctor named Ahmed Kamal who was one of the guerrillas. And this Ahmed Kamal I had a lot of respect for. His thoughts were that it wasn't fair for us people to be brought here. We were innocent people. This was a war between governments, not between people, and we shouldn't have been brought here. He was very nice to us all.*

Kamal was an understanding and good person. He did everything in his power to make us as comfortable as possible. The ICRC doctors were stationed in a tent near the planes. Perhaps their mere presence had a beneficial effect. But they did not pass again among us after that morning. And, despite the ICRC's promise to immunize us all against cholera, since an epidemic was raging in the region, it never did so.[4]

In a house in Irbid, 1 PM

It was still the middle of the night when the six anxious men who had been taken off our plane arrived at this one-story, flat-roofed structure in a residential neighborhood in Irbid. The house had only four rooms: a "command" room and a small kitchen on the right; and across a hall, a "dorm" room where the six would eventually be placed and an adjoining ammunition storage room. The lavatory—just an enclosed hole in the ground—was out a side door between the kitchen and the command room. In front of the house stood a flagpole with the red and white PFLP flag fluttering atop it.

When the men first entered, they were directed into the command room. A large map of Israel *in Hebrew* hung on one wall, with pushpins through different cities. Berkowitz averted his eyes, pretending that he couldn't read it. A Palestinian captain in the Syrian army came in to address the men. The way he said "you'll sleep in this room tonight," they knew that they would be there for a while. The six were given blankets and went to sleep, one on a wooden chaise lounge and the others on the hard floor.

This morning they had been moved across the hall into the fifteen-by-fifteen-foot room that would be their prison for the next two weeks. The room was bare except for a large clay water urn, a single glass that the men would share, a tiny table, and two chairs. There were no mattresses. They were given no toothbrushes or toiletries. Whenever they needed the outhouse—which they tried to avoid—they would knock on the door to be let out. Their room had a single window that cranked out. Once in a while they managed to get it at an angle by which they could see the street's reflection. Eventually they were caught and ordered to keep the window shut.

To their surprise, lunch that first day was delicious, for the three non-Jews at least. A spiced meat dish, baked with humus on top. The three Orthodox Jews, however, made do with pita, bananas, and grapes. (Berkowitz did not even eat the grapes because he believed that grapes might transmit cholera.) But from then on, particularly as the fighting intensified, there would be little food for any of the men.

Heavy fighting between the Jordanian Army and the Palestinian guerrillas was already raging all around. Baghdad radio reported that "at 0630 today, Jordanian artillery began shelling Arab Liberation Front (ALF), Popular Liberation Forces (PLF), and As-Saiqa advance bases in . . . Irbid province. Following the shelling, Jordanian tanks advanced on these bases and clashed with an As-Saiqa base . . . near Irbid. The tanks are still on the outskirts. . . . Preliminary estimates indicate that fifteen fighters of the *fedayeen* organizations were martyred and several others wounded."[5]

London, noon

By noon, Her Majesty's Government had decided that it was quietly prepared to release Leila Khaled and return the body of the dead hijacker, "acquiescing" to the U.S. proposal. Although Britain expected the PFLP to reject the U.S.—now the ICRC—proposal and Switzerland or Germany to then go their own way, it vowed that if the two countries gave the "slightest indication" that they would stand firm, Britain would too. However, Denis Greenhill, Britain's permanent undersecretary of state, fretted about the legal "technical troubles" involved in releasing Khaled. The evidence strongly suggested that she was guilty of attempted hijacking over British airspace. "Other considerations apart, people here would probably wish to prosecute her," he remarked. On the other hand, it would be "extremely awkward" to charge her and then withdraw the charges if a deal were reached. Meanwhile, Scotland Yard continued holding her "pending police inquiries."[6]

Amman, 2 PM

The safety of the hostages at the Intercontinental Hotel was becoming increasingly troubling. Earlier in the day, sporadic machine gun and rocket fire, as well as explosions, echoed around Amman. Not only was the Jordanian army not in control, it was hardly around at all. The U.S. military attaché cabled, "[o]ne can even sense the fear of the soldiers to move about the city . . . there [are] essentially no soldiers in the city anyway, except for those serving at headquarters. . . . Guerrilla control of the city is almost total. For example, loudspeakers are stationed in the city's streets inciting against the government, and no one bothers them." The army was demoralized and near mutiny, threatening to take matters into its own hands for King Hussein's own good.

Although the rest of the day was relatively quiet, with traffic moving and shops open, the situation was volatile. The embassy believed it "highly desirable that American citizens [in the hotels] depart Amman no later than nightfall." Rochat objected, adding even that "it would be unfortunate if any of them had already left." His instructions were to get out *all* women and children irrespective of nationality or religion, and that meant that American women and children would have to remain until Israeli women and children were released.

The embassy faced a dilemma: should it unilaterally try to move out its citizens over Rochat's objections or have them stay put? The State Department wondered how Rochat could insist that they remain, "especially as danger to them in Amman appears to be increasing," and pressed the embassy to get Rochat to relent. He wouldn't.[7]

Bonn, 2 PM

"Even Hitler would not have been able to initiate a more malicious act," German State Secretary Paul Frank fumed to Israel's chargé in Bonn. What's more, he said, the world would be furious if the passengers were harmed. It would be a "disaster for the Arab cause even among their supporters." But to be honest, he continued, while Germany preferred a package deal, if the PFLP refused to release the Israelis, it would face a tough dilemma about striking a separate deal for its citizens.

In fact, later in the day, the German Cabinet decided to pursue a "separate approach." "If we fail to do so," Germany informed the United States, "we would run an intolerable risk for [the] security and life of [the] German citizens." The United States urged Germany to "not break ranks." Secretary Frank planned to see Chancellor Willy Brandt the next morning to get him to overrule the decision. But, admitted one German official, there were "shaky nerves" even in the Foreign Office.[8]

Washington, 9 AM

Probably the most famous hostage was Rabbi Isaac Hutner, 64, a world-renowned Talmudic scholar with a large and devoted following. While the TWA plane was still in the air, one of his students had informed the State Department that Rabbi Hutner was aboard. Not knowing where the plane would land, the Department promptly cabled its legations in Amman, Beirut, Brussels, Moscow, Cairo, and Rome that "among the passengers . . . is Rabbi Isaac Hutner . . . highly respected, elderly and ailing. . . . Insure to extent possible he is accorded appropriate treatment." President Richard Nixon too was informed that "one of the senior American Jewish rabbis" was on board and "would probably not survive a lengthy internment."

Relatives and friends of other hijacked Americans also inundated the State Department with phone calls, seeking information about their loved ones or providing details of their special needs or circumstances. The department forwarded special needs or concerns, particularly relating to health or citizenship, to its embassy in Amman. For example:

> TWA informs us [that] two children, Kathy and Martha Hodes, who are still held on aircraft, have severe allergy problem. Children's medications are Tedral and Quibron. Children are allergic to dust and animals. Please inform ICRC.

> Department has received urgent request from uncle of American citizen Zipporah Moraine traveling on [the] TWA flight . . . to have Embassy do everything possible to see that she does not come to harm. Miss Moraine is 8 years of age, traveling alone and possibly speaking Hebrew better than English, because she has lived in Israel for extended period in last year or so. It is possible she is traveling on Israeli passport although she is American citizen. Embassy [is] requested to do all it can to assure welfare of Miss Moraine and keep Department informed.

The guerrillas would never find young Zipporah Moraine's Israeli travel documents. Yaakov Drillman, a passenger who had become aware of her predicament, had eaten them.[9]

Dawson Field, 4 PM

Kicking up clouds of desert sand, a caravan of about twenty-five cars drove up to the airplane site, bringing with it a bevy of journalists. A rather bizarre press conference was about to take place. Some Orthodox passengers and TWA and Swissair crew members sat on the desert floor about a hundred yards from the planes; the reporters were told to stand a further distance away. The PFLP spokesman in charge of the proceedings, Bassam Abu-Sharif, barked at the journalists through his TWA megaphone: "Stay still! Our fighters have orders to shoot if you do not obey orders! Do not crowd in like that! You are not civilized!"

Questions and answers were then shouted back and forth, with Abu-Sharif intervening by megaphone. The Q&A revolved mostly around the conditions on the plane and the treatment of the passengers. Captain Woods described the sanitation as good but deteriorating, alluding to the nonflushing toilets. One passenger described the "unbearable heat" aboard the planes. A TWA stewardess added that it was "cold at night and hot during the day, and the plane is starting to smell."

Abu-Sharif deflected a question about whether the PFLP intended to blow up the planes, saying only that their fate hinged on the response to the PFLP's demands. In a separate conversation away from the media, however, Abu Maher, another senior PFLP official, told Rochat that if the governments refused the PFLP's demands, "no one will be able to guarantee the passengers' safety." And, he reiterated that "we would not hesitate to blow up the planes with everyone on board" if the United States intervened militarily.

When asked about the Jewish hostages, Abu-Sharif responded that "[w]e are not holding them because they are Jewish; they're being kept for interrogation" to determine their citizenship, and a number of U.S. citizens "are suspected of serving with the Israeli army." But the PFLP was singling out the Jewish hostages. As Abu Maher asserted, "It is out of the question to release Israelis or Jews if the Palestinians we have asked for, who are being held in Israel, are not released." TWA vice president Richard Wilson, who had arrived in Jordan, also reported that the "situation [of the] Israeli and other passengers of Jewish origin [is] positively more delicate."[10]

Amman, 5 PM

In the afternoon, the PLO and Jordanian government reached a second cease-fire agreement in four days. That evening, both the PLO and the Jordanian army broadcast their calls for cease-fire. Jordanian Army commander in chief, Mashhur Haditha, announced sternly: "No soldier, *fedayeen*, or citizen who violates the agreement will be excused. . . . Anyone who carries arms should fear God in using them."

But like its predecessor, this cease-fire would not hold. Almost immediately, Fatah claimed that the army was firing "unprovoked and indiscriminately" around Irbid at both *fedayeen* and civilians. Almost concurrently with Haditha's appeal, the PLO announced the agreement "null and void because the Jordanian authority has violated [it] . . . before the ink . . . was dry." It called on soldiers not to participate in the "plot against the *fedayeen*" and implored the "Arab masses" to defeat the "agent regime's" "campaign of annihilation" against the Palestinians.

Nonetheless, Amman quieted down for the evening and, in the telling words of one reporter, "life has been normal since the shooting stopped."[11]

Jerusalem, 5 PM

With its "primary concern being the fate of all the hostages, and particularly the Jews" and wanting "no separation and no discrimination," Israel pressed the Europeans throughout the day to maintain "the full package." It continued to show "absolutely no inclination" that it might release any *fedayeen.* The "only way to deal with Habash and company was to get tough," its Foreign Ministry director general, Gideon Rafael, suggested, and the PFLP would back down. Furthermore, Israel saw this as essentially a U.S. problem, not an Israeli one, especially if the Israeli mother and her children could somehow be gotten out.

Despite its tough and unyielding front, Israel was prepared to deal. At a Cabinet-level meeting, "none of those present had any illusions regarding the severity of the situation and the paucity of means at [Israel's] disposal." Thus, "in order to prevent a catastrophe and the loss of life," they committed to "focus all our efforts *on any*" nondiscriminatory deal that would be presented. Diplomats intimately familiar with Israel sensed this, too. U.S. Assistant Secretary of State Joseph Sisco, for example, believed that Israel would contribute if confronted with the "sentencing to death" of Israelis or dual nationals. The British ambassador to Israel, John Barnes, also felt that Israel's public position was not its last word.

European policymakers, in contrast, remained convinced throughout that Israel was simply unprepared to deal.[12]

Bern, 4 PM

Late in the afternoon, the Bern Group of Four met for the first time, with Switzerland chairing this and all future meetings. Israel was not invited.

Informed that the ICRC had agreed to intermediate with the PFLP, the group decided that the ICRC's top priority should now be to firmly determine when the deadline was and try to eliminate it. It also agreed to convene whenever any country felt the situation warranted. Despite the veneer of common cause, however, the group would be plagued over the next three weeks by mutual suspicions of independent action.[13]

Dawson Field, 5 PM

In the late afternoon, a truck towing a borrowed KLM generator unit drove up to the TWA plane. Over the next few days, the generator would be activated periodically, for very short periods of fifteen minutes to an hour. The generator ran on jet fuel, which the captain wanted to conserve. Nonetheless, the cabin crew took advantage of the times to clean up the toilets, and most of us savored the brief respites from the heat. The Swissair captain had agreed to allow the unit to service our plane and not his because of the number of people we still had on board, including so many women and children.

To the passengers in the back of our plane, though, the air conditioning created a problem. One passenger recalls, "The generator . . . drew in all of the stench from the bathrooms into the cabin. . . . We begged them to stop the generator. Some of us moved up front until the air conditioning was turned off because it [created] a horrible smell."

Toward evening, the tension of the day's luggage search and interrogations subsided somewhat. For dinner, everyone was given a plastic bag with three pita sandwiches—one cheese, one egg salad, and one spicy meatball—and another plastic bag with a cucumber, a tomato, some grapes, and a banana. The guards brought aboard a small stove and a butane canister to boil water for sterilizing baby bottles. The crew also figured out a way to brew coffee for themselves.

Most of the Orthodox passengers still refused to eat the nonkosher sandwiches. Whatever they did not eat, however, they gave to the other hostages. No food was thrown out. After a while, even the kosher passengers began to eat more of the questionable food, including the cheese and the hard-boiled eggs. "To us it was [becoming] a matter of life or death," recounted my mother. "I felt, at this time, we'd better start eating because I didn't know how much longer we would be on the plane. The children were starting to feel weak." Some mothers tried to convince their children to eat the nonkosher meat too, but the kids, seeing that their parents would not eat it, also refused.

The guerrillas continued into the evening to call people up front for interrogation. My mother was one of them—

> I sat in the first row in the first class section. The captain was sitting asleep in the corner on the left-hand side. The crew was sitting in the lounge with the Arab guerrillas, and I was sitting on the right-hand side with a male guerrilla. It was dark. . . . He spoke a very good English. It was dark in there because the light was coming only from the lantern in the galley. He had a gun. It was standing up in the corner. . . . His tone of voice was very frightening. . . . I was questioned alone. . . .
>
> They had taken my wallet and taken out my organizational membership cards. I had three Hadassah membership cards, and he said that I must be a very important member of Hadassah. I said, "What makes you think that?" He said, "Because you have three membership cards." The membership cards were . . . for 1968, 1969, and 1970. I never threw out the cards. He wanted to know what Hadassah meant. . . . I said that it was . . . an organization to raise money in Israel and America to support hospitals and outpatient clinics for Jews and Arabs in Israel. . . . I told him that Jewish people and Arabs sit side-by-side being treated equally. . . .
>
> He asked me if I was a Zionist. Because of my fear of punishment or harassment or whatever—I denied being a Zionist. I said I was a humanitarian. . . . [I was afraid because the] PFLP are sworn enemies of the state of Israel. They are sworn to drive Israelis into the sea and anyone that has anything to do with the Israelis, and I feared that referring to myself as a Zionist—from the beginning, we knew that they do kill Israelis and they do kill Jews. They have no qualms about killing children and women and raping them, and I was in their hands. I was terrified. I had to deny my Zionism. This was actually the fear that we all had because we had all been coming from Israel. . . . We were being used as pawns and we had real cause to be afraid. We knew they could kill us collectively or individually. This was the fear we were sitting under and no one of us was willing to put it into words, and therefore . . . we kept conversation [with the guerrillas] at a minimum. We were afraid that if we said the wrong word to anybody, we would be killed or molested. . . .
>
> He saw that I was very agitated, and he offered me a cigarette. I took it. I had completely forgotten that I had stopped smoking eleven years before. . . . I was just a bundle of nerves.
>
> I had some slips of paper that said "Car Wash," and he wanted to know what they were. I told him that if I collected ten of these I would get a free car wash. He said, "Here, have a car wash." The membership cards he kept.

The interrogation lasted an hour. When my mother returned to her seat, everyone was concerned and wanted to know what happened. She remembers that "My children were in tears not knowing where I was because the curtain was drawn and nobody could go in there."

To help her calm down, my mother got permission to listen to music on someone's transistor radio. "We went to the back of the plane where the door was open. We heard the news that a Swissair plane was hijacked. . . . It was in Arabic. Sarah Malka, who had come from the Sudan knew Arabic and she was translating for us. There was no mention of TWA. . . . We couldn't believe that here we were hijacked on Sunday and it was Tuesday night and the United States government hadn't come on their white chargers and do something to take us out of the plane. We just couldn't believe that here we were, United States citizens, and we had been incarcerated for two days and nobody helped us. It was unbelievable."[14]

Dawson Field, 9 PM

Even as my mother was being interrogated, the crew gathered in the first class lounge area to relax. They had some wine and talked in the semidarkness of the lantern about the day's events and the situation generally. The conversation strayed at times to family and other matters, but usually returned to what was happening on the plane. Adnan, a tall, bald bachelor with a bushy mustache, from the PFLP's office in Beirut joined them, as did Abu-Nidal, the interrogator. The crew talked with the commandos, who were friendly to them and repeatedly tried to explain their cause to the crew. Such get-togethers would recur nightly.

It was understandable that the crew needed this time to unwind. They were working very hard, serving over a hundred people twenty-four hours a day, without electricity, running water, functioning air conditioning or toilets. But as the crew sat up front socializing with the terrorists who had brought us there and who were interrogating the Jewish passengers, I and many Jews sitting in the darkness in the back, anxious about our fate, felt forlorn and forsaken.

These were highly stressful and confused circumstances, and I bear no ill-will to any crew members, who were themselves hostages. One stewardess was even taken advantage of by Abu-Nidal: She had nodded off, and when she awoke, she found him trying to kiss her. But some crew members did not fully appreciate the Jewish passengers' perspectives and plight. One stewardess, for example, could not understand how some of the Jews who were so ardently Jewish and totally kosher in front of the crew played dumb when interrogated concerning their knowledge of Israel and insisted they were *Americans* involved in Israel only as tourists. And, at one point, another crew member recalled, "I got so mad at one of the rabbis and some of these Jewish passengers. I told them to forget about the kosher and that it was cruel to starve the children just because the food was not kosher." He was also upset that many kosher passengers hid their food until the next day, by which time it was spoiled by the heat.

To an observant Jew, observing the commandments, including keeping kosher, becomes especially important when one is being singled out for one's Jewishness, which we were. And, as to hiding food, some hostages were survivors of the Holocaust, just twenty-five years earlier. One, Miriam Leser—traveling with her two young children, Millie and Manny—saw everything that was now happening through that prism. Throughout the week, she would teach her kids survival tactics. When the plane first landed, for example, Manny was as curious as anyone to see where he had landed and to watch the commotion outside. He pressed his face against the glass to peer out. His mother told him to get away from the window and pull the shade down, admonishing him that a Jewish child's face makes an attractive target.

Despite being in the desert, Mrs. Leser would not let her children drink very much at any one time from the water bottles that would be handed out. Certainly not to finish one. "You never know if or when you will get more," she cautioned. So the kids spent the days with parched lips. At one point during the week, Mrs. Leser approached an elderly non-Jewish couple from New Mexico. She gave them a letter she had written to her husband along with some valuables and asked them to deliver the items to her husband if she didn't survive. The couple became distraught and told her that she mustn't talk that way. But she responded that as a child of the Holocaust, she had to be realistic and that, as non-Jews, their chances of being released were greater than hers. Perhaps Miriam was one of those who, on seeing the world she had succeeded in building from the ashes about to be destroyed and reliving her bitter experience, instinctively instructed her children to put away a bit of the food for tomorrow.[15]

Amman, 9:30 PM

TWA vice president Dick Wilson had still not been permitted to visit his plane. He had come with four colleagues to help ensure the safety of the passengers and the plane and to negotiate—independently—for their release, which immensely disturbed the Red Cross. The PFLP tried to extort "monetary payment" from him "to assure [the] safety of [the] aircraft," but Wilson refused to talk money. He reported afterward his belief that the "crew and majority of [the] passenger problem will be resolved soon . . . [but] selected passengers may be detained, and we [are] gravely concerned about [the] aircraft at this juncture." He was slated to go to Dawson the next morning, but would not. In fact, he would not get there until it was too late.[16]

Amman, 11 PM

"No one will be killed tomorrow afternoon unless by accident." This was Rochat's good news when he briefed the American, German, and British diplomats in Amman. He had had a "very long" discussion with the Palestinians "most involved" in the hijackings and was confident that the PFLP would extend the approaching deadline, only thirty-six hours away. The PFLP would reply to the ICRC proposal early the next day, he asserted. Even so, the situation remained "extremely serious," he warned. The PFLP had reiterated that "not one person will leave the planes" unless all of its demands were satisfied. Rochat insisted several times "in the strongest terms" and on "best authority" that the hostages in the hotels were not free to leave. He confirmed that six passengers had been taken off the plane "for varying periods of time for interrogation." But, misinforming the diplomats and thus their governments, he claimed that "all are now back on [the] airplanes."

Rochat had failed, however, to extract from the PFLP the names of those in the desert—for "security reasons," he was told. He still did not know how many Israelis and/or dual nationals were actually involved. Nonetheless, he repeated several times that he was "extremely firm" in sticking to his mandate. Any attempt to move away from the multinational approach, he warned, and "we will withdraw completely and leave the place."

Rochat, however, was "not at all convinced that the situation will end successfully . . . There is perhaps one chance in two that we will get everyone out." "We may have to face a tragedy," he concluded.[17]

The Pentagon, 9:29 PM

Two and a half days into this morass and the United States still did not see a way out. Earlier in the day, Secretary Rogers had held a top-level meeting with Defense secretary Melvin Laird, attorney general John Mitchell, CIA director Richard Helms, FBI director J. Edgar Hoover, and assistant to the president for national security affairs Henry Kissinger. According to Kissinger, "considerable time was devoted to the possible use against the hijackers of some nerve gas that paralyzed victims without their knowledge. The lack of knowledge of whether a suitable gas existed in our arsenal impeded the discussion no more than the absence of a concept of how it was to be delivered." The men also ruled out a military rescue or relying on the Jordanian government to free the hostages. The only resort, they concluded, was diplomacy.

At 4:30 PM, President Nixon called a strategy session in the Oval Office with essentially the same group. Nixon, anxious to use the crisis as an excuse to crush the *fedayeen*, apparently ordered that Palestinian strongholds be bombed. A wary Secretary Laird adeptly responded that the weather was unsuitable, and Nixon dropped the idea. But Nixon sensed that the United States would need to project power in the area in order to deter the Soviets, Syrians, or Iraqis from mixing in. Under the pretense of preparing for "a possible military air evacuation" of the hostages, the Joint Chiefs of Staff (JCS) ordered U.S. Army, Navy, and Air Force Central Commands in Europe to initiate "readiness actions" and "preposition, at a forward staging base, as soon as possible, a sufficient number of military transport aircraft to evacuate, on order, approximately 150 hostages from Dawson's air strip . . . and approximately 125 hostages from Amman."

Shortly thereafter six C-130 transport aircraft were ordered to Incirlik, Turkey, only eighty minutes from Amman, ninety from Dawson. Contingency plans were reviewed for ground troops and tactical air support. The battle staff of the U.S. Strike Command at McDill Air Force Base in Florida was ordered to place itself in "a more responsive posture." Then, at 9:29 PM, the JCS ordered the Sixth Fleet's *USS Independence,* with four destroyers and two more that would join it later, to head to a position 33 degrees north and 33 degrees east. In the night waters of the Mediterranean, the ships struck an easterly course that would shortly bring them to within a hundred nautical miles of the Lebanese coast.[18]

MISERY LOVES COMPANY

WEDNESDAY, SEPTEMBER 9

Dawson Field, 9 AM

Wednesday, they took us outside for exercise. This time, though, nobody was forced to go out. Of course, every day was pretty bad, I should say. First of all, without electricity, the toilets had been clogged up completely and it became pretty impossible to go to the bathroom at all.

Although permitted to use the bathrooms, we tried to avoid the urge. There were no windows or lights in the lavatories, and the refuse spilled onto the floor. There was usually "overflow" on the carpeting in the surrounding area. Now, into the third day, the odor and the stench were terrible, not only in the lavatories but throughout the entire rear of the plane. Flies, drawn in from the desert by the smell, buzzed all around. Some passengers tried to alleviate the smell by spraying perfume, but the situation was just impossible.

Trying to keep the facilities as usable as possible under the circumstances, the crew had been manually forcing the refuse down the toilets, at first using coat hangers from the first class closet. Then, they began stripping off and using the plane's inside wall panels. But by Wednesday the plane's waste tanks had filled to capacity and shoving no longer helped. We joked that the only way to clear up the plumbing was for the guerrillas to blow up the plane. Something had to be done. So the crew asked the guerrillas to dig a trench beneath the rear underside waste disposal valves, to which huge vacuum hoses normally attach. There were three T-handles on three valves. Never having done this before, the crew assumed that there was one T-handle per lavatory. They decided that each crew member would open one handle by tying on a six foot piece of rope they had cut from one of the plane's escape ladders. Captain Carroll Woods, as the senior officer, was given the honor of pulling the first one. He latched the rope on, tugged, and opened it. Nothing. Then copilot Jim Majer opened the second valve. Again, nothing. Finally, Al Kiburis, the flight engineer, who was a bit shorter than the others, stood up on a rickety wooden box in order to reach the third T-handle. He tugged, and all of the refuse of the three lavatories over three days came pouring out. Kiburis almost lost his balance and fell into the pit. Woods and Majer broke into laughter but, for some reason, Kiburis was not amused.[1]

London, 9:30 AM

The previous evening, a Jerusalem judge issued a warrant for the arrest of Leila Khaled for attempted murder, conspiracy to murder, and assault and battery. This day, in London, Israel requested that Britain detain Khaled until Israel presented a formal demand for her extradition. Britain was unhappy with Israel's request, which put the government "into [a] most terrible legal tangle," as it would now be bound to release Khaled only with Israel's consent. Furthermore, negotiations could be "gravely endangered" if the PFLP suspected that the United Kingdom might surrender her to Israel. Foreign Secretary Sir Alec Douglas-Home sent his Israeli counterpart, Abba Eban, a personal note to "ask forthwith that this request should be suspended." Home assured Eban that "without a satisfactory agreement for the release of the hostages, the girl will not be allowed out."

Eban responded that he was sure that Her Majesty's Government was working for a solution acceptable to both governments that would include the "simultaneous release of all the hostages." In the meantime, however, Israel would "have to maintain our legal step." Home's promise of a "satisfactory agreement" for the release of "the" hostages fell short of Eban's desire for a "solution acceptable to both our governments" and release of "all" hostages. This disagreement would come to a head before long.

In truth, Israel would have preferred that Britain bring Khaled to justice, but Israel presented its request precisely to make it more difficult for Britain to free her and to preclude a deal from being struck behind its back. Britain was now obliged to hold Khaled for up to sixty days and to consult Israel on any deal. Plus, Israel now had time to monitor the situation and decide what it really wanted to do.

Meanwhile, under the British Aliens Order, Khaled could be held only five more days at the Ealing police station without being charged. Then, something would have to happen.[2]

Dawson Field, 10:30 AM

The days passed slowly and agonizingly.

> *The situation toward the end of the first week became pretty much unbearable. You know what it's like when kids, and people in general, are boxed up for a week, not being able to move. It's tough enough to spend a ten-hour flight on an airplane. Imagine spending a week on it, living there, actually living there.*
>
> *During the day the temperature rose well over a hundred. Of course, we were sitting in the middle of the desert. At night the temperature fell into the fifties. It became pretty unbearable both times. During the day they brought a KLM mobile unit to give the plane some electricity, some power, and they turned on the air conditioning and the lights every once in a while. That made it a little better, but not too much better.*
>
> *It was now a little bit roomier, as they had taken people off the planes. We were able to spread out over a couple of seats. We would push down some of the seats for more room. During the day we sat and played chess. We talked and just did nothing really for a whole day. We got some cigarettes from this Dr. Ahmed Kamal and some other people, and had a good time smoking. You know, we never smoked before. I don't know—we passed the time away. It was very boring. Everybody started to become a little restless, but we managed to survive.*

We passed much of the time speculating. We wondered where the U.S. government was and whether it even knew where we were. We wondered if TWA was doing anything to help us. Some people read. Others "just sort of sat there and looked out the window," my mother recalled. "We were very lethargic. When you are hungry and thirsty, you do not have very much energy. We just really sat there . . . [and] worried how much longer it would be." Every once in a while, a woman would break down and cry; one of her neighbors would comfort her. Jewish children and adults often prayed or recited Psalms. From time to time, the older girls would lead the children in singing songs like "London Bridge." The teens and adults would sing from time to time too. Songs like "Show Me The Way To Go Home" and "Up, Up, and Away with TWA." One pastime was to take current songs and make up more relevant lyrics. "I'm Living on a Jet Plane" was the most popular.

Some passengers passed the time in a stupor. My mother observed that many of the women slept all day long or "were in this almost comatose state." Dr. Kamal had been freely dispensing tranquilizers, primarily to women and teenagers. He even gave my eleven-year-old sister a tranquilizer without my mother's knowledge. Earlier in the day, Tikva, had been walking barefoot and burnt the bottom of her foot on a lit match or cigarette. She was in pain and hysterical. My mother took her over to the doctor, who was in the rear galley. He said to Tikva, "Your eyes are too pretty to cry," and put something on her foot. In the evening, Tikva was still in pain and distraught. Dr. Kamal, who had come back aboard, gave her a tranquilizer and told her that it was a vitamin. My mother found out only later.[3]

Amman, 11 AM

Night in Amman had passed relatively quietly, but, sure enough, by 10 AM both Jordanian police and *fedayeen* loudspeakers urged people to get off the streets within the hour. Downtown shops and schools quickly closed as families hurriedly stocked up on food. At 11 AM, the Jordanian Army Bedouins guarding the American embassy "donned steel helmets and have added rocket launchers to their weapons inventory." At 11:20 AM, the hostages at the Intercontinental were moved into the basement because there was already sporadic fire in the area. Finally, according to a news report, "life came to a standstill at noon with heavy exchange of gunfire heard throughout the capital. Two bomb explosions were heard."

By early afternoon, extremely heavy fighting, including mortar fire, raged. Jordanian Army headquarters were reported hit. At 1:45 PM, heavy fighting was reported around the U.S. embassy. At one point, the British embassy, about two hundred yards from the Intercontinental, took a direct rocket hit.

Heavy fighting continued around Irbid in the north as well. Jordanian tanks "poured the fire of hatred" onto the Palestinians there. The Jordanian garrison in Irbid, in turn, was surrounded by the *fedayeen,* as the PLO called on its men to "crush the machineries of suppression."[4]

Dawson Field, noon

On Wednesday, the Red Cross was able to bring to the planes the provisions that it had flown in the day before. These included approximately twenty cases of orange and lemon sodas, diapers, baby bottle sterilizers, rubbing alcohol, aftershave lotions and perfumes to be used as disinfectants for the lavatories, bottles of Vichy mineral water, jams, watermelons, canned meats, canned and powdered milk, talcum powder, aspirins, tranquilizers, disinfectants, cigarettes, lemons, napkins, paper plates and cups, cotton and gauze, toilet paper, canned peaches and fruit salad, jars and packs of Gerber's baby food, Similac baby formula, and vitamins. André Rochat claimed that he had brought kosher food, but that was not so.

The ICRC in Amman reported to Geneva that "relief work continues on both planes under difficult conditions and medical doctors [are] treating some cases." From most of the TWA passengers' vantage point, it was not clear exactly what the ICRC was doing for them, however. "The Red Cross doctor was very uncommunicative. . . . [The guerrillas] told us he was outside and he would be available if we needed him, [but] we never saw him. He never really came up or asked us how we were," recalled a passenger. "There was one pregnant woman. We requested that she be taken off the plane . . . to give her a night's rest because sitting up she couldn't sleep. We were afraid for her. . . . The Red Cross never replied to us." The Red Cross doctors also did not approach us when we were outside.

At lunchtime, the crew passed out bread, lemons, fruit, lunch meat and canned corned beef, and cold water. The passengers in the back of the plane complained that by the time the food cart got to them it had run out of cheese and tomatoes. They asked that the food be served from the back to the front but were told that that would be too complicated.

Later that day, watermelons were cut up, and we ate them warm. My brothers and I saved the pits, salted them with the salt shakers included in the Red Cross meals, and roasted them in the sun on the wing of the plane. For the next couple of days, we had our own little snack.[5]

Bonn, noon

Germany's commitment to the united front remained the big unknown. Earlier in the morning, acting on information that Germany was seriously considering a bilateral deal, the United States, Switzerland, and the United Kingdom each delivered Germany a strong message to persuade it to stay the course. Even the ICRC became concerned and, a few hours later, warned the four countries that it would renounce its mandate if there was any bilateral deal. With all this pressure and encouraged somewhat by Rochat's reports the prior evening, the German government backed off "for the time being" from "isolated actions." However, it "reserve[d] the right to make a new decision if imminent new danger arises." Despite the renewed commitment, a British diplomat in Bern continued to believe that "the Germans remain the weak link in this affair."[6]

Dawson Field, 1:30 PM

By Wednesday, it had sunk in that we were going nowhere soon. Bob Palagonia and George Freda, both businessmen, decided that it wasn't fair for the crew—themselves hostages—to have sole responsibility for caring for the passengers. So they organized their fellow passengers to help in the chores. One brigade distributed water, which had become somewhat more available today with the Red Cross delivery and a sudden supply by the guerrillas. The task was also a bit easier now that the brigade could distribute or refill bottles rather than endlessly pour from coffee pots into cups, as the crew had been doing. The brigade tried to ensure that all got their fair share, but some passengers who tried to get more didn't appreciate reprimands from their peers, questioning who had given them the authority.

A sanitation detail now dragged large garbage bags down the aisles after meals. Volunteers were also posted to politely but firmly make sure that each user cleaned up after using the pitch-black lavatories. Even with this "guard detail," however, the crew had to clean the lavatories a few times a day. Trying to keep the plane clean with so many people on board was a major but ultimately futile undertaking.

> *We really hadn't any water to wash ourselves with. At first we had a little. The guerrillas had brought water to the plane and it was possible to get water. After a while, I don't know why, they just stopped bringing water.*

Lack of water and, relatedly, personal hygiene were also becoming serious issues. One day, one of my brothers spilled his water ration and became quite hysterical because he was afraid that he wouldn't get any more. But everyone around us said that, if we needed water, they would share. What water did come aboard had its own problems. My brother Noam developed diarrhea. My mother recounts: "He was quite sick with it . . . but didn't want to go to the bathroom because of the horrible smell. I had no change of clothes for him. . . . It was getting to be an impossible situation, physically, with his trying to control himself with this diarrhea." Today, however, we actually had enough water for us all to come aft, one by one, and wash up. The crew also started passing out cotton drenched with rubbing alcohol so that the women could clean off their children.

The women had their unique challenges. Susan Hirsch recalls, "On the third or fourth day in the desert, I felt the cramping in my lower abdomen. As a young teen, I was naturally embarrassed about these female body functions. I was extremely distressed and humiliated by the lack of privacy, especially when faced with the male terrorists. I took my pocketbook with me on the way to the bathroom, with the provisory sanitary napkin rolled up inside. But before entering the toilet, my purse was searched. I was told I could not take it in with me and was forced to remove the pad under the guard's scrutiny. We had no opportunity to change our clothing during the entire time we were held hostage, and my stained panties combined with my minidress and the prying eyes of the terrorists caused me great anguish."[7]

Washington, 9 AM

Some Orthodox Jewish American leaders began to quietly challenge Israel's seemingly unyielding stance. On Tuesday, the Agudas Harabonim, a preeminent Orthodox group led by the renowned sage Rabbi Moses Feinstein, concluded unanimously that to secure the lives of the hostages, even Israel was obliged to yield to the PFLP's demands. Reaching a similar conclusion, another principal Orthodox leader, Rabbi Joseph B. Soloveitchik, cabled Israel's Ambassador Yitzhak Rabin that "the necessity to prevent [the] imminent slaughter of helpless captives, among them women and children, is and must remain [the] overriding consideration." Besieged by these and other appeals, the Israeli Foreign Ministry instructed Rabin "to act to calm the anxiety in the Jewish community." This sort of pressure continued nonetheless.

Some American Jews also began to consider raising funds to ransom selected hostages. Getting wind of this, the Israeli Embassy in Washington reacted angrily: "Woe unto anyone who would dare try—Heaven forbid—to discriminate [among the passengers], for example to try to ransom the rabbis as opposed to the others." A rumor would circulate the following week that a million dollars was being raised to ransom Rabbi Hutner. A rabbi close to Rabbi Hutner denied it as a vicious libel.

Christian groups around the United States deplored the hijackings and called for the immediate release of the hostages. Catholic groups and leaders such as Monsignor John Oesterreicher, Sister Rose Albert Thering, and Sister Donna Purdy of Seton Hall University sent cables to Pope Paul VI. Terrence Cardinal Cooke of New York issued a statement. Over the next few days, the leaders of other Christian groups including the Southern Baptist Convention, National Association of Evangelicals, the National Council of Churches, the Christian Church (Disciples of Christ), and the United Church of Christ cabled President Nixon. A group of non-Jewish dignitaries and attorneys would offer themselves as alternate hostages. And, of course, countless Americans of all faiths offered their prayers daily for our safety and release.[8]

Amman, 3 PM

"The internal situation here has taken a sharp turn for the worse," cabled British Ambassador Phillips. Jordanian army units were acting independently and Commander in Chief Haditha resigned because he could not control them. In the late afternoon, heavy weapons—machine guns, artillery, mortar shells, and rockets—rocked the city. Smoke billowed from burning buildings in several neighborhoods. *Fedayeen* units penetrated the embassy section on Jabal Amman for the first time. The Reuters news agency building came under shellfire and its radio went silent. Jordanian helicopters patrolled the sky. By 3:45 PM, Amman was "[an] open battle field." The capital was "paralyzed" and "on the brink of chaos." It was cut off from the outside world, its power supply failed, and its street traffic ceased. A mortar shell crashed near the Intercontinental, and at 5:55 PM, heavy firing broke out again around the hotel. The hostages and other guests "rushed to a downstairs night club for safety. Management opened a bar there . . . guests used candles stuck in red fire buckets. Children played cards while their parents tried to gossip while the fighting raged. Some pulled out mattresses to spread in hallways. Scores of newsmen . . . used the [battery-powered] television lights to write their stories." The situation was so chaotic that, when a U.S. embassy official called the palace, King Hussein himself answered the phone.

The intense fighting disrupted the hostage negotiations. Rochat was to have met the PFLP at 4 PM about extending the deadline but was trapped in the Intercontinental. Furthermore, the fighting was distracting the PFLP leadership from the hostage issue. In the end, however, Rochat managed to reach the PFLP by phone and extend the deadline, given that negotiations could not proceed under the circumstances. But he wasn't sure for how long, and he was "fearful [that] we are approaching a very serious night."

Negotiations between the Jordanian government and the *fedayeen* were dead too. King Hussein was under mounting pressure from high-ranking officers to crack down on the guerrillas. But rather than doing so, King Hussein ordered General Haditha to reassume "full powers" and take "necessary measures to establish order and calm," i.e., restrain the army. While not actually apologizing, the government seemingly accepted blame for abrogating the cease-fire in the Irbid area, claiming that some units had acted on their own. It promised to punish the perpetrators and prevent a repetition.

Half an hour later, Haditha ordered his armed forces to cease fire. "I will take the severest military action against anyone who contravenes this order." The announcement was broadcast several times. An hour and a half later, Yasser Arafat broadcast a personal statement ordering all *fedayeen* and militia to cease fire at once. All calls, however, went unheeded.[9]

Dawson Field, 4:30 PM

We see all around us again that the guerrillas are so excited and so happy, jumping up and down, applauding each other, and shaking each other's hands. We wondered what happened. About an hour later—around five o'clock—we hear a big noise over us, ZOOOOMMMM. Looking out our windows, we see a BOAC jetliner coming down from above us. Our first reaction was that we applauded. It was great to see that other people had come to join us. We felt that we had power in numbers. We knew we were up for some type of trade and therefore the more people we had, the better our chances of getting out. So when this plane landed, we were very, very happy to see it. Now we had company.

A British Overseas Airways Corporation (BOAC) VC10, Flight 775 from Bombay-Dubai-Bahrain to London was hijacked on its Bahrain-to-Beirut leg.

Ten crew and 145 passengers were on board; 24 were children unaccompanied by their parents. In Bahrain, the crew had been assured by a self-confident head of security of the scrupulous measures he had taken to ensure the plane's safety. Nonetheless, about forty-five minutes before the scheduled arrival in Beirut, a PFLP man burst into the flight deck with a gun in his hand. At first, First Officer Trevor Cooper thought it was a prank, given Sunday's hijackings. He quickly realized, though, that the man was deadly serious. The hijacker was extremely agitated, sweating profusely, and had a desperate look about him. The gun was cocked, pointed at Cooper's and the captain's heads, and his finger was on the trigger. Captain Cyril Goulborn very calmly said, "Sit down and have a talk about it. Tell us what you want us to do."

There were, in fact, three male hijackers, traveling on Egyptian, Syrian, and Jordanian passports. Two sat in first class. All three had automatic weapons and had boarded in Dubai. One had deplaned in Bahrain and returned with an attaché containing explosives. According to British Security Services, no one boarding in either Dubai or Bahrain had been subjected to any physical or electronic search. Before taking off from Bahrain, Goulborn had noted the "odd circumstance" that a first class passenger was "wearing poor quality clothes, had little baggage, and appeared to be in a somewhat nervous state." Unfortunately, his curiosity had been piqued no further.

The hijacker first ordered the crew to proceed to Beirut. But after circling once or twice over Beirut, suddenly, amazingly, he said, "Now we go to Tel Aviv." The crew said he must be mad, but he insisted. "No, we go to Tel Aviv." After several nerve-racking moments, as they neared Lod and the hijacker became increasingly agitated by getting no response from Lod air traffic control, despite the fact that he "talked and talked and butted in on other conversations," the hijacker instructed the crew to return to Beirut.

When they reentered Beirut airspace, they had only an hour's fuel left. The hijacker did not instruct the crew to land because he first needed word from the ground. Rather, he commanded them to "go up, go down . . . and there was a general period of uncertainty, climbing, descending, circling, turning here, there, and everywhere. None of us knew what was happening at all." Eventually, after "talking to an awful lot of people" on the ground, the hijacker told the crew to land. It took a while, but finally the captain received a radar course into Beirut International. Just as they headed in, one of the accomplices handed the lead hijacker a large black canvas briefcase apparently filled with explosives. He warned Beirut air traffic control and the crew that he would blow up the aircraft if anyone attempted to interfere with it. Cooper turned to him and urged him to strap himself in and "hang onto that." He declined. Cooper tried again to convince him, but the man would not strap on his seatbelt.

The plane landed with its fuel tanks almost empty. It was directed to a relatively remote area and just sat there. After assuring Lebanese authorities that no explosives would be brought aboard since the plane "is supplied with the necessary explosives," Abu-Khalid, a PFLP representative in Lebanon, boarded. He had shown up at the airport on Sunday too, when the hijacked Pan Am 747 landed there. Soon, a truck approached to supply fuel for a three-hour flight. The crew pleaded for much more—not knowing where they were headed—trying to convince the lead hijacker that the fuel would be free, so why not take it? But he refused and again threatened to blow up the plane if anyone approached it during refueling.

After nearly two hours on the ground, Abu-Khalid deplaned and a "very excitable" woman and a man came aboard. The man was later reported to be our plane's male hijacker. The British ambassador, in the control tower, pleaded for the release of the women and children. He was refused. "[A]dequate accommodation is available in Amman," he was told, probably with a smirk.

At about 2:30 PM, the plane took off. The hijacker instructed the crew to fly to Revolution Airport and handed them only a "very vague let-down chart." Once in our general vicinity, they proceeded toward Amman, descended to six thousand feet, and asked all the hijackers to come into the cockpit to try to spot Dawson. None could. Very soon, over Amman, the hijackers "started getting absolutely out of control. They were shouting at one another, arguing amongst themselves, waving guns in the air, pushing and shoving around. It was extremely tense at this stage." Plus, the plane was again starting to run low on fuel. They did a U-turn over Amman and backtracked. "Luckily, we went right over the top" of Dawson Field, Cooper recalled. "All we could see was the other two aircraft parked there. . . . [The] runway looked long. But the only trouble was Swissair [was] parked . . . slap-bang in the middle." This time, the crew got the hijackers all strapped in, "which was a major achievement in itself."

Word came to us aboard TWA at around 3 PM that a BOAC plane had been hijacked. Our guards were quite excited. So were we—we kept watching excitedly for signs of the plane. An hour later, our crew was asked to help talk it down. Jim Majer turned on the emergency radio. "This is Revolution Airport GCA (Ground Control Access)," he announced and gave them landing instructions.

The BOAC jet made a first approach, coming in low over the planes, but overshot the runway. "Again [the guerrillas] got desperate—they thought we were mucking about, but there just didn't seem anywhere to land because the Swissair was right slap-bang in the middle," Cooper recounted. Plus, trucks and jeeps were driving in all directions as the guerrillas on the ground became very excited. "So we came downwind again, the visibility was very poor, a lot of sand blowing about, and we made another approach and we landed slap-bang on top of the Swissair. It was an extremely good landing, very, very good indeed." At 4:30 PM, the BOAC jet was on the ground and disappeared into a great cloud of smoke and sand, which had to settle before the plane could turn around to taxi toward the TWA and Swissair planes. The BOAC plane was quickly surrounded by "all kinds of armored cars, trucks, everything, with waving, screaming guerrillas on board. They all had machine guns." The plane eventually parked diagonally in front of our plane, and the crew shut everything down. "That was the last any of us saw of the flight deck," Cooper later reported. "We weren't allowed back on there. . . . We are certain that they wired up explosives on the flight deck immediately [after] we landed. . . . Someone was on guard in the flight deck throughout every minute we were there." About 150 commandos gathered in front of the plane and the minute the forward cabin door opened, they all danced and jumped up and down. They threw their caps and rifles in the air and "shouted some words over and over again. It was as a scene like out of a movie."

Dawson Field was becoming a busy international airport.[10]

Bern, 4:30 PM

When the Bern Group reconvened, Great Britain proposed that Israel be invited "to join our consultations." The proposal came, however, only after Foreign Secretary Douglas-Home had audaciously asserted that "the Israelis have only themselves to blame for their exclusion hitherto from the talks (which have been limited to representatives of those governments interested in a settlement)." At any rate, Britain acquiesced since "it is clear that no settlement will be possible without Israeli cooperation" and the group needed to know whether the Israelis were "prepared to modify their hard line."

Switzerland hesitated, but Israel's ambassador to Switzerland, Arie Levavi, was invited to join the Bern deliberations. Quickly surmising that the motive behind the belated invitation was to "now have the 'Israeli contribution card' in order to make it easier for Rochat," the Israeli Foreign Ministry instructed Levavi not to formally join the group.[11]

Dawson Field, 6 PM

There was not much for dinner Wednesday night because fighting in Amman had apparently prevented the terrorists from bringing in fresh food and supplies. The crew served leftovers from lunch. The situation aboard the TWA plane was "serious," admitted Rochat.

At night when it became too dark to do anything, we'd sit around and talk. But tonight would be different for my siblings and me after they called my mother up front for a second interrogation. She recounted:

> I was sitting and all of a sudden I was called up front, by an armed woman guerrilla, to be interrogated again, a second time. To describe my feeling is practically impossible. I was frightened, extremely frightened, because I knew that six men had been taken off the plane. They had already interrogated me on Tuesday night about Israel and about my visit there. When they called me this time, I didn't know what they wanted with me. I thought perhaps they were going to take me off the plane and away from my children. My children, the little ones, were crying hysterically, "Don't go, don't go." And the others were in a state of shock. They just didn't know what to say or do. I just kept saying [to the older ones]: "Take care of the children."
>
> I was sitting on an oil can at the lounge table. It was pitch black, except for one of the lanterns that was swinging back and forth. . . . The captain slept in the corner. . . . Everybody was holding guns. . . . A woman was interrogating me . . . and translating into Arabic to a man who was sitting next to her taking notes. . . . She had the slip that I had filled out, and she asked me what my husband's profession was. My husband is a rabbi, but I was afraid to say that . . . so I said he was a teacher. They weren't satisfied. They wanted to know what did he teach and I told them "languages." And again they weren't satisfied. They asked, "What kind of language?" I finally said "Hebrew."
>
> Then they wanted to know where I had been while I was in Israel. I'm a very poor liar, so I actually told the truth. I mentioned some of the places, not knowing there would be places that would upset them very much. I mentioned the Golan Heights, which is new territory gained in 1967, which was a tourist attraction. They wanted to know why I went to a military installation. Then they mentioned another place, and I said, yes, I had been there. They said "Did you know that it's a military installation?"
>
> They asked me if I had an Israeli passport. Again, I said that I was born in Jersey City and that I was an American citizen and my children were all Americans and my husband was an American.
>
> And the more these answers were given, the more excited they became. They kept talking back and forth in Arabic. They were getting very agitated at my answers . . . I got very agitated. This was the most frightening experience of my life . . . All I kept thinking was, "My God, what's going to happen to me? What is going to happen to my children?"

The questioning went on for about an hour, the questions repeated over and over. My siblings were beside themselves. People tried to console them and assure them that everything would be all right, but they were extremely upset.

After the interrogation, my mother recalled, "as I was going down the aisle, everybody wanted to know what happened. . . . They could see that I was very agitated. Somebody offered me a cigarette. . . . I took it readily." Somebody offered her a tranquilizer, which she refused to take. "I tried to quiet myself down . . . and I went back to the back of the plane to cool off and sort of gain my senses. I put the radio on and we were listening and all of a sudden we heard that President Nixon announced that he was giving Israel Phantom jets." Golda Meir had asked Nixon a year earlier for twenty-five F-4 Phantoms and a hundred A-4 Skyhawks in light of increasing warfare with Egypt along the Suez Canal. The decision had been delayed—until now.

Evidently, the guerrillas were listening to the same broadcast, because as soon as it was over, a bunch of them came on board and shouted at us to sit down immediately! Again, as my mother recalled: "The guerrillas became very agitated and ordered us, screaming, really ranting. They never before had really raised their voices at us, but at that point they were very upset and they were ranting and running up and down the aisle saying, 'Everybody sit down!' And they were shoving us, like with the gun. They didn't touch us, but practically. We assumed if we didn't move fast, they would have swatted us. Near the first class cabin, the PFLP woman again shouted that they were no longer responsible for our safety. She was shouting at the top of her voice that the PFLP was no longer responsible for our safety.

"It seemed like [their agitation lasted] all night. We didn't sleep very much. I was too upset by what happened to me in the evening, so I couldn't sleep. I was talking to the woman who was sitting opposite from me and it seemed we spent most of the night talking and smoking and whispering about what was happening. That we were just becoming very frightened, very depressed. We didn't think we would ever get out of this mess."[12]

Amman, 7 PM

The earlier cease-fire call from General Haditha did at last yield a brief respite. Power was once again restored at the Intercontinental. The area seemed relatively quiet for the moment. The hostages were fed in the dining area and lobby. Some were "discussing the possibility" of going up to their rooms to spend the night. Morale remained "reasonably good given the strain of [the] present situation."

Later that evening, however, the PLO once again blasted the Jordanian "lackey authorities" for abrogating their agreements. Clashes resumed and continued throughout the night in Amman, Jarash, and Irbid. One of the most intense battles in Amman took place across the street from the hotel when *fedayeen* captured a building and began sniping at Jordanian soldiers from it. Army commandos then penetrated the building, and floor-to-floor and door-to-door combat ensued. The platoon of soldiers guarding the hotel shot at anything attempting to approach. During the battle, shells hit the hotel, shattering many of its windows. Power and water were yet again cut off. The hotel guests could see bodies being removed from the building.

During the course of the evening, the PLO Central Committee formally called for Hussein's overthrow. Civil war was now inevitable.[13]

Amman, 8 PM

Still pinned down in the hotel, André Rochat learned by phone that the deadline had been extended by seventy-two hours to 6 AM Sunday morning. While asserting that the passengers on all three aircraft were safe, the situation, he claimed, was "extremely serious." He still hoped for a definitive PFLP response the next morning to the ICRC's proposal, but suspected that its demands would remain "extremely tough." He foresaw a "very long negotiating process," extending perhaps for "several weeks." U.S. chargé Jerry Odell reported a "note of real pessimism creeping into Rochat's attitude."[14]

Dawson Field, 10 PM

That night, six-year-old Connie Pitparo, traveling alone, fell sick and became very scared. Using a megaphone, the guards called over a Red Cross doctor. He gave her an injection and said that someone needed to wake her every hour throughout the night to give her water and medication. Jim Majer and stewardess Linda Jensen alternated. An elderly lady became sick too. The doctor borrowed a thermometer from one of the passengers and then gave the woman an injection and some medication. The two had come down with bad cases of tonsillitis.

At night, the temperature would drop to nearly 50°F and we had no heating. There were not enough blankets to go around—this was to have been a day flight, not a sleep-away camp—so, the crew took off the divider curtains, cutting them up using someone's cuticle scissors. But sleeping upright was extremely uncomfortable and fitful. Millie Leser recalls, "I can still hear the toddlers crying 'Abba, Ima' [daddy, mommy], in the black of night on the plane. Perhaps they cried for a bottle of milk, or from being uncomfortable, or from fear. We were all so very, very frightened because we did not know what the next day would bring." My brothers Noam and Yaron didn't sleep very well either. Every time my mother looked, they were up. They wanted reassurance that everything would be all right. They wanted to know if their father knew where they were. They wanted to know when they were going home.[15]

Trenton, 6 PM

My father had learned of our hijacking on a radio newsflash as he drove from Trenton to pick us up at Kennedy International airport on Sunday. This entire week, back at home, he agonized that he might lose his whole family in an instant. He feverishly worked the phones, maintaining constant contact with the State Department, TWA, congressmen and senators, the Red Cross, and anyone else of influence he could think of. He would sleep only two, three, four hours a night with the radio on.

He was not alone, though. His personal physicians checked up on him regularly, making sure that he was sleeping, eating, and keeping his stress under control. His mother and siblings came to spend the long days and nights with him. He received hundreds of letters and phone calls from colleagues, friends, and even anonymous well-wishers around the country. And, as a congregational rabbi, the principal of the local Hebrew day school, and a known community figure, from the start of his vigil, our living and dining rooms saw a constant flow of friends, neighbors, and sympathizing strangers both within and without Trenton's Jewish community.

With his eyes glued to the television set, one ear to the radio, and bated breath, he waited to hear whether the deadline—now only five hours away—for the destruction of the planes and his entire family might be extended. Then he sat back and allowed himself a brief smile. The deadline, he learned, had been put off unofficially. His family would survive, at least for the moment.[16]

"THEY FORCED ME INTO THE GRAVE"

THURSDAY, SEPTEMBER 10

Intercontinental Hotel, 6 AM

After considerable fighting the previous night, the *fedayeen* now controlled the building across the road. The hostages had spent the night, as had the other hotel guests, in the rooms, on mattresses in the hallways, and in the basement nightclub/bomb shelter. No one was injured but several cars in the hotel's front parking lot were struck. The hotel itself took several hits, one knocking out the water system and flooding the first floor lobby and offices. At 6 AM, breakfast was served and then, suddenly, heavy fighting erupted again around the hotel.

During the morning, shooting was occasionally heard elsewhere in the city. Hussein's own palaces engaged in periodic rocket volleys, and one palace was directly hit. While power was back in most of Amman, telephone contact with the outside world was still cut and the airport was still closed. Vehicular and pedestrian traffic moved furtively through the streets. Several pharmacies and grocery stores opened their doors, but only for a few hours. Food prices were rising appreciably as a result of shortages and hoarding. Any Ammani who could now fled the city, heading up to Damascus.[1]

Dawson Field, 6 AM

Every morning, I got up very early—actually I never really slept. I was usually up all night and then I slept afterward for a few hours. So around four-thirty, five o'clock I would put on my tefillin and say the "Shema" and its blessings, as well as the "Shemoneh Esreh" [the silent meditation]. I davened [prayed] as quickly as I could and then I took off my tefillin. I didn't want them to see what I was doing. I wore my yarmulke only when I ate, and I ate only when there were no guerrillas around because I didn't want them to see me wearing a yarmulke.

It was the month of Elul, when we recite Psalm 27, For David: The Lord is my light, twice a day. Every time I said it, it seemed very, very appropriate. It seemed very coincidental that we had been hijacked just at the time when you say this particular chapter in Psalms. For example, one verse is, "Though a host should encamp against me, my heart shall not fear; if a war should be waged upon me, in God's succor I put my faith." Now, you can't really ask for a better verse than that. It fit the situation completely. It seemed to express my feelings. It was very reassuring; like God was telling me: Don't be afraid because in these types of situations I come through. The last sentence of the chapter seemed to have the strongest influence on me. It says, "Await the Lord; be strong, and let your heart take courage. Yes, await the Lord." It was all very comforting to me, especially since the psalm began "For David."

Dawson Field, 8:30 AM

Now into our fifth day, the plane was filthy and smelly. The crew asked the guards if the passengers could get off so that it could be cleaned up. The guards agreed. It was quite a job. As some crew and passengers went through the seat pockets, they found old food, soiled napkins, and other garbage that contributed to the stench. Meanwhile, beneath the plane it was still cool-ish, and the other crew members served breakfast.

Halfway through the cleaning, Jim Majer had a brainstorm. Within minutes, three 145-pound life rafts were thrown overboard onto the desert floor. The first one didn't inflate, which the adults found morbidly amusing. The other two rafts did inflate. After the guerrillas checked for knives, the children and young women, with a glee that had been absent for almost a week, raced to jump into the bright yellow crafts. They put up the canopies for shade and took the candies and the gum out of the waterproof bag on the raft. The kids devoured the treats and, for a brief moment, they reconnected with their former worlds and some sense of normalcy. Soon all were singing and clapping hands, with the young women leading the children, while other passengers jumped rope with the yellow connection rope. This incongruous sight offered a welcome relief for everyone.

Observing the goings-on, the BOAC crew and passengers who were outside at the same time decided to follow suit. (Although we could see each other, passengers from the different planes were not permitted to approach one another.) Only one of their three rafts inflated properly, however. In the understated words of their first officer, "I think that is worthy of some attention."

After an hour and a half of revelry, everyone had to go back inside. The party was over.[2]

Amman, 9:45 AM

Without notice, twenty-one Arab nationals and the British fiancée of one of them were whisked off the BOAC plane and driven to the Intercontinental Hotel, escorted by a joint Army-*fedayeen* patrol. They were permitted to depart Jordan immediately but did not.[3]

Dawson Field, 11 AM

Abu-Nidal came aboard and announced that the PFLP was going to inspect the luggage and confiscate items made in Israel. Helplessly, we watched the guerrillas take the luggage out of the hold and set it down by one of the wings. One by one, passengers were called out. A TWA crew member stood by and observed as the suitcases were rifled through. They were surrounded by four or five machine gun-toting guerrillas.

My mother was summoned in the early afternoon. Being seventeen and knowing that I was considered an adult by the Arabs, I tried to maintain a low profile. So my brother Moshe, fourteen, went down with her.

> *Our family was afraid of this luggage-checking business because we had a few things we didn't want them to see. First of all, we had a picture of three Israeli soldiers holding up a Jordanian flag in Israeli-held Jordan [the West Bank]. That, we didn't really want them to see. We also had a dog tag of a dead Jordanian soldier and an insignia medal that goes on the beret of a Jordanian soldier. We didn't want them to see those either. So we became pretty nervous. . . . I took my brother Moshe's little Psalms book that my Aunt Leah had given us in Israel (she had given one to each of us; mine was in my suitcase) and I recited Psalms until my mother got back. I put it in my pocket when I'd finished, forgetting to return it.*

One guerrilla conducted the search. My mother described the scene:

> As they went through each suitcase, they took out everything that was made in Israel. . . . Things that were made of gold or silver, they put into a box. The other stuff they threw into the dirt. . . . I had a watch that I had bought my son in America, but the back of the watch had a map of Israel. They took that, even though it was a Swiss watch. . . . I had a gold bracelet that I had bought for my mother. They took that and threw it in the box. The heat was intolerable. I was standing there for about three hours because they read every label of everything that I had in my [six or seven] suitcases. I had to help them read words they couldn't read: store labels and company labels and the like.

> I had a bag of candy made in Israel. An Arab took it. He opened it and he was eating it and passing it around to all of the guerrillas who were there. . . . Then he spit it out in front of me. He said "I spit on Israel. I spit on Zionism. I spit on the Jews."
>
> One man had . . . a large dent in his head. He kept lifting his hair and saying, "See? That's an Israeli bullet." He kept pulling it up to show me. It was raw and just awful. Another man was telling me all kinds of stories of what Israelis do to Arabs. . . . You can just picture the burning heat and my standing on swollen feet watching my things being thrown into the dirt and having this man talking to me and showing me the scar and the other one telling me all these things. . . . They kept repeating this over and over again.
>
> One of the crew members saw me. I looked like I was going to faint from the heat and standing on my feet—I could hardly stand on them because they were swollen. He told me to sit down, but they wouldn't let me sit down. They said I had to stand and watch them. I had to stand and watch them going through my luggage and throwing out everything that I had bought. I was beside myself.

When it was over, my mother was in shock. "This scene is indelible. . . . It was like a nightmare."[4]

Dawson Field, 1 PM

There was little food on Thursday. One woman started crying hysterically, wailing, "How long can we go on?" My mother started crying too. "The children were hungry and complaining about their stomachs, that their stomachs hurt," she recounted. "We were given no food during the day until late afternoon. We ate the pita that was left from Wednesday when we had gone outside. We were eating what we had saved." In the evening there was finally some food, as the guards brought some cold chicken, bread, tomatoes, hard-boiled eggs, tea, and fruit.

The plane had also run short of diapers. The women had used gauze and cotton provided by the terrorists and then the Red Cross. Now, some of the women ripped the gold first class napkins in half and made provisional diapers out of them. The bottled water brought by the Red Cross had also run out. The crew began dropping the disinfectant that the Red Cross had provided into the water being brought by the commandos in the hope of fending off the cholera epidemic. But it made the water vile tasting, and the children did not want to drink it.[5]

Amman, 3 PM

The Jordanian government and the PLO reached their third agreement that week. This one was negotiated by the leaders themselves: Premier

Rifai, Commander in Chief Haditha, and PLO Chairman Arafat (who had approved the call the previous evening for King Hussein's overthrow). They agreed on the need "to put an end, once and for all, to the tragic incidents."

The airport was reopened, but tension and anxiety prevailed as everyone knew that shooting could resume at any moment. After all, neither of the two prior cease-fires had lasted more than a few hours. Indeed, there was still sporadic shooting in Amman despite the present cease-fire.[6]

House in Irbid, 4 PM

The six men who had been taken off our plane Monday night were an eclectic bunch. Group discussion was sparse, although the three non-Jews often discussed restaurants around the world. Mostly, the men sat around and listened to the fighting around them. When the shelling came particularly close, the Defense guys, Robert Schwartz and James Woods, instructed the rest of the group to sit on the window side of the room and cover their heads with a blanket. That way, if the adjacent ammo room was hit, the blast would go over their heads.

John Hollingsworth, a seasoned American diplomat, spit-polished his shoes every day, put on his tie, and shaved whenever there was electricity. The Harari-Rafuls, of Syrian Sephardic extraction and devoutly Orthodox, wore their black suits and black satin yarmulkes. They occasionally paced around the room trying to reconstruct from memory some of the *slichot* prayers recited daily before Rosh Hashanah, which was fast approaching. Jerry Berkowitz, a modern Orthodox Jew, spent his time trying to figure out what he was doing there. The guerrillas claimed that he was an Israeli, but he was pure American.

Schwartz had chronic diabetes mellitus, a mild form that required a special diet, liquid intake, and medication, which he had not brought off the plane with him. The Amman embassy was aware of Schwartz's condition and was concerned that the stress of the situation might aggravate it. But, contrary to its assurances, the Red Cross did not ensure that he was getting proper medical attention. He would get woozy from time to time, but under no circumstances did he want to leave the group, despite their urgings that he ask to be taken to a hospital. Fortunately, at one point, their captors gave them a tin of Kraft cheese from Australia, and whenever he'd feel faint, he would eat some of the cheese and feel better.

Throughout the next weeks, the guerillas would bring crates of ammunition to the room next door. Schwartz and Woods would peer through the window as it was brought in, identify it, and keep mental inventories. It was mostly American materiel, and they concluded that it was probably obtained through sympathizers in the Jordanian army. The guerrillas seemed to have an abundance of heavy weapon and small arms ammunition. For the most part, the PFLP fighters they saw were young men, almost none over thirty. Many appeared to have superior educational backgrounds; some had studied or received technical training in Western Europe. Their morale and esprit was extremely high.

The six got very little news from the outside, especially at first, and didn't know what was happening to their families on the plane. During their entire stay in Irbid, they got one *Newsweek* magazine and one copy of the *Beirut Star*. Both would eventually serve as toilet paper. The guards gave them a transistor radio, but took it away on the hour and overnight so they couldn't hear the news. The Harari-Raful brothers, who spoke Arabic with the captors who did listen to the news, gleaned only tidbits. When the hijackings ceased to be a main news story, however, the group had the radio all the time. Berkowitz was the "radio man" and listened most often to VOA broadcasts from Rhodes, the BBC, and Kol Yisrael. He would lull himself to sleep at night listening to Israeli folk songs playing softly on the radio next to his ear.[7]

Amman, 4 PM

At 4 PM, a second Red Cross plane arrived in Amman. On board were two doctors, three nurses, health supplies, tents, blankets, toiletries, medicines, and 1,200 meals. The first plane, which had brought Rochat, still sat at the Amman airport, available for a hostage evacuation. Rochat went out to meet the second plane "which (with his usual flair for the dramatic) he intended to fly direct to Dawson Field." But the PFLP refused to allow the plane to land at Dawson. Thus, the medical team and five tons of supplies it carried would have to reach the aircraft overland the next day. They would never make it.[8]

Dawson Field, 4 PM

For BOAC's First Officer Trevor Cooper, late Thursday afternoon turned into a hellish nightmare.

> We were allowed off again and that is when the incident happened. I had been playing cards all day with Major Potts's daughter, whose name was Suzy. We left the airplane together and got on the ground. I was then approached by the [PFLP] officer who was on the flight deck during the hijacking, who asked me to accompany him to his tent. I went along happily. The tent was, I should say, 50 yards away from the airplane. I got inside and there were two men with machine guns. I sat down in the middle of them on a sack.

> The chief hijacker then produced a pistol, stuck it at my head, and said that when I was leaving the aircraft I said to the girl I was with that I had got a sonograph on board, and he wanted that sonograph. I immediately tried to think back on what I had said when I left the aircraft and, having discussed it later, all I can remember was [that] I noticed a Lexicon set—you know, the card game. I remember saying to Suzy "there is a Lexicon set, we can play . . . it will be different from playing cards." . . . But again he was getting very excited, and I immediately said, "Well, what is a sonograph? I don't know what a sonograph is." He said, "I heard you say that you have a sonograph on board. I want that sonograph. I don't want to hurt you, but you have ten minutes to tell me where the sonograph is."
>
> He was getting very excited, clicking his gun; the other two with the machine guns aimed at me. And I said, "Look. Will you please come on the airplane with me, search it all, search everything I have got, search the whole airplane, and let me prove to you that I haven't got anything at all. I don't know what a sonograph is, I haven't got a clue." I pleaded with him to come and talk to the captain about it, but again he said, "I heard you say you had a sonograph—I want that sonograph. You now have five minutes to tell me where it is."
>
> At this stage, I was getting very worried. . . . They were becoming increasingly excited, demanding, demanding that I gave them this sonograph and—I mean, what can you say?—I just pleaded with them that I had nothing, that I would certainly give them anything I had, but they didn't believe me. So the ten minutes was up, and they pushed me out of the tent and into a van which was parked near there, and we drove. At this stage I was extremely anxious.
>
> Again they were clicking their guns, they had one stuck in my back, one was aimed at my head, not very far away, and we drove off into the desert for about a mile. They then parked the van and I was forced to get out. As soon as I got out, I saw that there was this grave that had been dug—at which stage I really thought I had had it. They forced me to get into the grave, kneel down, the three of them stood on top, on the bank—they all had machine guns at this stage—all pointing at me and they gave me sixty seconds to tell them where this bloody sonograph was or else I had had it. And I broke down. . . . I just thought I had had it. I just gave up pleading. . . . I started praying. . . . How long I was in there for I don't know. I just was curled up with my head down waiting for them to shoot, because I was certain they were going to at this stage. I just thought I had had it, you know.

The sun was going down as they drove Cooper back to the plane. When he got back on board, he broke down. The Red Cross wanted to inject him with a sedative, but he refused. He stayed up all night with Suzy, "and, well, I didn't sleep."

Upon her return to England, Suzy Potts protested that "this was one incident which illustrated that, whatever press accounts had said, relations with the *fedayeen* were by no means all sweetness and light. . . . It served to indicate the kind of people who were in charge."[9]

Bern, 5:15 PM

Earlier in the day, the PFLP offered a counterproposal. If the four powers would begin to return the European-held *fedayeen,* the PFLP would permit the immediate evacuation of *all* women, children, and sick from Amman and the three aircraft. The remaining male hostages would be released once Israel freed a still-unspecified number of Palestinians whose names would be provided by the PFLP. The counterproposal was provisional, though; interestingly, it now needed approval by the PLO "High Command," which would meet at 7 PM.

When the Bern Group met that afternoon to consider the counterproposal, the Israeli ambassador was in attendance. He hadn't "joined" the group; he was there merely "to get information." The group rejected the counterproposal outright because it didn't release all prisoners concurrently. The four countries were also clearly reluctant to hinge their male citizens' freedom on "the unpredictable extent" to which Israel might surrender any *fedayeen.* This was especially so since, as Rochat had cabled, "considerable international pressure" on Israel might be needed because the PFLP might demand as many as 600 prisoners.

The four asked whether Israel would in fact free *fedayeen* as part of a package deal. Ambassador Arie Levavi "stonewalled." British Counselor David West insisted that Levavi get his government's answer. To intensify the pressure, a follow-up meeting was scheduled for 11 PM that same evening for Levavi's answer. Britain was "not currently disposed to twist [the] Israelis' arms on this," mind you. It was "just asking."[10]

Amman, 7 PM

Following the *USS Independence*'s arrival off the Lebanese coast this morning, rumors again circulated around the Middle East that the United States was preparing to intervene militarily. Iraq took the possibility seriously and, in a startling move, publicly and forcefully commanded the *fedayeen* to free *all* hostages *unconditionally.* It demanded that Arafat announce the release immediately. Otherwise, he was warned, "we are not responsible for anything that happens to you."

Iraq's about-face was astounding. To this point, Iraq had been on close terms with the PFLP's leadership. There were even reports that Iraqi authorities had prior knowledge of the hijackings and that its forces helped prepare the desert airstrip for the planes. The Iraqi directive seemed to have an impact. So, apparently, did the increasing realization of the risks and logistical challenges of holding 450 people captive in the desert. They were diverting too much time and energy, and the PLO clearly no longer wanted to be distracted from "the basic issue" and preparing for the imminent "final battle."

The PLO decided to take charge of "supervising the detained passengers" and set terms markedly less demanding than the PFLP's. The PLO would release all passengers except "Israelis with military status" once the countries officially announced their readiness to free the European prisoners. The planes and their crews would be freed when those prisoners were returned. Only "Israelis of military capacity" would be held until Israel agreed to release *fedayeen* in its jails. The PLO did not define the term. As it turned out, it would essentially mean American Jewish men and women aged 16 to 35, including me.

The PLO then directed the PFLP to transfer all passengers including Israelis and crew to Amman. The PFLP reluctantly said okay. But it, in fact, did not yield "supervision" to the PLO, accept the PLO's new terms, or comply with the PLO's directive. The PFLP was still very much in control of us.[11]

Amman, 8:30 PM

"If everything goes well," André Rochat figured, "we will need at a minimum ten days." If not, "it may be a matter of months." But Rochat was on borrowed time, failing both as an intermediary and in his humanitarian mission.

The British were concerned about Rochat's slow progress and lack of urgency. They were also concerned about mounting tensions between him and the Jordanian prime minister over credit for certain amenities, like air conditioning, being provided to the hostages and over his refusal to let the hostages at the Intercontinental hotel leave.

Israel continued to be unhappy with him because of his "unreliability" and "independent" role, his "scare and extortion campaign," and his suggestion that everything depended on Israel. Rochat had just expressed his assessment to the European and American diplomats in Amman that the Palestinians were "desperados" who, he was sure, had taken a "very quiet resolution to extend the volume of their hijacking activity until, almost inevitably, something will blow up." He concluded that the "nub of the problem comes back in almost any conceivable scenario" to Israel. If Israel would refuse to budge, he hinted strongly, the danger to the passengers would be so great that "special and deep humanitarian considerations" might prompt the ICRC to drop its insistence on nondiscrimination.

Rochat was also not sufficiently pressing the PFLP. He had conveyed unchallenged the PFLP's claim that its prisoner demands of Israel would consist merely of female prisoners, prisoners in poor condition, and certain "particularly important or heroic fedayeen." And he had just passed on the PFLP's proposals, "which were so clearly unacceptable." Britain's ambassador to Switzerland, Eric Midgley, concluded that if Rochat would resign, no one would see it as a tragedy.

In addition, Rochat seems not to have reported to the countries the intense and intimidating interrogations of and threats to the Jewish passengers and the confiscation of their personal belongings. Even as we had very little food today, he reported that the food condition aboard the plane was "acceptable." Rochat also reported that our morale was "quite high" and that some passengers spoke of being "extremely well treated," obvious fallacies. Rochat asserted that the aircraft were not wired with explosives even though ICRC personnel had no way to closely inspect the planes.

When confronted today with TWA vice president Dick Wilson's report that the six who had been taken off the plane were still absent, Rochat replied that he had now been "assured" by the PFLP that the six were well and "simply being questioned." Rochat was not aware of where they were being held or their medical condition. Quite amazingly too, he had not insisted on a list of hostages and their nationalities, though he confessed that compiling such a list was "a basic Red Cross responsibility." And not having resolutely pressed the PFLP for an explanation, he could not account for why so many Swissair passengers had been released while most TWA passengers were still at the site. He should have known that no Jews from the TWA plane had been released.

But the following anecdote is perhaps the most telling. Buried in a report later that night, Rochat wrote almost offhandedly, "For your info, a young American woman gave birth today in [the] TWA plane in conditions you know." It would take a full day for him to learn that the information was false. But in the meantime, he did not insist that the baby and mother be taken to a hospital or at least a more sanitary facility. It is hard to fathom how he could countenance a new mother and newborn baby aboard a filthy, unhygienic, sand-filled, alternatingly hot and cold plane. Nor did he request formula, diapers, or even fresh water for the newborn baby. He did not even insist on knowing the mother's name.

Perhaps even more astonishing was the response of the president of the International Committee of the Red Cross: a pathetic telegram to the nameless mother. It read: "Madame: I do not know who you are, and I am still unaware of the name and sex of your child, but I make myself the mouthpiece of all those who are deeply moved by the difficult conditions in which you find yourself." He added that he had asked his representatives in Amman "to send you some flowers, if they can." Flowers![12]

Jerusalem, 8 PM

Responding to the pressure from Bern, Israel's cabinet went into emergency session. It decided to continue resisting any advance commitments. After all, the other four powers were now trying to get all passengers out in return for only the seven European-held terrorists; the UN Security Council had unanimously called for the passengers to be released; the PFLP had shown weakness by extending its deadline; and now, *mirabile dictu,* Iraq had called for the release of all passengers! Why commit to anything now? Israel's contribution, "with which it was not happy" either, was to abstain from "loud protests" against the release of European-held *fedayeen.* For Israel even to accept the release of these terrorists whom it saw as murderers was farther than it wanted to go.

So Levavi in Bern was instructed that "if we reach a situation where a deal cannot be struck without our participation and if the demands [on us] are specified, the government will deliberate about it. Right now, there is no need to decide."[13]

Amman, 9 PM

Thursday evening, with the afternoon's cease-fire tenuously holding, the Jordanian government appealed to "all citizens, businessmen, shopkeepers, and employers to resume their normal work now that the situation has calmed down, anxiety and unrest have ended, and everyone is working for a return to normal life." Amman's mayor urged municipal workers to report to work Friday morning.

Simultaneous with those appeals, however, the PLO was airing impossible demands "which the Jordanian regime must meet if it wants to survive." One amounted to complete capitulation: "Formation of a patriotic authority representing the people's force's groups, [which] should control all the government's departments." If its demands were not met, "the revolution, the masses, and all honest elements in the Jordanian Army will have before them only one choice—to carry out themselves the task of liquidating the plotters, one by one, group by group, until all Jordan has been purged of the traitor, agent, and plotting elements."[14]

Bern, 11 PM

Israeli Ambassador Arie Levavi, now with instructions, was duped into missing the reconvened, late-night session of the Bern Group scheduled specifically to get his input. As Levavi reconstructed the events, a Swiss official called him at about 10:45 PM and told him that the group was considering canceling the meeting. Levavi briefly conveyed Israel's position, emphasizing that he would be happy to expand on it when the group met. He wasn't told that the meeting would take place after all. Rather, at 2:45 AM he received a call that the group had met. Israel understood that Levavi had been excluded.

Meanwhile, the United States, and presumably the British and Germans, saw his failure to attend as "an effort to avoid pressure." They took his absence and telephonic communication, presumably conveyed by the Swiss, as "entirely negative" and signaling Israeli unpreparedness to liberate *fedayeen*. According to the U.S. ambassador to Switzerland, Shelby Davis, "the uncompromising negative attitude of the Israelis . . . came as a shock to all participants. When we adjourned [earlier], each of us had grounds for believing that [the] Israeli position had evolved."[15]

Dawson Field, 2 AM

Thursday night we went to sleep. It was the first decent night's sleep I had gotten in a week, because every night it was something else. I hadn't slept too well. This night I lay across the floor between two rows. I went to sleep and was sleeping very soundly. Then, I got up, ten-thirty, eleven o'clock. I lay across the chair, and I again was sleeping soundly.

At two-thirty in the morning, I was awakened with a flashlight shining in my face. Jim Majer woke me up. I knew automatically what he was going to say, but he told me anyway: They wanted me up front, for questioning. There was a guerrilla standing behind him—with a beat up nose and unshaven face. I asked him whether I should put on my shoes and socks and shirt—because I was sitting on the floor, I had wanted to be comfortable—and he said yes. So I knew I would be saying good-by to the plane. I knew I wouldn't see it again.

My mother happened to be awake at the time. She was turning over in her seat a few rows back. She heard them calling my name and she got up; she automatically knew what was going on. As I started walking up front, I started shaking all over; I couldn't control parts of my body anymore. I became very nervous. My mother told me then all the different stories she had told the guerrillas, so that we would have our stories straight in case they wanted to compare the stories. It's very amusing now and even then it was a little amusing, but it was a very serious situation.

I went up front and was told to sign a piece of paper. I was shaking like a leaf and Ben Feinstein happened to be there. He put his arm around me and pulled me close and told me not to worry, that everything was going to be okay. They told us to sign our names, but I couldn't sign it because my hand was shaking, so I had to print it.

Then they told us to get off the plane. Of course, this was a very sad situation: getting off the plane and not knowing where I was going, not knowing when I would see my family again. I really felt lonely.

I got off the plane. It was the desert in the middle of the night and it was in the fifties. I should have been freezing, but I really didn't notice the

> *temperature. It didn't make any difference, in fact. I really didn't care how cold it was or how hot it was, whether it was day or it was night; it really didn't make any bit of difference.*

I was sure I was being taken off to be killed. I left the plane with nothing but the clothes I was wearing. No money. No passport. Nothing.

> *We were put on board a bus. It was myself and nine other people. Ben Feinstein, Bob Palagonia, Rabbi Jonathan David, Yaakov Drillman, Meyer Fund, David Miller, Mark Shane, Mitchell Meltzer, and of course Jeffrey Newton, my friend from high school. Two guerrillas sat up front carrying machine guns facing us—as if we were going to run somewhere. And we were all very, very scared. They took us in front of the TWA plane and around to the other side of the BOAC plane. We stayed in front of the BOAC for a few minutes; then we were driven off.*
>
> *We started moving at three-thirty. At first, I tried to track our direction by seeing which way we were going, what routes we were taking. Because I knew what direction the planes were facing: The sun rose on the right side of the TWA plane, which meant that the nose of the plane was headed north, northeast. And we started off in the direction that the plane was facing. But then we made all kind of windings, and it was very hard to keep track, especially since it was night and we couldn't see too far to either side of us—I gave up. We had a jeep in front of us and a jeep behind us. I decided that since there was nothing better to do, I'd go to sleep; so I did. We came to a few roadblocks set up by the guerrillas. They asked the driver who we were, and every time we got through.*
>
> *We decided that my watch was probably the most important thing that anyone of us had; nobody had too much with them. I had my watch that had the day and the date on it. The month wouldn't be too hard to remember. So we decided that I must wind this watch every day and make sure it kept running because this would probably be the only way we'd keep track of time and date and how long we'd been there.*

As I was being led to the plane's front, my mother had followed until a guerrilla said to her "No, mama, sit down." She continued a bit further. They picked up a gun in first class and pointed it at her, repeating "Mama, sit down." She ran back to the rear exit to try to get a last glimpse of her son. But she saw nothing. "It was just pitch black. They just disappeared. . . . I stood there for about—I don't know how long. I didn't care whether they shot me. . . . I just wasn't going to move." And she recited the *Shema.*

When she realized we were gone, she went up to the galley. "I just pushed my way through and I sat down. . . . I was shivering from the cold. . . . I [sat] there until the sun rose and I could hear the children in the back yelling, 'Where's my mother?'" She went back to reassure them that she was there and okay. "Then, my son Moshe went into shock. He just sat and couldn't believe it. 'But he was right here during the night. What happened to him?' His eyes were glazed over and his lower lip was just hanging down." He sat alone, just shaking his head.[16]

CHAOS, CONFUSION, AND "FANTASTIC TENSION"

FRIDAY, SEPTEMBER 11

Dawson Field, 5:30 AM

"I [had] struck up a relationship with one of the few teenagers close to my age," Susie Hirsch recalls. "When the sun went down and the light faded, David and I whispered together, talking about ourselves and our summer experiences. This was a comfort to me and certainly helped to keep my mind off the situation. Here we were, two teenagers who felt the bond of our common fate. On Friday morning, when I awoke, David was gone. Even now [thirty years later], as I write these words I feel the fear and sorrow of that morning, and tears come to my eyes."[1]

Amman, 5:30 AM

And there I was. A seventeen-year-old American kid. An A student, president of my high school honor society, captain of my high school chess team. Supposed to have started college in New York two days earlier. Instead, I was in a minibus in Jordan, huddled with nine other guys, hostage to Palestinian terrorists, being driven in the dead of night to who-knows-where. Scared out of my wits.

> *I'd say it was an hour and a half ride. We were taken to an Arab refugee camp [Wahdat] or, if you will, a refugee section of Amman. We were brought into a small compound.*

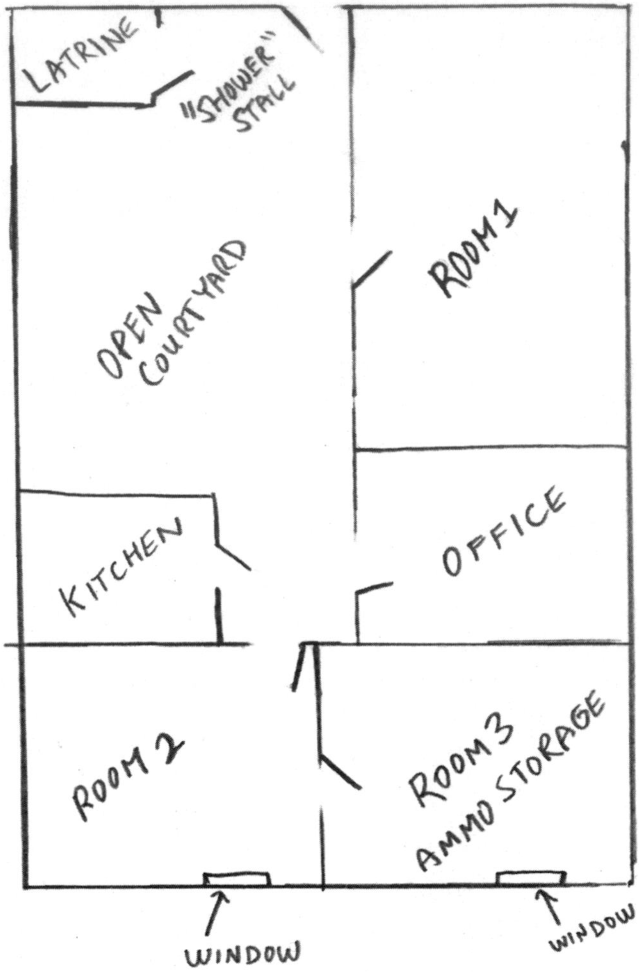

Figure 1 Our Compound in Wahdat

We were very frightened, as you can imagine. As we came in, it was early morning. The sun had just risen and the Arab music was screeching away—high-pitched violin music. Some of the guerrillas who had been sleeping outside were now just getting up. We were taken into the office. We stood there, not knowing what was going to happen. Then we were moved into another room which was larger (Room #1), and then we moved into Room #2. They brought us blankets to put on the floor, and then they brought us more blankets to put on top of us. And there we sat.

The first thing they did was bring us tea. In other words, they started treating us well right away. Every time we asked for it, they brought us tea. At first we didn't ask for it but they brought it every once in awhile. They gave out packs of cigarettes, which we gladly took. And there we sat.

For two days, the going was really rough; really, really rough. Here we were, ten people sitting in a room that was ten by thirteen at most and had two small windows: one on the door and one opposite the door. Two very, very small windows. The temperature during the day went up into the hundreds. And we were sweating bullets, "shvitzing" like crazy. It was just pouring out of us. It was so humid in there.

At first it was very difficult telling the men that we had to go to the bathroom. We kept asking for the WC—finally they understood what WC was. And every time we said WC, they would unlock the door and let us go to the bathroom [a hole in the ground with no toilet paper]. We noticed that when someone had to go to the bathroom, they would leave our door open until we got back. So we decided that in order to get some fresh air in the room, one would go and they'd leave the door open; when he came back, the next person would go—even if he didn't need to—just to go outside and to get some fresh air and to leave the door open so we would get some fresh air inside. It worked.

Of course, they got a little suspicious when everybody went to the bathroom around eight or nine times a day, and they decided to keep the door locked even then. We asked them, motioning with our hands—we couldn't speak Arabic—"Please leave it open, it's hot." One guerrilla motioned to us "if I leave the door open" and then put one wrist on top of the other, which meant of course he'd be imprisoned, he'd be tied up. In other words, he was under orders or he felt he was under orders to keep the doors locked.

It was extremely hot and we had nothing whatsoever to do. They hadn't told us that we were going to be out taking a "vacation" anywhere, and we didn't bring anything along with us except the clothes we were wearing. It was really, really difficult passing the time away. We looked at our watch every five minutes, and you know how long it takes for a day to pass when you keep looking at your watch.

The ten of us were aged 16 to 40. I was the second youngest. We were all Americans, none Israeli, although David Miller was born in Israel. Other than Bob Palagonia, we were all Jewish. Bob, 25, from New Rochelle, New York, who had boarded in Bombay, liked to collect visa stamps in his passport and had gotten off in Tel Aviv to get an Israeli stamp. We and the three Jews in Irbid were the "Israelis of military capacity" whom the PFLP intended to hold for the long term. The world would not learn of our abduction for several days. It would not know until this whole affair was over that we had been held in the Wahdat refugee camp, a PFLP stronghold.

As we sat there, our spirits swung dramatically, soaring one minute as we imagined that we were surely about to be released and plummeting the next as we convinced ourselves that we were doomed. Once, when we were down, Bob blurted "Thumbs up," jabbing up both his thumbs. This soon became our mantra. We would repeat it throughout our ordeal to lift our spirits.

Dawson Field, 7:30 AM

Apparently, both the PLO's insistence that nearly all passengers be released and overnight radio reports of an imminent foreign (probably American) military intervention had set off the guerrillas guarding the planes. After breakfast, Abu-Nidal came on board, hopping mad. He ordered all passenger hand luggage and coats off the plane and searched again. One by one, the passengers brought their hand luggage forward, and the guards proceeded to throw everything off onto the desert floor.

Outside, the situation had become even tenser. The ICRC medical team stationed near the planes, led by a Dr. Frascani, was ordered to leave the area. This left Ahmed Kamal as the only doctor for three aircraft. Other "draconian security measures" were also imposed, André Rochat anxiously reported to Geneva, including the "installation of dynamite in these planes with passengers prisoners aboard."

The Jordanian army surrounding the planes also reported a change for the worse:

> The situation at the site of the hijacked planes is very bad. The Red Cross is dismissed from the site. All vehicles are evacuated from around the plane. It is forbidden for anybody to get near the planes or to get on them. . . . The two [*sic*] planes are ready to be exploded if they suspect any movement afoot. The way of treating the passengers is changed.

A short while later, the ICRC relief convoy carrying the supplies flown in the previous day was stopped en route to the planes, about five miles away. The Frascani team, heading to Amman, met the blocked convoy, and both convoy and medical team would sit there for over twenty-four hours.

A Palestinian "principal leader" in Amman insisted that André Rochat immediately obtain assurances that there would be no foreign military intervention. Rochat urgently cabled Geneva.[2]

Dawson Field, 9 AM

A tremendous sandstorm kicked up in the desert, sending sand swirling over the luggage and through the plane. The brown blizzard was so intense that the passengers couldn't see out their windows. The crew quickly shut all doors and window exits, but in only a few short moments, the plane's entire inside was engulfed in sand. For the next two to three hours, the hundred or so remaining passengers sat with no ventilation, sand heavy in the air, and temperatures rising again above 100. The heat became intolerable, breathing difficult. The hostages didn't know how to protect themselves. Some covered their mouths and noses with moistened shreds of cloth or with their undershirts. Some parents told their children to lie down on the floor, while others told theirs to stand up high. My brother Noam, and others with respiratory problems, had an extraordinarily hard time. Noam began wheezing and couldn't catch his breath.

Finally, the storm cleared. The crew opened the doors and windows again, and everyone drew a deep breath. But with the humidity and perspiration, the thick yellow sand now stuck to everyone's skin and clothes. The luggage outside was completely coated. Very soon it was time for lunch, but the commandos brought no food at all. The crew passed out whatever leftovers there were. The copilot cut up and served limes, apparently from the first Red Cross shipment.[3]

Amman, 10 AM

Amman itself quieted down on Friday. The cease-fire of the prior day appeared to be holding. Amman airport reopened to inbound traffic. Joint army-PLO patrols roamed Amman's streets, exhorting citizens to resume their normal activities. The Education Ministry urged schools to reopen the next day. Communications with the outside world resumed although they were still sporadic.

Despite the momentary respite, the situation remained tense. About 140 people had been killed in the fighting over the prior eleven days. New fighting could break out any time. In fact, the PLO claimed that the Palace Guard, in an attempt "to escalate the crisis," had shot and killed a civilian.

The Jordanian Cabinet, meeting in emergency session, was increasingly concerned about the ongoing drama in the desert and the escalating tensions with the PLO. Though still essentially hamstrung, it formulated a "strong new approach [to the] entire *fedayeen* issue." It warned the PFLP that it would be held responsible for the increasing danger and hardship of the hostages on the planes. And, it made "crystal clear" to the PFLP "in terms [of] inherent plausibility to [their] fanatic mentality" that blowing up the aircraft and passengers "would result in [a] wholesale government assault upon the *fedayeen* movement." King Hussein too was becoming restive. He told British Ambassador John Phillips that if the *fedayeen* blew up even empty planes, not one would emerge alive.

For the moment, though, the government's engagement in the crisis remained limited to frustrated bluster.[4]

Amman, 11 AM

Concurrent with the dangerously worsening conditions at Dawson, the PFLP in Amman asked the Red Crescent to organize a convoy and immediately bring all passengers and crews to Amman. A sizable convoy of buses, ambulances, and other vehicles departed Amman to retrieve the remaining passengers.

Meanwhile, at about 11 AM, a PFLP representative suddenly appeared at the Intercontinental and handed back sixty-two passports—twenty-two for TWA passengers (eighteen Indian, one Saudi, and three U.S. nationals) and forty for Swissair. He pronounced their owners free to leave Jordan. Others would follow, he said. The passport return seemed random; some families were even split up. There was no discrimination, as several Jewish families were permitted to depart. The PFLP in Amman had seemingly concluded that it no longer needed the large group of hostages it was holding to achieve its objectives.

The guerrillas at the site had other ideas. They barred the convoy from nearing the planes. This day was fast turning into a "hectic rash of ostensibly contradictory events."[5]

Bern, 11:30 AM

Unaware of the PLO offer or the unfolding events, the group reviewed Rochat's morning cable which, unfortunately, was "in telegraphese" and "rather obscure." Rochat strongly urged the group to now agree to his own proposal: "three Palestinians against all women, children, and sick." With a quick positive response, he believed he could get these out by early the next day, latest. He wanted an immediate reply.

While Germany was open to it, the group rejected Rochat's compromise despite the "urgency of the matter" and the "risk of the situation's turning sour." Britain felt that Leila Khaled could be released only with "the release of every single passenger and aircrew." Switzerland found Rochat's proposal "totally unacceptable" as it would only make negotiations for the male hostages more difficult. Even the ICRC slapped Rochat's wrists. "Please avoid absolutely" presenting proposals to the group without first getting the ICRC's okay.

While the Bern Group was meeting, another, "panic-stricken" cable arrived from Rochat.[6]

Amman, 12:35 PM

Rochat had been summoned to an "immediate conference" with PFLP leaders at their headquarters. "Fantastic tension" reigned, he cabled. "We now see these people as they really are . . . angry and desperate." Rumors of a possible military intervention and internal disagreements were causing a "very grave situation." The *fedayeen* leaders were taking "various decisions" to demonstrate their anxiousness. They canceled the passenger transfer and the Sunday-morning deadline. TWA's Wilson now expected "dramatic events this afternoon, probably TWA aircraft destruction." And, in Washington, Joseph Sisco frantically informed Henry Kissinger of Palestinian threats to kill the remaining hostages because of the Sixth Fleet's menacing moves.

Rochat had tried to "calm their angry mood" and to persuade them to ignore the rumors and trust the Red Cross. He even proposed his unauthorized compromise. But the PFLP ordered him to return at 3 PM, when it would inform him of further "warning measures" it planned to institute.

The Bern Group cabled Rochat to categorically assure the *fedayeen* that no armed intervention was contemplated. At about 4 PM, Rochat held a press conference in Amman to do so. The Swiss and U.S. governments later issued statements to the same effect. But the chaos persisted.

By late afternoon, the PLO believed that all passengers were now in Amman. Presumably, it was incredulous and furious when it learned that, despite its prior evening's directive, passengers were still on the planes. So the PLO sent out its own contingent of ten buses and an armed escort (the third convoy of the day) to retrieve the passengers. The PFLP guards at Dawson, however, refused to allow the deputation to near the site. The buses idled until evening, but no passengers were released. The PLO's frustration with the PFLP's insubordination was mounting.[7]

Amman, 3 PM

Escorted by a lone Jordanian police vehicle, a convoy of about sixty-six Swiss, German, and American nationals left the Intercontinental hotel for the airport. The PFLP and "all others concerned" had agreed to their departure with "no conditions attached." The convoy took a circuitous route, skirting guerrilla-held areas, but it did pass near skirmishes between *fedayeen* and government forces. A Royal Jordanian Airline aircraft, standing by at Amman airport for several hours, flew the sixty-six to Nicosia, Cyprus. They arrived "tired but in generally good shape." With a cholera epidemic raging in the region, the freed hostages were all given medical exams and cholera shots. They would leave for home the next day at noon. The twenty-two released BOAC hostages also finally left, heading to Beirut under "private" arrangements.

Rochat believed that the remaining hostages at the hotel were also "on the verge of moving" to the airport for evacuation. Nicosia expected a second Jordanian airliner. But no one else moved, and the flight was cancelled.[8]

Bonn, 4 PM

Skeptical of prospects for a common solution, Germany sent two emissaries to Jordan: Hans Wischnewski and another senior member of Chancellor Willy Brandt's Social Democratic Party. Learning of this, the United States urgently pressed Germany to not make a separate deal and to not have Wischnewski proceed to Amman, or, if he was already en route, to deal only through Rochat. Germany's State Secretary Paul Frank defended the "visit" as a "private effort." Wischnewski was merely going to talk to his good friend, the president of the Palestinian Red Crescent Society, about the "possible alleviation" of conditions aboard the aircraft. Three times Frank repeated that the common front remained unchanged. But Germany had clearly just initiated a back channel for its own citizens.[9]

London, 4 PM

As the days elapsed, anxiety in London grew over how to deal with Leila Khaled. Under the Aliens Order, she would have to be transferred to a prison on Sunday. The British were apprehensive about how the PFLP might react.

Attorney General Peter Rawlinson was becoming "restless" too. He had sufficient evidence to charge her and the press was puzzled at his silence. He had thus proposed to institute formal proceedings against Khaled. However, following a Cabinet-level debate, the British Secretary of State "put it to [him] very strongly" that "the public interest" demanded that Khaled not be prosecuted at this stage. Rawlinson obliged.[10]

Dawson Field, 5:30 PM

As the setting sun began to cast the plane's long shadows over the desert floor, the Jewish Sabbath was approaching. The Sabbath, *Shabbos* or *Shabbat*, is very special for an observant Jew. It is ushered in shortly before sunset by the women, who light the *Shabbat* candles to radiate a peaceful glow over the home and the *Shabbat* table. After evening prayers in the synagogue, the *Kiddush* is recited, sanctifying the Sabbath with blessings over a cup of wine. The *Shabbat* meal begins by reciting a blessing over two braided challahs and sharing the bread. The meal is festive—the most special meal of the week; delicacies and treats are served. Then throughout *Shabbat*, the day of rest, observant Jews refrain from various activities, such as turning electrical appliances on or off, writing, or driving. So, as sunset approached, the thirty-five or so observant Jews still on the plane anxiously wondered what their *Shabbat* would be like as captives in the Jordanian desert.

Trying to maintain as much of the tradition as possible under the circumstances, the Jewish women asked the crew for candles. When the crew responded that it didn't have any, some women raised their voices. A commando came over and asked what the problem was. He went away and returned shortly after with two candles. The doyenne, Mrs. Rachel Harari-Raful, lit them on behalf of all the women. (By agreement, the guerrillas blew out the candles shortly afterward so as not to create a fire hazard.)

After the candle lighting, Millie Leser recalls, "We were all so depressed and very sad at not being able to usher in the *Shabbat* properly. I will never forget one passenger, Mrs. Raab, who gave each of us a small handful of soup nuts [bought in Israel] and said 'in honor of the holy Sabbath.' We celebrated as best we could—similar to the Jews during the Holocaust who used whatever was available to mark the various holidays."

It looked like no new food would arrive for supper, so the crew for the second time that day served whatever leftovers there were. Then, suddenly, the guerrillas arrived with a hot meal, some of which was offered to the passengers. Abu-Nidal insisted that he and the crew dine together. None of the hostages knew it was to be their last supper on the plane.[11]

Wahdat, 5:30 PM

Of the ten of us, five were religious. We realized that "Shabbos" was approaching, and we felt it was time to get ready. We were wondering what "Shabbos" would be like in the hands of the Arabs. We just hoped we wouldn't have to desecrate the Sabbath. As it got dark, we all davened [prayed]. We then waited, as we wondered when we might make "Kiddush." Of course, we didn't have any wine. But then they brought us supper and they brought bread—pita. The Halacha [Jewish law] is that when you don't have wine, you can make "Kiddush" over bread—pita, challah, or whatever bread there is. So when they brought in the pita, Rabbi David made "Kiddush" for us all. As soon as he finished, I realized that when the Red Cross came on Tuesday with box lunches, these box lunches had little packets of salt and pepper that I had stuck in my pocket. So now I had salt that we were able to put on the bread, which is, of course, the Halacha. We considered it very amusing at the time.

Sleeping was very difficult, as we had only blankets. We were very crowded and we were all stretched out. We had to use other people's arms and stomachs as pillows. It became pretty uncomfortable.

Dawson Field, 7 PM

Shortly after the trash had been collected from dinner, at about 7 PM, the guerrillas instructed the captain to get all adult male passengers off the plane and to do so with the least possible fuss and commotion. It went very quickly. The men all exited through the forward galley door where a truck with a ladder was waiting. For some reason, Al Kiburis was called back onto the plane to disengage the movie projector. (Did the guerrillas want to keep the movie?) When he left the plane a few minutes later, the remaining passengers had started singing.

But the singing was to distract and console themselves. The women, mostly Jewish, were distraught. With no men around, they felt highly vulnerable though somewhat comforted that the female crew members, whom they viewed as authority figures, had remained. My mother organized the Jewish women into a guard detail, which took turns staying up to make sure that no one was molested during the night. At one point, a male guerrilla did walk through the plane and bother one of the passengers. Halla Joseph was informed and immediately threw him off the plane.

Meanwhile, after they deplaned, the eighteen men, including the captain and the other male crew members, were herded into a small minibus. Rabbi Hutner, the eminent Orthodox Jewish leader, was thus forced to desecrate the Sabbath and leave behind a manuscript of a book he was writing. (It had been confiscated by the guerrillas and has never been recovered despite numerous approaches to the Palestinians.)

Four armed guerrillas rode inside the minibus with the men; it was cramped. A jeep with a mounted anti-aircraft gun and two armed soldiers led the way; a similar jeep followed. The forlorn men bumped and banged through the desert, swallowing dust for over an hour. Suddenly they stopped, and the hostages thought that the driver had lost his way. It turned out that the jeep behind them had a flat tire, and after about half an hour the convoy started moving again.

Finally, they came to a paved road. They drove past a few old stone shacks, an irrigated field, and a herd of about twenty dark brown sheep with curled horns. The guards were in a good mood and began to sing. The pseudoserenity was jolted, however, when a Land Rover bearing Jordanian soldiers passed them, and the soldiers pointed their guns at the bus. The guerrillas bolted upright and grabbed their guns. The hostages ducked, sure that shooting would soon follow. Fortunately, it didn't. At another point, they came to a roadblock manned by Jordanian soldiers. The hostages' guards just brandished their rifles and the convoy was waved through. Wittingly or not, the army had just let the hostages it sought slip through its fingers.

After driving about an hour and a half, they saw lights twinkling in the distance. They had come to the outskirts of Zarqa. The convoy wended its way through a network of small unlit alleys and streets, crowded with armed guerrillas. Finally it pulled into a small, unlit street, blocked by a disabled car.

There it stood for about fifteen minutes. The guards left the bus, possibly to find the best route for the convoy not to be discovered. When they returned, the bus then backed up and drove very slowly for another ten minutes until it came to another small street. Everyone got out, and the men were led single file in pitch darkness through a clutter of adobe-like houses and tangles of alleyways. They trudged slowly up a hilly, crooked alley and then around a corner where they found themselves standing in front of stone steps. They climbed the steps and walked through a green doorway into a courtyard. They had arrived at their new residence.

The group split into two: ten men went into one room, eight into the other. The rooms were bare except for a wooden bench, some small wicker stools, a wooden table, and a couple of sewing machines. (The rooms had served as classrooms where children were schooled and taught sewing.) One room had a bed with a mattress. Large posters of Lenin adorned the walls and stacks of communist literature were piled on the floor. The men sat on the wooden benches in those rooms for about fifteen minutes, awaiting their fate. Soon, guards came with a tray of glasses of sweetened hot tea. They gave the men blankets and told them to go to sleep. The men slept on the floor.[12]

Amman and Dawson Field, 7:30 PM

It would become obvious that even the PFLP leadership in Amman was unaware that these men had been secreted. This was apparently a rogue operation by some of the *fedayeen* at Dawson who felt that their leaders were yielding too much to pressure.

Meanwhile, hard-headed negotiations were taking place at Dawson between PLO and PFLP representatives. The PLO was applying "considerable pressure," humiliated that the extremist group not under its control was running the show and concerned that its public image was being tarnished by worldwide condemnation.

At 12:30 AM, an agreement was finally reached to release all remaining passengers at 10 AM. But the PFLP extremists at the site had another—outrageous—plan in mind.[13]

West Bank and Gaza, midnight

Without warning, Israel unilaterally upped the ante. Banging on doors and rousing sleeping families in darkened Arab villages, Israel rounded up 350 West Bank and 100 Gaza Strip residents, including about eighty women. In some cases, whole families were arrested. The pretext for arresting the 450 was suspicion of "being active in the Popular Front," a supporter, or a relative of PFLP members. Two were said to be George Habash's uncles.

There had been vigorous disagreement among Israeli policymakers about the wisdom of the move. Its objectives were murky. One West Bank mayor claimed being told that "we're collecting counterhostages." A respected military analyst wrote that the Israeli action hinted at the brutal measures at its disposal if anything happened to the hostages. Abba Eban, however, soft-pedaled the arrests as merely an operation to gather intelligence on the PFLP. What prompted Israel to act, especially since its approach had been arm's-length until now? Did it not worry that the PFLP might take revenge against the hostages? A PFLP spokesman would in fact call Israel's move "barbaric" and threaten "cruel reprisals that know no mercy."

In the end, after an "investigation" over the ensuing eight days showed that the 450 had no connection with the hijackers, they would be released, bringing the poorly conceived escapade to conclusion. As Shlomo Gazit, then coordinator of Israeli Government Operations in the Occupied Territories, would later write, "everybody preferred to forget this affair."[14]

Bern, midnight

The Bern Group reconvened at midnight and met into the wee hours of Saturday morning, reviewing the PLO proposal of the previous evening. The British were encouraged both by the PLO's intervention—indicating that it might be getting "rather sick of the whole business"—and by its proposal to let everybody out except for "some smallish number of Israelis, who are said to have military capacity." However, Israel's Ambassador Levavi pointed out that, since there were no Israelis of military age or position among the passengers, the PLO obviously intended to hold on to either dual nationals or American Jews. The United States too rejected the proposal since it discriminated among American citizens.

Levavi's protestations notwithstanding, he was pressed yet again by the Swiss and British about what Israel would contribute if the proposal were improved. They pointedly asked him whether Israel appreciated the criticism that the European governments had incurred for their readiness to yield their prisoners. Levavi "calmly and intelligently" responded that as a matter of fact, Israel regretted the Europeans' decisions. It understood their humanitarian motive, he said, "but considered [the] method mistaken."

In the end, the group realized that the PLO proposal only confused matters. With whom was the ICRC really negotiating now? On whom was the PLO proposal binding—the PLO who had issued it, the PFLP who was to implement it, or somehow both? And, as there were no "Israelis of military capacity," who exactly did the PLO intend to hold? And who of those imprisoned in Israel did the Palestinians wish freed?[15]

Rhodes, 1 AM

ICRC vice president Jacques Freymond was now on his way to Amman. Disillusionment with Rochat had been mounting; he was clearly not on top of the situation. The ICRC had recalled him to Geneva, but he refused to come. "I am employing my time to defuse the existing extreme tensions to prevent a tragedy that is at our door," he claimed and sent two subordinates instead. So if Rochat would not come to Geneva, Geneva would come to him.

Freymond arrived in Rhodes, Greece, after midnight and met Rochat's subordinates. They told him that the six men taken off the TWA plane on Monday had been transferred by the Palestinians "to an unknown place" and "had a special military status: they are supposed to be officers in the Israeli army." The ICRC had again taken the PFLP at face value.

How the ICRC did not know the truth is hard to fathom. Israel knew by this time that all six were U.S. citizens. By Tuesday at 6 PM, in fact—three days earlier and less than 24 hours after the six had been spirited away—Kol Yisrael had already reported that they had been taken off the plane and had even broadcast their names except for Schwartz's.[16]

EXPLOSIONS IN THE DESERT

SATURDAY, SEPTEMBER 12

The Country Club, Zarqa, 4 AM

They dubbed it "The Country Club" because they could sun themselves and "it was a lot pleasanter than the stinking, stifling plane we left behind." The quarters for the eighteen men in Zarqa were two small, fly-infested rooms: one eight feet by eight feet, the other ten by ten. "We had filthy blankets to sleep on," recounted George Freda. "The cold floor was our bed. The rooms opened onto the courtyard, as did the kitchen and bathroom, if you could call it a bathroom. [It] was a hole in the floor. I got diarrhea for four days and I wasn't alone."

This morning started around 4 AM. The men had been awakened about an hour earlier by two very loud bangs. Commandos had bombed two Jordanian houses in retaliation for a Jordanian soldier wounding a commando. The men managed to fall back asleep but were now awakened by the Islamic prayer call, blaring from a transistor radio.

Breakfast was served at 6 AM—pita, green peppers, tomatoes, hard-boiled eggs, lunch meat, and hot tea. For the rest of the day, the men were allowed to do as they pleased: sleep, read (they were given Marxist propaganda in English), or just sit outside on the wooden benches and talk. Early morning was nice and comfortable, but by 10 AM the heat became unbearable, and the men sat inside mostly. The day did not seem to pass, however, and the men tried conversing with the guards who spoke only broken English.

"Our [Palestinian] cook [Raja] was a character," recorded 42-year old Freda from Belpre, Ohio. He had just wrapped up a business trip in West

Berlin before boarding the TWA plane in Frankfurt. Raja had worked in Germany for eight years and spoke to the men in pidgin German. "The food was good, sort of combination German and Arab style. . . . He scrounged boxes of grapes, fresh figs, hot Arab bread. . . . But the fruit and dishes were not well washed." Raja even rounded up some cans of Pepsi. When Rabbi Hutner frowned, Raja asked "what's wrong?" To the mortification of the others, the rabbi said he preferred his drink cold. Raja ran out and came back with cold Pepsis. When the rabbi wanted bananas, Raja ran out and got them. He even got a truck seat for the rabbi to sit on. A country club indeed![1]

Dawson Field, 6 AM

The women's guard detail on the TWA plane had taken on the sanitation rotation too. However, one woman—someone surely far removed from such activities in her real-world life—refused to take her turn plunging the toilets. My mother, wife of a distinguished rabbi and a stately woman in her own right, confronted her. "Lady," she said, "if you don't shove, you don't shit!" The woman was flabbergasted, but refused to join the rotation. "We'll see about that!" she snorted. The other the women laughed hysterically.

Amman, 6 AM

Shortly before midnight, twenty-two Indian and Ceylonese passengers were taken off the BOAC plane and brought to the Intercontinental. The next morning, twenty flew to Beirut. A Ceylonese woman and her son remained behind; she had slipped and broken her arm during the night. Sixty-three passengers now remained aboard the BOAC jet.

At about the same time the twenty took off, Rochat arrived at the airport after caucusing all night with Palestinian leaders nearby. He discovered that, despite all the assurances he had received and "continuing rumors of the impending arrival of additional passengers," no one else showed up. He also had no inkling that eighteen men had been carted off to Zarqa.

A short while later, Rochat sent "a long, rambling and incoherent message" to the ICRC. His "exasperated" cable "displayed signs of strain" and was "somewhat diffuse and obscure." He bemoaned the "amounts of most fantastic information" that had swirled around Amman the previous day. The ICRC's "credit and confidence" had gravely declined, he claimed, apparently due to Palestinian accusations that he and his colleagues had "dishonestly declared" that passengers were being "subjected to physical and emotional torture." Without access to the planes, he admitted, he no longer had a way of knowing for sure, but he surmised that the "human problem is doubtless getting worse hourly." But "one way or another," he promised, he would get to the planes the supplies that were stuck en route.

Despite it all, Rochat took the opportunity to pat himself on the pack. "[T]he members of our delegation are all agreed to congratulate themselves [for] a miracle permitting us up to now to avoid the worst."[2]

Wahdat, 10 AM

Saturday morning was a regular morning, I guess. At first, the door was kept closed and we did the same thing we did the day before—sat and watched the rays of the sun. In the morning, we decided that since we had nothing to do, we'd play a game of ghost. Out of the ten, I think eight or nine decided to play. So we started playing around and were really enjoying ourselves for the first time. We were having a lot of fun. Then, all of a sudden, Hajji—who was the head of the place—walked in and said, "Don't speak!" That of course shut us up pretty well. Not a single word came out of our mouths for two or three hours. But when he brought in lunch, he became pretty friendly. He sat down and started eating with us. I didn't eat. He asked me to eat, but I didn't. They brought us a pail of water so we wouldn't have to go out every time to get water. We'd just have to put in the cups that they gave us and drink from the bucket in our room.

Dawson Field, 10 AM

At about 10 o'clock, the women and children aboard the plane were told that they were being taken off. My mother recounted:

> Those people who did not have their luggage gone through on Thursday or Friday had to go through it on Saturday. I was heading for the bus and the guerrillas stopped me again. They told me to put my hand luggage on the ground and they wanted to go through it again. I said, "How many times are you going to go through my luggage? This is inhuman. Why are you doing this to us?" They said that they wanted . . . to spoil the Israeli economy by taking our things away from us. I gave them a whole lecture that they shouldn't think they are the only country in the world suffering. . . . I said I had no gun and I couldn't fight with them and therefore I don't know why they are taking advantage of us with their guns. . . . A woman came over to me, "Remember, your son is a hostage. Don't anger them." When I realized that I might jeopardize the life of my son, I stopped questioning any more.

The passengers then boarded battered old brown minibuses, and the convoy proceeded to Amman in a "triumphal commando cavalcade led by a jeep-mounted machine gun and a woman guerrilla singing the Popular Front anthem over a loudspeaker." An armed guerrilla was aboard each bus, and Jordanian police accompanied the procession.

My mother further recalled:

> This was the first time that my children or I had ever ridden on a Sabbath. Because it was really a matter of life or death, we got on the bus and we rode. . . .
>
> We were told we must keep the windows closed. . . . They were afraid hand grenades would be thrown in the buses by bystanders. . . . It seemed like about a two-hour trip, and it was scorching hot. The windows were closed, and we were unable to open them. We hadn't had anything to eat that day and no water to drink. . . . My children were complaining all the time how hungry and thirsty they were, and "Where is David?"
>
> As we were riding in these hot buses with the windows closed, we heard shouting by the passersby. "Yahud!" [Jews!] and fists were waved at us. . . . On the bus a male guerrilla gave us a lecture on the PFLP position and anti-Israel feelings. We didn't know where we were going. . . . We thought maybe we were being taken to some internment camp or some prison.

At about 12:30 PM, the convoy arrived at the Intercontinental. A total of 120 passengers unloaded, including 68 from TWA, 47 from BOAC (all women and children), and 5 Swissair stewardesses. The Israeli woman and her two children were among those released. The women and children who arrived at the bullet-pocked hotel looked tired and drawn. Several women broke down and cried as they entered the hotel lobby; a British woman fainted.

Shortly after she walked into the hotel, my mother met TWA's vice president Richard Wilson. "He tried to quiet me down because I guess I was pretty hysterical. I came into the lobby and he right away took my hand and said, 'Okay, okay . . . everything will be all right.' I said 'My son, he was taken away from me,' and he said, 'OK.'"

The hotel lobby quickly became a mad, joyous scene. Food and drink began flowing for the weary, hungry, and bedraggled passengers who had just spent a grueling and terrifying week aboard a plane in the Jordanian desert. The embassies tried to get an accurate list of their citizens. The press swarmed around, each trying to scoop the most titillating story. My mother spoke with any reporter willing to listen about her missing, seventeen-year-old son. My six-year-old brother, Yaron, was wearing his bright blue velvet *kippah.* A Jordanian soldier came over, picked him up, and took his *kippah* away. "Give it back," demanded Yaron, who had refused to take it off all week. Instead, the soldier put his own beret on Yaron's head. As the media saw this, they quickly came over and began snapping away. Inspired, the soldier also gave Yaron his submachine gun . . . with the magazine still loaded!

By midafternoon, Wilson decided to move the TWA passengers to the Philadelphia Hotel where, he felt, they would be more comfortable. In the taxi to the Philadelphia, my mother "saw panic in the streets. People were not walking, they were running. They were in a hurry . . . I said to the taxi driver 'What's going on.' He said, 'Very bad trouble. Terrible trouble.' You could just see that people were scared. He was driving like a maniac to get us to the hotel because it was getting dark and unsafe to be in the streets."

Meanwhile, an ICRC convoy sent to pick up the remaining men on the planes was halted by *fedayeen* three kilometers away from their destination. The ICRC reported that a "logistical problem" would make transporting the men to Amman difficult today. Apparently, Rochat's leg was being pulled again. He was also unaware that several TWA women still remained at Dawson.[3]

Dawson Field, noon

About an hour after most of the women and children had departed, the guerrillas shifted the remaining BOAC and TWA passengers to the Swissair plane. The BOAC men carried their luggage across. Before they boarded, a water truck was brought over and they were permitted to wash up and change their clothing. "The water just gushed out of it, and we stripped ourselves down," recalled BOAC First Officer Trevor Cooper. "We just ran and cavorted under this and it was so marvelous." The crew's briefcases were confiscated, however.

Now, all crowded again on a single plane, "it was very, very hot, extremely unpleasant. We just thought if we have got to spend the night like this, it is going to be hell." They sat on the plane for about an hour and a half. With one exception, the remaining TWA passengers were young women—aged 15 to 22—and they were petrified. They thought they had been singled out for rough treatment. Finally, the PFLP came on board and said that everyone was going to Amman. There was a mad rush to get off, but the guerrillas ordered everyone to sit down. They then called a few people by name. The BOAC crew, called first, thought that they were possibly being summoned to fly their plane out. Then the names of five Jewish women from TWA were called: Barbara Mensch, Sarah Malka, Mimi Beeber, Fran (Foozie) Chesler, and Bruriah (Mrs. Jonathan) David. These women also thought that they had been chosen to be released first. When Barbara Mensch heard her name, she turned to a friend with whom she was traveling and apologized for abandoning her. No one imagined that this nightmare might continue. "We thought it was all over—finished with."

It took at least an hour until the passengers deplaned. Everyone picked up their hand luggage and got on the little buses that had come to pick them up. One carried most of the BOAC and Swissair cockpit crews, about ten other male European passengers, and the five American Jewish women. "They drove us to, I would say, between 100 and 200 yards away from the airplanes and parked," Cooper remembered. "They were becoming hysterical at this stage. Fanatical. Rushing around, screaming, arguing amongst themselves. Really getting in a very, very bad state."[4]

Dawson Field, 2:59 PM

At 2:59 PM, successive explosions pierced the desert silence. One after another, the hijacked planes blew up, catapulting metal fragments in all directions and hurling balls of fire and plumes of black smoke up to the heavens. First the forward section of the BOAC went, then its aft. The TWA plane was next, followed in short order by the Swissair plane. When the dust settled, only the tails of the three aircraft and TWA's number four engine and wing outboard remained intact. Before long, neighboring villagers, Bedouin nomads, and even Jordanian soldiers would swarm over the site to scavenge through the debris, looking for souvenirs and useful spare parts. Soon no trace would be left of the drama that had transpired at this place.

"It was an extraordinary sight," recalled Sarah Malka. "We had to sit and watch the airplanes destroyed," recounted BOAC's Cooper. "The VC10 blew up first, and we were so close it almost turned the bus over. [Our minibus] was rocking from side to side, as bad as that." The commandos had kept the minibuses close at hand to use the hostages as human shields upon their departure, believing that the Jordanian army would otherwise capture them or worse, once the planes were blown up.

The commando guards and hostages then "drove off past the army detachments that had observed the scene helplessly all week." Cooper, who was not on the bus with the other BOAC cockpit crew members, recalled:

> The Jordanian Army tanks which had surrounded us all started closing in as we left for Amman. We got, I suppose, about a mile away from the airplanes when everything ground to a halt. Once again, they became extremely excited, arguing among themselves. All the [shit] came out to the forefront again and it was obvious they were having some trouble with the Jordanian Army. . . . But the moment we were through, all the tanks started waving and following alongside, and they didn't seem to bear much animosity toward the Popular Front people at all. This scene lasted nearly half an hour. It was again an extremely tense few minutes, because the rear doors of the buses were open, the machine guns were pointed at the passengers. A lot of the girls from the TWA airplane who were on the same bus as I were petrified and certainly very, very worried. But they let us through in the end.
>
> It was a very nasty ride through the desert. Everybody held handkerchiefs over their faces—the sand was everywhere. I could hardly see the driver at times because it was coming in everywhere. We eventually got onto

> a reasonably tarmaced surface and the journey took in the region of two hours to get to the hotel. . . . [I]t seemed to us they [the PFLP] were heroes. They were cheered and waved, people kept rushing out, applauding, singing.

As the convoy neared Amman, the first buses forked off to the right and proceeded to the Intercontinental. The last bus in the convoy veered to the left. The seventeen men and five women in that small bus were driven to a different section of Amman. As they rode through the streets, their bus was accosted by a mob of "violently angry" Palestinians who banged on the vehicle, "screaming, celebrating, supporting the revolution. Victorious." At one point the throng tried to overturn the bus but was warded off by the PFLP escorts who fired into the air. After a while, the bus stopped and the hostages were led into an apartment in Ashrafiyeh, a Palestinian enclave in Amman.[5]

Amman, 3:30 PM

Just as he was conveying the PLO proposal to the ICRC's Freymond, Yasser Arafat received word that the planes had been destroyed. Arafat was "profoundly shocked." This was not what he had ordered. The PFLP was out of control.

Quickly recovering, the PLO updated its demands: Six Swiss citizens, six Germans, and six Britons would be kept as hostages pending the arrival in Amman of the seven *fedayeen* prisoners. Israeli citizens "with military status" and dual U.S.-Israeli nationals with "military status in Israel" would be held pending an exchange with Palestinian prisoners in Israel. All others would be freed unconditionally. "About 30" Israelis and dual nationals would remain hostage, Freymond was told and was (again) promised a list later that night. The governments could choose their hostages, and the British schoolchildren were free to leave "immediately and unconditionally."

This was blackmail! retorted Freymond. The ICRC would not countenance it and especially not suggest to the governments to select their own hostages. Then, to everyone's shock, Freymond announced that the ICRC was pulling out; he and Rochat would leave forthwith. The PLO reacted with "great surprise" and pleaded to let Rochat remain. Freymond flatly refused. He and Rochat were going.[6]

Wahdat, 4 PM

> *Saturday afternoon we were all sitting around when this guy, Hajji, points his finger at me and pulls me out. I looked at the guys. I didn't know when I would be seeing them again, because I didn't know where he was going to take me. So I looked around and said good-by to them.*

He took me to his office, which was right next door, just two or three feet from our room. He took me in and sat me down. I thought I was about to be interrogated. But, it turns out, he wanted to learn some English. He took a piece of paper, and he wrote down the Arabic word for something. Let's say cigarette, which is "du'-khan" in Arabic and he had a cigarette in his mouth. So he wrote down "du'-khan," pointed to the cigarette, and said "Arabi du'-khan. Anglasi?" I told him "cigarette," and he wrote it down transliterated into Arabic. "Thank you" was "shok'-ron." And so it continued.

Then, a black person came in, a guerrilla also. He said he was from Ethiopia. I don't remember exactly what his lineage was. At first he said "Do you like the black people?" I said, "I like anyone who likes me." Then he said, "Do you have any black friends in the United States?" As I was about to answer him, Hajji told him to be quiet, and we continued talking back and forth, me and Hajji.

After a little while, this black person—whom we called Hercules because he had once seen a movie of Hercules and he mentioned to us that Bob Palagonia looked like Hercules—came and told me that the airplanes had been blown up. I immediately became very frightened. I asked him "what about the people?" He said: "Don't worry, the people are in the hotels." Meanwhile, I looked very frightened and Hajji told me not to worry about it, and he shouted at this guy. I figured he told him to stop, but I don't understand Arabic. When I got back into the room, I told all the guys that he said that the airplanes had been blown up but that the people were in hotels. We also got reports from some other people who looked into our small window every once in a while that the airplanes had taken off, so we were very unsure of what happened. Of course we were very frightened.

So now we had the news—or what they told us—that the airplanes had been blown up. But we didn't know what to believe, and we didn't find out until the next day or Monday what actually had happened. We speculated, as we had done throughout the whole period. We speculated back and forth. Usually we didn't get anything right, but we speculated. It passed the time.

Amman, 4 PM

After Freymond left, the PLO Central Committee was in a snit. The PFLP had violated its order to release all "nonmilitary" passengers. The committee thus "wash[ed] its hands" of the PFLP's exploits and expelled the group. The PFLP was "very surprised" by its ouster and would ask to be reinstated. But the expulsion was more show than reality. With plans for Hussein's overthrow, the PLO did not truly want to alienate PFLP fighters. And, the ICRC would note, despite the "expulsion," the groups "have not severed working relationships."[7]

Amman, 5 PM

At a 5 PM press conference, the PFLP announced that it had released all but *forty* passengers. The hostages would be transferred to "a more cozy place," there would be no reprisals against them, and there were no longer any deadlines. We, the hostages, would simply now be held as prisoners of war.

The PFLP was in fact still holding fifty-six hostages. In the Ashrafiyeh apartment were six Americans (including serviceman Ken Hubler who had been on the Swissair flight), eight Britons, six Swiss, one German, and one Dutchman. I was in Wahdat with nine other Americans from the TWA plane; six other Americans from the TWA flight were in Irbid; and, sixteen Americans, one German, and one Dutchman from the TWA jet were in Zarqa.

Unbeknown to us, the negotiations for our release, almost a week into our captivity, were in total disarray. No one knew how many hostages were being held, who was holding them, where they were being held or under what circumstances, what the conditions were for their release, who was mediating on the countries' behalf, or even with whom they needed to be dealing on the Palestinian side.[8]

Wahdat, 7 PM

Saturday night a doctor came, not Ahmed Kamal but a different one. It seemed that he was much respected, because as he came into our room, the guerrillas who were sitting outside stood up and shook his hand. It looked like he was held in high regard, like they really liked him. He came in and saw what conditions we were living in and became very upset. Whether his being upset was real or not, I don't know. But he looked very upset. He immediately told them to open up the room (Room #3) adjacent to our room so that we could spread out some. So the guerrillas emptied out all the ammunition—the room next to us was an ammunition storage room—and put it into another room and opened up the door for us. But they locked the door to the office, which was adjacent to that room.

Then the doctor asked us what we needed. We told him cups, toothbrushes, toothpaste, soap, towels. Some of the men asked for razor blades. So he brought all this stuff after a little while, plus diarrhea pills and constipation pills. He also brought Russian pajamas. We also got more blankets and we were able to sleep a little more comfortably now. We were very happy to see what he had brought, but then we realized that it was nothing more than the bare essentials. But it did pick up our spirits. We saw that people were still thinking about us. We hadn't seen anybody in two days, and now we finally saw that people still remembered us.

Ashrafiyeh, 8 PM

The seventeen Swissair and BOAC men and the five TWA women were in a three-room apartment in a low building on Jabal Ashrafiyeh, one of Amman's hills. On the southern side of Amman and with a large Palestinian population, Ashrafiyeh abutted the Wahdat Refugee camp to its south. In the evening, Mrs. David began crying and acting hysterically until the guerrillas brought her husband over from our group, and she saw that he had not been executed.

That evening, the five American women and Ken Hubler wrote to President Nixon and Golda Meir asserting that "[t]he lives of women, girls, and men are literally in jeopardy every moment," and asking that "human consideration transcend all other political considerations so that we may be immediately released and returned to our homes." The British Embassy would receive a similar letter from its citizen-hostages. So did the ICRC the previous day from Rabbi Hutner, who expressed fear that "blood will flow" if the hostage problem was not solved soon. The next day, German TV crews would film German hostage Klaus Jeschke accusing his government of callous neglect. The PFLP was using the hostages to pressure their respective governments.[9]

Amman, 9 PM

With the planes destroyed, Jordanian officials urged the United States to get its released citizens out, tonight—passports or not—because the security situation could fast deteriorate. Rochat too exhorted the embassy to take "the first opportunity" to get its citizens out, even tonight. The two Red Cross planes at Amman airport were readied, and Nicosia airport was alerted to receive them. Freymond, the airline representatives, a Jordanian general, the new U.S. chargé William Brubeck, and others held a long meeting at the Intercontinental to plan the extraction. King Hussein and Prime Minister Abdul Rifai both telephoned to urge departure yet tonight. But the group decided to hold off until daylight.[10]

London, 7 PM

In an emergency meeting, the British Cabinet decided that it was now "increasingly urgent" to "press the government of Israel for a clear indication" of its contribution. While the meeting was still ongoing, British permanent undersecretary of state Denis Greenhill called U.S. Ambassador Walter Annenberg. The "Israelis must *now* make up their minds," he said, and the United States needed to persuade them. Then, dismissing the advice of its ambassador in Israel that it was "premature" to press Israel and that even an "implied threat . . . would be counterproductive," at 1 AM in Israel, Ambassador John Barnes was directed to do just that. So was Ambassador Eric Midgley in Bern.[11]

Washington, 5 PM

The U.S. now wanted Jordan to act, despite the missing thirty-eight American citizens. Secretary of State William Rogers summoned Jordanian Ambassador Abdul Hamir Sharaf to impress upon him that King Hussein needed "to demonstrate to all concerned" that he was able "to exercise clear-cut authority throughout [his] kingdom," especially in light of "incidents of the past week." Not only was such authority necessary right now but, "even more important," it would affect the ability to reach a peace agreement in the Middle East. Israel, he told Sharaf, had already questioned with whom peace could be reached in Jordan. Rogers stressed that he was not suggesting destroying the *fedayeen,* but he hoped "that [a] stronger stance over [the] coming days will provide [the] answer."[12]

Bern, 10 PM

In a confrontational meeting, Ambassador Midgley conveyed a sharp message to Israel: "We fully understand the Israeli difficulty," but "clearly the Israelis will have to contribute by releasing detained Arabs, and they will have to make their intentions known soon." If Israel was not prepared to do so, the United Kingdom might have to consider abandoning the nondiscriminatory approach. The Israeli ambassador "though shaken" remained calm.

Switzerland's Foreign Minister Pierre Graber also made a sharp and "lengthy appeal." There were limits to all hard lines, he said, and Israel could not afford the luxury of quarrelling with her friends "for the pleasure of maintaining her intransigence."

To everyone's surprise, the American representative, echoed this tough line too, saying that "Israeli intransigence was being directed against her allies, not the *fedayeen,* and solidarity, on which the Israeli laid so much stress, could not be a one-way affair."[13]

Tel Aviv, 1:30 AM

Shortly after Israel took a pounding in Bern, Britain's Ambassador Barnes, as instructed, roused Gideon Rafael, Israel's Foreign Ministry director general, and read him the riot act. "John Barnes, normally an example of diplomatic courtesy and calm," recalled Rafael, "snapped without introduction: 'I am instructed by my Prime Minister to demand the immediate release by your government of a number of Arab detainees in order to complete the arrangements agreed between all the other parties concerned.'" Rafael's response was "adverse and hostile." "Listen John," he replied slowly, "I want to remind you that the British High Commissioner [for Palestine] departed from these shores on 14 May 1948." Israel was not going to release any *fedayeen*.

A short while later, Israeli foreign minister Abba Eban called Barnes directly to say that he would "passionately oppose" the British view but would pass it on to the cabinet. Israel's sharp responses prompted the British Foreign Office to reassure Eban "that we are issuing no kind of threat." But the point was made. The British had obviously decided that either Israel released some *fedayeen* or they would withdraw their commitment to a package deal.

Israel's stance was not a reckless one. It had established a crisis management team to analyze every scrap of information. It had experience parsing hostage-holders' patterns of behavior under stress, ways of negotiating, reactions to counteraction, and mental stamina during ultimatum periods. Looking at the situation retrospectively, Israel's approach, so far at least, had proven valid as passengers were being released with absolutely no quid pro quo. And, as Israel saw it, a frustrated PFLP had just given up another valuable negotiating card—three planes—for nothing in return.[14]

Washington, 10 PM

An urgent cable went out about me from the State Department to Amman:

> We understand [that] David Raab, age 17, is among missing male TWA passengers. Father here informs us [that] David boarded aircraft in Tel Aviv wearing uniform of Israeli officer as a joke. Relatives point out David [is a] native born American, not Israeli national, never out of [the] United States before summer visit to Israel this year with family. Father says it [is] ridiculous that he could actually be [an] Israeli officer.
>
> COMMENT: It seems probable this is part of background to fedayeen claim earlier today that they are holding six Israeli officers. [We] suggest [that the] info above be passed to ICRC for whatever benefit possible, especially protection of American citizen Raab.

The State Department's assessment was wrong, still giving credence to the PFLP bluff that six Americans in Irbid were Israeli army officers. State's cable was clearly a memorable one, though, because Hume Horan, then a U.S. embassy official in Amman, recalled thirty years later: "Among [the hostages] was an American teenager who had decked himself out in the uniform of an Israeli Army major!"[15]

MY FAMILY IS FREED

SUNDAY, SEPTEMBER 13

Amman, 7 AM

The flight to freedom for 252 hostages got underway early. Jordanian army buses under heavy guard took them to Amman airport. At about 7 AM, 65 or so BOAC passengers departed the hotel. They took off an hour later in a chartered Royal Jordanian Alia airliner for Nicosia. About 80 TWA passengers—including most of the American citizens—departed their respective hotels at about 7:30 AM and flew out of Amman two hours later aboard a Red Cross DC6B, also for Nicosia. At 11:10 AM, the second Red Cross plane took off for Nicosia with over 100 Swissair passengers.

Many of those departing had to make wrenching decisions whether to leave family members behind. Mrs. Potts and Mrs. Wallace left their husbands. "Both ladies were deeply disturbed," wrote Joseph Godber of the British Foreign Office who met them the next afternoon in Heathrow, "but Mrs. Potts was in a very distraught condition and it was difficult to have any effective discussion with her. . . . [She] was in need of sedation."

My mother too recalls that, on Saturday, "I didn't want to leave. I wanted to stay, and I spoke to . . . the State Department. They told me that I should go home because there was no guarantee when my son would come home. So I called my husband, and he advised me to come home. The next morning, I finally realized that we were going home. I took some kind of tranquilizer because I just was in complete hysteria. Women had to put me on the bus. I refused to get on the bus to go home, because I realized that was it. That it was final."[1]

Amman, 8 AM

War, implied Yasser Arafat, was at hand. "The fact is that the Jordanian government and authorities want to liquidate the Palestinian resistance," he said. "It is our natural right to defend ourselves." Amman portended imminent war. The city was under the "absolute control of the various guerrilla groups; neither soldier nor police officer is to be seen," reported the German official who had accompanied Hans Wischnewski to Amman. "The Intercontinental is in a no man's land . . . taking stray bullets from both sides. There is no trace of a Jordanian government. All senior Foreign Ministry workers are 'on vacation.' The telephones work only sporadically, and only the airport and the main road to it are under army control. . . . Most 'dignitaries' had already escaped to Europe or Beirut."[2]

Amman, 9:30 AM

The united front was dead. Germany had just struck a bilateral deal for its two hostages, reported Reuters. (Contrary to prior reports, only Swissair copilot Horst Jerosch and TWA passenger Klaus Jeschke remained captive.)

Later in the day, the PFLP also offered Swiss Ambassador Charles-Albert Dubois a bilateral deal. Dubois urged his government to consider the offer. "In the present situation, it is the only way to save the lives of the remaining [Swiss] passengers and crew." The British ambassador, John Phillips, urged his government likewise. "Seeing that the united front seems to be crumbling . . . we should not be left out on a limb." He feared that the British hostages would be lumped with the Israelis and Americans or that the PFLP might "carry out some lunatic action against the hostages." The prospects for us American hostages did not look so good right now.[3]

Wahdat, 10 AM

Somebody who spoke English pretty well came in and told us to write our names and addresses down and that we could send telegrams.

The U.S. Embassy in Amman refused to receive the letters we wrote to our families claiming, according to the PFLP, that "we do not care about these letters which say that the U.S. subjects are well treated and are living well." The PFLP promised to get the letters to TWA.

My parents received the actual note I had written but didn't believe that it was really from me. They didn't recognize my handwriting, as I had written in block letters for legibility, thinking that it would be transcribed to a telegram. And, not wanting to call attention to myself, I had written "DEAR DAD" rather than referring to my father by the Hebrew Abba, as I always did.[4]

The Country Club, 10 AM

At around 10 AM, the PFLP's Dr. Ahmed Kamal and Halla Joseph, the female commando from our plane, paid the group a surprise visit, bringing with them playing cards, Pepsi and orange soda, and eight bottles of beer. The hostages were thrilled, since none of them had thought they would see these two again. Kamal told them that he was going to bring medical supplies and shaving gear (most of the men had not shaved since the hijacking), towels, soap, toothbrushes, clean underwear, and clean shirts. Joseph told them that they could write quick notes to whomever they wanted and that she would make sure that they would be delivered. Their hour-long visit lifted the group's spirits.

Dr. Kamal had brought the men some English language newspapers—the first that they had seen in a week—which they devoured. Their guards also now let them use a transistor radio to listen to English language broadcasts on BBC and Kol Israel a few times a day. At last, they had some contact with the outside world.

The men tried to make the best of a bad situation. They organized themselves into work details and put up a duty roster. They were quite amused when the next day their PFLP guards put up their own. The men drew a checkerboard on an old piece of cardboard and used bottle caps as their checkers, and they put up a sign that read "PFLP COUNTRY CLUB: CABANA THIS WAY, POOL THIS WAY." They organized a regular poker game on the picnic table in the courtyard, using pieces of ripped-up propaganda material as chips. When their guards asked about the game, the group told them that poker was a good Marxist game—it was all about redistribution of wealth! They described how there were two kinds of chips: dings and lings, where five dings equaled one ling. They anointed Lennett Cain, the sole African American hostage, King of the Ding-a-Ling Republic.[5]

Irbid, morning

The six hostages were given a copy of a Beirut Arabic newspaper with a picture of the planes being blown up. The men with families aboard the planes were distraught; they did not get a straight story about whether their kin were spared. (Jerry Berkowitz would not know for sure until he saw them upon his return.) James Woods, on the other hand, sat in a corner and began scribbling in a little pad. When Berkowitz asked him what he was doing, he said that he was creating an inventory of what he had in his suitcase to file for insurance.

Shortly afterward, a transformer nearby was hit. Huge explosions followed and suddenly their electricity went out. For the next two weeks, the men would have no electricity. Nor would they ever receive a change of clothing. The Red Crescent would show up from time to time, as they could plainly see through the reflection in their window, but no official ever came in to see them.[6]

Bonn, 10 AM

German Chancellor Willy Brandt decided to reject the deal conveyed by Hans Wischnewski after all and to stick to the common front for the moment despite strong domestic pressure. The cabinet ministers decided to keep Wischnewski in Amman, however, remaining highly concerned that, as with the planes, "uncontrolled elements might suddenly decide to massacre the hostages." In the meantime, a German Air Force jet was readied to fly Germany's three prisoners to Jordan.[7]

Northern Jordan, afternoon

In the afternoon, Jordanian and *fedayeen* forces clashed around Tura, near the Syrian border. The *fedayeen* claimed that an army unit opened fire on a Fatah patrol, destroying two vehicles and killing twelve *fedayeen.* Jordanian authorities expressed "profound regret." The chief of staff's office announced a committee to investigate and "determine responsibility and punishment." Despite the government's contrition, the PLO called the incident "a new massacre" and a "malicious, criminal incident," all part of "the plot to liquidate the resistance movement." The *fedayeen* demanded "the execution of the killers."[8]

Jerusalem, 1:30 PM

Nerves were raw, even between Israel and the United States. Gideon Rafael complained to U.S. chargé J. Owen Zurhellen about the United States' having "joined in the pressure" on Israel in Bern. Rafael reiterated that it was not up to Israel to bail out hostages with criminals who would "turn around and come right back for more." Quietly, however, the previous day the Israeli Foreign

Ministry authorized M. R. Kidron, its ambassador to the United Nations in Geneva, to inform the Red Cross that, "from our point of view, the two Algerians will not constitute a hurdle to the conclusion of this affair."[9]

Amman, 4 PM

Jacques Freymond and André Rochat of the ICRC were scheduled to depart Amman at 3 PM and arrive in Geneva by 10 PM. Freymond was then scheduled to be in Bern by midnight, and the Bern Group would convene immediately afterward. At 4 PM, however, the two were still in Amman. They delayed their departure believing that they were about to receive a hostage list from the PFLP. When they finally left after several hours, they still had not received the list.

With the departure of Freymond and Rochat, "special delegate" Louis Jacquinet was now in charge. His mandate was narrow: protect the hostages, try to visit them, and help in the logistics of any exchange. A 57-year-old professor who had spent a large part of his life in Turkey, he was deemed by Freymond "fine for the present role." The five powers did not agree; they had no confidence in him.[10]

The Country Club, 7 PM

At around 7 PM, Dr. Kamal returned. He wanted four TWA crew members to come with him. The cockpit crew and Rudi Swinkels went, leaving Frank Allen behind. Jim Majer promised to return that same night. Kamal took the men in his jeep, with armed guards, to PFLP headquarters in Amman. They were led up some steps and ushered into a room with a desk and several chairs. The door was immediately locked and an armed guard stationed in front of it. Inside was a French Jewish journalist who spoke with the crew for about ten minutes. Then, a commando motioned with his gun to Jim Majer and Al Kiburis to open one of the doors and go through. When they entered the adjoining room, they were taken aback as flashbulbs went off and questions were fired by waiting press and photographers. The two—shocked, unprepared, and with guns implicitly at their back—gave a brief press conference. It took all of about ten minutes and they came back to the room again.

At 7:40 PM, probably while Majer and Kiburis were giving their press conference, Captain Carroll Woods telephoned the U.S. embassy, in the presence of his captors. He reported that his group of eighteen was in "fair" physical condition, although one was suffering from dysentery, and another seemed to be coming down with it too. He complained that the hostages' general situation had "not changed one bit" despite no longer being in the desert and said he hoped that everything was being done to secure their freedom.

All four men were then led into another room where a high-ranking commando officer sat at his desk and Richard Wilson and Claude Girard (TWA director of International Flight Operations) greeted them. As the two had promised, the ten-minute conversation remained strictly informal. They reassured the crew that they were doing everything possible for the hostages. Woods asked Wilson whether "if this goes on much longer, could you please get them to move us to other accommodations?"

The PFLP held its own press conference too and now admitted to holding over fifty hostages. One spokesperson, Abu Maher, alleged that there are "Phantom pilots and a number of Israeli military men among the detainees" but refused to disclose how many. He asserted that American and Israeli hostages would now be treated equally because of the U.S. support for Israel, but vowed that their lives would not be endangered. Another spokesman reiterated that the PFLP would accept nothing less than "unconditional surrender" for their release.[11]

Amman, 7:25 PM

There were rumors that at least some of the hostages were in a house in Amman. This accurate though vague tidbit probably came from a Dutch hostage, G. H. W. de Koning. He had been aboard the BOAC flight and had been released this afternoon following an appeal by Michael Adams, a British Palestinian supporter who had arrived in Amman a few days earlier.

The locations of the hostages remained a well-shrouded secret. "Jordanian army has neither precise knowledge of [the] whereabouts of [the] hostages nor any involvement in security arrangements under which they are held," wired U.S. chargé William Brubeck. His best information indicated that the hostages were in two or more groups in and around Amman, with at least one being in Wahdat. Switzerland's Ambassador Dubois reported that a PRCS official had seen the hostages in groups "all in the vicinity of Amman." The next day, Bassam Abu-Sharif would assert that the hostages were scattered "three in each place." Israel Defense Forces' intelligence would pass on to Britain "in strict confidence" a report from a "highly confidential and sensitive source" that the hostages were in several groups. One, considered "particularly sensitive," was now in "a former women's militia camp" in Amman, in a building that was primed for demolition to foil any thought of a rescue attempt. No report seemed to account for the twenty-four in Zarqa and Irbid.

After meeting for several hours with his top staff, Secretary of State William Rogers decided that a rescue operation was still out of the question since the United States did not know "where the hostages were being held, exactly who was holding them, [or] how many [hostages] they have."[12]

London, 7 PM

The British were becoming increasingly frustrated with an "obdurate" Israel and, as a result, disappointed with a United States unwilling to pressure Israel. Exasperated, Foreign Secretary Alec Douglas-Home cabled Ambassador John Freeman in Washington: "The Prime Minister and I are very concerned at the apparent passivity of the Americans in this. . . . The situation in Amman is so unstable that there is more urgency in this matter than the Americans think." Did Rogers, he asked, really believe that a comprehensive solution could be attained without an Israeli contribution of *fedayeen*? And how long could the countries stay united without an Israeli contribution? "Please have a frank talk with Rogers and let me know what he thinks."

Freeman got in to see Rogers in Washington at 4 PM but left empty-handed. "Rogers takes a somewhat more optimistic view than we probably do," he cabled. Rogers reiterated his assessment that the current strategy had gotten 375 people out and "cost no concessions," and now there were sharp divisions within the PFLP. Rogers couldn't understand why the Europeans felt so pressured and had little doubt that Israel would, however reluctantly, contribute to the package once what they needed to contribute became apparent. "[W]e might well face some moment of crunch with the Israelis," he said, but this would come, if at all, only once a concrete deal was on the table. "I do not think we shall get any U.S. support for squeezing the Israelis," Freeman concluded.

Douglas-Home was not satisfied. He instructed Freeman shortly afterward, to "please see Rogers again urgently," this time to convey a "personal message":

> [If,] like us, you want to hold the group together, I am sure that you must exert the maximum pressure on the Israelis, and soon. For unless this is done, you will find yourself in the position you want to avoid of being left alone with the Israelis to bargain for the return of American citizens. . . .

He also instructed Freeman to make several blistering arguments, including one that Israel was acting in bad faith:

> They expect consultations and solidarity, but they have taken unilateral action in bringing in 450 Arab prisoners without consulting or informing other members of the group. . . . We cannot leave the future of our hostages in the hands of the Israelis, who are fighting a war with the Arabs in which we have no part.

Freeman roused Rogers late at night. More sensitive than his Foreign Office, he muted the volume substantially and, while covering "most of these points orally," did not go into "detail on every one." "Rogers said very little," he reported back, "no doubt because we had been over most of this ground earlier."

Separately, urgent exchanges were taking place in London about Leila Khaled. Under the Aliens Order, she needed to be moved to a prison this night, and the British feared that such a move could lead to violence particularly because of the extent to which Khaled had become "a symbol of Palestine resistance and a folk heroine." In the end, the Home Secretary amended the Aliens Order, designating the Ealing police station holding Khaled "an approved place of detention," thus extending the period that she could be detained there uncharged.[13]

Wahdat, 9 PM

Sunday night we were brought foam-rubber mattresses, foam-rubber pillows, and more blankets. So we had these mattresses to sleep on, and it was pretty comfortable. We were about to fall asleep. The lights were off already, and we were five in my room—#3—the order was Ben Feinstein, Bob Palagonia, Jeffrey Newton, myself, and Mitchell Meltzer.

We were about to fall asleep when they turned on the lights. Ben mumbled to Bob, "Okay they're coming to take us away. This is it. It's been nice knowing you." We got up and went to the door and there we saw the crew standing with their beards half grown, looking very fuzzy. It was really, really great seeing them. When I saw Jim Majer, we were so happy to see each other because he was the one who had taken me off the plane and had felt sorry for me, and here we were seeing each other again. Everybody looked in great condition. The captain looked very, very tired. He had wrinkles on his forehead that were very thick, very deep. He had been through a lot. But we were really, really happy to see them. The guerrillas brought in some watermelons, and we cut them up.

After their brief stay at PFLP offices, the crew members had been led back to the car that had brought them. As they drove off, they thought they were heading back to Zarqa. But after driving for about half an hour, they stopped in front of a similar-looking adobe structure, also well hidden and in a hilly area. The guards unlocked a prison-type door—it was heavily padlocked—and when the door was opened and they went inside, they found the nine of us. Recalled Rudi Swinkels of our reaction: "they danced around, shouted for joy, and embraced us, so happy they were." After about an hour, the captain informed the guards that the crew was ready to return to Zarqa but was told that they were staying with us. In the meantime, Frank Allen also arrived from the Country Club carrying most of the crew's hand luggage.

It was really good to see the crew again and be together with them once more. So we split up the crew. Some of them slept with us. I think Jim and Rudi slept in our room. Frank went into room #2, and the captain slept on a bed in the office and Al slept on mattresses.

The guards distributed blankets to the new arrivals who made themselves as comfortable they could under the circumstances. But it was very difficult as we crowded into two smallish rooms where the only ventilation came from two small windows high in the walls.[14]

Bern, 1:15 AM

The Bern group went into immediate session once Freymond arrived. The meeting lasted until 3:40 AM. Freymond described Saturday's "indescribable confusion. . . . Convoys to the airfield were blocked, as were convoys coming from the airfield; the various fact[ion]s would not agree to the same conditions; and the dynamiting of the plane surprised the moderates." The planes were evacuated in such confusion, he said, that no one could keep track of the numbers because some hostages had been spirited away.

Freymond was particularly disturbed that, "despite all the assurances," the PFLP was apparently holding women hostages. He also complained that the PFLP never gave him a hostage list and, despite having "announced several times" that it would give him a list of *fedayeen* it wanted freed, appeared unable to agree even internally on numbers and names. By late Saturday, he said, it was clear that negotiations had "reached the point of diminishing returns." Pulling out was a "shock tactic" to jolt the PFLP out of "continually adding to their demands" and to force the "hopelessly divided PFLP" to become a viable interlocutor. Freymond advised to let the PFLP "temporarily stew in its own juice."

The United States, Israel, and Switzerland agreed. Britain and Germany disagreed and demanded that the ICRC "at once" send in someone senior to Louis Jacquinet, as "time was not on our side." Freymond rebutted that "we had time and should above all not appear anxious." Whereupon he set off on a five-week trip to Africa. The five governments did, however, succeed in convincing the ICRC to reassume its mediation mantle.

This was "an unsatisfactory meeting" to the British and Germans because the United States had accepted "without question" Freymond's assessment that the immediate urgency had subsided. For his part, the American representative, Shelby Davis, figured that Freymond's report had bought "another 48 hours or so of solidarity."[15]

NEGOTIATIONS AT A STANDSTILL

MONDAY, SEPTEMBER 14

Jerusalem

A short, stocky, elderly woman strode determinedly up to the Western Wall. She had been there every day of the prior week; she had even slept there one night. The Rabbi of the Kotel had noted in his diary her wailing and crying. Now, she thanked God for the release of her daughter and four grandchildren. Then, turning her eyes heavenward, she pleaded with God to please watch over her grandson, David, and free him soon. For two weeks, she and her friends and neighbors would keep my continued incarceration a secret from my grandfather, inventing all sorts of excuses as to why he had not yet heard from me. She knew he would die of heartbreak if he learned that I had not been released with the rest of my family. Keeping the secret would not be easy. The next Friday night, my grandfather asked her to "celebrate" my "release" by singing a tune that I enjoyed singing at the Shabbat table. With tears welling in her eyes and a choked voice, my grandmother sang the melody, never letting on.

Wahdat, 8 AM

After breakfast, Dr. Kamal arrived again, bringing us clean shirts, underwear, toothbrushes, toothpaste, towels, and soap. He promised more supplies the next day. He also left us some orange and Pepsi sodas, which we drank with lunch. He said that he was looking for larger and safer housing for us. When he left, he took Jim Majer with him. Jim, who had promised the other group he would return, was driven back to the Country Club in Zarqa in a Volkswagen Beetle.

> *We got two newspapers. One, I think, was a Lebanese newspaper. We decided that one person would read out loud so not everybody would jump up and rip at it. I was reading one of the articles and all of a sudden I came across my mother's name, one of her quotes. Then I came across my name and I was pretty excited. I really didn't expect to see my name in a Lebanese newspaper, but there I was. When I found out that the rest of the family went home I was pretty happy. I figured that if I didn't make it, at least five out of the six did. It was pretty good news to hear that they had left.*
>
> *Today they brought in a whole branch (not just a bunch) of bananas. We really had a great time eating bananas. They brought in grapes. Those who didn't eat kosher didn't have it so bad. They had all types of meats and chicken and all kind of stuff. For lunch today, the guards brought a large pot of the local beef stew with rice on the side. It was the first hot food in over a week for those who could eat it. I stuck to cheese and eggs and the fresh fruit and vegetables and onions. I once made myself an onion sandwich, and another time I made myself a cheese, jam—there was always a lot of jam—and pita sandwich. They sent in some tomatoes every once in a while. It was pretty good. There we had enough food. Whenever we wanted water, we got it. Once they even brought us ice-cold water. I don't know where they got it, but we had ice-cold water and it was really, really great.*

The rest of the day was quiet. A commando brought us a large electric portable radio so we could listen to the English broadcasts. We played cards and read the newspapers papers left behind by Dr. Kamal. We played chess and checkers on a chess set that Jeffrey Newton and I fashioned out of pieces of cardboard. Jeff and I had been high school chess teammates.

> *During this time—the first few days in the refugee camp—I said Psalms every once in a while. I decided it would be best to read them straight through from the beginning until wherever I stopped. I still had in my pocket the little book of Psalms I had borrowed from my brother when my mother was taken for questioning. I had forgotten to give it back to him. So now when I became very frightened, I started reading. I read until I reached a verse in the first chapter of the second book. Things were looking up and I figured it was a good place to stop. The words were "therefore I will remember you from the land of Jordan." I thought it was very fitting, a very nice place to stop.*
>
> *Another memory: I was wearing an Israeli watchband, and all along they had been confiscating things that were made in Israel. My Israeli watchband had a tax sticker on it, which almost everything made in Israel had. I figured, why should I take the chance, my watch isn't made in Israel. Let me scrape off the tag so that in case they check it, they won't take the whole thing away from me. So I scraped it off. Ten minutes later, one of the Arabs called me over. He wanted to see*

my watch, to see where it was made. I thought that was pretty interesting, how I thought of it a few minutes before it actually happened.[1]

Amman, 5 PM

The PFLP bluff was finally unmasked. ICRC delegate Louis Jacquinet managed to cobble together a fairly complete and accurate list of the hostages and their nationalities. There were now fifty-five hostages: thirty-two Americans, eight Britons, six Swiss, two Germans, one Dutch, and six "unknowns" (who were, in fact, also Americans). The ICRC estimated, based on Jewish-sounding names, that the PFLP might consider as many as nineteen dual citizens.

U.S. chargé William Brubeck was worried about the "disturbing conclusion" that there were no "exclusively Israeli" hostages, which presented "obvious" and "dire consequences." Indeed, it would now be more difficult to pressure Israel, the Europeans might then fall away, and the United States would be left alone with citizens stranded in Jordan. The State Department, however, already knew the situation—its chargé in Tel Aviv had cabled the determination a week ago—but had not let on.

Later in the day, the United States would also conclude that only three hostages at most were duals. The next day, Israel would confirm that the Harari-Raful brothers were the only dual citizens. Joseph had served in the Israeli army between 1959 and 1960 as a clerk in the Chaplain's Office. Abraham, as a rabbinical student, had been exempt from military service altogether. A third hostage, David Miller, had been born in Israel, but Israel had no record of his citizenship. There were no "pure" Israeli hostages, certainly no "officers or soldiers."[2]

Amman, 7 PM

Fighting was erupting all over the country as civil war drew nearer.

In southern Jordan, the Jordanian army shelled *fedayeen* bases in the countryside where there had been pro-*fedayeen* demonstrations and fighting over the past several days. The shelling was followed by a major Special Forces operations and an attack by Bedouin troops on *fedayeen* offices. In the end, over seventy *fedayeen* were killed, many others wounded, and several taken prisoner. The operation was so successful that the *fedayeen* presence in southern Jordan was soon eliminated.

The army was less successful in northern Jordan where several firefights took place throughout the day. A *fedayeen* ambulance carrying wounded was allegedly hit at a Jordanian army checkpoint near Irbid. The ambulance crashed on the highway. The PLO reported clashes near Malka, fifteen miles northwest of Irbid and stridently claimed that "the forces of the authority are continuing to provoke the revolution in the north." By evening, reports filtered into Amman that the *fedayeen* had gained control of Irbid, Jordan's second largest city, about forty miles north of Amman. Travelers reported *fedayeen*-manned roadblocks at all entrances to the town barring Jordanian personnel. Not a single Jordanian soldier or policeman was to be seen in Irbid, and the population was reported to be cooperating with the *fedayeen.* After bitter fighting, the *fedayeen* also gained control of the main Irbid-Jarash road. A hundred Iraqi armored vehicles and tanks were also reported moving from Zarqa toward Mafraq and Irbid.

On the surface, Amman itself seemed to be returning to normal. There had been no serious outbreaks of fighting during the night. Traffic flowed normally; almost all shops were open. Most *fedayeen* were off the street, and some of their roadblocks had been dismantled. "There are other indications, however," Henry Kissinger noted later in a memo to the president, "that the present lull in the fighting may only be temporary. Most *fedayeen* strongholds in Amman have been reinforced and some army units are also digging in." Monsignor Pio Laghi, the apostolic delegate in Jerusalem who had come to Amman, described the situation as bleak, with streets abandoned and commandos—including armed children—in control. Only a miracle, he believed, would save the situation.

In late morning, *fedayeen* and royal forces clashed near the Wahdat refugee camp, where we were being held. The incident was brief and caused no casualties. But, the *fedayeen* accused the authorities of bringing in reinforcements and violating the cease-fire.

In addition to the fighting, the tenor of the PLO's diatribe against the Jordanian authorities rose to an incendiary pitch. Asserting that Jordanian "death squads" were perpetrating "massacres throughout Jordan," it declared that "[t]hose who killed our revolutionaries in Irbid, Az-Zarqa, and Amman are enemies of the people. . . . Our revolution will accept nothing short of rule by the masses . . . and of liquidating all the killers involved in all the massacres." The PLO sent out invitations for a "Jordanian National Congress" in Amman on Thursday to "discuss the demand for [a] national authority to fulfill the wishes of the people" as the only way to put an end "to the provocations and plots." The *fedayeen*-dominated Jordanian Trade Union also called a general strike starting Saturday to shut down the country if *fedayeen* demands were not met by then.[3]

Amman, 7:30 PM

The PFLP now definitively avowed that it would not provide a list of the prisoners in Israel it wanted freed before Israel indicated its willingness to free

Palestinian prisoners. It feared that Israel would harshen the treatment of those on the list. Nor, it announced, would anyone be permitted to visit the hostages. There were severe internal debates over how to treat us meanwhile. Many felt that we should be treated "no better than refugees in the camps" and should "try eating the same food as Palestinian refugees." The PFLP's attitude was hardening, the PRCS's Ghazi al-Saudi warned the British, and it was increasingly difficult "to keep them in control."[4]

Wahdat, 8 PM

For dinner the guards sent somebody to a local store. He returned with some hot fried spicy fish croquettes, relished by the ten who partook. Shortly after dinner, Dr. Kamal showed up yet again. He had found larger and safer housing, he said, and we would be moving the next day. (We didn't.) He also promised that we could take a bath or shower the next day, which we were all thrilled about, as we had not washed ourselves in over a week.

Kamal then called Rudi Swinkels aside to break the good news. Rudi was to be released. Rudi was clearly happy to go, but also sad to leave us behind. Many of us hastily scribbled our home phone numbers on a scrap of paper and begged him to let our relatives know that we were okay. He promised that he would, said good-by, and left. Swinkels, a Dutch citizen, was released because the PFLP was now convinced that Holland would not request Leila Khaled's extradition despite her having boarded the El Al flight in Amsterdam. Once back at the Intercontinental Hotel, Swinkels told TWA's Richard Wilson and Claude Girard that the elderly Rabbi Hutner was quite weak and that William Burmeister's morale was low, as he was convinced that he would not survive.

When Swinkels later arrived in New York, he met with the hostages' families. (He also called my mother.) The families described their loved ones to him and he related how each was faring. When Rivke Berkowitz asked about her husband, Jerry, Swinkels looked at her quizzically and responded that he did not know who that was. This was Rivke's first alarming clue that her husband was being held apart.[5]

Bern, 8 PM

Britain had waited long enough for the ICRC's Jacquinet to produce results. "Neither appearance nor fact" of negotiations were possible under him, it now asserted. Germany agreed. At 8 PM, the Bern group met for three and a half hours at the request of both countries. Both, concerned about public opinion, insisted that the ICRC urgently send in a top-flight negotiator. Both also laid it on the line to Israel. And, both made it abundantly clear that they were prepared to go their separate ways if they did not get satisfaction. (Reporting later on the meeting, Israeli Ambassador Arie Levavi was incredulous: "It is difficult to grasp that Germany, of all countries, with its infamous past and with only two citizens among the hostages, is preparing apparently to release them for three Israeli-murderers in Munich and to forsake Jewish captives.")

The Swiss representative—who had been outside talking to the ICRC—broke into the discussion to inform the others that the ICRC had just tapped a senior man after all—Marcel Boisard. Boisard was head of the ICRC's delegation in Cairo and had helped obtain the release of the Israeli TWA passengers in Damascus in an earlier hijacking. He was, even according to Levavi, "personally popular with each side" and "exceptionally qualified." Boisard was to arrive in Geneva on Tuesday night and leave for Amman immediately.

This was not enough for either Germany or Britain, however, who asserted that an Israeli declaration of principle was "indispensable." "The solid front showed real danger of breaking up," U.S. Ambassador Shelby Davis later reported. "This was [a] depressing evening," he summed up sadly.[6]

BOAC exploding. © Bettman/Corbis

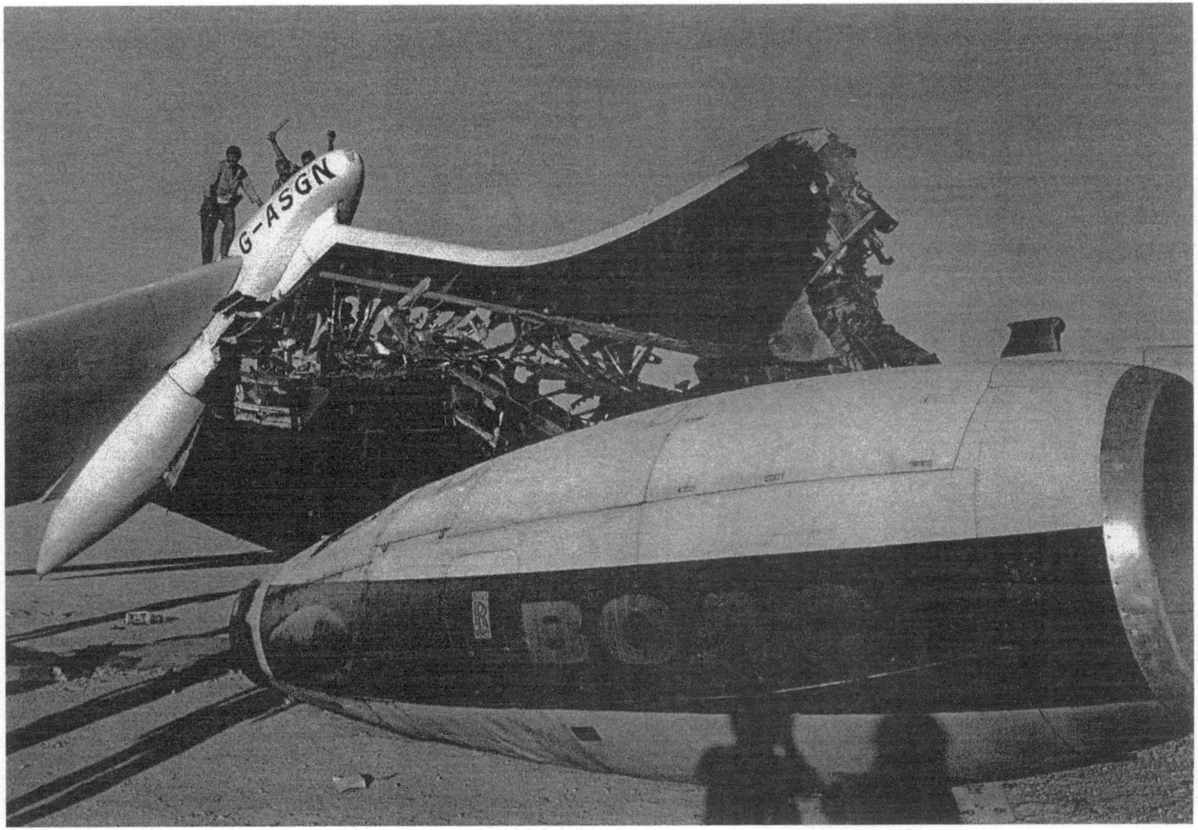

Wrecked BOAC plane. © Hulton-Deutsch Collection/Corbis

My brother Yaron held by Bedouin soldier at Intercontinental Hotel. My brother Noam looks on. © Bettmann/Corbis

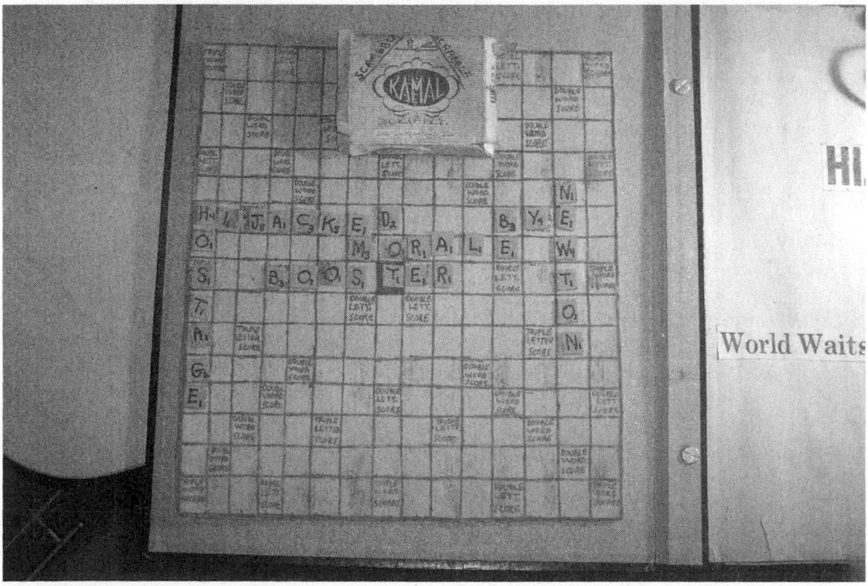

Our Scrabble set. © Jim Majer

My parents receiving news of my release.

President Nixon and me in Rome. © Bettmann/Corbis

Press conference at JFK.

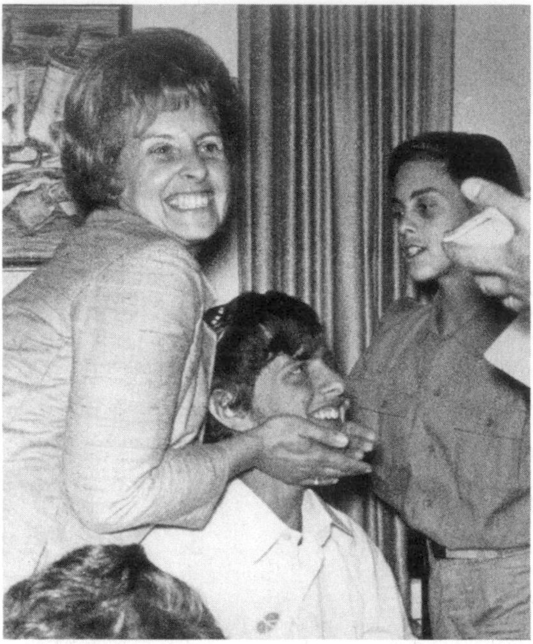

Hugged by my mother upon my return home. My brother Moshe looks on. © Elwood Smith/Philadelphia Daily News, reprinted with permission.

My sister Tikva kissing me at home.

My siblings, mother, and me near Dawson Field, 1996. © David Raab

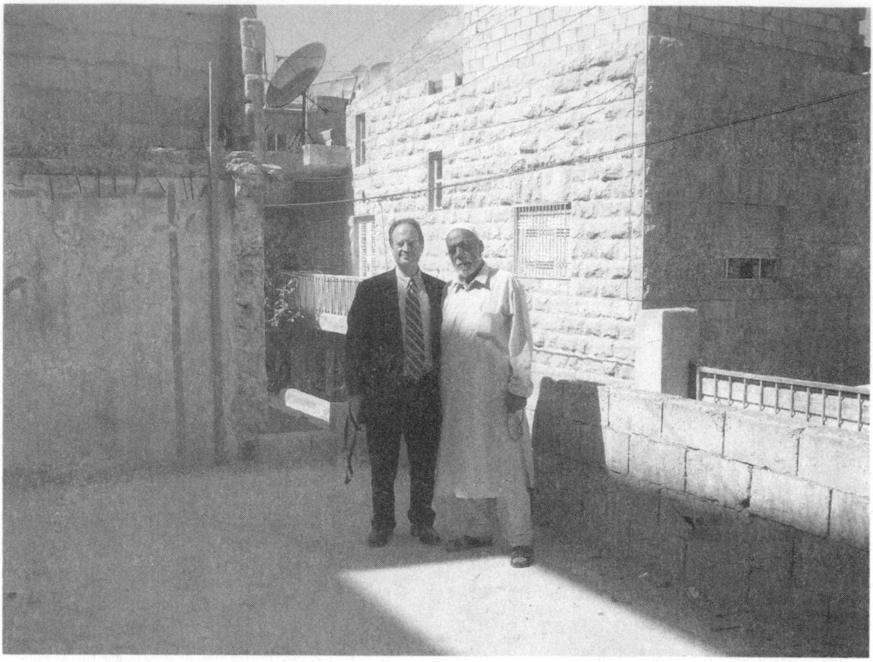

With Ismail Ahmed Hussein in front of my house of captivity in Ashrafiyeh, 2004. © David Raab

With former captor Bassam Abu-Sharif, 2004. © David Raab

"I JUST WANT TO BE NEAR MY DAUGHTER"

TUESDAY, SEPTEMBER 15

Amman, 8 AM

"The present situation in Jordan cannot last," King Hussein declared. The commandos needed to respect their agreements, he warned, "or bear the consequences." The army's morale was deteriorating, its officers "fed up." "They have had enough. They are [not] used to being so abused, disparaged, and unceasingly provoked." Then, after reading an intelligence report later in the morning, he soberly declared to those present: "If [the situation] continues any longer, I am afraid we shall lose Jordan *and* Palestine. We have decided to . . . restore law and order to the country and put an end to this chaos." At long last, he was taking his fateful step.[1]

Wahdat, 9 AM

> *Tuesday was a major event: We took showers! All this time we'd been asking Dr. Kamal, who came in every once in a while, for showers. He had said he would take us for showers that day or some time to a hospital somewhere. Anyway, he never took us. So we rigged showers ourselves. The guerrillas brought us soap. We took a piece of wood, laid it catty-corner across the top of the latrine wall and outer wall of our compound, and hung a rug on it. We put a pan behind the rug and took buckets of water. We soaped ourselves up and washed ourselves. It was really a lot of fun, I guess.*
>
> *On Monday, they had brought us new clothes and clean underwear, which I have kept as a memento. It was good to change out of all our filthy stuff which*

stank to high heaven. So today we also washed our clothes. We took a can, filled it with water. We had some Tide. I have no idea how we got hold of it. But we had Tide. We stuck in all our clothes and we pushed and we scrubbed and we hung them up to dry. It was all really, really nice. And, after they were all dry, one of the guerrillas came over to the whole group and said he had a good idea: he'd take them to a laundry and have them ironed for us. We figured it was great. So he took them away. I'd like you to know that we haven't seen those clothes since.

For a day or two we had been asking for a cold soda, Pepsi Cola, and—to our amazement—we got it. We got it on Wednesday too, and we enjoyed some Pepsi Cola. We got razor blades. Of course I couldn't use them on my face. It was against the Halacha [Jewish law]. But I asked Bob Palagonia to give me a trim on the neck and he did a very good job. It felt very refreshing after I washed off the soap and all the loose hair. We had also been asking Dr. Kamal for cholera shots, because the epidemic had been really great at the time. We didn't get the cholera shots.

What were our relations to the guerrillas? Well, by this time they were pretty friendly. At night we would play cards with them, or they would come in and sing with us or talk with us sometimes. It was a pretty close relationship. We even played blackjack with one of our guards. I almost panicked when one of my companions cheated. We would joke around with them all the time. We got very friendly with them. Here are some of the names: Hajji, Abu-Nadir, Hercules, and Sheikh. And there was Joseph Safi and Feisal. I can't remember all the names now. But let me give a brief description. Hajji was a pretty nice guy. He was the one who looked sorry for me all the time. He was the commander of the place. He was the one who called me in to learn English. He was a nice guy, gray hair, crew cut, big, very big. After we left this place, we saw him again. It was very good to see him. Abu-Nadir I considered the most intelligent of them all. He was the one who spoke English, and he was our main mode of communication with the guerrillas. He was very friendly. He joked around with us. We were able to talk to him and able to say that we wanted to get home as soon as possible. He really understood. He really felt sorry for us. Hercules was the black man. Sheikh looked like a kid but he was twenty-two or twenty-four, I don't remember exactly, and he couldn't stand it when someone would rub his stomach.

Amman, 10 AM

Louis Jacquinet's meeting with the PFLP the previous evening was "difficult" and "distrustful." The PFLP accused the ICRC of "attempting to buy time for . . . the imperialist states." It now rejected ICRC mediation and insisted on government-by-government negotiations. The PFLP made clear too that it, not the PLO, controlled the hostages and was the sole address for negotiations. And it again raised the price, now demanding that Israel release a Swiss national arrested for belonging to the PFLP and ten Lebanese soldiers captured in January.

The PFLP decried as "lies" the rumors that it threatened to execute the hostages by firing squad to thwart a possible Jordanian attack. Nonetheless, it warned again, "any stupid attempt by any party to try to retake these hostages would endanger their lives."[2]

Bonn, 11 AM

Still worried about Germany's commitment to concerted action, Israel now played its Holocaust card. Ambassador Yitzhak Rabin was instructed to ask the chairman of the Conference of Presidents of Major American Jewish Organizations to "immediately" complain to the German ambassador about reports that Germany was "preparing to abandon the Jews captive in Jordan" by doing a separate deal. "It is not possible to contemplate that Germany, of all countries, would act this way," he was asked to say.

Ambassador Eliashiv Ben-Horin in Bonn was also instructed to "[r]equest an immediate audience with Brandt" to make plain the angry reception Foreign Minister Walter Scheel would receive in the United States from both Jews and non-Jews if he arrived for the upcoming UN General Assembly session "after the abandonment of the Jews by his government." Ben-Horin was also asked to get the *New York Times* correspondent in Bonn to quote him as having said that "it is unconscionable that Germany—of all countries—would be prepared or would permit itself to discriminate against the Jews."

Germany did not yield to Ben-Horin, however. While understanding Israel's position and difficulties, Germany feared waking up one morning to find its citizens killed. An Israeli contribution was needed for a quick solution. However, the U.S. ambassador in Bonn also delivered a strong message, and, later that day, Chancellor Willy Brandt decided to stick with the unified front. The United States felt now that Germany was likely to stand firm "for some time yet."[3]

London, 10:30 AM

The British, for their part, were becoming "exasperated" with Israel. The four countries were now in a bind because of Israel, Britain felt; there was serious question whether Britain could "continue to cater to the Israelis." The "key to the entire problem," they concluded yet again, was for Israel to agree in principle to release some *fedayeen.* And it was "obvious" that the United States had to take the lead in persuading Israel. (Joseph Sisco, of the U.S. State Department, on the other hand, felt that Israel's committing in advance would be buying a "pig in a poke.")

British officials also remained convinced that the United States was far too relaxed about the situation. Rather than softening its demands, as the United States expected, the PFLP might raise the stakes by, for example, periodically "dropping a hostage body over the wall." Any such action would spark a public outcry against the British government for not having done more.

Beyond its penchant for a separate deal, Britain still had a sticky problem: Israel's request for Khaled's detention. Its international treaty with Israel wasn't easily circumvented; senior British officials struggled over several days to find a legal loophole. Britain was entitled to refuse extradition only for a "political" offense or one that would "render the accused liable to the death penalty in Israel." But Khaled was not wanted for the death penalty, nor could her offenses likely be regarded as "of a political character," advised a Foreign Office attorney. Rather, he recommended that Britain justify its refusal to extradite her "on the grounds of overriding humanitarian considerations. This, of course, is not a legal argument . . . [and] may put us in breach of the extradition treaty with Israel." Israel would then "be entitled to take us to the International Court of Justice." John Graham, counselor to the Secretary of State, scribbled on the attorney's memo: "I think it unlikely that the Israel Govt would take us to the International Court." And with that, Britain's sacrosanct international treaty with Israel was conveniently cast aside.[4]

Ashrafiyeh, 2 PM

Mustafa Zayn was led into the apartment in Ashrafiyeh. He had received a call the previous night from Bassam Abu-Sharif asking him to come from Lebanon, where he was a political figure and midlevel government official. Richard Dunn, Zayn's administrative assistant, was a BOAC hostage. Dunn had requested to see Zayn, who he knew had contacts in the PFLP.

Zayn found the conditions in the apartment dreadful, with seventeen men crowded into a twelve-by-twelve-foot room. (The five American women had a separate room; he may not have even known they were there.) Sanitary conditions were "appalling," and hostage morale was low. The hostages were being guarded by eight commandos, whose leader said that if the Jordanian army began firing at them, the commandos would fire back to draw return fire and then leave, letting the Jordanians kill the hostages in the return fire.[5]

Amman, 6 PM

Heavy fighting, including machine guns and tanks, broke out in Zarqa and lasted over three hours. Three soldiers were said to have been killed, four tanks destroyed, and another five damaged. Several civilians were also reported killed. The *fedayeen* put up roadblocks on the Zarqa-Amman highway, stopping and searching all vehicles.

Fighting continued around Irbid too. Though the cease-fire had held through the night for the most part, artillery shelling of Palestinian positions in Tura started at about 5 AM. Shooting in the north erupted periodically throughout the day. Irbid remained under *fedayeen* control; Jordanian units patrolled outside only.

On the surface, Amman, with its airport open, appeared calm during the day, but the tension pulsated underneath. The "situation is brittle . . . the present calm in Amman might be short-lived," concluded the just-arrived U.S. ambassador, Dean Brown. *Fedayeen* patrolled downtown streets, and artillery fire—intermittent throughout the afternoon and at times very heavy—was audible from the direction of Zarqa. By about 6 PM, "continuous artillery" was coming nearer to Amman and "sporadic machine gun fire can be heard."

A senior Jordanian official reiterated to the U.S. embassy that his government's will and ability to put the *fedayeen* in their place were still high. The *fedayeen* demands were presumptuous, the government was fed up with "*fedayeen* misconduct," and the army was urging action. A group of tribal sheiks was also threatening to brush the Jordanian authorities aside and take matters into their own hands. The government, he felt, would not back down this time.[6]

Geneva, 6 PM

In the end, the Red Cross decided to send not one, but two senior representatives to Amman. The second, Pierre Boissier, 50, was an "old hand," a "confirmed diplomat who understands negotiations." He had served with the ICRC during and after World War II and was currently the director of the Red Cross research institute. Boissier, like Marcel Boisard, would be a "special delegate," but would be Boisard's superior.

Boissier, who was to arrive in Amman Wednesday night, was to be the liaison with the Jordanian government and the various embassies. Boisard, now scheduled to arrive Friday night, was to similarly function with the Palestinian organizations. Jacquinet was to return to Geneva.

The rationale for a second delegate and the division of responsibilities is unclear. The United States and Switzerland worried that the ICRC's musical chairs and Boisard's delayed arrival in Amman could harm negotiations.[7]

Amman, 7 PM

Despite the best efforts of the United States, Martin Mensch was in Amman. Mensch had made up his mind to go as soon as the TWA plane had landed in

Jordan. "I had to be where she was," he recalls. Now that his daughter was still being held, his mission became all the more urgent. Sixteen-year-old Barbara was the youngest hostage.

Martin Mensch and fellow New York attorney Robert Van Lierop flew first to Athens. Then, hearing that released hostages were being flown to Cyprus, they flew to Nicosia on Sunday to meet two of Barbara's travel-mates. Mensch, a rational, low-key person, understood the risks he was taking. The Jordanian consulate in New York had already turned down his visa request. He knew that, as a Jew, he was not particularly welcome and that in Amman he could be taken hostage. But he was determined to at least let his daughter know that he was nearby. Perhaps he might even succeed in freeing her and was considering offering himself in her stead. Van Lierop was a young black attorney with contacts in the radical movement in the United States. Someone in the movement had furnished him with a contact in Amman. Both men recognized that they were taking a shot in the dark, but they believed that this might be the only way to free Barbara quickly.

From Nicosia, Mensch called "one Bassam [Abu-Sharif] of the PFLP." Bassam replied that a PFLP interrogation indicated that Barbara was a "special friend of Israel" who carried "circulars promoting [an] Arab-Israel friendship center [Givat Haviva]." However, Bassam promised to personally interrogate Barbara and, if he found that she was a "socialist," he would try to get her released.

On Monday morning, U.S. Ambassador to Cyprus David Popper tried to dissuade Mensch and Van Lierop from proceeding. Their mere presence in Amman, he suggested, could complicate negotiations. The men assured him that they had no desire to deal with the larger political issues; they simply wanted to arrange a quick release for Barbara.

Later in the day, Mensch chartered a plane and the two flew to Beirut. The State Department cabled its embassy in Amman that it considered the trip "not advisable at [the] present time and could complicate [the] delicate ICRC role." It wanted to block the men's way. "While we realize [that it is] extremely difficult [to] prevent their onward travel, [we] would propose Embassy Amman inform the Jordanian government of Mensch travel plans, stating [that] we [are] attempting [to] discourage them. Without explicitly asking that the Jordanian government take action [to] prevent their entry [into] Amman, you should suggest that [it] may wish consider such procedure."

That night, the U.S. chargé in Beirut reached Mensch "in an effort [to] dissuade him" from continuing to Amman. The chargé implored him to at least consider waiting a day before making a final decision. Mensch responded that he did not want to complicate matters; "I just want to be near my daughter."

The next morning, he and Van Lierop boarded a Middle East Airlines flight to Amman.

The U.S. embassy in Amman did "attempt to forestall" Mensch's entry but failed. So on this evening, Mensch met with PFLP representatives in the Intercontinental Hotel's lounge. (Not wanting journalists at the hotel to get wind of his mission, he told them that he represented an insurance company investigating the loss of one of the blown-up planes.) He remembers the PFLP men as polite, polished, and sophisticated. At first they told him that they would take him to his daughter. But then Bassam informed him that he would not be allowed to see her and that the PFLP would not swap him for her, because "she possessed a card from a kibbutz indicating membership in the Israeli women's defense force"—an absurd charge.

The next evening, the PFLP would advise him to leave. There would be war, they said. Mensch didn't leave, choosing instead to spend a week under fire in the hope of somehow letting his daughter know he was near.[8]

Trenton

At one point during my captivity, one Fahik al-Badri, who lived in New Jersey about fifty miles from our home, contacted my parents. Saying that he wished to repay a kindness—Jews had once helped him out of a business predicament—and claiming that his brother was an Iraqi general based in Jordan, he offered to have his brother obtain my release. My parents checked out his claim with Alexander Haig and were advised by the State Department that the facts were correct. After some soul-searching, however, my parents decided not to take a chance and separate me from the rest of the group.

Amman, 11 PM

The chairman of the Five Member Committee sent in by the Arab League announced that, under its auspices, the government and PLO had reached a new agreement. "We have accomplished not a little," he proudly proclaimed. "What we have already achieved shows that we . . . have begun to pursue the correct path leading to a solution of all problems." Nothing could have been further from the truth.

It had been an acrimonious meeting. There was a lot of yelling. Hussein sat in on part of the meeting but, contrary to his normal mien, was not pleasant. In the end, both sides agreed, among other things, to withdraw from recently occupied positions and stop interfering with vehicular traffic. These steps were to be implemented in Amman by 6 PM the following day and later elsewhere.

But it was too little too late. The king could not take it any more and had made up his mind. Despite his self-doubt—"How can I kill my people and the children?" he asked an officer that day—and despite his awareness of the clear danger to the fifty-four helpless Western hostages sitting in his country, Hussein was set to act.

At about the time the agreement was announced, King Hussein concluded a parallel, eleven-hour, secret meeting with his top advisers and army commanders. At the meeting, he was severely criticized for his reluctance to act, which had enabled the situation to deteriorate into near anarchy, with the northern districts no longer under army control and the state itself near collapse. Claiming that they could no longer tolerate the insults and abuse being hurled at them and the king, the officers concluded: "We are determined to save you, even against your will." They demanded that a decisive blow be struck immediately, before the situation became irreversible and were sure that strong, determined action would rout the *fedayeen* from the cities. Two to three days was all the time needed, they felt, to restore law and order and renew respect for Jordan's sovereignty.

By the end of the meeting, King Hussein had decided to appoint a military government headed by Palestinian-born Brigadier Mohammad Daoud. Daoud, a well-respected, Western-oriented, career army officer, was selected primarily for his Palestinian roots, to convey that this was a push *for* law and order, not *against* the Palestinians. Hussein also appointed another Palestinian, Adnan Abu-Odeh, as information minister.

But the King was advised on the cabinet formulation by his confidante, Wasfi Tall, a strict law-and-order man when it came to the Palestinians. The strongman of the cabinet was, in fact, not Daoud, but Deputy Prime Minister Mazin al-Ajluni, a non-Palestinian. As a whole, the cabinet was hostile to Arafat and the PLO and was bent on asserting Jordanian authority over the *fedayeen* by force. Plus Hussein decided to appoint Field Marshal Habis Majali as commander in chief. Majali had served once before as commander in chief and was the leader of an important tribal group in Southern Jordan, fiercely loyal to the king and with little love for the guerrillas.

Announcements would be made early in the morning with army units prepositioned outside the city. Hussein was still prepared to give the *fedayeen* a last chance to remove their forces from Amman. The army would engage only if the *fedayeen* did not comply.

King Hussein informed the U.S. embassy that he was moving to an "all or nothing showdown," although he admitted that he did not have a good sense of how it would all play out. He doubted that Iraq would pose a problem, despite the persistent American inclination to worry about it. Nonetheless, he alerted Ambassador Brown that, depending on what happened, he might call for U.S. *and Israeli* assistance. Hussein made clear that he was "betting all his chips," was prepared to use any force necessary, and was determined not to lose. He came across relaxed and confident, now that the die had been cast.

Brown was skeptical that Hussein would follow through, though. Hussein had been here before and always seemed to pull back just before the moment of truth. Nonetheless, the United States worried. "This may blow the hostages," wrote Deputy Assistant Secretary of State Rodger Davies. "I wish they had gotten them out before this happened." Henry Kissinger predicted that if the king went through with his plan, "the 54 hostages . . . will be in grave danger." Brown pressed the king to at least warn "of most serious consequences should *fedayeen* injure any hostages that may now be or may fall into their hands."

Hussein similarly informed the British of his plans and that he might call on the United States *and others* for help. The British were not as sanguine as Brown. Now, at 1 AM in London, the Foreign Office, in a telex conference with its embassy in Amman, discussed what might be done about its hostages:

> LONDON: Does [Hussein] realize the danger to Western hostages, possibly death? . . .
> AMMAN: Yes, but he feels that he has to do this in the interests of law, order, and unity.
> LONDON: What prospect is there of a bilateral deal on our hostages before the situation deteriorates?
> AMMAN: None.

Despite its doubts that Hussein would act, the U.S. embassy quietly battened down its hatches.[9]

Washington, 9 PM

At 9 PM, Alexander Haig took a hotline call at the White House from 10 Downing Street. Denis Greenhill, the Foreign Office permanent undersecretary, was calling to say that Prime Minister Edward Heath was very concerned about Hussein's decision. Greenhill insisted on knowing what the United States planned to do if the king called for Israeli intervention. Haig responded that the United States did not preclude direct intervention "or indeed for Israelis, if Hussein asks them." Her Majesty's Government, Greenhill responded, did not see how the United States could agree to leave hostages in Jordan if a free-for-all developed or to further jeopardize them by joining the fray, or even by having the Palestinians believe that it was about to.

At 10:30 PM, Kissinger convened an emergency meeting in the White House Situation Room of the Washington Special Action Group, a top-level crisis management team that he had activated. Many of the participants were in dinner jackets, having been unexpectedly summoned from a banquet in Virginia. Kissinger did not want a Palestinian victory. "I'd have to reach far to find a positive evolution in a Palestinian victory," he would say. "[The] Palestinians want [the] extinction of Israel." There was a unanimous sense in the administration too that "we can't let the king fail." But what to do?

The previous year, the National Security Council had concluded that "except as a last resort" to protect or evacuate American citizens, introducing U.S. forces into Jordan "must be ruled out." Such an action would "arouse the Arab world . . . against us and might lead to clashes and bloody incidents with the local population." And, "we would be caught in a long-term commitment, since the situation would be so unstable that the departure of U.S. forces after only a short time would precipitate chaos."

Then, in June 1970, the National Security Council and the Washington Special Action Group evaluated various responses to a possible appeal from King Hussein for assistance against either *fedayeen* attacks or Syrian or Iraqi intervention. Their conclusions were "somber." Without access to bases in the eastern Mediterranean, which it did not have, the Sixth Fleet could provide some air support, but it would be difficult to send in a sizable ground force. If serious military action were required, Israel would be far better positioned to provide both ground forces and air cover, particularly on short notice. But this solution was politically charged.

And again, at a Washington Special Action Group meeting on September 8, Joint Chiefs of Staff chairman Admiral Thomas Moorer and Deputy Secretary of Defense David Packard had reiterated the limitations of U.S. military power for a sustained operation. They repeated their admonition that the United States make every effort to avoid being drawn into any large-scale military action in Jordan. Three days later, the Joint Chiefs—concerned about basing rights, supply lines, the commitment of U.S. forces in Southeast Asia, and the unhelpful attitude of the NATO allies—said again that the United States could not even mount a "credible deterrent" to Soviet military intervention in the Middle East. And tonight once more, the Joint Chiefs opposed U.S. intervention, calling it "a very high risk venture from a military point of view."

Against this pessimistic backdrop, the group concluded that if the king could not defeat the *fedayeen*, the United States would need to help him somehow in order to reward his friendship and moderate foreign policy. And since Israel would surely act in that case too, the primary American military role should be to prevent the Soviets from retaliating against Israel. The most effective action to take right now, Kissinger decided, was to rapidly and threateningly augment forces in the Mediterranean in order to ward off Iraqi or Syrian intervention, provide a psychological boost for the king, and deter, but also match and overwhelm, if necessary, a Soviet response.

At around 10:45 PM (3:45 AM in London), Kissinger and Sisco, spoke by phone with Greenhill, echoing Haig's earlier comments. The conversation then turned to the hostages. Greenhill told Kissinger and Sisco that the PFLP's terms "do not seem so bad to us, as you know." Whereupon, Sisco broke in and a heated dialogue ensued:

> SISCO: Can I say a word on this? Let me tell you what the problem is with these terms, so you will understand. . . . The Israelis have been very resistant, as you know, to the idea of accepting the principle before they know what the totality of the demands are. Our efforts over the last four or five days have been to try to force the PFLP to give a concrete list. In other words, the strategy we have felt and feel is that we have got to get the other side to put on the table . . . their total demands so that we and you and the other two concerned can consider how we can influence our Israeli friends. But how in the hell are we going to influence the Israelis if the *fedayeen* won't even tell us . . . just how many *fedayeen* they want exchanged in the situation? That is the problem, you see.
>
> GREENHILL: The only comment I can make on that, Joe, is that it does not require imagination to guess what the *fedayeen* terms are or who would appear on their list when the time comes.
>
> SISCO: Well, you are a lot clearer than we are, because we have had three different numerical terms cited in the press—200 *fedayeen*, 400 *fedayeen*, 600 *fedayeen*—and you and we would be much more effective to the Israelis if we knew concretely what the other side had asked for.

Earlier in the day, Sisco had complained to Yitzhak Rabin that "the British have shown themselves as terrible" in dealing with the hostage situation and that, over the past four days, the United States had been battling with them to prevent a separate deal. "You can't do anything with the Europeans," said Sisco. "They are not prepared to confront the Russians or the Arabs at all."[10]

THE EVE OF WAR

WEDNESDAY, SEPTEMBER 16

Wahdat, 6 AM

Wednesday morning—now this I remember exactly—we heard some great news on the radio. We were all up because we all got up every day very early, five-thirty, six (except for one day in Amman later on, when I think I slept to nine or ten). We were listening to the BBC on the guerrillas' radio at six o'clock, and we heard the news. The announcer said that the five powers, who had been meeting in Bern, Switzerland, all this time, had been up for a few hours already discussing our issue. We thought, when we first heard this, that this was going to be great news, that we would be out very quickly and very soon. We were very happy because if it was six o'clock here in Jordan, then it was five o'clock in Bern. We knew that politicians don't get up early in the morning just to fool around and waste their time. Something was going to be done, and this was what we were hoping for.

Little could we imagine the behind-the-scenes disunity, discord, and chaos among the parties deputed to gain our release.

Amman, 6 AM

At 6 AM, Radio Amman announced the military cabinet. Hussein admitted his failure to rein in the situation before it had reached a point of "maximum danger." But now the country had reached the point "of serious probability of its destruction." So, Hussein said, he was acting to "restore order." He then broadcast a moving plea to his people to "unify your ranks, your hearts, and your voice" and support his move.

Soon afterward, the PFLP rejected the new "fascist" government which, it claimed, intended to destroy the resistance movement. The PLO Central Committee concurred and went into emergency session. It decided unanimously to prepare for armed confrontation and appointed Yasser Arafat commander in chief of all Palestinian forces. It called for a general strike the next day to last until the collapse of the military government and appealed to Jordanian soldiers—"comrades in arms and brothers in struggle"—to defy orders and not harm the *fedayeen.* And, no surprise, it rescinded the PFLP's suspension.

Fedayeen units throughout Jordan were put on full combat alert. They set up roadblocks on Jabal Ashrafiyeh and elsewhere, barricaded side streets with hasty piles of rubble, reinforced the sandbagging of their strongholds, and dug trenches. Jordanian troops too dug in. War was at hand.[1]

London, 10 AM

London moved closer to striking out on its own. "The situation is now so serious that we [can] not afford the delay which further lengthy negotiations between the Israelis and the *fedayeen* over precise numbers to be released would involve." Israel, in other words, needed to cave in.

The British assessment "borders on hysteria," Israel countered. Now was the time for the five powers to restrain themselves, cut off contact with the guerrillas, and direct their demands to Jordan's government to release the prisoners without further concession. What's more, it believed, in the current circumstances the British would not be able to find anyone authorized to reach and implement a separate deal, even if they wanted to. But, just to be sure, Israel reaffirmed its request for Leila Khaled's detention, warning that Israel would regard her release without its okay "as being contrary to the letter and spirit of the Extradition Agreement."[2]

Amman, noon

Despite the king's announcement, life in Amman went on for the moment. Schools and food shops were open. Pedestrian and vehicular traffic were below normal but flowing in all directions. The number of uniformed, armed *fedayeen* was noticeably lower and few civilians appeared armed. Roadblocks to the west and north of Amman were manned at "normal" levels. But an anticipatory hush was settling over the city.

Outside of Amman, "dozens of violations were being committed [by Palestinian guerrillas] in most of the towns and villages of the kingdom with complete disregard and irresponsibility," according to government reports.

"Houses were broken into, citizens kidnapped, public highways blocked, cars stolen, men and officers assaulted, and checkpoints set up in the streets."

Yet the government still hoped to find a way out of the impasse. At 10 AM, Prime Minister Mohammed Daoud called Arafat in a last-ditch effort: "I beseech you in the name of God, in the name of Jerusalem, in the name of the martyrs, and in the name of Palestine to let us sit down and put an end to this chaos." The government also contacted the Committee of Five throughout the day to broker a meeting with the PLO in order to avoid a showdown. At 2:20 PM, the committee returned the PLO's negative reply. At 10 PM, the PLO itself informed Daoud that "we have decided not to cooperate with the military cabinet."[3]

Mediterranean, 4 PM

The U.S. high-stakes bluff intensified. The Sixth Fleet drew closer to Lebanon's territorial waters and stepped up its monitoring activities. Its radar was causing severe interference on the local TV channel, raising both official and public ire. But the Soviets too were initiating an evolving game of cat and mouse, as Fifth Eskadra warships positioned themselves among the American battleships and between the American ships and the Lebanese coast.

Despite U.S. escalation, Henry Kissinger, chillingly, advised President Nixon that if Jordanian forces were to lose control and there was complete chaos in Amman, armed intervention could not assuredly save either the American community or the hostages. If, however, the army could retain control of parts of the city and the Americans could gather there, armed intervention could save them. But even in that case, "it seems unlikely that the hijacking hostages could be saved."[4]

Bern, 4 PM

Fearing a major conflagration in Jordan, British Ambassador Eric Midgley was told to reach a common negotiating stance in Bern "now" that "must include an Israeli contribution." Otherwise, he could "imply," his government would feel free to "seek other means" to secure its hostages. Israel's Ambassador Levavi was asked to call Israel for an answer. There was "no point," he responded. Negotiations like these were a war of nerves. It was important not "to stimulate the Arab appetite by premature concessions," he said and counseled continued patience.

U.S. ambassador Shelby Davis suggested a compromise: that the five governments inform the ICRC that they would "consider" a PFLP proposal that specified its *total* demands, including who it wanted freed. This was still problematic to Levavi because "five governments" would include Israel in the Red Cross's mandate—which, to date, was from the other four countries only—and it implied Israel's willingness to consider PFLP demands. Nonetheless, Levavi cabled his deep concerns that the package would fall apart unless Israel accepted the United States' compromise. "The British are creating terrible panic regarding the situation in Jordan," he wrote. The Israeli Foreign Ministry also hesitated to reject the U.S. proposal outright. "We don't want to be blamed if something, God forbid, happens to the hostages."[5]

The Country Club, 4:30 PM

"We're taking you to a safe place," Ben Hasim, a guerrilla guarding the Zarqa hostages, told the group as shells began flying overhead. Derrell Suttles was upset; he didn't want to leave. He was having a great poker game and didn't want to lose all his dings and lings. The men were herded into a convoy of Volkswagen Beetles and driven off. They ran into a number of army roadblocks along the way, but the *fedayeen* simply brandished their guns and the army let them pass. Once in Amman, "we saw people in civilian clothes behind barricades," recalled George Freda. "They were all armed. Our little convoy climbed up a steep hill, around winding roads and stopped at the house we were to be quartered in."

A bit earlier in the day in Irbid, two *fedayeen* came into the room and told the six Americans there that they had five minutes to get ready because they were being taken away. The six couldn't figure out why they needed the five minutes since they had absolutely nothing with them. They were taken outside and five of them piled into a big Chevy. Joseph Harari-Raful was directed into a truck with a bunch of PFLP guerrillas. The men were alarmed at their separation.

The two vehicles pulled into the street and shortly afterward into a gas station at the edge of town. The hostages were all obvious in the broad daylight, but no onlooker did or said anything. The guerrillas filled up their gas tanks and, without paying, pulled onto the road again. Almost immediately, the Chevy got a flat tire. Unfortunately, they had no jack. So everyone—including the hostages—got out of the car and the truck and stood at the roadside trying to flag down a passing car so they could borrow a jack. The surreal and tragicomic scene—six American hostages, including two sporting black suits and black yarmulkes, standing at a roadside in Northern Jordan, gesticulating wildly to flag down a car to borrow a jack so that they could continue on their way to who-knows-where—was not lost on the men.

Finally, the guerrillas gave up on the Chevy. They prodded all six men into the back of the truck and drove off again, southbound. After several minutes, they came to a junction (probably the strategic Ramtha junction), where

Berkowitz noticed a sign indicating that they were now only six miles away from the Syrian border to the east. They were thankful that the truck did not turn left. A while later, they came into Mafraq and pulled into a darkened dead-end alley. All but one or two of their guards left. Like a scene out of a movie, the six feared that they were going to be shot and have their bodies dumped there.

The guerrillas suddenly reappeared and the truck pulled out and turned around. To the men's amazement, they were heading back toward Irbid. There had clearly been a change of plan because by the time they returned, PFLP guerrillas had already moved into their room. The fighters were kicked out and trudged up to the roof. In all likelihood, the intent had been to bring the six to Amman to join the other Americans. Perhaps in Mafraq the guerrillas realized either that it was too dangerous to travel or that they might hit an impassable roadblock. The men were now fated to sit out the rest of their captivity alone in Irbid.[6]

Wahdat, 5 PM

Wednesday we were told that we would be combined and united with the other people, that all the Americans would be brought together that day. We waited and we waited. Then, in the evening, we twelve were taken to Amman proper.

There were three cars, and we decided that we should split up. We would have four people in a car, with each car having one crew member. One of the guerrillas followed behind us in a half-track. As we were going through to Amman proper, it was a very strange sight, because we saw everyone walking around with kaffiyehs on their heads and holding guns and it was fairly frightful.

We were taken to a building and brought into two rooms in an apartment in the back, and there we stood. After a few minutes, they brought in the five women and Rabbi David, plus a soldier, Kenny Hubler, a Vietnam vet on his way home, who had been on the Swissair plane. We found out that another group—British and other nationalities taken off the planes before they were blown up and brought here—had just been moved out. It was good to see that other people were alive and well. After approximately half an hour, the rest of the people [thirteen from Zarqa] came. So that completed our group of thirty-two people. And there we were to stay.

The European hostages were taken to Wahdat, apparently to the rooms that we had just vacated.

Our new residence was a three-room apartment at the back of a two-story building built into the north side of a steep hill up which Barto (now Badr) Street ran. The top, entrance floor was at street level. My room (with the others from "Hajji's Place," as we now referred back to it) was the furthest in. From one window, we could see the huddled houses on the neighboring mountain, Jabal Nadhif, and a tall antenna atop what we believed was a commando headquarters nearby. Out the other window was the building next door, separated from us by a narrow alley. The building's exterior was chiseled ecru stone.

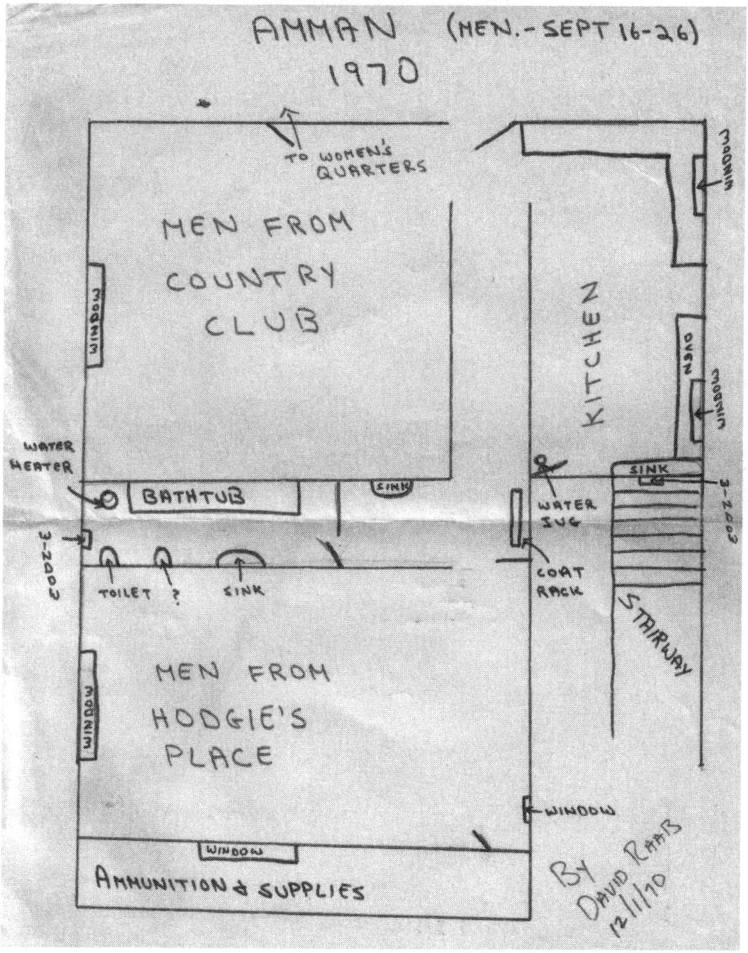

Figure 2 Our Quarters in Ashrafiyeh

When the people from the Zarqa Country Club arrived, we were all so happy to see each other again that we started singing. Then, settling into the apartment, we were each given a thin foam rubber mattress and two heavy blankets. I put my mattress near the middle of the inside wall of the room.

Now, not all of us had taken showers the day we rigged showers. So when we came to this place, we thought it was going to be great. There was running water, and we had three sinks, a toilet, a shower, and a bath. It really looked like we were going to have a good time here. So the ones who hadn't taken showers beforehand took their showers, and we really thought we were going to enjoy ourselves.

But our exuberance and the water would both evaporate the next morning.[7]

Irbid and Zarqa, evening

Northern Jordan was now a "Liberated Area," declared the *fedayeen,* claiming total control of Irbid. Not a single Jordanian soldier or policeman was seen in Irbid that day. The *fedayeen* also appeared to be in control of Zarqa, where there had been a clash in the morning. In the evening too, heavy fighting was reported, both sides using rockets and artillery. Most of the civilian population had left town. The PLO warned whoever remained that "the tanks of the agent's [Jordanian] regime are surrounding your city, seeking more than a massacre and a blood bath." The hostages from Zarqa had gotten out just in time.

Despite Hussein's judgment that the Iraqis would not engage, he could not be sure. Just a few days earlier, the Iraqi defense minister had inspected the expeditionary force and met with a PLO delegation. He encouraged all those opposed to the Rogers Plan for peace talks between Egypt, Jordan, and Israel to "translate their rejection into practical action." The Iraqi threat was very real and potentially devastating.[8]

Bern, 1 AM

Arie Levavi called Shelby Davis with Jerusalem's very quick and sharp response. First, Israel did not agree that the situation in Jordan was precarious. Second, serious negotiations could not get underway in any case for at least two days, until the new ICRC negotiators were on the ground in Amman, so why the rush? And, third, if the Jordanian government could prevail in its new, more authoritative posture, it could be the one to negotiate. Thus, Israel "hesitates to accept" the U.S. proposal. Levavi asked Davis to raise the matter in Washington, as Israeli Prime Minister Golda Meir had just arrived in the United States.

The United States balked at Israel's response. It had gone as far as it could in "considerable arm-twisting" of both the British and Germans to keep them from breaking ranks. So Secretary of State Rogers asked chargé J. Owen Zurhellen in Tel Aviv not only to encourage Israel to accept the U.S. proposal, but to prepare to be even more flexible. "Israeli failure to concur would leave us isolated from [the] British, Swiss, and Germans, and cause the package deal to fall apart," he asserted. And, for good measure, he asked the chargé to note to the Israelis the "increasing unhappiness" of "influential members" of the American Jewish community with Israel's failure "to engage themselves more actively."

At 3 AM in Bern, Levavi was called and told that the United States could no longer press Britain and Germany. The time had come for Israel to make some concessions.[9]

"A LITTLE EXCITEMENT"

THURSDAY, SEPTEMBER 17

Amman, 4:50 AM

War erupted in Amman just as dawn broke. Red and white tracers lit up the predawn sky over the rolling hills south of the capital. By first light, heavy gunfire opened up north and northeast of the city. In the first hour of fighting, the guerrillas hit a major fuel depot in the center of Amman, sending a cloud of black smoke curling skyward. Very soon, black and gray smoke spiraled up from many spots around the city. The rat-a-tat of heavy machine-gun exchanges and the booms of artillery and mortar shells reverberated throughout Amman's jabals and wadis. The telephone lines out of Amman went down immediately, electricity was cut, and the airport was shut down. The water supply in most parts of the city also ceased. Then "the unmistakable clank of tank tracks" echoed through Amman's abandoned streets as Jordanian armored vehicles and infantry made their way on two main axes into Amman in a "picture book pincer movement."

Amman in 1970 was a city of about a half million people, built upon several three-thousand-foot hills, or jabals, with deep valleys, or wadis, running between them. At Amman's heart were three jabals: Jabal Hussein to the north, running northwest-southeast; Jabal Luweibdeh in the center, running west-northwest to east-southeast; and Jabal Amman below, running west-east. To the east, the three jabals gave way to a wadi, Amman's downtown. PLO headquarters were on Jabal Hussein's northwestern edge; the Hussein refugee camp was at its south-center; Jabal Nuzha adjoined its northeast edge.

Jabal Luweibdeh, home to the U.S. and other embassies, was a largely middle-class Palestinian neighborhood. On its northwestern edge, in the Al-Abdali area, sat Jordanian army headquarters, only half a mile south of PLO headquarters. Farther northwest was the Shmaysani neighborhood. The northwest-southeast Salt-Amman highway entered Amman at Shmaysani's northeastern rim, continued onto the crest of Jabal Hussein, and then fed into the downtown area. The airport was two and a half miles northeast of there.

A road with three traffic circles, designated numerically from east to west, traversed Jabal Amman's crest. The Intercontinental Hotel was on the north side of the road between the Second and Third Circles. A multistory structure atop the jabal, it was visible from Luweibdeh and other parts of Amman. Separated from Jabal Amman by a deep wadi (which also led downtown) were Jabal Nadhif to its south and the steep and massive Jabal Ashrafiyeh, where we were being held, to its southeast. Abutting Ashrafiyeh on its southeast was the Wahdat refugee camp. Running north-south between Nadhif on the west and Ashrafiyeh and Wahdat on the east and feeding into the wadi below Jabal Amman was another deep wadi. The road through that wadi was the last leg of the Aqaba-Amman highway.

It was up this road that the 1st Infantry Division of the Jordanian Arab Army (JAA) thrust north. Providing the main punch, was a regiment of the 60th Armored Brigade. This Bedouin-dominated brigade was intensely loyal to King Hussein. Wahdat was the force's first objective, then Ashrafiyeh, and finally Luweibdeh. Wahdat, where I had been and now the European hostages were being held, was a Palestinian refugee camp, a center of guerrilla support, and home to a number of key groups including the PFLP. Wahdat had been dubbed the "Republic of Palestine."

Spearheading the west-to-east thrust astride the Salt-Amman highway, firing as it came, was a brigade-sized force led by the 4th Mechanized Division and another regiment of the 60th Armored, with desert-camouflaged armored cars, small tanks, and infantry with medium and heavy artillery support. Its objective was Jabal Hussein and its Hussein Refugee Camp, another *fedayeen* stronghold.

Confident that it would control the city in two days, as it had advised King Hussein, the army planned for the thrusts to meet downtown by dusk of September 19 at the latest.

Light and medium weapons fire poured out in most parts of the city. From about 6 AM on, the U.S. embassy area came under small arms fire from Jabal Amman. The roof of the Catholic Church adjoining the embassy was penetrated by a rocket or mortar. At 7 AM, 81mm mortars began striking near the embassy. Bursts of gunfire flattened the tires of the embassy guards' vehicles. Two mortar rounds exploded on the embassy roof and knocked out two

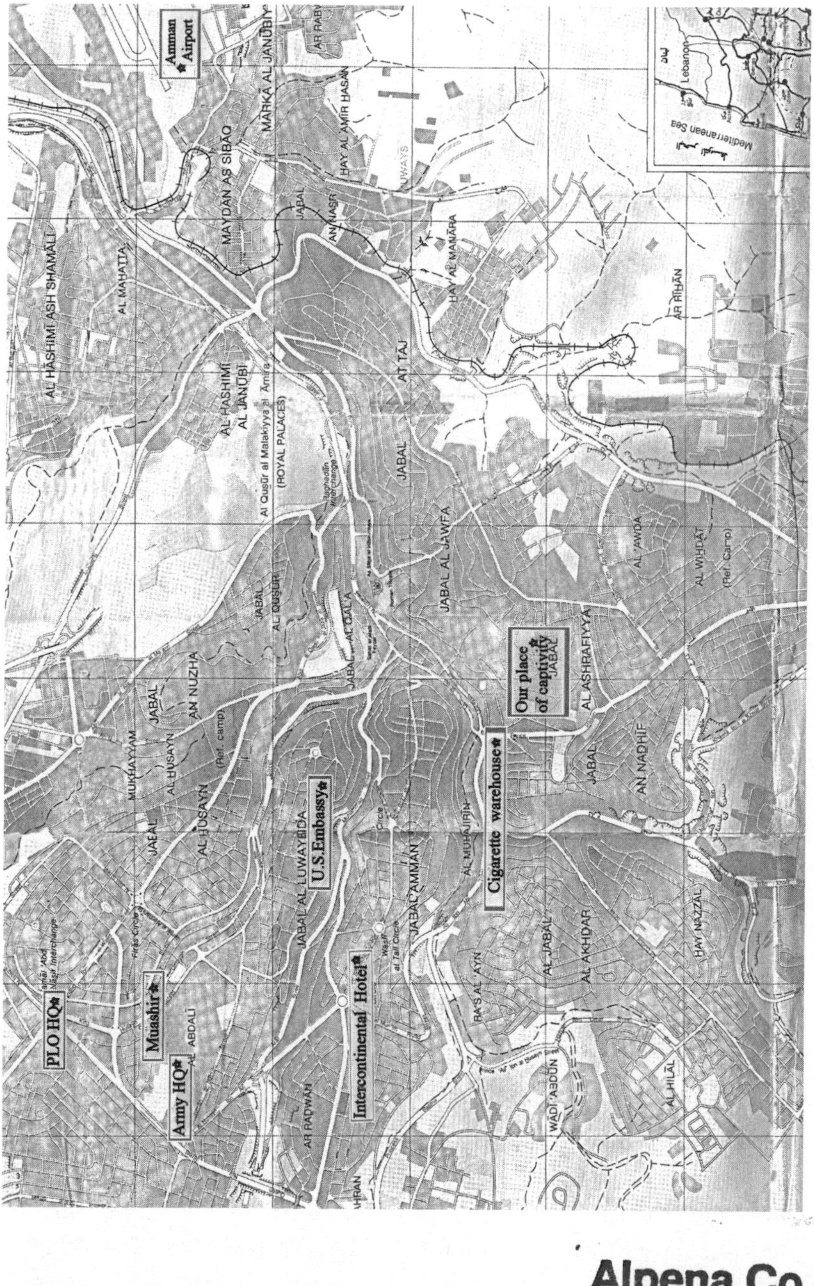

Figure 3 Map of Amman. © Royal Jordanian Geographic Centre

antennas. A bit later, gunshots penetrated the ambassador's office on the second floor and another office downstairs. The staff took cover in the code room and other interior rooms. At the British embassy, the windows of the operations room were smashed.

At about 7:30 AM, Jordanian troops, tanks, and other armored cars made their way eastward from the Third Circle, firing away at guerrilla hideouts. A gray pall of smoke began to blanket the city as the shooting intensified by the hour.[1]

Ashrafiyeh, 4:50 AM

That morning the war broke out—the civil war in Jordan. King Hussein was a smart cookie and turned off all electricity and all water supply. And that's when our troubles began, because now the guerrillas had to supply us with water every day, which, I must say, they did consistently. But, every day we had to ration our water. On average, we had around two cups a day except for the day before we were released when we had one cup for the whole day. That was very, very difficult.

The day the war broke out, we figured that war was the best thing that could happen to us. Otherwise, had the war not broken out, the governments could have dillydallied back and forth for days and months and years even. People would forget about us and that would be the end of it. But we figured as soon as the war broke out, there would be so much pressure on all sides to get us out of there. The United States would want us out because of public opinion. The American people would say, we hoped, "How are you going to let Americans sit in the middle of a civil war?" The guerrillas would want us out because they wouldn't want us dead. And the Jordanians would want us out because our being there was a very bad thing for Jordanian politics: They were harboring a group that was holding American citizens. So, we figured, as soon as the war was over we would be released within a matter of a very few days. All along Al—who, by the way, happened to be very precise in his judgments and was very resourceful—had said that we would be out by September 26. And Jim also all the time was saying, "don't worry, you'll be home for Rosh Hashanah."

We were not usually optimistic, however. As Mimi Beeber recounted, "the war started and the bombs started coming and . . . hit all around the house." We feared that we might die accidentally and spent the rest of our time there teetering between deep despair and equally irrational confidence that we would survive unscathed.

The war, as we suspected, did heighten the urgency of the countries. What we did not realize is that it also exacerbated the anxiety of the Europeans who were increasingly worried about their citizens. Nor did we realize that the war would throw a huge monkey wrench into the negotiations logistics and that PFLP members, now fighting for their lives, had no interest in being distracted by negotiations. What we further did not realize as shooting and shelling raged all around us was that the United States continued to believe that we were nowhere near it.[2]

Damascus, 9 AM

Even before the onset of fighting, Syria began rattling its sabers, viewing the appointment of the military government as an attempt to liquidate the *fedayeen.* "[I]t has become urgent to block the road to the plot and to raise the whip and fist in its face," Syria's ruling Ba'ath party railed, vowing to take "all measures to preserve the security and freedom of *fedayeen* action." Now, Syria warned that it would not "stand idle while the Palestinian revolution groups and the masses in Jordan are being exposed to massacres." Syrian President Nurredin Atasi openly endorsed the Palestinians and threatened to intervene. "We must give generously in blood, money, and everything else to . . . protect the Palestine revolution," he would proclaim the next day at a rally in Damascus.[3]

Amman, 10 AM

The army's mandate was to disarm the *fedayeen* and expel them from Amman and the other cities, not to destroy the resistance movement or kill the *fedayeen.* Nonetheless, during the course of the morning, the fighting in Amman became quite intense.

At 9 AM, Field Marshal Majali imposed "a strict curfew" in Amman. Any violator "shall be fired upon," he announced. (That is precisely what happened to British Ambassador Phillips when he tried to get a lift that afternoon with a passing tank column.) At 9:30 AM, a Jordanian armored personnel carrier was hit and its engine burned at the Third Circle. The *fedayeen* set up mortars and a rocket launcher near LaSalle College on Jabal Hussein. JAA tanks on Jabal Nuzha lobbed shells at Jabal Ashrafiyeh. Six tanks, led by a scout car, moved toward the city on a ridgeline southeast of Jabal Amman, firing at targets on both sides.

A major firefight broke out again for control of the unfinished apartment building across the street from the Intercontinental. An army vehicle slowly cruised by, guns ablaze, firing at all openings. Cement flew from the pillars like dust. A demented beggar caught in the crossfire scurried for his life. The building changed hands several times during the morning. The hotel too came under fire several times. Heavy-caliber bullets punched holes the size of a head in its walls and windows; the guests huddled in the basement. A Swedish cameraman was hit while photographing the battle from the hotel's second floor balcony.

The *fedayeen* also tried to capture the U.S. ambassador's residence, located between the First and Second Circles, but were beaten back by guards. A French photographer was wounded in both legs while documenting the attack from the garden of the Spanish Embassy. Armed exchanges continued around the embassy itself, where JAA shelling scored some direct hits on a Palestinian stronghold about five hundred yards from the embassy. About fifteen to twenty rounds exploded close to the embassy within half an hour, shattering some windows. A Bedouin guard was hit by light shrapnel. Another antenna would be hit, leaving only one to receive incoming communications.[4]

Northern Jordan, noon

Reoccupying the capital, Amman, was the army's main objective. It planned to turn its attention northward once Amman was subdued. Meanwhile, though, northern Jordan was turning into *fedayeen* country. Irbid, already under *fedayeen* control, was quiet. But ten miles away in Ramtha, astride the Syrian border, heavy fighting ensued. The junction two miles to Ramtha's southwest was the most strategic in northern Jordan, its control critical to both sides. About eight miles northwest lay Irbid and about twenty miles to the southwest, Jarash, with its road leading to Amman. Given the border topography, a Syrian incursion would necessarily flow through Ramtha. The junction was crucial to the Palestinians too for reinforcements and supplies from Syria.

By noon, the *fedayeen* claimed complete control of Ramtha. In fact, the PLO Central Committee proclaimed Jordan's entire north "totally liberated" from the "regime of the agents." It created three "liberated provinces" and appointed a governor for each. Radio Amman did not dispute *fedayeen* control. The border itself also heated up as Syrian troops amassed at Dar'a opposite Ramtha and, with apparent Syrian acquiescence, Syria-based Palestinian commandos attempted to infiltrate into Jordan. They were stopped at the border by Jordanian tanks. This time.[5]

London, 11 AM

The outbreak of war rattled Germany. It pressed the United States and United Kingdom on the urgent need to pursue bilateral deals. The United States responded with a very strong demurral and Germany backed off yet again.

But British patience with Israel was close to an end. Prime Minister Edward Heath called Israel "obstinate and uncompromising." While no one wanted to submit to blackmail, he argued, there was no denying the guerrillas' victory in having captured the planes and hostages. Plus, one had to remember that the Arab war was against Israel, not England, and that England had important interests in the Arab world. And now the situation in Jordan further endangered the hostages.

In addition, Britain was still having a difficult time internalizing the fact that there were no pure-Israeli hostages. This became apparent when British Foreign Office undersecretary Denis Greenhill and American assistant secretary of state Joseph Sisco argued—by phone—over possibly scrapping the unified approach:

> GREENHILL: [T]here are three possible courses if you abandon the five-power approach. One is that the four of us say that the European prisoners could be exchanged for all hostages except the three Israelis, or whatever the number of Israelis are.
> SISCO: Well it is really three, but these three are also Americans.
> GREENHILL: They are not pure Israelis?
> SISCO: No, no, they are Americans.
> GREENHILL: So, it is three duals and, so, that deal would only be a feasible one for you if it was the European prisoners for all the hostages, period?
> SISCO: Yes. As you cannot distinguish [among Americans], that deal is no deal for us.
> GREENHILL: Yes, but, I mean, if we could get all the Americans and the duals . . . are there no pure Israelis involved?
> SISCO: No.
> GREENHILL: You are certain of that.
> SISCO: Well, we are satisfied that these two or three . . . have American passports.
> GREENHILL: Yes, I see.
> SISCO: So, that is the problem, you see.

Nonetheless, Greenhill persisted, trying to convince Sisco to let the Europeans go their own way. The conversation became heated, the tension palpable, with some harsh British words for Israel and the United States' relations with it.

> GREENHILL: Well now, another deal would be, and I am talking in theory, that in view of the danger to our people, that the Germans, the Swiss, and ourselves swap our prisoners for our hostages, leaving you unprovided for. The final stage is that we should agree amongst ourselves that nobody would mutually reproach the other if each person did the best they could for their own people.
> SISCO: Right. Well, Denis, obviously I can tell you we would have difficulty with all three of these approaches. And moreover I think your government would want to weigh very, very carefully the kind of outcry that would occur in this country against your taking this kind of an action as well as the Germans. . . . It would be very strong indeed, and be very sure your Ministers understand that.

> GREENHILL: Well, they do, Joe. But there is also an outcry in this country on the lines of, because your visitor [Golda Meir] won't lift a bloody finger and put any contribution to a bargain, our people get killed. And can you imagine how bad that would [play]? And if it all comes out that we could have got our people out but for the obduracy of you and the other people, so to speak. . . .

Later, an American diplomat in London "strongly" pointed out to the Foreign Office that the absence of "pure" Israelis only underscored the importance to the United States of a united front because this was an American issue more than an Israeli one. As Henry Kissinger wrote to the president, "the *fedayeen* are conditioning the release of our citizens on the performance of a third country—Israel. Israel is in fact being asked to ransom the nationals of third countries." The diplomat's argument seemed to have had the opposite effect. At least one official believed that Israel would now be even more reluctant to contribute since its "interest in securing the release of the hostages is so slight." U.S. pressure on Israel would thus need to be correspondingly greater. This, in turn, made "the early release of the British hostages" less likely and strengthened the case for a bilateral deal. So Britain instructed its ambassador in Israel, John Barnes, to "make it clear" to Israel that "by refusal or delay they will make themselves responsible for placing the lives of the hostages in jeopardy. This is bound to be damaging to Israel's relations with ourselves."

But the United States also began to pressure Israel. As instructed, its chargé in Tel Aviv reminded Israel's foreign minister, Abba Eban, and the Foreign Ministry's Gideon Rafael that the United States had "carried the ball" in keeping the countries unified and had not till now pressed Israel. However, he said, Israel had to do something in order to preserve the common front, especially since the Europeans were becoming jittery with the fighting. He requested that Israel agree to the American formula that Ambassador Shelby Davis had proposed in Bern. The United States might not be able to hold the group together otherwise, he hinted.[6]

Amman, 2 PM

Fighting was fierce throughout the day. Shells hit downtown and the northern slopes of Jabal Ashrafiyeh where a fuel storage dump was hit. There was intense fighting along Embassy Row where hundreds of armed guerrillas had apparently dug in. U.S. embassy guards were now firing back against increasing small arms fire directed toward them.

Automatic weapons fire could be heard around the First and Second Circles. In most quarters in Amman, explosions went off, fires blazed, and smoke billowed upward. At one point, Hussein's palace itself was hit, killing about fifteen soldiers and wounding many others. Loss of life was rising and the number of wounded civilians "reached several hundred." Armored half-tracks bearing the Red Crescent's insignia evacuated army casualties from the thick of the fight. But for the most part, wounded civilians lay in their own blood where they fell, as no ambulances braved the withering crossfire to rescue them.

The army's progress was much slower than anticipated, as armored units bogged down in the built-up areas of Amman despite having received permission to fire at residences from which guerrillas were sniping. So far, they had not penetrated beyond the Second Circle. Though the army had received its orders to move only this morning, King Hussein's cousin, Deputy Chief of Staff Zeid bin-Shaker, had worked with his staff flat out for two weeks to prepare attack plans. The army had hastily massed the bulk of its combat units, about 35,000 troops, into the Amman area—pulling many away from the border with Israel—and had even conducted some urban warfare exercises outside the capital.

Still, the army was clearly inadequately trained and equipped for such warfare. The 60th Armored, which carried the brunt of the initial attacks, did not coördinate well with accompanying infantry, whose units included a high percentage of less-trained Palestinians and small-village Jordanians. The army had old guns—single-shot M-1 carbines—versus the *fedayeen*'s Soviet Kalashnikov and Simonov submachine guns, and their armored personnel carriers were wheeled vehicles, vulnerable to bullets. Plus, the *fedayeen* were using civilians and their homes as shields.

Amman was a defender's dream. Jordanian armored units were not suited to fighting in Amman's narrow streets and steep hills; maneuvering in narrow twisting streets filled with rubble, they were easy prey. The army had too few riflemen to track down the numerous *fedayeen* who wove in and out of buildings, fired upon advancing Jordanian troops, and, when finally spotted by the Jordanians, simply moved a hundred yards to another house and resumed firing. Also lacking hand grenades and other close-combat tools, the army had only its Centurion and Patton tanks to fire their main guns at near-point-blank range at every building where they suspected even a lone sniper. But most buildings in Amman were constructed of heavy limestone blocks, almost impervious to even direct fire by a 105mm tank cannon.

For their part, the Palestinian guerrillas viewed this war as the "final confrontation" with Hussein and vowed to fight to the last drop of blood. But they were poorly prepared and short on heavy weapons. They had no offensive plan, nor a joint defense plan, for Amman or elsewhere. They had not put in place the rudiments of warfare, such as a clear command structure; their unified command had been established only hours earlier. Even where joint operational or sector commands were in place, they were not integrated. For example, two thousand well-munitioned *fedayeen* sitting in Jarash only a few miles away were never summoned to Amman. They also lacked a secure communications system and used public radio to broadcast coded messages like: "The grapes are ripe. Strike!" and "Gift delivered. Thank you." Another *fedayeen* broadcast—"We are waiting for orders"—was indicative of the chaos.

Nor had the guerrilla groups made adequate provision for shelter, food, water, or medical supplies. And they hadn't provided for hiding places for their leaders. In fact, the entire PLO leadership, including Yasser Arafat and Abu Iyad, was at the military operations center that morning and had to escape "without losing another moment."

There were many reasons for the lack of Palestinian preparedness, almost all having to do with hubris. Over the years, Arafat and the *fedayeen* had taken to believing their own press reports of military prowess, when in fact their military accomplishments were minor. They believed that "Jordan is weaker than us" and that King Hussein was no more than "a paper tiger, whom we can topple in half an hour." They also misjudged Hussein's willingness to use force against them, "for fear of triggering a massacre within the population." Some were confident that the army would rebel and overthrow Hussein in the opening hours of any confrontation. All that was needed was for Arafat to give the word.

What the *fedayeen* did not realize, though, was how devoted the army was to King Hussein and to Egypt's President Nasser who, unlike the *fedayeen*, accepted the Rogers Plan. So, the army remained overwhelmingly loyal to Hussein. The *fedayeen* failed to realize also that the public, who had once avidly supported them, had grown tired of the chaos. They now longed for law and order.[7]

Bern, 4 PM

A breakthrough of sorts was achieved in Bern. Israel quietly acceded to letting the "*four* governments" inform the ICRC that Boissier could point out to the PFLP that Israel had in effect previously agreed to the principle of exchange by exchanging prisoners for Israelis held by Syria during the earlier TWA hijacking and had also indicated its readiness to the ICRC to release the Algerians as part of a deal.

Germany objected because the declaration only implied a commitment, which Israel might not honor when the time came. Levavi, who had sat silently through the discussion, retorted that the only uncivilized people involved here were "the other side." Duly rebuked, Germany accepted the proposal.[8]

Amman, 6:30 PM

In late afternoon, Hussein's palace confidently asserted that the army would control all of Amman by nightfall, and Commander in Chief Majali claimed that the army now controlled all of Amman "except for a few pockets of resistance." By evening, the army's Patton tanks were atop Jabal Ashrafiyeh and in the wadi between Jabals Amman and Luweibdeh. Army units had also apparently reached and occupied the First Circle on Jabal Amman.

Majali's "few pockets," however, were the core commando enclaves. The *fedayeen* themselves claimed complete control over most of Amman and key positions along its approach roads. PLO radio announced the *fedayeen*'s own clean-up operations.

Regardless of the assessments, we hostages were about to spend the first of many nights amidst war.[9]

Chicago

The outbreak of war and the naval buildup in the Mediterranean were all very stimulating to President Nixon, who was in Chicago. "[T]here's nothing better than a little confrontation now and then, a little excitement," he said to Henry Kissinger. Nixon deemed Hussein's survival essential, but he disagreed with Kissinger and William Rogers over Israeli air intervention. Rogers's argued that Israeli intervention would be preferable to deploying American forces. "[T]he reasons are so strong. It would be in line with their national interests; it would help in preventing the Iraqis from having a hand in the government of Jordan. The King can give as the reason the Israelis are on his soil is because of the acts of the *fedayeen.* Third, if we are going to have any peace, Jordan and Israel will have to work together anyway." He also speculated that if U.S. military intervention failed, "For Israel to bail us out would be awful." Kissinger agreed, adding, "No matter how we slice it, the question would be what are we doing there?" The president's instincts were the other way.

Indeed, in what was to have been an off-the-record briefing, Nixon told the *Chicago Sun-Times* that if Iraq or Syria intervened, "there are only two of us who can stop them, the Israelis or us. It will be preferable for us to do it." He then added, in a scoop that the paper printed, apparently finding it too hot to suppress: "We will intervene if the situation is such that our intervention will make a difference."

Saving Hussein was not the only consideration. Nixon and Kissinger tended to see the Jordanian crisis through the prism of the U.S.-Soviet balance of power. The insurrection was directly attributable to Soviet mischief, Nixon believed. "If it succeeded, the entire Middle East might erupt in war . . . [and] the possibility of a direct US-Soviet confrontation was uncomfortably high. It was like a ghastly game of dominoes, with a nuclear war waiting at the end." Nixon wanted to respond not only with a strong message but a credible threat: "I am more interested in the effect [of the U.S. military movement] on the Russians than on Iraq and Syria," he told Kissinger, inquiring whether there were enough B-52s with bombs in Europe. "I don't see this as just an exercise," Nixon continued. "If we hit, we hit with everything we've got. I want a plan available so it's a massive strike."

Nixon reinforced his view to Kissinger again that evening. "I want Europe mobilized in readiness. If we do [a strike], I want to hit massively. Not just little pinpricks. I want them to know we are hell-bent."

That day the United States ordered in an imposing naval force. The carrier *Saratoga* which had been stationed near Malta was instructed to head east to join the *Independence* off the Lebanese coast, accompanied by a cruiser and twelve destroyers. The Sixth Fleet's flagship, the guided missile cruiser *Springfield*, had also moved into the eastern Mediterranean. A third carrier, the *John F. Kennedy*, was dispatched to join the Sixth Fleet. When the Soviets would see the *Kennedy* come through the Straits of Gibraltar, Nixon commented, "they will know that we are ready to do something." The Sixth Fleet's 1,200-person Marine amphibious element and supporting helicopter carrier and landing ships, which had just finished training off Malta, were ordered to stay in position off the Lebanese coast.

The helicopter carrier *Guam* and an accompanying task group were on their way to Camp Lejeune to pick up another group of Marines. Additional C-130 transport planes were sent to Greece. An infantry brigade on maneuvers in West Germany was put on alert, as were elements of the 82nd Airborne Division at Fort Bragg. Twenty thousand U.S. troops were now on alert.[10]

AN EXTREMELY CLOSE CALL

FRIDAY, SEPTEMBER 18

Amman, 4:40 AM

The night had been quiet, the city totally blacked out except for a pillar of flame still rising from the fuel dump on Ashrafiyeh. But by 5:45 AM both light and medium weapons fire echoed throughout Amman.

Early in the morning on Jordan Radio, Commander in Chief Majali gave the *fedayeen* one last chance to put down their weapons and leave Jordan's towns "for the front" against Israel. There were no takers, and the army resumed its disciplined, methodical, albeit snail-paced advance through the city.

Shooting was particularly intense on Luweibdeh. The U.S. embassy took rifle shots through the windows of several offices. The British embassy was also "getting rocked now and then." British Ambassador John Phillips was "furious and frustrated" that the embassy was cut off from the Foreign Office for almost twenty-four hours because of the power and communications outages. His embassy was also unable to reach King Hussein by phone.

Fighting was severe on Jabal Hussein, downtown, and near the First Circle where massive clouds of black smoke billowed upward. A fierce battle raged for control of the Second Circle. The Intercontinental Hotel was rocked by numerous explosions, shattering glass all around. The noise was deafening, the din constant.[1]

Irbid-Ramtha, 6 AM

Fighting was intense in the north as well. At 6 AM, tanks of the Jordanian 40th Armored Brigade began shelling Irbid. A tank battalion was also sent to Ramtha, and a violent battle ensued around the town.

The six Americans in Irbid, recalled Jerry Berkowitz, were far from secure. "Our building was strafed daily. . . . Schwartz and Woods [claiming that they could differentiate between Jordanian Hunters and Israeli Phantoms] believed that it was the Israelis strafing us. I think the Jordanians shot at us as well from the air. We also were barraged by mortars, etc., from the ground . . . I spent a lot of time making clawing marks on the floor as shells exploded around us."[2]

Mafraq, 7 AM

Worryingly, Baghdad continued rattling its sabers. The Iraqi Ba'ath party announced that all its resources were ready "to fight the battle side by side" with their *fedayeen* comrades. The party's secretary general cabled the PLO that "history will not forgive those who fail to support the heroic Arab *fedayeen.*" But, so far, Iraqi forces did not interfere with Jordanian tanks and artillery moving north. In fact, that day, they announced their intention to shift eastward, away from the battle zone toward Mafraq. Unbeknown to the Jordanians, though, Iraq was coordinating with Syria for what was about to occur.[3]

Amman, 11 AM

Confusion over the hostages' whereabouts persisted. One "untested source" reported to the United States that the hostages had been moved near to the Iraqi border. Ambassador Phillips telexed, "I simply do not know anything about the fate of thc hostages." Yitzhak Rabin would tell William Rogers that Israel had no information on the hostages' whereabouts. At one point this morning, Hussein's palace thought that some of the hostages had been located. "Special units" were detailed to get them out, "if they are still alive."

We were still alive. We were, in fact, sitting in one of the epicenters of the fighting, in great danger of being hit by shells or bullets.[4]

Allenby Bridge across the Jordan River, 11:30 AM

A lone U.S. embassy official walked up to the Allenby Bridge, an unimpressive, steel and wooden structure spanning the Jordan River at a narrow point between Israel and Jordan. He carried a box marked "special foods for [the

Red Crescent] Amman." Inside were canned Israeli goods and a note that read "Kosher food for Rabbi Hutner."

Two days earlier, the American embassy in Amman learned that Rabbi Hutner, "a strict adherent to the dietary laws of Judaism, has refused to accept food which he believes to be not kosher." (In fact, eight other hostages, including me, were doing the same.) The embassy asked other U.S. embassies in the region to "obtain canned kosher items and forward [them] to Amman as soon as possible for relay to the captors." The next day, the U.S. embassy in Tel Aviv offered to do so. The Amman embassy advised it to deliver the food in "inconspicuous packages" to the Jordanian police at the Allenby Bridge and request that it be turned over to the ICRC in Amman. Despite a day-long effort, the Amman embassy could not reach the ICRC to alert it to the possible arrival of the food.

Now the official walked across the bridge hoping to find someone on the Jordanian side willing to accept the package. Finding no one at the Jordanian end of the bridge, he walked about a kilometer into Jordan, where he finally encountered a group of Jordanian soldiers. The corporal in charge was sympathetic but had no clue what to do; he phoned an officer. Instructed not to accept the parcel, the corporal suggested that it might be possible to deliver it in a couple of days, perhaps on Sunday. So, the official returned to the Israeli side and entrusted the parcel to the bridge commander, one Captain Ilan, who agreed to hold onto it until new arrangements could be made.

The food never reached Rabbi Hutner.[5]

Washington, 11 AM

Golda Meir met with Richard Nixon in the White House to discuss the cease-fire violations along the Suez. Jordan was a secondary topic. Both Nixon and Meir felt that Hussein would prevail, and they did not discuss military intervention. No mention whatever was made of the hostages, their safety, the negotiations for their release, or an Israeli contribution to the deal.

At Meir's earlier meeting with Secretary Rogers, however, Rogers expressed bewilderment as to why the Europeans were so agitated. Meir responded that the Swiss were good but that the "Germans and British were awful." Rogers then reiterated the U.S. position, which sounded much like Israel's. "First, there would be no deal with [the] *fedayeen* unless all hostages were given over." Second, the United States "did not like [the] idea" of the demand on Israel to accept an exchange "in principle." And, third, quite surprisingly, he urged that "Israel do nothing under pressure."

Meir reaffirmed that Israel would not release any terrorists. They were murderers who had blown up cafeterias and killed civilians. She thus was hesitant to make promises, such as in the proposed U.S. formula, that Israel could not keep. When Rogers expressed concern about a possible rift among the five countries, Meir responded that while unsure about Britain, she was convinced that Germany would never agree to a separate deal that would leave Jews hostage. "This would be too much, and they would not do it."[6]

Bern, 4 PM

The fighting in Amman of the past two days had completely disrupted the hostage negotiations. The PFLP had more important things to do. Pierre Boissier, unable to fly into Amman as planned, tried driving there from Beirut, but had to turn back. So, in a major shift, ICRC President Marcel Naville informed the group that the ICRC could no longer concentrate primarily on the hostages but would now focus on assisting war victims. Nonetheless, Boissier would still try to get to Amman by car, while Marcel Boisard would travel to Beirut and contact PFLP leaders there.[7]

Amman, 6 PM

The Jordanian army's tactics were wreaking massive destruction on Amman. As Ambassador Phillips described, "I am not altogether confident that the army are mopping up quite as efficiently as they might. They seem to retaliate to being fired at, particularly from buildings, by wrecking the building with gunfire rather than sending in infantry to ferret out the *fedayeen.*"

By evening, it was evident that the army's armored attack was bogged down in Amman's solid, stone-built neighborhoods. The 4th Mechanized assault was being held in check a mile from the center of town. The 1st Infantry assault on Wahdat had met with stiff resistance and an unbelievable volume of automatic weapons fire. And the army, despite a major thrust, was repelled as it tried to penetrate Ashrafiyeh.[8]

Ashrafiyeh, 6 PM

> *Friday evening was Shabbos, and that was the worst attack of the war, when the battle came very close to us. Tanks rolled up the streets very near us. Shells were coming extremely close. We were put into one room and there we sat. Outside our door, a guerrilla stood, sweating like crazy, with a hand grenade in one hand and a machine gun in the other. We could hear the tanks coming up the street firing their shells. It became very difficult, very bad, very frightening.*

> *But during the attack, one of the girls, Foozie (Fran) Chesler, asked me how I was. My answer to her was, "Good Shabbos." In other words, it's the Sabbath, don't worry, nothing will happen. What a way to spend Shabbos. We talked about how next Shabbos we'd be home sitting at the supper table and everything would be okay. Of course, we weren't right, but it was a good thought to think.*
>
> *The guerrillas promised—I didn't hear them, but I was told that they made a promise—that in case anything serious would come about, they would jump on top of us to save our lives. I don't know how true it is, but this is what they said. Meanwhile, these tanks were rolling up the street.*

"There was heavy shelling," George Freda also recounted. "The guerrillas told us to keep down. It was eerie sitting on the floor, hearing the boom of shells and stutter of machine guns around us. The guerrillas said [that] two Jordanian tanks came within 25 yards of the house but were driven off." Locals recall how the lead tank was hit by a *fedayeen* shell, swerved onto the sidewalk, and got stuck there.

It occurs to me now that if there was ever an opportunity for escape, this was it. The thirty-two of us were being guarded by a lone guerrilla, with all of the doors of our apartment and building not only unlocked but wide open and the army only twenty-five yards away. We never really seriously considered escape, because we had no clue where we would go or how we would survive once we got away. When I did fantasize of escape, I tried to figure out how I would find my way back to Israel. It never occurred to me that I, as a Jew, might have safely turned myself in to the Jordanian army.[9]

Moscow, 8 PM

At a diplomatic reception, a Soviet official sought out U.S. Ambassador Jacob Beam. He said that he hoped that the United States had no intention of intervening in Jordan. Such action, he said, would make a bad situation worse and create serious difficulties for nations like the Soviet Union who had interests in the area. In Washington too, the Soviet Union delivered an "urgent note" cautioning against outside intervention. While neither message made explicit threats, the warnings were clear.[10]

Damascus, 9 PM

Many historians criticize Richard Nixon and Henry Kissinger for seeing the Soviet Union behind every Middle East tremor and for not accepting Soviet statements on the events in Jordan at face value.

There is also significant debate as to whether Syria's Hafez Assad initiated what was about to happen. Many point to the fierce internal power struggle raging in Syria between President Nureddin Atasi, General Salah Jadid, and Yusuf Zu'ayyin, heads of the "civilian wing" of Syria's Ba'ath Party and Assad, defense minister, air force commander in chief, and head of the Ba'ath's "military wing." They claim that Zu'ayyin, after visiting Jordan shortly after the clashes began, recommended Syrian intervention and that Jadid, who had a long relationship with Arafat, was the one who ordered the forces to move. Assad, they claim, had lost his enthusiasm for the "squabbling irregulars" who were not only ineffective militarily against Israel, but invited Israeli retribution and sowed anarchy wherever they were allowed to bear arms.

New evidence, however, proves unequivocally that Nixon and Kissinger were right—the Soviets goaded Syria to act. It also shows that Assad himself ordered the Syrian intervention. At 3 PM and again at 7 PM, the Soviet Ambassador in Damascus, Nurradin Mokhidinov, met with Atasi and urged him to send forces into Jordan to help the Palestinians overthrow Hussein. Now was a golden opportunity to remove this vestige of Western imperialism in the Middle East, Mokhidinov pressed, and to strengthen Atasi's left-leaning civilian faction against Assad's right-leaning military. Intervention was a "moral imperative" of the first order that "would be credited to Syria for many years to come," encouraged Mokhidinov.

Persuaded by his Soviet patrons, Atasi exhorted Assad throughout the afternoon to order military intervention. Assad's own military intelligence and senior officers, who had heard the embattled *fedayeen*'s desperate pleas for help (probably at Ramtha) over field communications, concluded too that, without assistance, the Palestinians faced catastrophe.

That evening, Atasi and Assad had a tough, tense meeting. Mutual recriminations and pitched arguments flew all around. Assad argued that a Syrian penetration into Jordan was an unbelievably dangerous and useless act and rebuked Atasi for having allowed the guerrillas free reign over the prior four years. Calling Assad distrustful and paranoid, Atasi accused him of ignoring the plight of his Palestinian brothers who were being mowed down in Jordan.

Assad finally realized that his stature would be harmed more by inaction than action. Despite his reluctance, he gave the order for the Syrian invasion of Jordan.[11]

Ramtha, 10 PM

Earlier in the afternoon, fifty Syrian tanks had congregated at Dar'a on the Syrian side of the border across from Ramtha. They fired at Jordanian positions but did not cross the frontier. Now these fifty Soviet-built, World War II vintage, T-34 tanks with Palestine Liberation Army (PLA) markings crossed the Syrian border at Ramtha. (The PLA was a small, conventional army established at about the same time as the PLO. To keep it reined in, though, its units were dispersed among various Arab states, including Egypt, Iraq, and Syria, and placed under their respective control and whims.) These tanks took up positions near the Ramtha-Dar'a road, about 250 yards inside the Jordanian border. About a thousand *fedayeen* also crossed over from their bases in Syria. At nightfall, reinforcements were still moving southward through Ramtha and the *fedayeen* were digging in to guard the key junction. Late at night, commandos from Syria raided Shajara and Tura, Jordanian border villages further north, and physically repositioned the Syrian border fence three kilometers beyond Tura.

Although Syria officially denied the crossing, it had sent a militarized probe across the border into a fellow Arab country.[12]

HUSSEIN'S MOMENTARY EDGE

SATURDAY, SEPTEMBER 19

Amman, 2:30 AM

By this time, the blaze was dying down around the U.S. embassy in Amman. Everyone appeared to be unharmed. There had been a big scare and the staff had started destroying official papers, believing the embassy might be overrun. Firefights had broken out around midnight as a group of thirty *fedayeen* attacked twice; two were shot dead, and a building in the embassy compound caught fire. A Jordanian tank finally appeared and drove the guerrillas away. At 2 AM, Ambassador Dean Brown sent the embassy staff, who had huddled in the communications center, back to their makeshift beds. Fighting had raged around the British embassy too, and Ambassador John Phillips "passed a peaceful night among the more important files in the strong room."[1]

Ashrafiyeh, 7 AM

As the morning sun burst over the horizon, the cannons and machine guns erupted. Shooting and shelling could be heard once more around the city. *Fedayeen* snipers had reinfiltrated during the night and were proving difficult to dislodge. The army again went after them with its heavy guns. Intense fighting was underway in the Wahdat and Hussein refugee camps, the greatest problem areas for the army. The *fedayeen* claimed to have beaten back an attempt by Jordanian tanks to break into Jabal Amman, destroying ten of them.

During the day, the army succeeded in overrunning PLO headquarters and capturing several PLO leaders including Abu Iyad, Arafat's deputy and intelligence chief. Fighting was fierce in the area and one Jordanian officer, Mohammad Olaimat, lost three men and had his own armored vehicle destroyed. But his unit succeeded in destroying the PLO's broadcast and printing facilities. Olaimat then tried to get area residents to leave so that he could battle the guerrillas without harming civilians. But the *fedayeen* shed their fatigues, ran with the residents, and, using the civilians to shield them, shot at the soldiers as they went.

Some days, the shelling came pretty close to us. This morning a shell hit the house next door, taking off part of its roof. Machine gun fire also slapped into the wall of the house, biting out chunks of concrete. Other houses around us were hit directly by artillery shells too.

> *Fragments came in all over the place. The smell of gun powder had really such a bad odor. . . . Just sitting there every time a shell exploded, your tongue would shake. It became close to unbearable.*

Jim Majer, who went out once to look for water after shaming our captors who were afraid to go out, saw rocket launchers, mortars, 105mm cannons, and possibly even 155mm howitzers all around our house. Somehow, though, our building remained unscathed.

> *I was pretty frightened at times in that place. During shelling attacks, which happened many, many times, we would evacuate from my room into the other room which, as a less-exposed room, we felt would be safer. As we went from my room to the other, we would pass through the corridor with the bathroom perpendicular to it. I had the irrational fear of a grenade being thrown in through the bathroom and into the corridor as we were going through it. I was very, very frightened, really afraid, but I didn't tell anybody about this.*
>
> *The first day of the war, the guerrillas had come in very, very happy and said that, "By tonight Hussein shall be overthrown." And then the next day they came in and said, "By tonight Hussein shall be overthrown." The next day they didn't come in anymore; they were pretty nervous. They didn't think that they were really going to win anymore. All along, though, we thought that they were being victorious. We didn't know that they were really being smashed.*

Though the situation remained confused, the army was in fact making steady progress and gradually gaining the upper hand.[2]

Beirut, 9:30 AM

Boissier and Boisard, the ICRC's representatives, were both stuck in Beirut. Aware of the negotiations shutdown, Mustafa Zayn, the Lebanese government official with PFLP contacts, reentered the picture and tried to jump-start talks. He met that morning with Boisard and Boissier, explaining that he was meeting with them first because, by Arab custom, initial contacts were typically conducted through a third party. Once preliminaries were out of the way, he would withdraw and leave the negotiations to PFLP officials. He would never take himself out of the picture.[3]

Northern Jordan, noon

The northern towns of Irbid, Ramtha, Mafraq, Ajlun, and Jarash were all under *fedayeen* control today. But they were also under siege. The previous day, with the Amman campaign progressing well, albeit slower than planned, the Jordanian army had begun shifting its attention to the north. It had sent two brigades with artillery support and tanks to Irbid and ordered the *fedayeen* to vacate the city. At noon, the PLO claimed that the Jordanian army was "savagely" shelling Irbid, particularly around the refugee camp.

The battle around Ramtha still raged as well. The Jordanians had counterattacked the invading Syrian force, and the tanks retreated into Syria. The Jordanians believed that after having repulsed the Syrians, that would be the end of it. They were mistaken.[4]

Amman, 2:30 PM

This afternoon the palace claimed to have "broken the back" of the resistance. Wahdat and Hussein camps were "subdued," and the city would be cleaned up by nightfall. The U.S. embassy was assured that Wahdat had been taken "with the safety of the hostages" in mind. The army was severely pulling its punches in order "to recover the hostages alive." Its red berets, who were among Hussein's best soldiers and had received "special instructions," were now spearheading a house-to-house search. However, as no hostage had yet been found, a very concerned Hussein made it known that he held Arafat accountable for their well-being.

Despite the pronouncements, the fighting remained intense. At 5 PM, a Bedouin guard at the U.S. embassy was wounded. At the British embassy too, Phillips telexed: "Please forgive some incoherence. A soldier outside the embassy was hit by a sniper just before this conference started. Since then a field gun and a tank have blasted the building to bits. . . . The noise has been very considerable indeed." But by late afternoon, the battle subsided and, Phillips cabled, "the main holocaust in Amman itself may be nearly over."

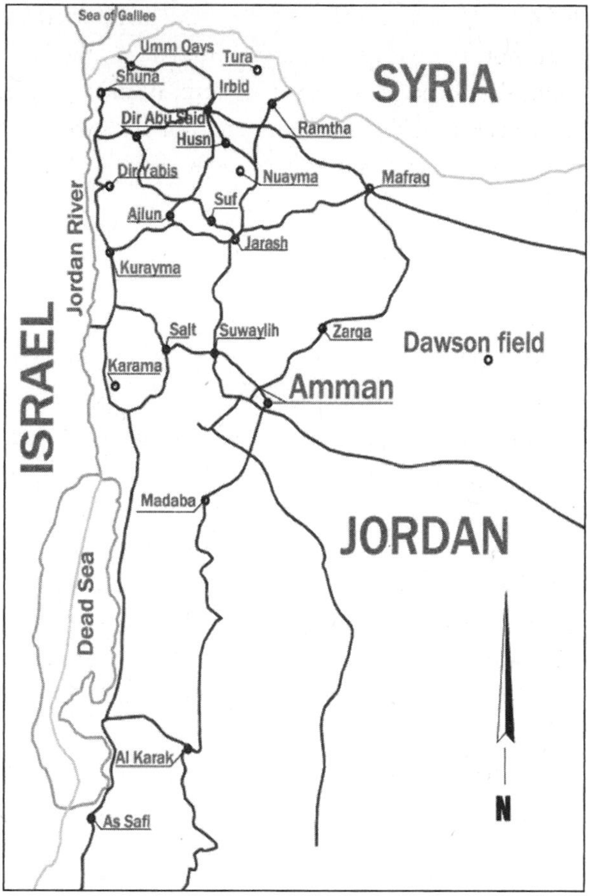

Figure 4 Map of Jordan. © David Raab

The Jordanians were staggered by the "incredible quantities" of the *fedayeen* arms, explosives, and ammo caches they had seized. The guerrillas were "ten times stronger" than the Jordanian army had estimated. Many weapons even turned up in government buildings. All of these arms, the Jordanians firmly believed, had been amassed for a *fedayeen* attack on the regime and declaration of a *fedayeen* government. The Jordanians came to the sobering realization that they had acted just in time.[5]

Ashrafiyeh, 4 PM

In this place, I had been wearing my yarmulke all the time. In the refugee camp I hadn't, because I really wasn't sure what they were going to do to me. But here I figured they weren't going to differentiate between religious and nonreligious people, so I put my yarmulke back on.

> *This was the first Shabbos in Amman proper during the war. The evening before, I had decided that in honor of the Sabbath, I would get dressed up. Most of the time I had been wearing the pajamas that they had given me. So I put on my short pants and my shirt and I was dressed up for Shabbos. Shabbos afternoon, Rabbi David offered me some cake in honor of Shabbos, which I gladly accepted. I had spoken to him a few times about various things: he had asked me about my background and where I go to school; he had told me not to be affected by the discussions that Al Kiburis was having about religion with Meir Fund and Yaakov Drillman.*

Bern, 5 PM

In a "startling display of rapid unanimity" and a clear shift in light of the belief that Hussein would win, the Bern group—including Israel—now felt secure enough to issue its own demands:

> The five governments hold responsible for the safety of the hostages all those in whose hands they may be. The governments call upon those holding hostages to provide information on their whereabouts and well-being. They require that the hostages should be brought to a safe place. . . . The governments stand ready to consider at any time proposals for the release of all the hostages.

The group also cabled Boissier and Boisard its skepticism that Zayn had any authority or was in contact with the hostages' captors. It also informed the two that it was not prepared to seriously consider any proposals until it had a full list of the hostages and the names of the *fedayeen* in Israel whom the PFLP wanted.[6]

Amman, 8 PM

At first, Amman was dark, quieter than it had been in the past three days. A cease-fire that Jordanian Commander in Chief Majali had announced at 6 PM seemed to be holding. A Jordanian armored convoy made its way to the center of Amman, passing unmolested up the road astride Ashrafiyeh. However, the PLO soon rejected the cease-fire, claiming that it was a trap and that the *fedayeen* would stop firing only after the regime was overthrown.

The firing resumed shortly afterward. The Intercontinental was hit by small arms fire. The hotel still had no electricity, and food and water were rationed. Many foreigners remained trapped inside, including Martin Mensch, TWA's Richard Wilson and Claude Girard, and the international press corps. Across the way, all the windows of a BOAC sales shop were blown out by the blast of a recoilless rifle fired several times from the hotel's entrance. Soldiers ran in and looted many items, including provisions that the British embassy had purchased to send to the BOAC hostages before the war began. The fighting would remain heavy all night.[7]

Ashrafiyeh, 8 PM

During the war we didn't have any lights at night. So we took empty sardine cans (we had plenty of sardines) and filled them up with oil. We ripped up a burlap bag, used it as a wick, and lit it in the kitchen, so at night we had a few lamps. We would sit in the kitchen nightly, talking, smoking, and watching the flares and flashes of the shells go off.

But in the rooms there was no light. So whenever Meir Fund and Yaakov Drillman would go to their mattresses in the far corner of the back room—they'd come in later than everybody else, when everybody was asleep—they would walk all over everybody's feet and wake everybody up. "Where are you going in the dark?" they were asked, angrily. It was pretty amusing, I guess, under the circumstances.

Yaakov and Meir were really, really nervous during the shelling attacks. They jumped as soon as they heard an explosion; they would jump and run into the other room. Meir was always the first one out. We joked and kidded them about it. One night as we were about to sleep, a really very close explosion came. As Meir, who was at the very far end of the room, far from the door, ran up, Ben Feinstein grabbed an arm and said, "Gotcha!" We were all very amused by it.

Northern Jordan, 8 PM

After dark, seven convoys of Soviet-built tanks wended their way south to Dar'a. Syrian infantry was on its way too. Jordan's and the West's worst fears were about to become reality.[8]

OUR FATE IN THE BALANCE

SUNDAY, SEPTEMBER 20

Northern Jordan, 2 AM

At 2 AM, a Syrian armored force violated Jordan's border at Dar'a. As it struck out southwest toward Ramtha, however, Jordanian armor quickly intercepted and severely crippled it, destroying several tanks and taking prisoners. The remainder of the invading force withdrew over the border. But that was not the end of it.

At 5 AM, a larger force, including scores of Soviet T-54 and T-55 tanks masquerading as PLA vehicles, with freshly painted red, black, and green insignias, accompanied by troops wearing "Palestinian uniforms" penetrated the border again at Ramtha. These advance units of the reinforced Syrian 5th Infantry Division succeeded in occupying two locations near Ramtha. At 7 AM, the Syrian 88th Tank Brigade launched its main thrust along the Ramtha-Jarash highway, knocking out five or six Jordanian Centurions around the Ramtha police post.

Hafez Assad personally directed the operations from his advance headquarters in Dar'a. Soviet advisers were intensely engaged in the attack's preparation and execution, defining objectives, advising military strategists, and relaying commands. Some Soviet troops and advisers accompanied Syrian units right up to the Jordanian frontier.

The Jordanian-Syrian border area is flat from about five miles southeast of Ramtha to about ten miles to its northwest. From there, deep ravines drop hundreds of feet, making the border nearly impassable for mechanized units.

West of Ramtha lies a fifteen-mile square plain. Although Irbid sits at its western edge, it is reachable from Syria only through a narrow passage, because starting five miles east of Irbid and running north to the Syrian border is Wadi Shallala. With near-perpendicular banks rising a hundred to two hundred feet above its dry water-course, Shallala is an impassable antitank obstacle. And to Irbid's south, bounding the plain along the Irbid-Jarash-Amman road, is a ridge that runs from Husn to Nuayma, forming a crest several hundred feet high overlooking the Ramtha plain. This crest is the front end of a mountainous area west to the Jordan Valley and south past Amman. The north-south Irbid-Jarash-Amman highway wends its way through a valley among these mountains. To the southeast is another mountainous area, reaching Mafraq.

The Syrian move had been synchronized with Iraqi forces. Until the previous day, Iraq's forces had been deployed astride the Irbid-Ramtha-Mafraq-Zarqa road and controlled the entire area west to the Irbid-Jarash highway. As darkness fell, red and green flares fired by the withdrawing Iraqis lit the northern sky, informing the Syrians that the road was clear.

For its part, Jordan initially had only a squadron of Centurion tanks at Ramtha. The bulk of its 40th Armored Brigade was deployed in the Jordan Valley facing Israel. Its sole other armored brigade, the 60th, was mired in Amman. Learning that the Iraqi forces were side-stepping eastward, King Hussein quickly ordered the 40th and other units in the Jordan Valley to the Ramtha plain. Jordan's Centurions had an eight-hundred yard firing range advantage over the T-55s. Placing them along the Husn-Nuayma crest with Wadi Shallala to the north, the Jordanian army hoped to turn the Ramtha plain into a killing field for the advancing Syrian tanks.

Despite being severely outnumbered at first, the Jordanian tanks had in fact by 9 AM taken a heavy toll on the T-55s, managing to check the Syrian advance and even repel the force. Before noon, Syrian forces had retreated from some positions in Ramtha, and thirty Syrian tanks had been destroyed or damaged.

At noon, Syrian tanks and armor resumed the attack, apparently entering Jordan a bit north of Ramtha, at Tura. These units struck out toward Irbid but came to an abrupt halt at Wadi Shallala, as if somehow unaware of it. Jordanian air force Hawker-Hunter aircraft then entered the fray, attacking the Syrian tanks and setting some afire. The *fedayeen* claimed that the Israeli air force was attacking. The Israel Defense Forces denied it but was in fact patrolling the skies. Curiously, the Syrian air force did not enter the fray.

Setbacks notwithstanding, the Syrian forces made slow but sure progress. They penetrated about ten miles west into Jordan, and gained control of the Ramtha-Irbid area. Syrian units also advanced five miles south of Ramtha.

Jordanian forces there were faring poorly, outnumbered and underequipped. Another Syrian attack was carried out at 5 PM by "large armored units supported by Syrian heavy artillery." The critical Ramtha junction was now being reinforced by PLA and *fedayeen* infantry units. "A fierce battle is now taking place on the soil of our dear homeland," announced a worried Jordanian Commander in Chief Majali.

By 9 PM, Syria had over two hundred tanks in the area. The Jordanian forces withdrew to a defensive line atop the Husn-Nuayma crest. All that stood now between Syrian armor and Amman was a weakened armored brigade and a widely dispersed infantry brigade. And if Syria's MIG fighters joined the battle, Jordan's Hawker-Hunters would be no match for them.

Jordan's situation was desperate. King Hussein believed that Syria intended to topple his regime. He was determined to fight. This was a battle for his fate and the fate of Jordan. Our fate too stood in the balance: a Syrian and *fedayeen* victory would raise the price of our release and extend our incarceration. And it all hung by a single thread—the narrow road from Ramtha to Amman.[1]

Damascus, morning

Having cloaked its invading troops and tanks in PLA colors, Syria vehemently denied invading Jordan. The *fedayeen,* too, claimed that the invading forces were solely the PLA's Syrian brigade. Compounding the duplicity, Syrian President Atasi vilified Jordan for accusing Syria, calling the charge a diversion from "the killing and massacring of thousands on Jordanian soil." But the Syrians were lying. The PLA brigade possessed only a few old tanks; the invading force of two hundred was far larger than anything the Palestinians could muster and included new Soviet T-54 and T-55 tanks, which the PLA did not possess.[2]

Beit Shean Valley, 2 PM

Hearing of the Syrian invasion, reporter Christopher Dobson drove up north to the Beit Shean Valley just below the Sea of Galilee, where Israel, Jordan, and Syria meet, looking for a hint of Israeli preparations. As he sat in the sweltering heat listening to the rumbling of a continuous artillery barrage emanating from the Jordanian hills, all he saw was how "Israeli jets, shining silver in a burnished blue sky, flashed quietly over the quiet green waters and the kibbutzniks harvested their cotton and plowed the fields for next year's crops." With nothing to report, he headed south, back to Tel Aviv. "Suddenly, in front of the car, there appeared three tank transporters carrying Centurion main battle tanks. They turned off the road into a field which had been empty. . . . Now, it had troops lining up at a canteen, and tucked away among the trees were a squadron of Centurions. . . . [I]t soon became obvious that I had run in to the vanguard of an armored task force rolling up toward the frontier. There were more and more tanks, columns of half-tracks carrying recoilless rifles and automatic cannon, communications vehicles and truckloads of fully armed troops. The Israeli army was on the move."

Israel moved two armored brigades to battle stations in plain view of the Syrians. Several reserve units were also called up, and units on the Golan Heights—flanking the Syrian invasion force to the southeast—were put on alert. The Israeli air force too, according to the *Evening Standard,* was put on full alert anticipating that the Syrian air force might take to the air in support of its ground forces in Jordan.

Despite its overt and menacing moves, Israel was not rushing into battle. Official Israel viewed Hussein's possible fall with ambivalence. On the one hand, Hussein seemed Israel's best potential peace partner—he had usually maintained good, though *sub rosa*, relations with Israel. On the other hand, many believed that Jordan needed to be *the* Palestinian state and that Israel should actually support the Palestinians in their current endeavors. Ezer Weizman, for example, a future Israeli President, asserted that "now is the best time to liquidate the Hashemite Kingdom. . . . I believe that we should get rid of the little king."

What did concern Israel, though, was a possible Syrian and/or Iraqi takeover of part or all of Jordan. That would be unacceptable.[3]

Amman, 2:30 PM

Shooting continued throughout the city as the army began a major, new offensive. On Jabal Amman, the army blasted away at fedayeen snipers and its artillery fired at targets just below the ridge line of Ashrafiyeh. From our vantage point, George Freda recalled, "The firing was even heavier this day. Most of the time we huddled on the ground. We could peer out a window and saw some burnt out tanks and rounds and rounds of shells slamming into hilltops. The [guerrillas] told us they were destroying many tanks. We began seeing some wounded guerrillas."

Shelling continued near the Wahdat and Hussein refugee camps as well. On Luweibdeh, small arms, recoilless rifles, and rocket launchers could be heard all day, mortar fire sporadically. Several 12.7-millimeter armor-piercing rounds hit the U.S. embassy. In downtown Amman, Jordanian armored units were firing near the grand mosque. Several rounds hit about four hundred yards southwest of the Philadelphia Hotel.

By 5 PM, the *fedayeen* snipers were being slowly dislodged. The army had destroyed over three hundred of their bunkers, far more than it ever thought existed. But the battle for Amman was still far from won. The two assaulting divisions had been, as described by one military historian, "absorbed like water in a sponge in the alleys and byways of the packed houses and buildings of a congested Amman." Plus, the army had to proceed with caution as it battled amid essentially innocent civilians. The slogging would remain tough.[4]

Beirut, 3 PM

Mustafa Zayn had been taken aback and displeased. At 2 AM, Pierre Boissier had conveyed the Bern group's tough message. Here he was trying to create a suitable bargaining atmosphere, complained Zayn, but the ICRC was making this "most difficult." Its insistence on getting the names of *fedayeen* in Israel before Israel accepted the principle of exchange was especially troublesome. Boissier tried to mollify Zayn, pointing out that the fact that the group was asking for this information showed progress.

Now the PFLP delivered its angry response. It was unprepared, it said, to negotiate any more until the five countries accepted is proposals. And, it now viewed the four powers "on an equal basis with Israel" since they chose to link their nationals to the Israelis. It would hold the five countries responsible for any harm to the hostages, as the countries were taking the hostages' situation "very lightly and have been dragging their feet."

Boissier later advised Geneva that he believed that Zayn's PFLP counterparts in Beirut were in fact "very influential figures, among the most important of the organization" and in a "position of authority to negotiate." And, while having the "impression of negotiating with 'rug merchants,'" he was convinced that the difficulty in getting the list of fedayeen that the PFLP wanted was due simply to "lack of organization," not bad faith. Boissier thus concluded that it was "essential" that he be authorized to discuss Israel's openness to an exchange.[5]

Amman, 5 PM

Humanitarian conditions in Amman were rapidly deteriorating, becoming more unbearable each passing day. In many areas it was almost impossible to find food. Water and electricity were still cut off. The fighting was unpredictable and deadly, the number of killed and wounded high and growing, and movement around the city nearly impossible. Marcel Boisard, who had flown in that day, called the situation "absolutely catastrophic." An Egyptian news correspondent reported:

> Hundreds of houses in Amman are destroyed. . . . Thousands of others are severely damaged. No one dares go out into the street. To cross the street is to risk almost certain death. Amman's narrow streets are littered with rocket and mortar shells. Broken glass and burnt-out vehicles are strewn in all directions. Utility poles are collapsing and electric wires are "electrocuting" desolate sidewalks. . . . Hundreds of wounded lay strewn in the streets and doorways. Yet, it is impossible to approach them in order to give them medical care. The *fedayeen* periodically snipe at the Jordanian Red Crescent people who scurry to help them, assisted by the International Red Cross.

Jordan appealed for medical assistance to "cope with a catastrophe comparable with the aftereffects of an earthquake. . . . Estimated casualties, which existing resources cannot deal with, may be as many as 5,000, excluding the dead. All hospitals are already cramped, and wounded are lying in the streets . . . medical aid is required for civilians and *fedayeen* even more than for Jordanian troops. . . . If possible, whole field hospitals are required."[6]

Ashrafiyeh, 6 PM

> *As the days went on, things got worse. Some days you could smell the stench of dead people being burned up in the street. It was a very bad smell.*

"We were told that the bodies of the dead were being burned in the streets," George Freda recalled. "From the kitchen window we could see many fires in a populated part of the city."[7]

Our own situation too became quite difficult. At first we had plenty of canned goods, some of it from Red China.

> *During the war things became very difficult. The food supply got much smaller and smaller, especially toward the end. We had no fresh fruits or vegetables, except, I think, for a total of five lemons for thirty-two people. This was our entire fresh fruit supply for nine days: five lemons. But, whenever we got a lemon, we ate it gratefully. We cut it into a few parts and we ate it gratefully because we didn't know when we'd be getting more fruit and we didn't want to get any type of disease. So food started getting low, and the water supply became very low. Of course, no water to drink means no water to wash yourself, so health conditions were very poor. If one person would have gotten sick, it would have spread like wildfire. Fortunately nobody got sick. Al Kiburis would take some of the water and dump it down the toilet to get rid of all the junk. It became very difficult to go into the bathroom because the stench became so unbearable.*

It was probably around this time that I had one of my most life-scarring moments. Fairly trim at the start of the saga, by now I had probably already lost ten pounds—I would lose fifteen in all—keeping to my kosher diet. A hostage for two weeks and under bombardment for the last several days, I did not know if the ordeal would ever end, if we would get out alive. And with our water and food supply dwindling, none of us knew when, or even if, our next meal would come. I was becoming melancholy, and I was hungry. To this day, I still see myself sitting glumly on my mattress, as dusk darkened not only our room but my spirits, with a bowl of some type of nonkosher hash. It was a life-and-death situation, I decided, and I needed to eat. Very sadly, I put the fork to my mouth and did what I have never knowingly done before or since.

Washington, 1 PM

Secretary of State William Rogers issued a scathing condemnation of the Syrian invasion of Jordan, demanding an immediate withdrawal and hinting at military intervention and a broadened conflict. He also urged "all other concerned governments" to "impress upon" Syria the importance of withdrawing. Then, Joseph Sisco, assistant secretary of state, handed Soviet chargé Yuli Vorontsov a blistering *Note Verbale* that called upon the Soviets ". . . to impress upon the Government of Syria the grave dangers of its present course of action and the need both to withdraw these forces without delay from Jordanian territory and to desist from any further intervention in Jordan. The Soviet Government cannot be unaware of the serious consequences which could ensue from a broadening of the conflict."

In addition to hard diplomacy, President Nixon also wanted Henry Kissinger to plan "some punishment . . . because we said we'd hold them responsible. And we've got to keep our pledge in that respect. . . . I want to have something we can do—not just a big statement. We just go in with a merciless air strike on somebody—even the Syrians."[8]

London, 9:30 PM

Believing that the Syrians were heading south and that his regime was imperiled, King Hussein had ten hours earlier called for "Israeli or other air intervention or threat thereof." The British, through whom the plea was made, were not sure how to deal with it. Foreign Secretary Alec Douglas-Home cabled Ambassador John Phillips asking him to reiterate the "precise terms of messages received from the king today." Phillips sent back a very confused but seemingly desperate response: "Syrian troops massing. Call for intervention by HMG and USA may come soon. King just now ask Israeli air strike now."

Despite Hussein's dramatic plea, it took ten hours for Douglas-Home to cable the following tentative message to his ambassador John Freeman in Washington: "We are at present uncertain how to interpret this and other messages apparently appealing for intervention. . . . We should be glad if you could find out from the Americans whether they have received any messages which they interpret as appeals from King Hussein for U.S. armed intervention." Freeman was not instructed to inform the Americans that the British had received such an appeal for U.S. or Israeli intervention.[9]

Washington, 7 PM

A few weeks earlier, King Hussein had twice indicated obliquely to the United States that he was prepared for Israeli assistance in saving his throne. Now, even before the United States had received an appeal from him, Sisco alerted Ambassador Brown in Jordan that the "option as to *our own possible intervention or other intervention* remains open and . . . under active review." [author's emphasis]

At 7 PM, the Washington Special Actions Group met in the White House Situation Room to develop a final recommendation for the president on whether and how the United States or Israel should intervene, if asked. Within twenty minutes, the group concluded that it would be preferable for Israel to act, with U.S. forces "holding the ring" against Soviet intervention.

Only at 9 PM did Denis Greenhill, the Foreign Office undersecretary, call the White House to pass on Hussein's desperate plea for immediate air strikes, a request that Hussein had initially made about thirteen hours earlier, had repeated seven and a half hours earlier, and that Greenhill had verified unequivocally two and a half hours earlier. Despite knowing the message's urgency and that "the U.S. embassy is out of touch with the King," Greenhill baldly refused to relay the message to Israel at all and, finally passing it on to the U.S. chose to convey it with his own predilections:

> We had confirmation here at 2330 our time that King Hussein had definitely requested HMG to pass on to the Israelis a request for an air strike on the Syrian troops which are massing. The request seems to have been made first this morning and then at about 1830 Jordan time this evening.
>
> We believe there is an obligation to pass the message on but believe that the U.S. Administration are in the best position to do so since Mrs. Meir is in New York. We think that it is important to handle the matter this way since you are closest to the Israelis and will be able to influence them on whether or not to act upon the King's request. If the Israelis do act, you of course are most closely affected.

After receiving the message, Kissinger and Sisco tracked President Nixon down to the Executive Office Building bowling alley. They updated him as he held a bowling ball in one hand. Nixon was determined to stop the Syrian attack and was adamant that any action had to succeed. With his approval, at about 10 PM, Kissinger called Ambassador Yitzhak Rabin who was in New York attending a dinner honoring Golda Meir. In the first known instance of operational military cooperation between the two countries, Kissinger asked whether Israel could fly reconnaissance at daybreak, three hours away in Jordan, and give the United States its assessment. (Despite the passage of thirty-seven years, the transcript of this conversation remains classified.)

Meanwhile, the United States upped its own state of readiness. It moved the airborne brigade in Germany to its airhead, thus reducing its alert time to four hours. The entire 82nd Airborne Division was placed on combat alert—which Moscow and Damascus were expected to learn of quickly—and *all U.S. forces* were placed on a low-level alert. Nixon ordered the Sixth Fleet to move closer to the Lebanese coast. A U.S. navy reconnaissance plane conspicuously flew from a carrier to Tel Aviv, broadly hinting to anyone watching (like the Egyptians and Soviets) that a U.S. attack could be imminent.

At about the time Greenhill was speaking to the White House, King Hussein finally succeeded in getting through to American Ambassador Brown in Amman and asked him to convey an urgent message to President Nixon. Kissinger received the jolting text shortly afterward:

> Situation deteriorating dangerously following Syrian massive invasion. Northern forces disjointed. Irbid occupied. This having disastrous effect on tired troops in the capital and surroundings. After continuous action and shortage [of] supplies . . . I request immediate physical intervention both air and land as per the authorization of [my] government to safeguard [the] sovereignty, territorial integrity, and independence of Jordan. Immediate—repeat, immediate—air strikes on invading forces *from any quarter* plus air cover are imperative. Wish earliest word on length of time it may require your forces to land when requested, which might be very soon. [author's emphasis]

"Any quarter" was Hussein's signal for Israeli intervention. At 10:10 PM, Kissinger, Rogers, and Sisco decided to recommend that President Nixon endorse an Israeli air strike. Fifteen minutes later, Nixon approved. At 10:35, Kissinger called Rabin again, informing him that, if Israeli reconnaissance confirmed what King Hussein had said, the United States would "look favorably upon an Israeli air attack" against Syrian forces in Jordan.

An hour later, Rabin called Kissinger. Israel would fly reconnaissance at first light. However, Rabin said, the situation around Irbid was "quite unpleasant"; air operations might not do the trick. Israel would take no action, though, without further coordination.

There is still debate among historians as to whether Hussein really asked for Israeli air strikes. Even putting aside the foregoing evidence, there should be no doubt. At 1:30 AM in Amman, the British embassy received an urgent letter signed by Hussein reporting his cabinet's authorization "to request *all aid necessary* to ensure [the] independence and integrity of Jordan." [author's emphasis] Hussein had also made it plain in no uncertain terms, Phillips cabled, that he wanted the gist of his message to be passed "in strict confidence" to the Israelis "in the hope that a hook in the Syrian ear plus air will teach them a lesson."[10]

A DESPERATE SITUATION

MONDAY, SEPTEMBER 21

Ashrafiyeh

What did we do all day? In the Wahdat refugee camp, Jeffrey Newton and I worked on a little chess set. The doctor had brought medicines and all kinds of stuff in boxes. So we took those boxes and we made a chess board out of it. We had pens, and I think somebody even had a magic marker, so we made pieces and a board. It was really, really nice. We had cards, of course. Then in Amman proper Jeffrey Newton made a Scrabble set. We had a heck of a time trying to figure out how many tiles of each letter there were. So we took a consensus of opinion on each letter and we got approximately the amount of letters. We played Scrabble with points and passed the time away.

We would sing every once in a while or talk. Some of the kids talked about drugs, and there were many discussions about religion. Al Kiburis who was an admitted atheist got very angry at Yaakov Drillman and Meir Fund about their being religious. He said that when a community is involved, it is better for the community that you not be religious and that kind of stuff. He said that it was causing an extra heavy burden on Sarah Malka who had been cooking for everybody in the apartment. She was cooking nonkosher and yet several people always wanted kosher. But I think what Al failed to realize was that Sarah Malka herself kept kosher and that it was he and the rest of the group that was causing the trouble for her, not anybody else.

During the war, when it became very bad and the shells came very close, we were not really afraid of death. And this was one of the things that kept us going. Because we figured—and I spoke to Ben Feinstein about this—we figured that if we were blown up, it would not be in vain. You know, many times we joked around about it: We saw forty caissons, each one pulled by a black horse, down Pennsylvania Avenue in a state funeral, etc. [President Kennedy had been assassinated only seven years earlier; images of his funeral procession were still fresh in our minds.] We figured that if we were to die, Israel and the United States would come in and just wipe out all operations of the guerrillas. We had heard that the Sixth Fleet was off the Israeli coast and the guerrillas had told us that the United States was going to invade. We knew that if anything happened to us, they would come in and do something. So we felt that we would be dying for Israel. And that was one of the things that kept us going.

Northern Jordan, 8 AM

Syria had now relocated the headquarters of its 5th Infantry Division into Jordan. It now had 250 to 300 tanks and sixty 120mm artillery pieces between Ramtha and Irbid; the stretch also swarmed with a second echelon of equipment, including supply vehicles and bulldozers. Photo reconnaissance indicated "massive" defensive construction, seemingly entrenching for the long haul "to gain effective control of Jordan," but southward movement remained possible.

Confronting the Syrian onslaught, Jordan had only three infantry brigades and 120 to 140 tanks in the area, "pathetically inferior to the Syrians" in Yitzhak Rabin's assessment.[1]

Bern, 8:30 AM

Now it was the Swiss who were anxious. The Swissair passengers freed the previous week were waging a public relations campaign to get their crew and fellow passengers out. Swiss public opinion had shifted dramatically with the war. Eighty percent of those polled favored a separate deal for the Swiss hostages. The Swiss called a morning meeting of the Bern group. They wanted the ICRC to "insist" on visiting the hostages and determine who they were and how they were faring. The United Kingdom and Israel continued to question whether talking with the PFLP in Beirut was "divorced from reality," given that even Yasser Arafat was out of contact, and whether the Lebanese intermediary Mustafa Zayn could "deliver the goods." The group did not consider Pierre Boissier's request for permission to discuss an Israeli concession but encouraged him to maintain his contacts while bearing in mind the group's skepticism.

Later in the afternoon, U.S. Ambassador Shelby Davis met with an unhappy Swiss foreign minister. The Swiss had maintained solidarity and were prepared to persist, Pierre Graber explained, as long it offered "a real possibility" for a hostage release. Yet, Switzerland couldn't tell whether Israel's tough stance was merely tactical hardball or "negative and/or permanent," which would be "tantamount to abandoning the hostages" indefinitely. So, said Graber, "the moment has come for the Israelis to speak as to whether hope is possible or not."[2]

House in Irbid

During the fighting, food was a sometime thing—for the guards as well as their six hostages. No hostility or discrimination was ever shown toward either the three Jews or the three U.S. government employees. They were never searched or interrogated, except for when two men in suits once came to ask the Harari-Raful brothers why they had hidden their Israeli passports. The questioning was neither detailed nor prolonged, however. The closest they ever came to violence from their captors was one day when the group was under heavy shell fire and one Jewish prisoner who was keeping to a kosher diet and was probably hungry repeatedly insisted on a banana for breakfast. A guerrilla finally pressed a revolver against the man's stomach and said that he was about to directly feed him a banana.[3]

London, 10:30 AM

Her Majesty's Government decided that "in no circumstances could we ourselves intervene in Jordan by military means," as it would strain resources, harm British interests in the Arab world, and, at best, merely prolong, "possibly for only a short time, the increasingly precarious regime of King Hussein." Taking its position a step further, the Cabinet decided that it would oppose U.S. intervention and not even provide logistical assistance for such intervention. The next day, the international diplomatic community would buzz over Britain's opposition to U.S. intervention and Prime Minister Edward Heath's intent to say this "very firmly" to President Nixon. Britain was prepared to see King Hussein's regime fall.[4]

Washington, 5 AM

At 5 AM, Yitzhak Rabin called Alexander Haig. Although reconnaissance information would not be available for another two hours, Rabin said, Israel deemed air strikes alone inadequate. Ground action might be needed. "If we're going to do this, Al," Rabin counseled, "we should do it right." And to be sure that Israel would not be putting itself out on a limb, Rabin posed seven questions for clarification and assurances regarding the precise stance of the United States on Israeli intervention. He requested a response within three hours.

Haig immediately called Henry Kissinger. "That's frankly exactly what I expected," said Haig. "That's just common sense. . . . I was shocked that [CIA director Richard Helms] said that air would be enough because I've known all along it would not be, at least it wouldn't if I were in charge." The two decided to give Israel twenty-four hours to gear up, pending a final U.S. decision. Kissinger hoped that Israeli mobilization, which would be visible and take up to forty-eight hours, might alone "spook" the Soviets and Syria and provide time for a diplomatic solution.

At 5:35 AM, Kissinger called the president, rousing him, to recommend an early morning meeting with his advisers. Nixon preferred to decide then and there about an Israeli ground action and reviewed the pros and cons with Kissinger. He asked Kissinger to get Joseph Sisco's input, but before Kissinger could reach Sisco, Nixon called back. "I have decided it," he said. "Don't ask anybody else. Tell [Rabin] 'go.'" At Kissinger's urging, given the far-reaching repercussions of an Israeli invasion of Jordan, Nixon backed off and agreed to the early morning meeting after all.

At 6:45 AM, Haig spoke again with Rabin. Israeli reconnaissance had spotted Syrian units south of Irbid but couldn't tell whether they were security forces or the forward tip of a thrust south. In either case, Israel estimated, Hussein could "maintain his position for at least another day or more in Amman." Rabin also wanted a "political" quid pro quo from Hussein: a promise to maintain order in Jordan if Israel helped reestablish his authority.

At the morning Oval Office meeting with the president, Kissinger and Rogers disagreed strenuously over Israeli land-based intervention, with Rogers opposed. In the end, however, Nixon again gave Israel the go-ahead in principle for ground troops, subject to getting King Hussein's assent before a final decision.[5]

Amman, 2 PM

For the moment, however, the U.S. embassy could not contact the king. The backup generators for its main communications facilities were low on fuel, and it had no secure communications. The radio-phone at the embassy residence was compromised, with *fedayeen* getting on the line from time to time and taunting in English. The only working phone at the embassy was at the other end of the compound, and Ambassador Dean Brown would have had to dash back and forth across an exposed area to get at it. The U.S. embassy remained physically isolated too, as machine gun and sniper fire still reverberated among the stone buildings of Jabal Luweibdeh.

Other parts of Amman were now relatively quiet. Field Marshal Majali announced that the water system had been repaired (though not where we were) and lifted the curfew in northern and northeastern neighborhoods during the afternoon. It was still risky to venture out, as pedestrians were periodically peppered by *fedayeen* sniper fire or stopped by Bedouin troops for identity checks.

Later in the afternoon, King Hussein called a cease-fire in Amman as of 5:25 PM. At about 10 PM, the guerrillas rejected the cease-fire and vowed to continue fighting until "the fall of the reactionary regime in Amman."[6]

Northern Jordan, 4:30 PM

Sometime in the afternoon, according to Hussein's palace, a column of Syrian armored vehicles set off down the road south to Amman, thirty miles away, seeking to punch through the defensive line that Jordan had set up the previous evening. The advance was intercepted by Jordanian armor entrenched on the Husn-Nuayma ridge and eight Hawker-Hunters that gave the Syrians "a bloody nose," destroying fourteen tanks without suffering any major losses. The palace wanted information about the Syrian thrusts passed to "all concerned," specifically including Israel.[7]

Ashrafiyeh, 9 PM

Sarah Malka, 19, was called out yet again for questioning by our PFLP captors, who accused her of being an Israeli spy. The accusations had started on the plane. After collecting the passports and seeing that Sarah had been born in the Sudan, they asked her in Arabic whether she spoke Arabic. She pretended not to understand. After the third time, they pulled out a gun, and she admitted that she did. Then they found the pictures in her luggage of her summer in Israel: one of her atop an Israeli tank, another aiming a rifle with Israeli soldiers surrounding her. Many teenage American tourists in Israel that summer had similar mementos, but it was hers they found.

Now in Ashrafiyeh, they would come almost nightly into the women's room, wake her up, and summon her to an office in the building. Sometimes they took away her glasses, either to harass her or simply so that she would not be able to identify them. They would have long discussions, several hours at a time. Sometimes she would be questioned by several people. They asked her to identify guns in the light of the flares. How did you get on the tanks in the photos, they asked, and where were they? They could not accept that she was just a young American. Her arguments that she wasn't a spy—why wouldn't she have flown El Al and how could Israel know that this plane would be hijacked—didn't seem to faze them.

There were evenings when they would take her outside to the street or up to the roof, to show her what had happened during the day, the ferocity of the fighting, its brutality. Other nights, she would have long political discussions in which she defended Israel's right to exist. She also pleaded for our release, to let us out as we had come in. She argued with them about how history would remember their actions, that it was imperative that they release us without bloodshed, that we were more valuable to them alive than dead. She had the feeling though that they were capable of going either way, letting us go or killing us. But there was a tremendous thirst for bloodshed, she recalled.

Fortunately, neither she—nor any other of the captives in our group—was ever touched or molested. We were never individually or collectively threatened. The repeated interrogations that Sarah went through were essentially the total extent of any psychological pressure brought to bear on us.

Sarah Malka was truly the heroine of our story at Ashrafiyeh. She was our mediator with our captors, bravely passing on our many requests—typically for food, water, and medical supplies—and bringing back to us tidbits of information. She cooked for the whole group while maintaining a kosher diet for herself. And she stoically never discussed her nightly or daytime questioning with the rest of the group, not wanting to upset us.

Sarah apparently made a powerful impression on her interrogators. Thirty-four years later, I returned to the house at Ashrafiyeh. As I wandered about with my Jordanian guide, a curious group gathered. An older man, who was sitting outside a few doors down, walked over and, after being told the nature of my visit, said, "Yes, this is where you were held. There was a Jewish girl there too who came out every once in a while and spoke Arabic. Sarah."[8]

Beirut, midnight

The PFLP's message that Mustafa Zayn handed Pierre Boissier at midnight contained two apparent breakthroughs. If the four governments would accept the principle of exchange, the non-Israeli and nondual citizens would be released. The remaining hostages would be moved to a "secure place"—possibly a Beirut hotel—during negotiations for their release, which were "liable to take longer." The concluding sentence of the message, however, cast doubt on the proposal's authenticity: "These proposals are submitted by the third party [Zayn] to the Red Cross in order to pass them to the countries concerned. Should these countries accept these proposals . . . [i]t is felt that the PFLP will respond positively." Nonetheless, Boissier pressed the Bern group for an urgent response.[9]

Washington, 10:30 PM

At 10:30 PM, the United States responded via a *Note Verbale* to the seven questions Rabin had posed that morning. No, the United States would not formally request Israel's involvement. Israel would have to rely on the verbal understandings and "the fact that our common interests would be served." No, the United States was not sure that King Hussein had requested Israeli ground intervention. No, the United States could not commit how it might vote on UN Security Council resolutions other than to "veto a resolution which condemned Israel for this act of self-defense." Yes, the United States would not hold Israel responsible for the fate of the hostages based on its actions against Syria. No, the United States would not agree to confirm all this in writing.

So, while providing Israel with some political and military cover, the *Note Verbale* clearly indicated that Israel's action would be portrayed as unilateral rather than at the behest of either Hussein or the United States. This response surely made Israel a bit wary. It also showed that, in the larger scheme of things, the fate of the hostages was secondary.[10]

POISED TO INTERVENE

TUESDAY, SEPTEMBER 22

Northern Jordan, 5 AM

The protests to the Soviets had no effect. At dawn, Syrian and *fedayeen* forces tried again to punch through the Jordanian lines toward Amman. The Jordanian army again repelled them.

Knowing that his little air force would be badly mauled if the Syrian air force engaged with it, King Hussein had so far declined to commit it seriously to battle. Now, in the face of the incessant Syrian pressure and the assemblage of Syrian tanks, armored personnel carriers, and transport vehicles "packed bumper-to-bumper" on the Ramtha plain along the road to Jarash, he reluctantly authorized his two Hawker-Hunter squadrons to attack at dawn as "our last shot." Swooping in at half-hour intervals in relays of eight aircraft, they recorded hitting twenty to thirty tanks. Jordanian armor, reinforced by tanks sent north from Amman, also joined the fray.

With the Jordanian air and armored barrage, Syrian tank strength was impaired, but reinforcements and logistical support continued streaming across the border. At 10 AM, the Syrians once again launched south-bound thrusts. Once more they ran into heavy Jordanian artillery fire and were badly beaten, losing twenty tanks. Fierce fighting continued throughout the day as major tank battles raged and the Jordanian air force continued its relentless forays. The morale of the Jordanian military was becoming buoyant as it continued to contain Syria's invading forces.[1]

Ashrafiyeh, 8 AM

At times I felt so restless; I used to walk back and forth, just jumping up and down, moving around. Beginning Tuesday or Wednesday, some of the guys decided to do exercises. They did push-ups and sit-ups. I would go out into the hall and jump up and down and flex my knees a little. We became very, very restless.

Water and electricity remained cut off. Although we could no longer cook, we still ate three times a day . . . bread, cheese, fruit, canned vegetables, and tins of meat that the kosher Jews declined. Whatever the guerrillas brought was in small amounts. Close to the end of our captivity, they brought us a whole case of raisins that we devoured.

Every once in a while we heard rumors that Hussein was going to turn on the water again, and in some places he actually had. So every once in a while I would go over to the water faucet and turn it on to see if any water came up but nothing did. Once, though, Al Kiburis had a brainstorm. He remembered that there was a water heater in the bathroom, and he decided to empty it. So we emptied it out and we had a few extra quarts of water which were very good to have.

In the refugee camp, I think Bob Palagonia had a handkerchief that we cut up into small pieces, and we used that as toilet paper. Then they brought us cotton; the doctor brought us alcohol also. We washed our faces, our pimples, whatever. So we had cotton and we used that for a little while. They did bring us one roll of toilet paper, but it stuffed up the hole there, so our guards told us not to use it. Then, in Amman proper during the war, some of the men had shirts. They ripped up the shirts and we used that as toilet paper.[2]

London

As we innocent civilians sat under fire and with little food and water, terrorist Leila Khaled sat contentedly at Ealing station. "The place is comfortable and I find the people friendly and they treat me well," she wrote her mother. "I get up in the morning and drink coffee. I then leave the room to read. I read the daily papers which are published here. . . . Then, I go to another place for exercise. This I do twice a day, in the morning and in the afternoon. Of course, I get all the food I need and it is good. In short, my life is like a dream here; it is as if I were an official state guest."

Khaled urged her mother not to worry and assured her that she would return home soon. And indeed, unbeknown to her, Britain had put two air force jets on six-hour stand-by to transport her to the Middle East.[3]

Eastern Mediterranean, 2:30 PM

The U.S. military maintained its heightened alert. By this time, it had set in motion a massive naval array. Two carrier task groups—with a cruiser, 14 destroyers, and 140 aircraft—and an amphibious task force with 1,200 Marines were positioned off the Lebanese coast. A third carrier task group, a second amphibious task force with 17 helicopters and a battalion of nearly 3,000 Marines, 2 attack submarines, and 4 additional destroyers were headed for the Mediterranean.

But tension was rising on the waters, as there were now dozens of ships standing-to, with the Soviets intermingling their combat vessels with U.S. forces. As military historians Lyle Goldstein and Yuri Zhukov describe the scene:

> The [Soviet] Fifth Eskadra, increased from forty-seven to sixty ships, took up battle positions and ran missiles onto launcher rails in plain view of the U.S. forces; its fire-control radars began tracking American aircraft. At one point, seven surface-to-surface-equipped Soviet ships were within striking range of the U.S. carriers. In response, Sixth Fleet escorts armed with rapid-fire guns were given orders to trail the Soviet ships so as to, if need be, destroy most of the cruise missiles before they could be launched.

The Soviet naval posture certainly caused American commanders to worry about their own defenses and substantially reduced the number of sea-based sorties they could fly. This was especially problematic since, without landing rights for its planes, the United States was counting solely on its sea-based air power. Plus, a possible "interdiction of Soviet forces" had to be considered, which, the Washington Special Action Group reckoned, would require "increase draft calls, Defense budget augmentation, call-up reserves, [and] go to war-footing" as well as "activating part or all of the civil air reserve fleet, emergency requisitioning of shipping, and ultimately, to fuel [*sic*] mobilization." The situation was becoming critical and volatile.[4]

Bern, 4 PM

The Europeans were "rather tempted" by the PFLP's latest proposal since "only" two or perhaps three dual nationals, as they understood it, would remain captive. This, however, was unacceptable to the United States who would not tolerate discrimination among its citizens, period. Plus, both Israel and the United States suspected that the PFLP would hold *all* nineteen Jews, even if they were exclusively American.

At the same time, skeptical of the proposal's vaguely worded ending and its messenger, the Bern group hesitated to take the proposal too seriously. But it eventually agreed to respond that it "took for granted" Israeli participation in an exchange. Even Israeli Ambassador Levavi agreed to this "without hesitation" and, when asked whether Boissier could offer Israel's two Algerians, he answered that "if he were Boissier, he would already have given them away."

But before they could finalize the agreement, Britain's Ambassador Midgley received a call from London. Prime Minister Heath found the PFLP proposal "very attractive," and Foreign Secretary Douglas-Home felt that it should be accepted. While acceptance would involve "some discrimination," freeing fifty-two hostages and significantly improving the lot of the remaining two justified it.

When the Bern group reconvened at 8 PM, though, all agreed to ask Boissier to get Zayn to specify exactly which hostages the proposal's elements referred to. It also asked him to request that *all* hostages be transferred immediately to a safe place where they could be visited by the ICRC. "Beirut would be ideal."[5]

Northern Jordan, 5 PM

The ferocious battle had raged for twelve hours. The Royal Jordanian Air Force had conducted fourteen sorties in what one senior Jordanian pilot called a veritable "turkey shoot" with the Syrian tanks being easily spotted and hit on the open terrain. Despite strenuous demands by his Ba'ath party rivals and the Soviets, Hafez Assad refused to unleash the Syrian air force. Syria's ground forces, left to the ruthlessly effective Jordanian air force, suffered heavy casualties. Numerous tanks and other vehicles were destroyed or damaged, as were gun positions, vehicle concentrations, and ammunition and fuel dumps. (King Hussein specifically asked Britain to pass this battlefield information on to Israel.)

Harried by air and outgunned on the ground, the Syrians continued to be frustrated in their repeated attempts to break through Jordanian forces ensconced on the ridge. It was becoming apparent that Syria would not succeed without committing additional forces. The tide was turning, and Jordan now planned a counteroffensive for early the next morning.[6]

Amman, 6 PM

Sensing that the climax of the crisis was passing, Hussein met late in the day with foreign correspondents. He was upbeat. He was amazed, he said, at how well equipped the *fedayeen* were and how they had infiltrated his intelligence service. Even his personal staff had been penetrated: his driver and his cook were discovered to belong to the *fedayeen*.

Also sensing a shift, Martin Mensch packed his bags, now fairly confident that his daughter would be released soon and knowing he could do no more where he was. After a war-ravaged week at the Intercontinental Hotel, he and his fellow attorney joined eighty-six others and headed to the airport. Barbara Mensch never knew that her father had been so near.[7]

Cairo, 7 PM

An emergency Arab summit was to convene in Cairo. Although many Arab heads of state had flown in, some key leaders chose not to. Neither King Hussein nor Yasser Arafat showed up, and the PLO publicly reasserted its determination to "fight on to the end, to overthrow the throne and the military regime." Syrian President Atasi, who was in Cairo at the time, refused to attend. Instead of a summit, after a series of separate meetings, Sudan's President Jaafar Nimeiry was dispatched to Amman as head of a high-level, four-man "peace mission."

Prime Minister Heath, believing that the summit would be rescheduled for the next day, sent a letter to Gamal Abdel Nasser, Egypt's president. Without consulting his Bern group colleagues, Heath asked Nasser to intervene on behalf of the hostages and committed to the release of the seven European prisoners. He assured Nasser that "nothing would do more" to enhance the relationship between Britain and Egypt "than that you should be able to arrange this exchange." None of the other countries was aware that Heath had thus unilaterally brought Egypt into the picture and put a concrete deal on the table. Douglas-Home wanted to keep it that way and instructed his diplomatic corps: "You should not, of course, reveal the existence of [Heath's] message to your colleagues."[8]

House in Irbid, night

At night, the six hostages were told to get dressed. The Jordanians, they were warned, were going to kill them. (Given the battlefield developments that day, it is quite possible that the Palestinians may have begun to panic, fearing a Jordanian incursion into Irbid.) The men were hustled across the street. As they crossed the open terrain, they saw on the street heavy armored vehicles with powerful searchlights atop searing the darkness. The men hunched over and quickly zigzagged to the other curb.

They were led into an enclosed, open-air courtyard with no internal walls other than those around a privy with no toilet. The men slept in a tiny, mosquito-infested, basement bomb shelter, which, oddly enough, had a street-level window frame that the men covered with a piece of cardboard. The room was so small that the last person to lie down had to keep his feet on the steps going up.

Over the next several days, the bombings were intense and the men truly thought they were going to be killed. "Once," recalled Jerry Berkowitz, "when one of us was in the bathroom . . . a piece of shrapnel flew in and bounced off the door. I know I wasn't inside [since] I saw it. If it had been me I'd have suffered permanent constipation."

Another night, there was an explosion right outside their building. The cardboard over the window blew in with a gust of dirt. They found out the next morning that a donkey had stepped on a land mine. So much for any thoughts of escape.[9]

Washington, 4:50 PM

Israel was still hesitant to deploy its ground forces in Jordan, certainly not after the response it had gotten from the United States. At a long Israeli cabinet session that morning, a number of generals questioned the wisdom of appearing to be mercenaries for the United States against the Palestinians. In the end, the cabinet agreed in principle to act, but to require another decision to initiate action.

So now Yitzhak Rabin met with Henry Kissinger and Alexander Haig to try to get further assurances. Since Israel would not undertake *any* action unless it could be fully successful, it wanted advance approval for a ground attack in case air strikes proved insufficient. In addition, Rabin asserted, Jordan needed to specifically ask for Israeli air and ground intervention and meet to coordinate operations. Kissinger responded that Israel could have "immediate full approval" for air operations but that "full consultation" was needed before any ground operations; he asked whether the "air portion" could be executed as soon as Friday morning. Rabin replied that it could be done sooner; the timing was up to the United States.

In the meantime, U.S. Ambassador Dean Brown contacted Jordanian Chief of Diwan Zeid Rifai to clarify King Hussein's desire for Israeli intervention. As no embassy lines were secure, the two double-talked. The king "prefers action from up high," Rifai said (in other words, air strikes were okay). But, "if anything is to be done low, it should not be here but away" (in other words, ground action only on Syrian territory). Hussein was obviously not anxious for an unopposed Israeli ground advance on his soil: There would be too much political fallout. On the other hand, air intervention could be written off as a unilateral action by Israel and even publicly condemned.

While both the United States and Jordan welcomed Israeli intervention, neither was prepared to admit that it had asked for it. And no one, it seems, was anxious for this to actually happen. Everyone was stalling for time.[10]

SWITZERLAND AND GERMANY CAVE

WEDNESDAY, SEPTEMBER 23

Amman, 7:30 AM

The fighting in Amman persisted. Heavy artillery fire had begun again at dawn, and considerable machine gun and small arms fire raged for several hours. Fighting continued in the afternoon but was more subdued.

Two attempts to stop the fighting failed this morning. Sudan's President Nimeiry left Amman angry. He had not gotten to see Arafat, who was hiding somewhere in Amman, and his entourage had been fired at. And, at 7:30 AM, Radio Amman broadcast an appeal from captured PLO leader Abu Iyad for a cease-fire and a deal. King Hussein broadcast his acceptance shortly afterward. At noon, however, the PLO rejected Abu Iyad's proposal, claiming that since he was imprisoned, he lacked "clear vision" and could not "represent the revolution."[1]

Washington, 8 AM

Henry Kissinger reported to President Nixon that Jordan seemed to be fending off Syria's ebbing southward thrusts. Jordan now claimed tank parity given the number of Syrian tanks it had knocked out. It was confident that it could handle the situation if Syria did not reinforce and if Iraq did not intervene. But Kissinger was concerned that a standoff might be developing and that Syria might consolidate its position. He presented Nixon with the pros and cons of air strikes. The earlier they occurred, he argued, the less opportunity the *fedayeen* would have to consolidate their position and the more the Syrians could save face by claiming that they had intended only an in-and-out incursion. On the other hand, holding back would enable the king to try to repulse the Syrians on his own, which would be the best possible outcome *if* he succeeded.

Then, meeting with the president alone five times in less than five hours, Kissinger pressed to further augment U.S. forces in the Mediterranean, arguing that "perhaps the most critical moment occurs when the opponent appears ready to settle . . . it is the natural temptation to relax and perhaps ease the process by a gesture of goodwill. This is almost always a mistake."[2]

Beirut, 2 PM

Mustafa Zayn was "indignant and inflamed." The Bern group's "enormous conditions" to get the hostage names and nationalities were "outlandish," he declared to Pierre Boissier. Zayn "almost jumped in the air to the ceiling" at Boissier's assertion that the four countries were beginning to doubt the PFLP's ability to deliver. He "replied heatedly" that he in fact had "both lists" (the hostages and the desired Israeli prisoners), which he could deliver "in 10 minutes." But, he said, he would not provide the hostages' names. The PFLP felt that it had already made a "gigantic" concession in its most recent proposal, and it was now the Bern group's turn to make the next concession. Zayn threatened that if the Bern group did not move on the proposal, either he would sever contact with the ICRC or the PFLP would publicly accuse the four powers of having refused "reasonable" demands.

Boissier, in turn, urged the Bern group for a "more positive commitment" and requested that it sign a letter to himself, which he drafted, authorizing him to enter into direct negotiations with the PFLP accepting the principle of exchange. Accepting the principle was "immutable," cabled Boissier, and the talks were stuck unless the group consented to his letter.[3]

Northern Jordan, 2 PM

After dusk on the previous evening, the Syrian 5th Division had begun to retrace its tracks back to Syria. Despite this promising sign, tank battles thundered throughout the day. In the afternoon, Jordan's Commander in Chief Majali claimed that "[f]rom dawn today, our forces carried out fierce interactions . . . forcing [the Syrians] to retreat in disorder permanently. . . . The Syrian forces suffered heavy losses in equipment and vehicles." Fires in Irbid could be seen from Ramtha. The Jordanian Air Force's massive bombardments were visible from the Golan Heights.

The situation was clearly turning in King Hussein's favor. Britain's Ambassador John Phillips cabled that "the king is extremely grateful for the information received from Tel Aviv. Could you please kindly pass to Tel Aviv . . . the answer to their query about King Hussein's intentions . . . which are to clear the situation in the north if he can, but not pursue the Syrians into Syria. He would be grateful if Tel Aviv could confirm that [the Syrian] brigade reported in Irbid is infantry and not armor."

By 6 PM, Israel Defense Forces intelligence was reporting that all Syrian army tanks were out of Jordan; "187 were counted as they withdrew." Jordanian army units now eased back into Ramtha and the outskirts of Irbid. By the time it had completed its withdrawal, Syria had lost 62 tanks, 60 armored personnel carriers, and over 600 men killed and wounded, including 450 *fedayeen.* The Jordanian army had taken about 200 Syrian prisoners who had been told that their mission was to liberate northern Jordan because Israel had captured it. The ill-advised, poorly planned and even more poorly executed Syrian invasion was over. The bald-faced Syrian adventure had failed, accomplishing nothing.

Two key reasons are suggested as to why Syria's defense minister Hafez Assad surprisingly did not engage his air force. First, he wanted to prevent escalation, as he told his biographer. And, second, he hoped to have neighborly relations with Jordan and could not very well admit to having attacked it. While ground forces bearing PLA markings could be explained away, MIG jets could not.

Iraq did not intervene probably because its supply lines were too long, running five hundred kilometers across Jordan's eastern desert, and it feared Israeli or American intervention. Much more prosaically, it was said that a senior Iraqi general had taken a huge bribe from Jordan to keep his forces out of the fighting.

There is no question that the United States astutely manipulated diplomatic and military levers—both its own and Israel's—but it was lucky that its bluff was not called. As Undersecretary of State Alexis Johnson later described: "Those of us who were involved in planning . . . were appalled at the—let's say—inadequacy or limited resources and capabilities that we had to bring to bear if we had been called upon to do so." What's more, the United States would have had to act without allies. Britain, France, Italy, and Spain were unwilling to provide military landing and base rights, and Turkey was willing to provide a base for "humanitarian" purposes only. And, finally, U.S. action would surely have jeopardized our lives.[4]

Ashrafiyeh, night

Tuesday night we had found out that a large group of people had gone to Cairo to negotiate a cease-fire. But of course we didn't know for sure. The next night was Wednesday night. We knew that the negotiations were going on for a cease-fire and we were very happy because we knew that that meant our release. Wednesday night (this is the 23rd) we were sitting in the kitchen when I thought I heard a plane. And I said okay, we're going to be leaving soon. That's the plane to take us out. The next morning we learned that a group of diplomats had come to Amman to negotiate a cease-fire and I figured that the plane I heard must have brought them in.

Bern, 8 PM

The Bern group meeting was "dramatic." Switzerland had had enough. It could no longer justify holding its citizens hostage to Israel's "arbitrary attitude." It had "no option" but to agree to the principle of exchange for Israel's prisoners in order to obtain the release of the nondual nationals. It would insist only that the PFLP immediately move *all* hostages to safety. Switzerland was essentially capitulating without knowing what it was getting in return, since it had no idea what the Palestinians meant by "dual nationals" and, without a hostage list, it would not even be able to determine whether *all* hostages had been moved. (Even at this late date, the British believed that there were only fifty-three hostages.)

"With some embarrassment," the Swiss tried to claim that their decision was "consistent with" a package deal, since it aimed at the "eventual" release of all hostages, "though in two phases." Switzerland recognized the "difficulty" of leaving the remaining hostages for the United States and Israel to work out with the PFLP. This was "not unjust," it rationalized, given the United States' "special position" as Israel's "protector."

Germany then also accepted the PFLP proposal with the Swiss caveat. The United Kingdom too accepted its "general terms" though not the principle of exchange (which is confusing since the principle was the crux of the proposal).

Israel's Ambassador Levavi fumed that accepting the PFLP's terms would be a most abject surrender to blackmail. What was being suggested was not a global solution. U.S. Ambassador Davis too rejected the proposal.

Trying to avert a rupture, Switzerland suggested that Boissier's requested letter might be a simple "technical" way to get the ball rolling. If Boissier could get the hostages to a safe place, it could be possible to "evolve" a global solution. Without this "little something more" to offer, it felt, Boissier "was at the end of the road." Levavi agreed to the letter, but insisted that *all* hostages be moved to safety *before* negotiations for their release were initiated. And, he requested appending a secret letter to remind Boissier that his objective remained a global solution.

The group agreed to reconvene the following evening. The British saw the meeting the next day as an opportunity to "make one further attempt to persuade the Americans to join us before a final decision is taken on going ahead with the Swiss and the Germans." Despite the twenty-four-hour reprieve, Ambassador Davis sensed that the Europeans were prepared to get their citizens out and leave the American Jews to their fate.[5]

WHAT ABOUT THE HOSTAGES?

THURSDAY, SEPTEMBER 24

Ashrafiyeh, 7 AM

The previous afternoon, hearing that the Syrian tanks were withdrawing and satisfied that the United States had broken the back of the crisis, Kissinger noted that "there remained only the pleasant aftermath of success." Nixon marked the day by going golfing with Secretary of State William Rogers. Historian Alan Dowty wrote: "In the glow of success through which U.S. policy-makers viewed events . . . there seemed to be almost no problems remaining. . . . There is a striking lack of references to the hostages during this period."

But the hostages' situation remained as unclear and precarious as before. British Ambassador John Phillips cabled: "As regards the hostages, we really are in a helpless position because the Red Cross here are not dealing with this problem." The previous day, the French foreign ministry informed the United States that the hostages had been removed from the Amman area before the fighting broke out, were being held in small groups of about six persons each, and were safe. British sources in Beirut indicated that the PFLP might have transferred the hostages to the Iraqi army headquarters outside of Amman.

At our apartment in Ashrafiyeh, the guerrillas came in frantic. They really looked wild. They came in and said that we could be blown up any second. All along during the war they had said, "Don't worry, you are in a safe position, you are on a side of a hill, you have houses surrounding you, you'll never be blown up. Don't worry about it." Now, they were telling us that "you can be blown up any second, write to the president, write to the Red Cross, write to anybody!" So we wrote! We wrote telegrams to

> *Nixon, we wrote a telegram to the Red Cross, we wrote a telegram to the five powers who were meeting in Bern. We wrote a telegram to the press. We Jews were so desperate we even wrote a telegram to the pope. We didn't know what to expect. They took the crew members outside and showed them the area, and they came back really shocked. They saw dead bodies here and there; they saw shells all over the place. They were really shaken.*[1]

Amman, 9 am

The Jordanian Army was now working hard to eliminate the pockets of resistance in Amman. Twenty thousand soldiers were now engaged, moving down from the heights of the various jabals, pushing the *fedayeen* into the center of town. Sporadic firing and repeated explosions rocked Wahdat. Late afternoon was particularly noisy as tank guns and quick-firing "Chicago pianos" took out snipers just south of the Third Circle and on Luweibdeh.

The humanitarian situation in Amman had reached dire proportions. "The town is an absolute shambles, heartbreaking to anyone who knew it before," wrote Ambassador Phillips. Hundreds of houses were reported destroyed with thousands of bodies under the rubble. As Phillips reported:

> Casualties cannot be estimated properly but we have had one report from the Red Cross of between 700 and 1,000 casualties lying at one severely damaged hospital. Mass burials are taking place. Casualty collection is dangerous and difficult, if not impossible. . . . Few parts of the city can be considered safe. It is thought that a considerable number of casualties may be lying uncollected in the streets and concentrated particularly in heavily shelled refugee camps where little protection is available. . . . Some hospitals are damaged. . . . Food even in hospitals is short and getting shorter. Water is in short supply and distribution facilities seem inadequate. Power supplies and most telephones are not working. There seems to be a shortage of medical [supplies]. . . . Fighting continues in some parts of Amman and casualties increase hourly. . . . Urgent action is required now to save lives.[2]

Beirut, 5 PM

Mustafa Zayn called Pierre Boissier to reassure him that the hostages were "in good health, in [a] secure place safe from fighting, and being well-treated." The hostages listened to BBC broadcasts, he said, and could hear any messages their families might convey through it. He offered to deliver letters to the hostages too. But he "exploded" when Boissier expressed his doubt that letters might reach the hostages when the PFLP could not even get him a hostage list. Zayn once again insisted that the PFLP had the list but would not deliver it before the Bern group first offered a concession.

We in Ashrafiyeh were not safe and did not have a radio. Throughout the entire week and a half of war, we knew very little of what was going on outside other than the shelling and devastation that we could see and hear out of our windows and whatever our guerilla guards chose to tell us or let us see.[3]

Amman, 6:30 pm

Unaware that Britain had refused to pass on his desperate message to Israel, opposed U.S. intervention, and was loath to even aid a U.S. intervention, King Hussein sent his thanks to Prime Minister Heath. Even this small gesture, though, caused consternation. Ambassador Phillips, through whom the message was passed, advised the Foreign Office: "If it is given any publicity, this should be in general terms. We should not give the impression in [the] face of *fedayeen* suffering of having been entirely committed to the king's side." The Foreign Office agreed.[4]

Bern, 9 PM

Perhaps because it had asked Nasser to intervene, it was now, surprisingly, the United Kingdom that hoped that Switzerland and Germany would not break ranks. Its ambassador in Bern was instructed to impress upon the two countries the importance of a common front and, at the very least, of consulting with the British before embarking on a unilateral course.

Meanwhile, in Washington, "after careful consideration," Secretary Rogers decided that a "fresh approach" was "highly desirable." The time had come for Israel to become a full participant in the Bern process and for the *five* powers to propose a concrete deal: the seven prisoners in Europe plus the two Algerians in Israel for all hostages, and the PFLP would move all hostages to a safe place while the logistics for their release were being arranged.

Before the Bern group met at 9 PM, U.S. ambassador Davis was able to get to Israeli ambassador Levavi to ask Israel's concurrence, which was not a simple task. Israel believed that the Jordanians might soon liberate all the hostages without any payment. Nonetheless, Davis got Israel's support. The British went along too. The Swiss too, realizing that Boissier had never been made aware that he had been authorized by the group a full week earlier, on September 17, to indicate to Zayn that Israel "obviously" accepted the principle of exchange. It then took two hours of persuasion, "a good deal of argument," and a long telephone call to Bonn before Germany's representative in Bern was authorized to accept a text that essentially conveyed the Rogers proposal. Finally, the group sent Boissier the text to share with Zayn with a secret cover letter.[5]

Amman, 10 pm

Sudan's President Nimeiry returned once again to Amman, this time leading an eight-person peace mission. At 10 PM on Amman Radio, he broadcast a request to Arafat for a meeting:

> Brother struggler, Yasser Arafat. In my name and on behalf of the delegation which arrived in Amman tonight, we ask how we can contact you and the place and time of a meeting, by any possible means. Since the case is important and urgent, I request you to respond immediately. I repeat, immediately. Thank you.

About an hour later, Arafat responded via Damascus radio:

> Your Excellency, brother chairman, staff Major General Jaafar Muhammad Nimeiry: I have heard your appeal. I say: let the meeting take place at about 0100 tonight. We suggest you come in your cars on the road connecting [the] Caravan Hotel, Alia School, and the UAR Embassy in Jabal Luweibdeh. Our delegate will meet you there to lead you to the meeting place. We have instructed the revolution forces in Jabal Luweibdeh to safeguard your arrival and not challenge your cars. It will be safer for you if you stress to the other side that they abide by a cease-fire in Jabal Luweibdeh tonight.[6]

New York, 4 PM

At the operations level, the State Department consistently tried to get hostage family members to pressure Israel. The previous day, a two-person delegation went to see an Israeli embassy official after having been at the State Department. They adamantly insisted that Israel needed to contribute to the deal if it did not want to be held accountable for the fate of the hostages. The two said that they would feel obliged to go public if this didn't happen. Today, a number of meetings of hostage parents and families were held, the "stormiest" of which took place in the late afternoon at the New York Statler-Hilton hotel. State Department and TWA officials attended and made a push to get the families to pressure Israel. Some families even considered taking out an ad in the *New York Times,* threatening to harm United Jewish Appeal fundraising and U.S. supplies to Israel. My father recalls getting up at this meeting and stating very clearly that he was a U.S. citizen and his son was a U.S. citizen who had traveled on a U.S. carrier on his way home to the United States. My father's address, he said, was the U.S. government, not Israel. Others then rose to support him. The ad was never taken out.[7]

EUROPEAN HOSTAGES RESCUED

FRIDAY, SEPTEMBER 25

Ashrafiyeh, 8 AM

Amman had had a relatively quiet night, but firing resumed in the morning. Armored personnel carriers shooting at point-blank range blasted snipers out of their hideouts. Tanks were deployed to clear out an area about a mile south of the British embassy. A very large explosion, presumably of an ammunition dump, shook the neighborhood. Ashrafiyeh and Wahdat were shelled yet again.

Despite the winding down of the war, this was a tough day for us. We had enough for only one cup of water in the morning and then nothing until late at night. Some of my fellow hostages became despondent. "The guerrillas were talking about their dead soldiers. The tide of the war seemed to us to be turning against them. Some among our 32 were feeling quite up-tight, saying they thought they would never get out of this. I tried to cheer them up," recounted George Freda, "but in fact, I wrote a letter to my wife thinking it might be the last one I ever wrote."[1]

Amman, 10:30 AM

At 10:30 AM, the Jordanian army discovered the European hostages. "The guerrillas were on the roof firing," described the Swissair captain, Fries Schreiber. "They left at the last possible moment before the [Jordanian army] regulars got in. We heard women and children screaming 'Khalas! Khalas!'—it's over, it's over—and then there was silence." Then, recounted British hostage Major Fawkes Potts:

"All of a sudden, one of the Swiss chaps . . . started shouting out 'Ingleez! Ingleez! Help! Help!' . . . Then he stuck the stick with the handkerchief out of the window. What he'd seen was the top six inches of a rifle coming round the corner of the gate of the courtyard. . . . There were one or two loud noises very close. And then there was a burst of fire into the little office alongside us. Luckily, nothing came through the door.

"And then some soldiers opened the door which we'd already managed to unfasten, and we were up and out. There was a typical tough little Bedouin soldier. He flung his arms round me and kissed me, Arab fashion, and I must say I was delighted to kiss him back. Then off we went. I noticed a body in one of the rooms: I think it was a chap who'd been killed the night before.

"Then we ran along the lane, and one of the soldiers was shouting 'Stop . . . Go . . . Stop . . . Go' . . . Somehow, we managed to get away, in spite of all the sniping and countersniping that was going on all round us. One of the Swiss tripped up and sprained his ankle. We ran up this ridge and came up against a tank which fired over our heads and scared the life out of us. . . .

"They got us into a three-ton truck and told us to lie down, which was quite wise: there was some bazooka-ing going on round us. At last we bumped away though the rubble—and what a mess it was. That place—Wahdat Camp—was . . . as battered as anything I ever saw in Italy during the war. We then drove off to Amman."

Despite the loss of its European bargaining chips, the PFLP insisted that it remained the full deal or no deal. "It is only logical while death and destruction are raging in Jordan these days that the rest of the hostages are facing now a very critical situation and future," asserted a PFLP communiqué. The PFLP "officially considers the delaying tactics of the countries concerned only endangering the lives of the hostages." Apparently, the PFLP believed that our lives were in danger after all.[2]

Amman, 12:45 PM

Acutely aware of his political and military predicament, Yasser Arafat acceded to Nimeiry's cease-fire proposal. King Hussein immediately afterward broadcast his acceptance. It was to be a temporary agreement until a more comprehensive one could be worked out in Cairo over the coming days.

Arafat, disguised as a Kuwaiti—clean-shaven and wearing a long *dishdasha* and headdress rather than his trademark stubble, kaffiyeh, and fatigues—then flew out of Jordan with Nimeiry. Many Jordanians claim that no disguise was needed; Hussein knew of Arafat's departure and welcomed it.

Arafat met with Egypt's President Nasser at the Cairo Hilton. He and the eight Arab leaders who had flown to Jordan related their assessments of the situation, all stressing Hussein's "cavalier behavior" and the belief that he was out to crush the *fedayeen* at all costs. Arafat blamed the Jordanian army for human rights violations and (falsely) claimed twenty thousand killed. Nasser, hearing these stark reports, accused Hussein of a "ghastly massacre." In a vituperative press conference the next morning, Nimeiry too charged the Jordanian army with genocide against the Palestinians.

For their part, the Jordanian soldiers were angry that a cease-fire had been declared before they had totally recaptured Amman. They also doubted that the *fedayeen* would honor it. But, other than several stubborn pockets of resistance, the Jordanian Arab Army had in fact retaken control of the city. The Palestinian checkpoints had disappeared, and the *fedayeen* were ready to stop fighting.[3]

Ashrafiyeh

As soon as we heard about the cease-fire Friday afternoon, we knew that we would probably be getting out pretty soon. Because, as I said before, everybody would want us out. We were very happy. We got our shoes together—when we had come to this apartment, we had put our shoes into a little cabinet right next to the gas tank under the oven so we wouldn't dirty up the place. There were slippers there and some of the people had slippers or sandals. So after the cease-fire was declared, we gathered our stuff together. Everybody got all their cups and razor blades and razors together into their little bags. We wanted to be able to leave within a matter of minutes. I put on my clothes again so that if they told us to leave, I would be ready to go on the button.

Beirut 1 PM

Pierre Boissier departed Beirut for Geneva, oblivious that the European hostages had been freed. Not informed that he was en route, however, the Bern group urgently cabled him not to make any commitments based on the letters of the previous evening. Fortunately, Boissier had not spoken with Zayn.[4]

Amman, 3 PM

News of a hostage release was first announced on Amman radio an hour and a half after the capture, but did not mention the number or nationalities of those freed. At noon, Jordanian Chief of Diwan Zeid Rifai informed the U.S. embassy that "about half" the hostages were free and in the government's hands. The remaining hostages, he added, were apparently being held in Amman, and he expected them to be released "shortly."

Shortly before 3 PM, Rifai confirmed that only fifteen hostages had been released: eight British, two West Germans, and five Swiss. No Americans. But where was Walter Jost, the sixteenth European hostage, who, it turned out, carried a Swiss diplomatic passport? Somehow, he had separated from the rest of the group as they were escaping. Swiss officials told the British "in confidence that the Jost family is not, repeat not, Jewish." So that wasn't it. Where was he?[5]

London, 5 PM

Release of their citizens now presented the Europeans with a dilemma. Since only Americans remained captive, what should the United Kingdom, Germany, and Switzerland do with their seven prisoners? Yield them as promised and incur Israeli "indignation," or help the United States and Israel by keeping them available for a possible deal yet opening themselves up to possible reprisals?

The British also became highly concerned that the PFLP no longer held any quid against the British quo. Prime Minister Heath sent an urgent message warning "the pilots of all British aircraft, whether on the ground or in the air, and . . . all appropriate British air authorities" to take "the strictest precautions against the danger of hijacking." Swissair too was "in a panic," as it received anonymous threats against its aircraft. Swissair pilots were voicing reluctance to fly, and its board was considering whether to suspend service on certain routes or all operations. Britain also worried about bomb attack reprisals by teams that "might not necessarily be composed of Arabs."

The British were concerned too about a hostage "snatch back." Its embassy in Beirut refused to discuss security arrangements for the hostage extractions by phone "in case the PFLP are able to eavesdrop." The embassy in Amman was advised to search the aircraft that would pick up the hostages the next day, even though the crew would be all British and "as reliable as possible." The freed hostages themselves were similarly concerned, "conscious that they are prisoners who have been sprung by the Jordan Army, not voluntarily released by the PFLP." They did not want to fly to Beirut.[6]

Amman, 6 PM

Despite the putative cease-fire, at 6 PM the British embassy reported that "there has been little outward sign that the order is being heeded by either side. . . . Based on what we can see and hear from the embassy and Jabal Amman . . . sniping and army counterfire have been as brisk and movement in consequence as hazardous as ever." The army was apparently determined to make a final push to take its remaining objectives and did complete its seizure of Wahdat and most of Ashrafiyeh. But the *fedayeen* held on tenaciously to parts of Jabal Luweibdeh, the city center, Jabal Amman east of the First Circle, the Hussein Refugee Camp, and where we were on Ashrafiyeh.[7]

Ashrafiyeh, 8 PM

Friday night, a few of us were sitting in the kitchen. (Sitting in the kitchen at night it wasn't so bad; but sitting in the kitchen during the day usually meant that you wanted to drink some extra water. Every once in a while someone would dip a cup into the water urn and pass it around. Whoever was a little thirsty and wanted more than the usual rations would sit in the kitchen during discussions. Every once in a while if you really were thirsty, they would let you take the water because it was there to be drunk; they tried to limit it to make sure nobody hogged it, but if you were thirsty, you could have it.) This night a few of us were sitting in the kitchen and a shell suddenly exploded right outside, within ten feet of us, I'm sure. And we were really, really frightened because we knew that had the mortar or whatever it was—the cannon that had fired the shell—been aimed a fraction of a degree differently, we would have been up in smoke. Of course we were very frightened.

After a while we calmed down.

OUR PERILOUS WALK TO FREEDOM

SATURDAY, SEPTEMBER 26

Ashrafiyeh, 8 AM

At around eight o'clock—and that means we were awake already two or two and a half hours—the guerrillas came in and told the captain that he could go to the Egyptian embassy and start making arrangements for our release. They told him, though, that he may not come back to us and might not even get to the Egyptian embassy, but he said he was willing to go. So he went.

"I was released 8:30 in the morning," TWA Captain Carroll Woods recounted. "I was taken part way through the city . . . on foot . . . probably four miles and then ran into the Jordanian Army. I was stopped there. I didn't know what was going to happen; I didn't have any identification on me or anything. I had been told to play the role of an engineer of some type; [that] supposedly I was found wandering on the street. They kept me there about thirty minutes. Then a tank came up and I got on the tank and rode to their temporary headquarters. Stayed there about thirty or forty-five minutes. And from there I got on another tank and got to the Egyptian embassy."[1]

Amman, 10:30 AM

The cease-fire was generally holding today, but there were occasional bursts of gunfire. At 10:30 AM, a Middle East Airlines Comet jet chartered by the British embassy took off from Amman with the sixteen Europeans aboard.

Walter Jost had been found; he had sprained his ankle in the escape and had been taken to a "first aid post." The hostages were flown out with an all-British crew to the Akrotiri RAF base on Cyprus. The official destination had been Beirut, but with no intent to land there; all feared a snatch back. An RAF aircraft awaited them at Akrotiri for their forward journey to Gatwick. The Europeans were now free.[2]

Bern, 10 AM

Events on the ground were fast outpacing the Bern group's deliberations when ICRC president Marcel Naville and special delegate Pierre Boissier met with it. Boissier claimed that he had had no chance to read, let alone use, the group's September 24 letters because they had been received "badly garbled." This was quite possibly just an excuse; his unannounced trip to Geneva more likely reflected his unhappiness with his instructions. Boissier "seemed much wedded to his own formula," noted U.S. ambassador Shelby Davis. He was "quietly disabused" of this and was pressed to pursue the group's new approach. He promised to return to Beirut and work with his new instructions "for the time being." Meanwhile, the European countries confirmed that they would hold their prisoners until all remaining hostages were released, as originally agreed.[3]

Cairo, 4 PM

Muhammad Hassanein Heikal, Egypt's information minister and Nasser's confidante, called the British ambassador in Cairo, Sir Richard Beaumont. President Nasser, Heikal told Beaumont, apparently responding to Heath's note, believed that he could secure the release of the remaining hostages provided that the three European countries would assure him that they would free their *fedayeen.* Israel did not have to contribute, he added. This message was being passed only to Her Majesty's Government, he said, who should "give the undertaking" on behalf of the other two governments. Heikal wanted an answer within an hour; Beaumont promised it in three.

Our release process had already been set in motion by the time of this phone call. Further, at about 4 PM in Amman, or about an hour after Heikal's call and certainly before the British had responded, the PLO announced that the remaining thirty-eight Americans would be freed immediately and unconditionally. The hostages would be handed to the Egyptian embassy in Amman this afternoon, it said. Clearly, the PFLP had already acquiesced.

At about the same time, a man claiming to be a confidante of the Egyptian embassy in Amman handed a note, apparently from the PFLP, to journalists at the Intercontinental Hotel, which stated that the remaining hostages would be yielded to the embassy within forty-eight hours for transfer to the ICRC. The statement added that the hostages were being released per the PLO decision of September 24, most likely the agreement reached with Nimeiry that night.

From this sequence of events, it appears that we were in fact being released unconditionally. Phillips too cabled that "it looks as if the *fedayeen*, faced with the inevitable prospect of having all the hostages recovered by the army and thus of losing their bargaining counters, are making it appear that they had already voluntarily decided to hand them back as a gesture to ensure the release of the *fedayeen* prisoners held in Europe."[4]

Ashrafiyeh, 5 PM

Around five o'clock—in fact, almost at five o'clock on the button—we were told by a guerrilla with a smiling face that we were going to leave. Of course, we all were really happy. He told us that the Red Cross was going to pick us up by car and take us to their headquarters. He told us that our release was unconditional and that we should just impress upon people to make an exchange of prisoners—I don't remember exactly what.

It was Shabbos, of course, and I didn't want to carry anything. On the other hand, I wanted to keep all my little belongings. So I gave them to Kenny Hubler, I think it was. I explained to him that it was Shabbos and I couldn't carry anything. So he carried all my stuff.

We were taken out into the streets. We were led out behind the house, where we were supposed to meet up with the Red Cross cars. Now, of course, in this life-threatening situation, riding on Shabbos would have been completely permissible, but it would have been the first time that I would be desecrating the Sabbath in those three weeks. Of course, it was a matter of necessity, and I had no second thoughts about it. But, for some reason, the Red Cross didn't show up and we ended up not riding on Shabbos. [Apparently, the vehicles that had been sent to our rendezvous point had been fired upon and turned back.]

The guerrillas decided we would walk through the city. So we did. We had somebody leading us, carrying a white flag. We thought he was from the Egyptian embassy. He wasn't wearing any uniform or anything, so I don't know exactly who he was.

The Egyptian was not a diplomat, in fact. He was Youssef Azziz el-Dien, an Egyptian Intelligence officer who had accompanied Nimeiry's team as secretary and had based himself at the Egyptian embassy.

Anyway, somebody was carrying a white flag, and anybody who had something white on them raised it. We didn't want any potshots taken at us. And there we walked through the city. As we were walking through there were some people standing around, waving to us, applauding, smiling. It was a pretty strange feeling.

As we walked, we saw fires burning and were told that the bodies of the dead were being burned to halt the threat of disease. George Freda recorded shortly afterward: "We started walking down the hill. I borrowed Rabbi Hutner's cane and converted it to a white flag with a piece of underwear. On the way, we met a man and a woman, both in anguish and in tears. The man carried a baby and he held the baby out for me to take. I didn't know what to do. I stood there staring into his wet eyes for a moment before I turned and continued the descent."

> *As we were walking down a hill—we were ten minutes away from what would have been virtual freedom—when a group of guerrillas came out of a building in front of us with machine guns ready to fire at us, ready to kill us. Fortunately this Egyptian, or whoever he was, was able to convince them not to shoot us. They were so convinced that we were so important and not to be shot that they decided to join us and escort us, which was a very, very good feeling.*

We were taken to a cigarette warehouse on Ali ibn Abi Talib Street, at the corner of the terminus of the Amman-Aqaba road, and Azziz el-Dien left us. The warehouse owner's son asked Jim Majer if he should get the Jordanian army to come in and rescue us; Majer said no, we would wait for the Red Cross. We waited on the loading dock for about an hour and a half, anxious but cautiously happy. We were safe for the moment—the loading dock was under three feet of reinforced concrete—and there were working water fountains! Al Kiburis took the opportunity to smoke a good cigar.[5]

Washington, 3 PM

Six hours after Heikal's call, London contacted Bern, Bonn, and Washington for their agreement to Egypt's offer. But given the awkwardness, Britain again instructed its diplomatic corps: "You should not, repeat not, reveal that President Nasser has made the offer in response to a personal message from the Prime Minister." As for Israel, "further consultation with [it] is unnecessary" because Israel was not being asked for a new contribution and its hostages "have always been treated primarily as a U.S. concern." Plus, the message went on, "[w]e are keen to clinch this offer since it relieves us of many legal complications." As Peter Tripp, head of the Foreign Office Near East department, put it: "by taking the Israelis into our confidence we might provoke them into pressing for the extradition of Leila Khaled before we had been able to get rid of her."

The Swiss and Germans quickly agreed to the British undertaking. So did the United States at first, provided that the prisoners be released only after the hostages were in a safe place and that the onus was on Egypt to get them there. But shortly afterward, hearing preliminary reports that thirty-two hostages would be released, the State Department proposed that the British "wait two hours or so" until the situation clarified and see "whether we could not get them all out without giving anything in exchange." But London was anxious "to clinch the deal quickly," concerned that failing to close the deal and retaining Leila Khaled could expose it to PFLP reprisals.[6]

Cairo, 8:40 PM

Mohamed Riad, the Egyptian foreign minister, called the U.S. ambassador in Cairo to confirm that the remaining hostages—he presumed *all* remaining hostages but was not absolutely sure—had been turned over to the Egyptian embassy in Amman. His government was now trying to get the hostages to the ICRC as quickly as possible. Heikal called Beaumont, the British ambassador, too to say that the hostages—*all,* he believed—had been turned over to the Egyptian embassy in Amman, which then gave them over to the Jordanian authorities "for safer custody." In fact, the six hostages in Irbid had not been released.

Beaumont was "far from clear" about Egypt's role in all of this, whether it had "played an influential part" in obtaining the hostage release or "horned in on something that was already taking place." It is possible, despite the timing incongruities, that Egypt did catalyze our release since its embassy and official were directly engaged. If so, it made for some irony: The Egyptians did the British a favor by getting the American hostages released, yet the British could not take credit with the Americans because their arrangement with Egypt was secret.

In any case, Beaumont was instructed later that night to tell Heikal that the countries "remain ready to consider an exchange for all hostages, but we must be clearer that we are dealing with those who have control over them and can deliver them. Present reports are confusing."[7]

Cigarette Warehouse, 8:30 PM

It was dark by the time the Red Cross arrived. Without electricity, the neighborhood was shrouded in blackness. Just as we left the building to get into the Red Cross vehicles, machine gun fire erupted toward us from down the street. Tracer bullets whizzed by. We quickly flattened against the warehouse's outside wall. To this day I remember glancing up at the incredible sky, saturated with twinkling stars, and that somehow calmed me down. After a long minute, we made a dash for the four waiting vehicles and sped off to Muashir Hospital right behind Jordanian army headquarters in northwest

Amman. As Mimi Beeber described it, "It was really one of the most frightening times. We had to pass through the commandos and the Jordanian Army and into a no-man's-land, and we didn't know if there were mines on the road or if they were going to [shoot] or anything."

We made it, fortunately uneventfully, to Muashir, where we were greeted warmly and given food and drink. How delicious the orange juice tasted. After a while, we were taken to another building in the complex where we slept on cots in a hallway. The hospital was full with the injured, but Dr. Muashir could not turn down the Red Cross request to house us for the night. I remember lying on my cot awake, looking out the window at the sky. It was the first night of *slichot* and I remember feeling a great closeness to God; that His hand had protected me for three weeks under extremely threatening conditions. I felt very special, that I was exempt from saying *slichot* that night because somehow He and I had a special understanding.[8]

SIX MISSING HOSTAGES

SUNDAY, SEPTEMBER 27

Amman, 5:30 AM

We were up at first light, ready to go at 5:30 AM. We had breakfast, and by about 8:30 or 9 AM, we were on a bus to the airport where we boarded a Red Cross DC-6. Our flight plan, we were told, called for us to land in Beirut. We suddenly filled with dread, fearing that we might be rekidnapped there. But then, to our palpable relief, we were told that a medical emergency would be declared once we were airborne and we would not land there.

Sarah Malka was afraid to board the plane. She was terrified that *fedayeen* would come aboard and seize her. Jim Majer coaxed her on, telling her to lock herself in the bathroom. She recalled that Majer told her afterward, perhaps as a way of assuaging her, that guerrillas had climbed in looking for her, but that he had told them: "She's not here. Go, go, look, hurry. Get her." He then knocked on the bathroom door to tell her it was safe to come out. She sat with him in the back of the plane where he calmly reassured her.

Was it possible? Were we really going to be free? Finally at 9:45 AM, we took off, circled over the smoldering city, and took wing out of our Jordanian hell.[1]

Amman, 9 AM

The British Embassy could not confirm until about 9 AM that we thirty-two Americans had indeed been freed and were now on our way out. By the time the American embassy had tracked us down at Muashir and the officer dispatched to meet us arrived, we were long gone. Neither embassy knew where we were headed. Nor did they know where the other six American hostages were. The

U.S. embassy heard from "authoritative sources" that they had been released and were in the hands of the Jordanian Army. The British also heard from Wasfi Tall and Zeid Rifai that "all, repeat all" hostages had now been released and were in safe hands. Heikal too, even later that evening, thought that the remaining six hostages were "now safely in the hands of the Jordanian authorities" though he was not sure. They were all wrong. The six were still very much captive.[2]

Nicosia, 11 AM

We arrived in Nicosia, Cyprus, at 11 AM. The U.S. embassy there had received only fifteen minutes' notice of our arrival. None of us—other than Jim Majer—had a passport; Jim had managed to grab his jacket with his passport from the cockpit when he was taken off the plane that Friday night. All of us were reported to be "in good condition and good spirits," and we were immediately immunized against cholera. We were soon to be driven to a hotel to await our return to the United States the next day.

While waiting for our transportation, I heard a public address system announcement: "David Raab, please come to the nearest telephone. You have a phone call." I was petrified. Who knew that I was there? It could not have been more than half an hour since we had landed. Was it the PFLP somehow trying to separate me from the group and kidnap me again? I told a number of fellow ex-hostages that I was going to try to find a phone, but that if I did not return within a reasonable period, they should call the police.

When I did finally locate a phone, imagine my shock and joy to hear my parents' voices! An AT&T operator had worked some magic in tracking me down. It was wonderful talking to them—and knowing that I wasn't being kidnapped again.

We were then taken to the Cyprus Hilton where we were each given a room, new clothing, food, and as many drinks as we wanted, in all of which I gladly partook. I was finally able to shower and wash off the grime and odor of almost two weeks. I called my grandparents in Israel. The secret of my continued captivity had been successfully kept from my grandfather. Now that I was free, he was told the truth. But he needed me to speak to him to prove that I was truly out.

At the hotel, we were accosted by newspaper and television reporters in search of our story. I talked at length with one reporter and was cited prominently in the lead articles of the next day's *International Herald Tribune.* CBS newsman Bob Fenton spirited away six ex-hostages to Rome in a chartered Lear jet, intent on interviewing them en route and scooping the other journalists flooding into Nicosia.

We were scheduled to depart the next morning at about 9:30 on a chartered TWA plane "for a western European destination," thence onward to the States.

For security reasons, we were not told the exact departure time. Our three-week ordeal was about to be capped by an unexpected, this time pleasant, surprise.[3]

Cairo, noon

King Hussein arrived in Cairo at noon and was met by President Nasser. Their relations were strained, particularly after Nasser's blistering accusation. The summit talks with Arafat and other Arab leaders at the Nile Hilton began uneasily. Arafat and Hussein both wore revolvers on their hips; some of those present felt that neither man would hesitate to use his weapon. As the day wore on, the king successfully conveyed his side of the story. He showed a sampling of the "huge quantity" of documents captured during the fighting, "revealing the existence of well laid plans to overthrow the regime."

The summit lasted into the night. The fourteen-point Cairo Agreement reached at its conclusion was, technically, bad for Hussein because it basically called for a return to the status quo ante. His own throne was put under the supervision of an inter-Arab commission led by Tunisian Prime Minister Bahi al-Adgham. In addition, Ambassador Beaumont cabled, "the terms of the agreement are elastic enough to allow of a plethora of misunderstandings, genuine or deliberate" and were not backed by sufficient clout "to stop fighting if it were to break out again." U.S. and Israeli intelligence believed that the *fedayeen* would soon reinfiltrate the cities.

But King Hussein had clearly won the war and had the avid support of his army. He also had his own plan. Despite signing the agreement, he intended to finish the job that he and Wasfi Tall had begun. The next day's development would essentially give them a free hand to do so.[4]

Amman, noon

The six remaining hostages would be released today or tomorrow, Azziz el-Dien told reporters. "They are no longer hostages, but are just waiting to be brought [to] Amman." He had risked his life three times the prior day to free the thirty-two hostages, he told them. (I can vouch for one of those times.) The hostages were being freed unconditionally, he said, but hoped nonetheless that the Western countries would also free the commandos they held.

Later in the afternoon, both the United States and United Kingdom believed (incorrectly) that the six were now at the Egyptian embassy and that the ICRC was negotiating with UAR officials for their release. Four hours into the negotiations, the ICRC representative informed the U.S. embassy that he was not sure that he would succeed in securing their release. Neither the United States nor the United Kingdom had the facts right or understood the holdup.[5]

London, 3 PM

Egyptian authorities reiterated to Beaumont that Nasser could still arrange the release of the final six, but needed to know whether the British offer still stood. That afternoon, cabinet ministers concluded that Nasser's intervention placed the European governments "under a clear moral obligation to carry out the terms of the bargain." In addition, they believed it highly desirable, once the remaining hostages were freed, to "remove [Leila Khaled] from this country as quickly as possible," especially since Israel might seek her extradition. Thus, Britain concluded, "we should not be deterred from acting independently."

The Swiss and Germans decided to go along. But although the United States objected to the deal—Rogers wanted to wait a bit more to see whether the six might be released unconditionally—Britain informed Egypt that its deal held.

The RAF jet designated to fly Khaled out was now put on four-and-a-half-hour notice. Still worried that Israel might get wind of British intentions and pursue extradition, however, Foreign Office official Peter Tripp sought to speed up her removal.[6]

Bern, 7 PM

Israel—for the first time—called for a meeting the next morning of the Bern group. Feeling vindicated in sticking throughout the turbulent three weeks to its unyielding public stance, it now wanted a "session of retrospection and ideas for the future." The next day, however, Israel cancelled the meeting, offering no reason but probably just choosing to leave well enough alone. Other proposals would later be floated to reconstitute the Bern group (though perhaps without Israel) as a permanent body to deal with the issue of hijackings. None would take root. Thus the Bern group, overtaken by events and ultimately having contributed very little to the release of the hostages or their well-being, dissolved.[7]

NIXON AND HOME

MONDAY, SEPTEMBER 28

Fiumicino Airport, Rome, 11:30 AM

Monday morning, we were taken to Nicosia airport where a chartered TWA 707 waited to whisk us back to the United States. At 9:30 AM, we (minus the six who had flown off with the newsman) took off for Rome, arriving there at 11:24 AM. President Nixon, in Italy on a previously planned official visit, made a surprise and unscheduled side-trip to the airport to greet us. He was accompanied on the tarmac by Secretary of State William Rogers and Italian Prime Minister Emilio Columbo. I believe that I was one of the first to greet the president but saw that the photographers had not yet arrived to record the event. So once the "official" reception line was formed, I reentered, met the president again, and a picture was taken for posterity.

After asking each hostage "where are you from?" the president said a few words to each. For example, when Meir Fund, an obviously Orthodox Jew, approached him, Nixon reiterated to him what had been his guiding negotiating principle: "Anybody who's an American is an American." But when Fran (Foozie) Chesler approached the president, she somehow managed to take the initiative: "How are you, Mr. President? We were worried about you. We hadn't heard from you in three weeks!"

After the greetings and handshakes on the tarmac, the president boarded our plane to meet with us again and to say hello to some of those who hadn't come down to meet him. Most of us crowded around him. He was very relaxed and low key. It was very exciting being in such close and informal contact with the president of the United States. He asked us what we had eaten while we were in Jordan and other mundane questions. I got him to autograph that day's *International Herald Tribune,* in which I was quoted numerous times on the front page. (Twenty-odd years later, I got King Hussein's autograph on the same page as well. I would have occasion to get Arafat's signature on it too, but could not bring myself to shake his hand and ask him for it.)

Back on the tarmac, President Nixon described the scene to the press: "As I started to leave, they all held their thumbs up and said 'Thumbs up! That's the way we felt and that's the way we think the United States should feel at this time.' So from now on, as a result of what the hostages have done, we can say 'Thumbs Up!'" He also explained to reporters what had driven his policy during the prior three weeks: "We had the feeling that their captors might do something irrational in the event that we triggered it or somebody else triggered it . . . I am glad that we did show the proper restraint during this period while at the same time being very firm in our diplomacy and firm in the demonstration of our military strength in the event that that became necessary."

At 1:24 PM, it was wheels up for TWA charter flight 9346 to New York. The thirty-one of us—Al Kiburis flew home to Paris separately—anxiously anticipated our arrival at JFK.[1]

London, 11 AM

Reading press reports about the possible release of Leila Khaled, Michael Comay, Israel's ambassador in London, tried a second time to get a hold of Denis Greenhill. The message he left stated that his government hoped that in light of the extradition treaty between the two countries, Britain would not release Khaled "without the concurrence of the Israeli Government."

The treaty would not deter the United Kingdom from releasing her, but the British worried about Israel's reaction. They were so worried that one Foreign Office official suggested blackmail: If Israel threatened to go to the International Court of Justice, as it had the prerogative to do, the United Kingdom could bring murder charges against the El Al security guard who had shot Arguello. "[I]t seems to me that there is the making of a bargain in this," he wrote.

Earlier in the morning, the British had put Khaled's plane on a three-hour stand-by. Also in preparation, Germany decided to move its three prisoners to Munich, ready to be airlifted with Khaled. Almost ludicrously, the Germans worried that the three did not have visas for Egypt and asked the British if they knew whether requirements for such would be waived.[2]

Amman, 2:15 PM

The remaining six hostages were not in the hands of the Jordanian Army, the Red Cross, or the UAR after all. The UAR official asserted that the six were safe and well at a house outside Amman, but that he had lost contact with the captors the previous day and had not yet been able to reestablish it. Late that night, Israeli Intelligence would pass on a report "from a usually reliable source" that the hostages were still in Irbid, which was still in *fedayeen* hands with the Jordanian army waiting outside.

To Ambassador John Phillips, Youssef Azziz el-Dien was "the last, if not only, chance" of getting the hostages out, as Azziz el-Dien was the only real point of contact with any influence with the PFLP. Yet, in a "low comedy" at the Muashir Hospital, where the negotiations for the release were being conducted, Azziz el-Dien was arguing with the ICRC. He wanted to borrow one of their vehicles to go pick up the men. He had been waiting since at least 10 AM, but the ICRC wouldn't lend him a car. So, he "co-opted" the Abu-Dhabi Red Crescent representative, and they drove off in his Land Rover. But for some reason, perhaps because it was already getting late, they did not go to Irbid. The Egyptian now hoped to bring the men to Amman early the next morning.

London was growing antsy. It cabled Beaumont to ask Heikal why "cannot they hasten matters in Amman?" A couple of hours later, Beaumont reported that Heikal was under the impression that the six had already left Amman and gone to Beirut. Meanwhile, Azziz el-Dien informed the British that the PFLP expected Her Majesty's Government to exert pressure on Israel to be as "generous" as it could and release the two Algerians, especially since they had been taken off a British plane. The PFLP also expected Israel to release twelve *fedayeen;* a list would be forthcoming shortly.[3]

Cairo, 9 PM

Egypt's President Gamal Abdel Nasser was dead. Vice President Anwar Sadat announced on Cairo radio that Nasser had died some five hours earlier. He had just seen off the last head of state following the summit when he began to feel weak. He had suffered from diabetes, cardiac problems, and other ailments, and the stress of the last few days had taken its ultimate toll. As Nasser was the guarantor of the swap that Azziz el-Dien was trying to forge, the prospects of the six remaining American hostages suddenly looked dubious.[4]

Irbid, night

In Irbid, Jerry Berkowitz was getting a sinking feeling. Earlier in the day, he had heard Nixon say on the radio, during his stopover in Rome, that he was glad that the hostages had been released. "I asked our guards if I could send a cable to the American embassy stating that we were still being held." Now, tonight, the men heard the local muezzin calling from the mosque at an unusual hour. Learning that the muezzin had announced that Nasser had died, Woods, Schwartz, and Hollingsworth felt doomed. If Nasser was dead, they figured, so were they.[5]

Trenton, 9:30 PM

Our flight home was uneventful—no hijackings.

We landed at Kennedy airport at about 6 PM. Once off the plane, I rushed forward and passed all the other passengers, anxious to see my family again. I greeted my parents and was immediately escorted by them and a TWA representative to a press conference. It seemed that a hundred reporters were waiting there. I was the first of the released hostages to meet the press. Flashbulbs popped. Cameras rolled. Reporters fired questions. I believe that I was on live national television.

I remember being asked if I had heard the news. I said that I thought *we* were the news. They said that Nasser had died, which I had not heard. Here I was, a seventeen-year-old Jewish kid hearing that the individual who had initiated two wars with Israel had died. I was jumping for joy inside, yet I was on national television. What do I say? In an answer that still surprises me to this day, I responded something to the effect of "Well, we don't know who will follow him as president of Egypt, but I hope that whoever it is will help bring peace to the region." Indeed, Anwar Sadat replaced Nasser and did eventually sign a peace treaty with Israel.

I was asked how we were treated and if I was sympathetic to the hijackers' cause. I remember answering that we were treated fairly; that we had seen their human side, that they were not machines always fighting; that they had a cause but I disagreed with their cause. I was subsequently lambasted by Meir Kahane and others for appearing to applaud my hijackers. But that's how I saw it, and that's how I still see it under the circumstances.

Following the news conference, as we went to our car, we were greeted by hundreds of students from Yeshiva University and other area yeshivas. Over time, I learned of the tremendous emotions that our hijacking had evoked and of the millions of prayers that were said for us across the country by people of all faiths. Those prayers were certainly answered.

When we finally arrived in Trenton, we encountered police barricades a few blocks from our home. Once again I feared that something terrible had happened to us. Quite to our surprise and relief, it turned out that the area had been cordoned off for a huge block party of friends, neighbors, and hundreds of anonymous well-wishers. The Red Cross was there providing free coffee and donuts, a band played, and the police and fire department were there in force, as was the mayor. It was utter pandemonium. When we pulled into our driveway, I got up on top of the car, threw up my arms in greeting, and a great cheer went up! I was home!

LAST SIX FINALLY FREE

TUESDAY, SEPTEMBER 29

Amman, 11 AM

Normalcy slowly returned to Amman. The previous night had been quiet. Civilians now moved around "fairly freely" on foot; not many people were driving. Women and children appeared on the streets of Amman's suburbs, clustering around water and food distribution vehicles. Iraqi military vehicles bearing food started coming into the center of Amman; trucks carrying fruits and vegetables from the West Bank could be seen as well. The army was making a concerted effort to remove disabled and burnt-out vehicles. No *fedayeen* were to be seen.[1]

Amman, 1 PM

It was hard to get the Egyptian embassy staff to focus on the hostages. The building was crowded with mourners who had come to sign the condolence book for Nasser; the ambassador and staff were stunned by the news.

Nonetheless, at 12:30 PM an Arab Truce Supervision Team car and a Red Cross Land Rover left Muashir Hospital to fetch the remaining six hostages. The small convoy was provisioned with food for twenty-four hours. The Truce Supervision car was needed for the "penetration exercise" to get into *fedayeen*-controlled Irbid. The British persuaded Azziz el-Dien to take a doctor with him since neither of the two Red Cross delegates had medical training. Azziz el-Dien expected to be back at 6 PM at the earliest, but, depending on how things went, it could well be later.[2]

London, 10:15 AM

Israel's ambassador, Michael Comay, meeting with Denis Greenhill, was adamant that the "question of Leila Khaled" be dealt with under the extradition treaty and "determined by due legal process." Israel had taken the first step under the treaty, he reminded Greenhill, and Israeli foreign minister Eban's understanding from British foreign secretary Douglas-Home was that the treaty would be honored unless the hostages were released as part of a specific agreement with the PFLP. Furthermore, he argued, any justification that may have existed over the past few weeks to submit to the PFLP's blackmail—due to "human necessities"—had now fallen away. Greenhill equivocated: "It was impossible to say how the hostages had got out until all of them were free." Comay replied that there was no indication that the hostages had been freed as a result of an agreement. Greenhill did not let on that he knew otherwise.[3]

Irbid, 2 PM

The electricity came back on in Irbid. The hostages shaved using the Braun shaver that the Palestinian officer had left behind a few weeks earlier but had remained unused since the transformer blew. Most of the men were sitting around in their underwear when Woods, peering out of the courtyard door, told them that the Red Cross was across the street. Berkowitz went to check it out. The Red Crescent had been there frequently, but this time it was indeed a Red Cross vehicle, Berkowitz confirmed. Hoping that this might be it, they all dressed.

After what felt like an eternity, a delegation crossed the street: a bunch of guerrillas, Azziz el-Dien, and a couple of Red Cross representatives, who, according to Berkowitz, appeared "scared out of their minds." Now that the six men had cleaned themselves up, their scruffy guards looked more like hostages than they did, and the Red Cross men seemed confused at first.

What followed was a bizarre scene, as if out of a Fellini movie. The guerrillas made the six men a farewell party complete with juice, handshakes, photographs, and even an invitation by Hollingsworth for the guerrillas to come visit him in Europe. Azziz el-Dien told the men that they were being released unconditionally and urged them to "tell about their wonderful treatment."

The road out of Irbid to the highway was saturated with land mines, many of which were clearly visible. Two guides—one PFLP and one Jordanian army—walked alongside the vehicles to help navigate safe passage.

At about 6:30 PM, the six men arrived at Muashir Hospital where they met with the U.S. ambassador, TWA representatives, and the press. A TWA representative poured whiskey for the men. "In excellent spirits," pronounced the ambassador. "Some lost weight, but other than that in good shape, rapturous at being back with Americans . . . No problems, no dwelling on [the] past, all looking forward to future [of] everything OK. Neat suits, clean shirts, shined shoes."

Hollingsworth, who acted as their spokesman, said, "We are tired," and the men were put up for the night at Muashir. A Middle East Airlines Caravelle jet was scheduled to fly them out the next morning. They asked TWA to make an "immediate onward connection" for them to New York and to do everything possible to get the Jewish hostages home for Rosh Hashanah, which began stateside about thirty hours later.[4]

EUROPEAN CAPITULATION AND CULMINATION

WEDNESDAY, SEPTEMBER 30

Amman, 7:40 AM

At about 7:40 AM, the six hostages boarded the TWA-chartered plane. At 8:25 AM takeoff, it too was officially slated to land in Beirut, but its destination was changed to Cyprus and it landed in Nicosia at 9:30 AM. An hour later, the men flew out on a Cyprus Airways charter, arriving in Athens at around noon. Hollingsworth left the group there to fly to Berlin where his wife was. The others were scheduled to depart at 12:45 PM on TWA flight 881 and to arrive in New York at 5:25 PM. Would the three Orthodox Jews make it home by sunset at 6:40 PM?

They told a TWA official about the problem. He gave them a choice—stay in Athens, fly to Israel, or try to get to New York—but he assured them that they would get back to New York in time to get somewhere before sundown. They chose to try, and the plane took a faster but more fuel-consuming, route across the Atlantic, making an unscheduled fueling stop in Lisbon.

The five men finally arrived at Kennedy airport before sundown. The Harari-Raful brothers quickly went away to put on tefillin, which they had not donned in over three weeks, before heading home. Schwartz and Woods went in for an immediate debriefing. Berkowitz gave a short press conference. Then, under police escort to White Plains, with lights whirling and sirens wailing, Berkowitz arrived at his relatives' home just minutes before the onset of a very happy New Year.[1]

Amman, 12:15 PM

With all hostages now out of the country, Azziz el-Dien turned over to the American and British embassies in Amman the names of fifty-six detainees whom the PFLP wanted released as a quid pro quo for the release of the fifty-six hostages held after the planes were blown up. The list included the seven *fedayeen* in Europe, the two Algerians and ten Lebanese soldiers in Israel, and another thirty-six *fedayeen* in Israeli jails, characterized by Israeli Intelligence as "star performers." Azziz el-Dien announced that if the demands were met, the PLO would give its "word of honor" that there would be no future hijackings. "Frustration of this effort," however, could convince the *fedayeen* that "escalating violence is [the] only way to achieve results."

Less than two hours after the U.S. embassy cabled the list to the State Department, State instructed Ambassador Brown to "immediately" contact Azziz el-Dien to say that the United States government could not accept the list, would not serve as a conduit for PFLP demands, and would have nothing "directly" to do with the matter.

The British embassy in Amman, on the other hand, did accept the list. The next morning, the British Foreign Office sent it in an envelope to the Israeli embassy in London. The Israeli embassy used "the best means at our disposal" to open the envelope, photocopy the list, and reseal the envelope. It then politely but poignantly returned the "unopened" envelope to the British Government, basically telling the PFLP to shove it up its mailbox.[2]

Lyneham RAF Air Force Base, 9 PM

The RAF Comet revved its engines. Ignoring Israel's extradition treaty and protests, Britain boarded Leila Khaled onto the plane. The plane took off and stopped in Munich and Zurich to pick up the terrorists freed by Germany and Switzerland. After a nine-and-a-half-hour journey, the plane arrived in Cairo at 7:25 AM the next morning. The seven terrorists were ushered quickly off the plane, with Khaled in the lead. After a "most cursory reception" by the Egyptians, the *fedayeen* were "swept away in cars" accompanied, it was believed, by a Palestinian greeting party.

Within half an hour of arriving in Cairo, the six guerrillas, who had murdered and maimed, and Leila Khaled, who with her compatriots had terrorized nearly eight hundred innocent air travelers and triggered a devastating civil war in Jordan, drove off, scot-free.[3]

EPILOGUE

Sitting with my former captor, Bassam Abu-Sharif, having a beer at the American Colony Hotel in Jerusalem in May 2004, I couldn't help but reflect as to how much had changed and yet how much had not. Bassam, one of the masterminds of the hijackings, today preaches coexistence with Israel. Over ninety-five percent of Palestinian Arabs in Gaza and the West Bank are now self-governed. Yet Palestinian terrorism persists and the PFLP, Hamas, other Palestinian groups, and even many in Fatah remain adamantly committed to Israel's destruction.

The PFLP had hoped that the hijackings would bring recognition and glory to the Palestinian movement. In the end, the Palestinians were the main losers of the civil war that the hijackings engendered. Their image suffered, they were decimated militarily and politically, and they were demoralized. The hijackings were arguably the beginning of the end of Jordan's and Egypt's support for the armed Palestinian struggle. About a thousand guerrillas and a thousand to fifteen hundred civilians were killed, with five to ten thousand wounded. Most of those civilians were probably Palestinians, as it was their neighborhoods that were shelled most heavily.

This was far from the end for the PLO. Taking advantage of the leadership vacuum in the Arab world following Nasser's death, King Hussein sought to root the *fedayeen* out of his country. He appointed Wasfi Tall prime minister. Tall, the ultimate Jordanian royalist, was the archenemy of the *fedayeen* and known to brook no challenges from them to government authority. By the summer of 1971, he and the Jordanian army had totally eviscerated the PLO in Jordan, essentially forcing it out of the kingdom. Yasser Arafat and the PLO would shortly thereafter set up shop in Lebanon.

Because September 1970 was the start of their woes in Jordan, Palestinians began referring to it as Black September; for the same reason, many Jordanians refer to it as White September. In March 1971, Fatah, with Arafat's blessing, set up "a secret apparatus" to try again to topple Hussein's regime. Assassination was its method of choice. "Black September" was the cover name adopted. Black September's first spectacular act was murdering

Tall in November 1971 in Cairo. Its most infamous act was murdering eleven Israeli athletes at the 1972 Munich Olympics.

In addition to ridding Jordan of the PLO, the hijackings led to other major changes in the Middle East's political landscape. After Nasser died on September 28, Anwar Sadat became president. Six weeks later, in early November 1970, Hafez Assad would use Syria's abortive invasion of Jordan as his pretext for ousting President Atasi and taking total control of Syria. Two months later, an emboldened King Hussein compelled Iraq to remove its forces from Jordan.

In an ironic twist, Israel was a prime beneficiary of the whole episode. Its hostage negotiation strategy was vindicated. But more importantly, its willingness to engage the Syrian forces who invaded Jordan, though not motivated by pure altruism toward Hussein, enhanced its relationship with both Jordan and the United States. Jordan-Israel relations, though still *sub rosa*, became appreciably warmer. By the beginning of November 1970, Hussein had already held several meetings with Israel in London and Tehran. Three years later, in October 1973, King Hussein secretly flew to Israel to personally warn Prime Minister Golda Meir of the impending attack by Egypt and Syria.

Israel's willingness to cooperate closely with the United States in protecting American interests in the region altered its image in the eyes of many officials in Washington. Israel was now considered a partner, a valuable ally in a vital region during times of crisis. As Yitzhak Rabin later recalled, Henry Kissinger phoned him to convey a message from Nixon. "The president will never forget Israel's role in preventing the deterioration in Jordan and in blocking the attempt to overturn the regime there. He said that the United States is fortunate in having an ally like Israel in the Middle East." Israel's conduct launched a "strategic relationship" with the United States which persists to this day.

The PFLP failed on a personal level, too. At least fifteen of the seventy-eight American Jews who had boarded our plane decided over time to move to Israel. That includes my mother (and father), two siblings, and me. It took time to get over the nightmares, the quaking upon seeing flashing lights, the cold sweat each time I flew. But I pushed myself to overcome my anxieties—starting college immediately, taking TWA flight 741 out of Frankfurt again 14 years later, and eventually returning to Jordan twice. I have lived essentially a normal and successful life—I am a business strategist, have been married for thirty-three years, have three married children and six grandchildren—but I think about my experience in Jordan almost every day. My family and I celebrate a day of thanksgiving every anniversary of my miraculous release from captivity. It bothered me that no book had ever been written fully documenting the month. I have now written that history. It is said that history is written by the victors.[1]

NOTES

"We Are All *Fedayeen*"

1. Oren, p. 306; Cobban, p. 46; Salibi, p. 165; Sayigh, p. 143; Abu-Odeh, p. 147; Quandt et al., *Politics,* pp. 50–54, 75; Lunt, p. 78; FBIS, 9/16/70, pp. A2–3; MFA to Washington and New York, 3/9/70, MFA 4548/18.
2. Abu-Sharif, pp. 56–57; Cobban, pp. 25, 28; Quandt et al., *Politics,* pp. 72–74.
3. Quandt et al., *Politics,* pp. 66, 76–77; Shemesh, pp. 129, 135, 137; *Haaretz,* "Terrorist Attempt to Capture Broadcast Station in Amman Fails," 9/8/70, p. 2; Cobban, p. 50; El-Edroos, p. 437, 442, 445–47; Brown, p. 43; "Arafat Berates Amman Officials," *New York Times,* 9/3/70; Lunt, pp. 118, 125–28; Becker, p. 65; Hart, p. 307; Khalaf, p. 76; De Atkine interview; Horan; Sayigh, p. 252; Jordan interviews.
4. Quandt, *Peace Process,* p. 74; Quandt et al., *Politics,* p. 125; Rabin, p. 179; "Popular Front Most Militant Commando Group," *New York Times,* 9/10/70; "Guerrillas Warn Jordan's Regime," *New York Times,* 9/1/70; Garfinkle, p. 160; FBIS, 9/9/70, p. A6; El-Edroos, p. 446; Lunt, pp. 125, 131, 134; MER, pp. 834, 836; Amman 0940Z, 9/2/70, USSDA 2415; "Arafat Berates Amman Officials," *New York Times,* 9/3/70; Amman #4335, 9/4/70, USSDA 2415; Amman 1120Z, 9/6/70, USSDA 2415; FBIS, 9/8/70 p. D1.

"This Is Your New Captain Speaking."

1. MER, p. 837; MFA #127, 9/6/70, MFA 4464/1; Majer interview; Swinkels; Sara Raab deposition; Freda, *National Observer,* p. 1; Morse; Rosenrauch; *Hijacked* transcript; *Trenton (NJ) Sunday Times Advertiser,* 9/13/70, Part Two, p. 1; Bonn #10203, 9/6/70, USSDA 608; Paris #12039 and State #146334, 9/6/70, USSDA 683; Tel Aviv to British Ministry of Defense, 9/8/70, FCO 14/778; *Newsweek,* 9/21/70, p. 24; Frankfurt #3264, 9/7/70, USSDA 683; "TWA Passenger List," *New York Times,* 9/10 or 9/11/70; Amman #081125 to Ministry of Defense, 9/8/70, FCO 14/778; Minutes of 9/7/70 Ministers Meeting, 9/8/70, PREM 15/201; MFA #191, 9/8/70, MFA 4464/1.
2. *Haaretz,* 9/7/70, pp. 1–2; Zurich to MFA, 9/10/70, and #44 to MFA, 9/11/70, MFA 4464/2; Amman #4347, 9/6/70, #4359, 9/7/70, and #4424, 9/8/70, USSDA 665; Geneva #3054, 9/7/70, and Amman #4436, 9/8/70, USSDA 683;

State #132923, 8/14/70, USSDA 2388; analysis of passenger manifests and passenger dispositions; "Former Hostages Arrive in Nicosia," *New York Times,* 9/12/70; FBIS, 9/9/70, p. A2; Response of the Federal Council concerning the hijackings, 10/8/70, FCO 14/786; Zurich #41 to MFA, 8/20/70, MFA 4629/28.

3. *Haaretz,* 9/7/70, p. 1, 9/10/70, p. 2, 9/13/70, p. 2, and 9/22/70, p. 3; MFA #42 and #117 to London and #127, 9/6/70, #57 to London, 9/7/70, and #100 to London, 9/8/70, MFA 4464/1; London #29 to MFA, 9/7/70, and #100 to MFA, 9/8/70, MFA 4464/1; Khaled, pp. 184–85, 187–90; Bar-Lev interview; Bar-Lev, speech to the International Federation of Air Line Pilots' Associations meeting, 9/11/01; Robert L. Pollock, "'We Are Not Going To Be Hijacked'," *Wall Street Journal,* 9/25/01; Snow and Phillips, p. 80; Note re The Hijacking Crisis, 9/18/70, PREM 15/203; FCO ##13–15 to Montreal, 9/6/70, PREM 15/201; Note to Hanbury-Tenison, 9/11/70, FCO 14/786; Medical Report on Shlomo Vider, 9/9/70, MFA 6603/19; *UK Confidential;* Rosenrauch; Reuters Report, 9/14/70, RAW; London #7320 and #7325, 9/12/70, USSDA 608; Curtis cable to Commander, 9/12/70, FCO 14/780; Bulloch, p. 58; Abu-Sharif, p. 81. British police had a different version about how the two guards got onto the other El Al plane. Vider was admitted to Hillington Hospital at about 2:30 PM. He was resuscitated and at 3 PM taken to the operating room where 2.5 liters of blood resulting from internal bleeding were aspirated and several internal wounds located and closed up. He had taken two bullets in the front of the abdomen, one in the right shoulder, one in the left leg, and one just below the left ear.

4. Burton debrief, FCO 14/778; Sindall, memo re Hijacking of BOAC VC10, 9/13/70, FCO 14/780; *Haaretz,* 9/7/70, p. 2, 9/8/70, p. 1, 9/14/70, p. 1, and 9/17/70, p. 2; *Egyptian Gazette,* 9/7/70, p. 1, and 9/8/70, p. 3; Snow and Phillips, pp. 19–21; Ferruggio; Bar-Lev interview; Cronkite; Abu-Sharif, pp. 81–82; Haig, Memorandum for the President, 9/6/70, NPMC Haig 971; Clark, White House Situation Room Duty Officer, Memorandum re Aircraft Hijackings, 9/6/70, 1800EDT, NPMC NSC 330; MER, p. 837; Beirut #7405, #7411, #7419, and #7420, 9/6/70, and #7421 and #7437, 9/7/70, USSDA 683; Beirut #7409, 9/6/70, USSDA 608; Beirut #7797, 9/16/70, USSDA 609; Beirut #7425, 9/7/70, NPMC NSC 330; Cairo #2033 and #2037, 9/7/70, NPMC NSC 330; Cairo #958 to FCO, 9/7/70, FCO 14/778; Khaled, pp. 181–183, 187; Aviation Safety Network Accident Description, //http:aviation-safety.net/database. The Israeli Shin Bet, red-faced over its multiple lapses that day, reconstructs somewhat differently how the two additional hijackers ended up on the Pan Am flight. Almost all evidence supports Bar-Lev's description. Ferruggio claims that they were actually still 1,300 feet in the air, not a hundred, when the fuse was lit, and that it was a three-minute fuse.

5. Bern #2248, 9/14/70, NPMC NSC 330; Sayigh, p. 239; e-mails from Vassil Yanco, 8/7–8/03; Geneva #3054, 9/7/70, USSDA 683; Amman #4351 and #4353, 9/6/70, and #4355, 9/7/70, USSDA 683; FBIS, 9/9/70, p. A4; State #146354, 9/6/70, USSDA 683; Bonn #10211, 9/7/70, USSDA 683; Tel Aviv #4870, 9/7/70, USSDA 2415; Martin, NMCC Memorandum for the Record re Aircraft Hijackings, 9/6/70, 2300EDT, NPMC NSC 330; Ajeilat interview;

Makboul interview; JAA Operations Log, items 5–11 and 13–15, 9/6/70, and item 17, 9/7/70, JAAMA; MER, p. 839.

"Am I Leaving One Orphan Or Two?"

1. *Newsweek,* 9/21/70, p. 24; Swinkels; Bettie McCarthy-Kraut e-mail to author, 11/20/03; Majer interview; Sara Raab deposition, p. 69; Rosenrauch; "Freed U.S. Citizens Tell of Their Fears," *New York Times,* 9/14/70, p. 1; Tel Aviv to Ministry of Defense, 9/8/70, FCO 14/778; *Haaretz,* 9/9/70, p. 2.
2. "Hijacking: World Pact Seems The Cure," *New York Times,* 9/7/70, p. 1; "Popular Front Most Militant Commando Group," *New York Times,* 9/10/70; "Hijacking Mastermind Is No. 2 in the Popular Front," *New York Times,* 9/14/70; Cobban, p. 146; Cooley, p. 148; Convention on Offences and Certain Other Acts Committed on Board Aircraft, Signed at Tokyo on 9/14/63, http://www.kln.gov.my/TRITi/84/offences%20on%20board%20aircraft84.pdf, 1/5/04; list of Signatories to the Convention on Offences and Certain Other Acts Committed on Board Aircraft, Signed at Tokyo on 9/14/63, http://www.icao.int/icao/en/leb/Tokyo.htm, 1/5/04; Abu-Sharif, pp. 59–60, 64–65; FBIS, 9/16/70, pp. A2–3; list of terror attacks against civil aviation and El Al offices, MFA, 9/7/70, MFA 3210/7; Beirut #7442, 9/7/70, NPMC NSC 330; Tel Aviv #4877, 9/7/70, USSDA 683; *Haaretz,* 9/8/70, p. 2; "Seek Release of All," *TWA Today* 33, no. 18, 9/21/70. The PFLP also experimented, long before 9/11, with loading a plane with explosives in order to crash it into a Tel Aviv skyscraper.
3. MER, p. 838; FBIS, 9/8/70, pp. A1 and A3; Amman #4377, 9/7/70, USSDA 683; Abu-Odeh interview.
4. Sara Raab deposition, p. 55.
5. "US Aide Seized in Jordan Capital," *New York Times,* 9/8/70; Beirut #7429, 9/7/70, USSDA 683; Amman #4373, 9/7/70, USSDA 2415; MER, p. 837; FBIS, 9/9/70, p. D5; NEA Working Group Situation Report #2, 9/7/70, NPMC NSC 330.
6. Bern #220 to FCO, 9/7/70, PREM 15/201; Geneva #34, 9/8/70, MFA 4464/1; Haig, Memorandum for the President, 9/6/70, NPMC 971, p. 2; Bern #2086, 9/7/70, USSDA 608; MER, p. 838; *Haaretz,* 9/8/70, p. 1; Martin, NMCC Memorandum for the Record re Aircraft Hijackings, 9/6/70, 2300EDT, NPMC NSC 330; Geneva #3054, 9/7/70, USSDA 683; Washington #63 to MFA, 9/6/70, MFA 4464/1.
7. *Newsweek,* 9/21/70, p. 24; Swinkels; Sara Raab deposition, p. 82.
8. Martin, NMCC Memorandum for the Record re Aircraft Hijackings, 9/7/70, NPMC NSC 330; Amman #4355, #4372, and #4376, 9/7/70, USSDA 683; Amman #4576, 9/11/70, USSDA 608; London #7321, 9/12/70, USSDA 608; FCO #407 to Tel Aviv, 9/12/70, FCO 14/780; Amman to Ministry of Defense 081125, 9/8/70, FCO 14/778; Amman #470, 9/7/70, FCO 14/778; FBIS, 9/8/70, pp. A2 and H5; FBIS, 9/11/70, p. H1; MFA #169, 9/7/70, MFA 4464/1; New York #216 to MFA, 9/11/70, 4464/2; Tripp memorandum to Sir Denis Greenhill re Hostages, 9/27/70, CAB 164/795; Israeli Consulate letter to the International Civil Aviation Organization, 9/8/70, FCO 14/778.

9. *Newsweek*, 9/21/70, p. 24; Tel Aviv to British Ministry of Defense, 9/8/70, FCO 14/778; Ajeilat interview; Amman #4363, 9/7/70, USSDA 683; MFA #153, 9/7/70, MFA 4464/1; Sara Raab interview; Leser; Fried; Sara Raab deposition, pp. 71, 74; Rosenrauch; "Some Hijacking Victims Begin to Reach Amman," *New York Times*, 9/8/70; MER, p. 838; *Haaretz*, 9/9/70, p. 1; "Life on Jets Held in Desert Is Harsh," *New York Times*, 9/9/70.
10. Washington #2588 to FCO, 9/7/70, PREM 15/201; Bonn #1045 to FCO, 9/7/70, FCO 14/778; Bonn #10206, #10209, #10212, and #10214, 9/7/70, USSDA 683; *Haaretz*, 9/9/70, p. 2; MER, p. 838; Reuters, 9/7/70, 1836 GMT, NPMC NSC 330.
11. Bern #223 to FCO, 9/7/70, PREM 15/201; MER, p. 838; Bern #2087, 9/7/70, USSDA 683; Bern #2089, 9/7/70, USSDA 608; Bern #18, 9/7/70, MFA 4464/1.
12. *Haaretz*, 9/8/70, p. 2; Bern #2098, 9/8/70, USSDA 608; London #7090, #7095, and #7096, 9/7/70, USSDA 608; FCO #1969 to Washington, 9/7/70, PREM 15/201; Minutes, 9/7/70 Ministers' meeting, Cabinet Office 9/8/70, PREM 15/201; Brinson, memo to Head of Chancery, 10/20/70, FCO 14/786; FBIS, 9/8/70, p. H5; FCO #392 to Tel Aviv, 9/6/70, PREM 15/201.
13. Tel Aviv #4871, 9/7/70, NPMC NSC 330; MFA #137 to Zurich, 9/7/70, MFA 4464/1; MFA #152, 9/7/70, MFA 4464/1; Washington #63 to MFA, 9/6/70, MFA 4464/1.
14. Swinkels; McCarthy-Kraut; Sara Raab deposition, p. 82; Ajeilat claims that the Jordanian army provided much of the food that week and that the *fedayeen* ate it too.
15. NEA Working Group memorandum, State Department Operations Center, 9/7/70, NPMC NSC 330; State #146375, #146400, and #146411, 9/7/70, USSDA 683; Haig, Memorandum for the President and Memorandum for Henry Kissinger, 9/7/70, NPMC Haig 971; Kissinger, Memorandum for the President, 21799, 9/7/70, NPMC NSC 331; Memorandum of conversation, Secretary Rogers, Rabbi Schachter, et al., 9/7/70, USSDA 608; "Legal Help for Hostages Is Lacking," *New York Times*, 9/8/70; Washington #68 to MFA, 9/7/70, MFA 4464/1; FBIS, 9/17/70, p. H3; Kissinger, p. 601; Dowty, p. 123; Kissinger telecom with Flanigan, 9/10/70 3pm, NPMC Kissinger Telecons 6; Washington #2588 and #2590 to FCO, 9/7/70, PREM 15/201; FCO #1972 to Washington, 9/7/70, PREM 15/201; Bonn #10217, 9/8/70, USSDA 683.
16. Amman #4405 and #4430, 9/7/70, USSDA 683; Bonn #10211, 9/7/70, USSDA 683; Bern #2098, 9/8/70, USSDA 608; Beirut #7481, 9/8/70, USSDA 2415; NEA Working Group Situation Report #2, 9/7/70, NPMC NSC 330; FBIS, 9/9/70, p. D5; Washington #78, 9/8/70, MFA 4464/1; Amman to Ministry of Defense, 9/8/70, FCO 14/778.
17. Tel Aviv #4877, 9/7/70, USSDA 683; Bern #2089, 9/7/70, USSDA 608; UPI Press Report, 9/7/70, NPMC NSC 330; *Haaretz*, 9/8/70, p. 1; Geneva #31, 9/7/70, MFA 4464/1; Bern #223 to FCO, 9/7/70, PREM 15/201; *Newsweek*, 9/21/70, p. 26.

18. Swinkels; Rosenrauch; Berkowitz interview; State #149904 and Bonn #10542, 9/12/70, USSDA 608; State #146341, 9/6/70, USSDA 683; State #150426, 9/14/70, USSDA 684; Amman #4394, 9/7/70, USSDA 665.

"We May Have to Face A Tragedy"

1. Rosenrauch.
2. Rosenrauch; Sara Raab deposition, pp. 59, 70, 97, 106, 110; Swinkels; Nicosia #1710, 9/27/70, USSDA 307; CBS News, 9/27/70, VUTNA.
3. Beirut #7442, 9/7/70, NPMC NSC 330; Bern #226, 9/8/70, and #229, 9/9/70, PREM 15/201; Washington #2592 to FCO, 9/7/70, PREM 15/201; MFA #104 to Geneva and #296 to Washington, 9/11/70, MFA 4464/2; "5 Nations Firm on Hostages," *New York Times,* 9/15/70; MFA to Geneva, 9/8/70, MFA 4464/1; Geneva #34, 9/8/70, MFA 4464/1; Tel Aviv #789, 9/8/70, PREM 15/201.
4. Swinkels; Sara Raab deposition, p. 66; Washington #78, 9/8/70, MFA 4464/1; Amman #4419, 9/8/70, USSDA 683.
5. Berkowitz interview; Berkowitz e-mail to author, 9/24/03; FBIS, 9/9/70, p. D6. Amman #5474, 9/30/70, NPMC NSC 615 reports that the Palestinian was a captain in the Iraqi, rather than Syrian, army.
6. FCO 147 to Bern, 9/8/70, FCO 14/778; FCO to various embassies, 9/9/70, FCO 14/778; Cabinet meeting CM (70) 13th Conclusions, 9/9/70, CAB 128/47; London #37, 9/8/70, MFA 4464/1; London #7103, 9/8/70, USSDA 608.
7. "Jordan and Commandos Sign Short-Lived Truce," *New York Times,* 9/9/70; MFA #118/219, 091500, 9/9/70, MFA 6603/19; Kissinger, p. 603; Amman to Ministry of Defense, 9/8/70, FCO 14/778; Amman #4447 and State #146512, 9/8/70, USSDA 683; Bern #2107, 9/8/70, USSDA 665.
8. Bonn #30 to MFA, 9/8/70, MFA 4464/1; Bonn #10291, 9/9/70, USSDA 683; State #147019, 9/8/70, USSDA 683; Bonn #10356, 9/9/70, NPMC NSC 330.
9. Caspi, letter to Barosh, 10/27/70, MFA 4464/4; State #146337 and #146355, 9/6/70, USSDA 683; State #146692, 9/8/70, USSDA 683; Haig, Memorandum for the President, 9/6/70, NPMC Haig 971, p. 2; Martin, National Military Command Center, Memorandum for the Record re Aircraft Hijackings, 9/6/70, 1700 EDT, Attachment 1, NPMC NSC 330; Drillman conversation.
10. Bulloch, p. 60; Amman #4436, 9/8/70, USSDA 683; *Haaretz,* 9/9/70, p. 2; "Popular Front Most Militant Commando Group," *New York Times,* 9/10/70; Rochat, pp. 431–32; "Life on Jets Held in Desert Is Harsh," *New York Times,* 9/9/70; FBIS, 9/9/70, p. A2.
11. "Jordan and Commandos Sign Short-Lived Truce," *New York Times,* 9/9/70; FBIS, 9/9/70, pp. D1, D5–6; MER, p. 840.
12. MFA #41 to Bern, 9/9/70, MFA 4464/1; Tel Aviv #504 to FCO, 9/9/70, PREM 15/201; Maroz, memorandum to Bar-On re The Planes, 9/8/70, MFA

4464/1; MFA #182 to Bern, 9/8/70, MFA 4464/1; London #36 to MFA, 9/8/70, MFA 4464/1; Bern #19, 9/8/70, MFA 4464/1; MFA #80 to London, 9/8/70, MFA 4464/1; MFA #188, 9/8/70, MFA 4464/1; Tel Aviv #4900, 9/8/70, USSDA 608; Situation report, 9/9/70, MFA 4464/1; Rafael, pp. 240–1; MFA #199, 9/8/70, MFA 6603/19; Bar-On memo to Amir re: Airplane hijackings, 9/7/70, MFA 4464/1; Washington #2594 to FCO, 9/8/70, PREM 15/201; Tel Aviv #789 to FCO, 9/8/70, PREM 15/201.

13. Bern #2106, 9/8/70, USSDA 608; Daily activity summary, Israeli MFA, 092000, 9/10/70, MFA 6603/19; Hooper, memo to Burke Trend re Hijacking, 9/8/70, PREM 15/201; Bern #2106, 9/8/70, USSDA 608.
14. Amman #4419, 9/8/70, USSDA 683; Sara Raab deposition, pp. 83, 95, 105, 110–21, 128; Girard interview; Majer interview; Swinkels.
15. Swinkels; Fried; Leser.
16. Geneva #90 to MFA, 9/14/70, MFA 4464/3; Amman #4464, 9/8/70, USSDA 683.
17. Amman #4471, 9/8/70, and #4476 and #4478, 9/9/70, USSDA 683; FCO 508 to Bonn, 9/9/70, FCO 14/778; Geneva #3074, 9/9/70, USSDA 683; Bern #2108, 9/9/70, USSDA 608; New York #172 to MFA, 9/10/70, MFA 4464/2.
18. Kissinger, pp. 602–3; Miller, NMCC Memorandum for the Record re Aircraft Hijackings, 9/9/70, NPMC NSC 330; Kissinger, Memorandum for the President re Your 4:30 Meeting on the Hijackings, 9/8/70, NPMC NSC 330; Kissinger, Memorandum for the President re Hijacking Status 9 AM, 9/9/70, NPMC NSC 330; Quandt, *Peace Process,* p. 78; Hersh, p. 236; JCS #9479, 9/9/70, NPMC NSC 330; London #7186, 9/9/70, USSDA 2415.

Misery Loves Company

1. Sara Raab deposition, p. 92; Majer interview; Swinkels.
2. MFA #92 to London and #100, 9/8/70, and #136, 9/9/70, MFA 4464/1; Arrest warrant for Leila Khaled, 9/8/70, MFA 6603/19; London #47 to MFA, 9/9/70, MFA 4464/1; London #7189, 9/9/70, USSDA 608; Cabinet meeting CM (70) 13th Conclusions, 9/9/70, CAB 128/47; FCO #397 to Tel Aviv, 9/9/70, PREM 15/201; Tel Aviv #504 to FCO, 9/9/70, PREM 15/201; FBIS, 9/9/70, p. H2; Memo re Hijacking: Mr. Eban's reply, 9/10/70, PREM 15/201; FCO #149 to Bern, 9/9/70, FCO 14/778; *Haaretz,* 9/10/70, p. 1.
3. Sara Raab deposition, pp. 130, 137, 155–56; Morse; Rosenrauch.
4. Amman #4486, 9/9/70, USSDA 683; Amman #4477, #4488, #4498, and #4502, 9/9/70, USSDA 2415; London #7156, 9/9/70, USSDA 2415; FBIS, 9/9/70, p. D7; FBIS, 9/10/70, p. D5; Telex Amman-London, 9/9/70, PREM 15/201; MER, p. 841; Adams.
5. Swinkels; Sara Raab deposition, pp. 84, 99, 200, 205; MFA #107, 9/8/70, and MFA #112/212, 9/9/70, MFA 6603/19; Geneva #3085, 9/9/70, USSDA 683.

6. Bern #2129, 9/9/70, USSDA 608; Bern #229 to FCO, 9/9/70, PREM 15/201; Cabinet meeting CM (70) 13th Conclusions, 9/9/70, CAB 128/47; FCO #508 to Bonn, 9/9/70, FCO 14/778; London #7189, 9/9/70, USSDA 608; MFA #117/218, 9/9/70, MFA6603/19; Bonn #10297 and #10301, 9/9/70, USSDA 683; Cairo #2058, 9/9/70, USSDA 608; Geneva #45 to FCO, 9/9/70, FCO 14/778; Geneva #3084, 9/9/70, USSDA 683; Hanbury-Tenison, memo to Greenhill, 9/9/70, FCO 14/778; FCO #601, 9/9/70, FCO 14/778.
7. Rosenrauch; Swinkels; Sara Raab deposition, p. 94.
8. New York #123, 9/8/70, MFA 4464/1; New York #173 and #185 to MFA, 9/10/70, MFA 4464/2 and 4464/5; New York #263 to MFA, 9/15/70, MFA 4464/3; Washington #101, 9/8/70, and #112, 9/9/70, MFA 4464/1; MFA #258, 9/10/70, MFA 4464/2; Sitrep as of 111500, 9/12/70, MFA 3497/14.
9. Amman #480 to FCO, 9/9/70, PREM 15/201; Bern #2137, 9/9/70, USSDA 306; MER, pp. 840–41; "Heavy Fighting in Amman," *New York Times*, 9/10/70, p. 1; Amman #4500, #4501, #4504 and #4508, 9/9/70, USSDA 2415; Bern #2137, 9/9/70, USSDA 306; MFA #118/219, 9/9/70, MFA 6603/19; *Haaretz*, 9/11/70, p. 2; Geneva #3085, 9/9/70, USSDA 683; Amman telexcon to London, 9/9/70, PREM 15/201; Amman #4499, 9/9/70, USSDA 608; FBIS, 9/9/70, p. D2; FBIS, 9/10/70, p. D1.
10. Handwritten note re: Ambassador at Airport, 9/9/70, PREM 15/201; Amman telexcon to London, 9/9/70, PREM 15/201; Beirut #420 and #424 to FCO, 9/9/70, FCO 14/778; Beirut #423 to FCO, 9/9/70, PREM 15/201; Beirut #427 to FCO, 9/10/70, FCO 14/779; Beirut #433 to FCO, 9/11/70, FCO 14/779; Amman #487, 9/9/70, FCO 14/778; Sindall, memo re Hijacking of BOAC VC10, 9/13/70, FCO 14/780; Cooper debrief, FCO 14/785; Security Services report on BOAC Hijacking, November 1970, PREM 15/203; Shipp, note to Armstrong, 12/3/70, PREM 15/203; Amman #4520, 9/9/70, USSDA 608; FBIS, 9/10/70, p. A1; Swinkels; Majer interview.
11. Bern #2137, 9/9/70, USSDA 306; FCO #149 to Bern, 9/9/70, FCO 14/778; Bern #228 to FCO, 9/9/70, PREM 15/201; MFA #141/247, 9/9/70, 092350, MFA 6603/19.
12. Sara Raab deposition, pp. 158, 162, 166–168, 171; Amman #4499, 9/9/70, USSDA 608; New York #328 to MFA, 9/18/70, MFA 4464/5; Garfinkle, p. 224; *Haaretz*, 9/10/70, p. 1; Quandt, *Peace Process*, pp. 66–70.
13. Amman #4508, #4517, and #4524, 9/9/70, USSDA 2415; Amman #4525, 9/9/70, NPMC NSC 330; FBIS, 9/10/70, pp. D1, D5; *Haaretz*, 9/11/70, p. 2; Sayigh, p. 260; Shemesh, p. 143.
14. Bern #2142, 9/10/70, USSDA 306; Bonn #10361, 9/10/70, USSDA 2043; Amman #4517, 9/9/70, USSDA 2415; Amman #4520, 9/9/70, USSDA 608; Amman #4525, 9/9/70, NPMC NSC 330.
15. Swinkels; Fried; Sara Raab deposition, pp. 91, 127.
16. "Rabbi Raab Prays for Wife, Children," 9/8/70, p. 1; "Faith and Friendship," 9/10/70, p. 1; "Relatives Here Wait and Hope," 9/11/70; all, *Trenton (NJ) Evening Times*.

"They Forced Me into the Grave"

1. Amman #4530, #4531, #4534, #4549, and #4555, 9/10/70, USSDA 2415; FBIS, 9/10/70, p. D6; FBIS, 9/11/70, p. D1; MER, p. 841; "Truce Reached in Amman After New Wave of Battles," *New York Times,* 9/11/70.
2. Swinkels; Majer interview; Sara Raab deposition, p. 139; Rosenrauch; "Released Hostages Tell of Their Ordeal," *New York Times,* 9/13/70, p. 1; Cooper debrief, FCO 14/785.
3. Beirut #428 and Amman #491, 9/10/70, FCO 14/779; NEA Working Group situation report No. 8, 9/10/70, NPMC NSC 330; *Haaretz,* 9/11/70, p. 2; MER, p. 838; Amman #4545, 9/10/70, USSDA 608; Amman #4618, 9/11/70, USSDA 608.
4. Sara Raab deposition, pp. 182–92; Sara Raab interview.
5. Sara Raab deposition, p. 177; Swinkels; Fried.
6. FBIS, 9/10/70, p. D6; FBIS, 9/11/70, p. D2; "Truce Reached in Amman After New Wave of Battles," *New York Times,* 9/11/70.
7. Berkowitz; State #146403, USSDA 683; Bangkok #11295 and #11297, 9/8/70, USSDA 683; Crawford, Nicosia #1737, 9/30/70, USSDA 338; Amman #5474, 9/30/70, NPMC NSC 615.
8. Geneva ##3092 and 3093, 9/10/70, USSDA 683; Bern #234 and Amman #501 and #502 to FCO, 9/10/70, FCO 14/779.
9. Cooper debrief, FCO 14/785; Makins, note to Tripp re Hijacking: Miss Potts' Tale, 9/14/70, FCO 14/781 and PREM 15/202.
10. Geneva #3098, 9/10/70, USSDA 683; Bern #2160, 9/10/70, USSDA 306; London #7252, 9/10/70, USSDA 2043; FBIS, 9/11/70, p. D2; MFA #288 to Geneva, 9/11/70, MFA 4464/2; Cabinet meeting CM (70) 14th Conclusions, 9/10/70, CAB 128/47; Bern #236 to FCO and FCO #152, 9/10/70, FCO 14/779.
11. USCINCEUR #12449 and State #148727, 9/10/70, USSDA 608; Bern #2207, 9/12/70, USSDA 608; Beirut #7588, 9/10/70, USSDA 2415; Amman #4558, 9/10/70, USSDA 683; Amman #4683, 9/13/70, USSDA 2415; Amman #4629, 9/12/70, USSDA 684; FBIS, 9/11/70, p. A1; FBIS, 9/14/70, pp. A2, A4, A5, A8; *Haaretz,* 9/11/70, p. 1; Baghdad #614 to FCO, 9/15/70, FCO 14/781; Al-Sirhan account trans. al-Majali; Baghdad #605, 9/10/70, FCO 14/779; Baghdad #1 to FCO, 9/11/70, FCO 14/779; FCO #696 to Baghdad, 9/11/70, FCO 14/781; Baghdad #606 to FCO, 9/12/70, FCO 14/780; Salibi, p. 236; Sitrep as of 0800 9/12/70, 9/12/70, FCO 14/780; Amman #520 to FCO and FCO #157 to Bern, 9/11/70, FCO 14/779.
12. Amman #4553, State #148070 and Geneva #3103, 9/10/70, USSDA 683; Amman #4629, 9/12/70, USSDA 684; Amman #4576, 9/11/70, USSDA 608; Amman #485, 9/9/70, FCO 14/778; Amman #502 to FCO, 9/10/70, FCO 14/779; Bern #241 to FCO and FCO #157 to Bern, 9/11/70, FCO 14/779; Tripp, memo to Private Secretary re Situation in Jordan, 9/10/70, PREM 15/123; Geneva #49 to MFA, 9/10/70, MFA 4464/2; MFA #104 to Geneva, Geneva #61 and #65 to MFA, and MFA #296 to Washington, 9/11/70, MFA 4464/2; "5 Nations Firm on Hostages," *New York Times,* 9/15/70; Bern #2162

and #2170, 9/11/70, USSDA 306; Amman telexcon with FCO, 9/11/70, PREM 15/201; *New York Times,* 9/13/70.

13. Tel Aviv #812 to FCO, 9/11/70, FCO 14/779; Tel Aviv #4977, 9/11/70, USSDA 683; Daily situation summary, 9/11/70, MFA 6603/19.
14. FBIS, 9/11/70, pp. D2–D3.
15. Bern #35 to MFA, Washington #128 to MFA, and MFA #119 to Geneva, 9/11/70, MFA 4464/2; Bern #2168 and #2170, 9/11/70, USSDA 306; Bern #237 to FCO, 9/10/70, FCO 14/779.
16. Sara Raab deposition, p. 194.

Chaos, Confusion, and "Fantastic Tension"

1. Rosenrauch.
2. Amman #506 and #512 to FCO, 9/11/70, FCO 14/779; Geneva #63 to MFA and Bern #41 to MFA, 9/11/70, MFA 4464/2; Bern #2187, 9/11/70, USSDA 306; Bern #2219, 9/12/70, USSDA 306; Bern #2219, 9/12/70, NPMC NSC 330; Kissinger, Memorandum to the President re Overnight development on hijacking, 9/11/70, NPMC NSC 331; *Haaretz,* 9/13/70, p. 2; Amman #4594 and #4595, 9/11/70, USSDA 683; Amman #4588 and #4591, 9/11/70, USSDA 608; Swinkels; JAA Operations Log, items 19 and 21, 9/11/70, JAAMA.
3. Swinkels; Rosenrauch; Sara Raab deposition, pp. 198–202.
4. Kissinger, Memorandum for the President re Midday report on hijacking situation, 9/11/70, NPMC NSC 331; FBIS, 9/11/70, p. D5; MER, p. 842; FBIS, 9/14/70, p. D3; Amman #4596, 9/11/70, USSDA 608; Amman #4598, 9/11/70, USSDA 2415; Amman #515 to FCO, 9/11/70, FCO 14/779.
5. Amman #4584, 9/11/70, USSDA 683; Amman #4578 and #4588, 9/11/70, USSDA 608; Bonn #10540, 9/12/70, USSDA 608; Amman #510 to FCO, 9/11/70, FCO 14/779; Nicosia #1583, 9/12/70, USSDA 306; Washington #137 to MFA, 9/11/70, MFA 4464/2.
6. Bern #41 to MFA and , 9/11/70, MFA 4464/2; Bern #245 to FCO, 9/11/70, FCO 14/779; Bern #247 to FCO, 9/12/70, FCO 14/780; Hanbury-Tenison, note to Private Secretary re Hijacking, 9/11/70, FCO 14/779; Bern #2175 and #2192, 9/11/70, USSDA 306; Amman #4591, 9/11/70, USSDA 608; Geneva #74 to MFA, 9/11/70, MFA 4464/2.
7. Amman #516 and #520to FCO and Bern #245 to FCO, 9/11/70, FCO 14/779; Amman #4608 and State #148939, 9/11/70, USSDA 2415; Geneva #3112, Amman #4582 and #4588, and Bonn #10494, 9/11/70, USSDA 608; Amman #4594, 9/11/70, USSDA 683; Geneva #71 to MFA, 9/11/70, MFA 4464/2; Kissinger, p. 608; Bern #2187 and #2193, 9/11/70, USSDA 306; Hanbury-Tenison, note to Private Secretary re Hijacking, 9/11/70, FCO 14/779; State #148883, 9/11/70, USSDA 665; "White House Seeks to Allay Fears of Military Intervention," *New York Times,* 9/12/70; MER, p. 839; FBIS, 9/14/70, p. A2; *Newsweek,* 9/2170, p. 25; JAA Operations Log, items 23–28, 9/11/70, JAAMA.
8. Amman #517 to FCO 5179/11/70, FCO 14/779; Nicosia #1563, #1564, #1565, #1571 and #1572, 9/11/70, USSDA 306; Nicosia #1578, 9/12/70, NPMC NSC 330; Nicosia #1583, 9/12/70, USSDA 306; Amman #4595, 9/11/70, USSDA

683; Amman #4588, #4593 and #4618, 9/11/70, USSDA 608; Broomfield, note re Hijacking, 9/11/70, FCO 14/779; "Former Hostages Arrive in Nicosia" and "Arabs Release Some Passengers," *New York Times,* 9/12/70.

9. State #148818 and Bonn #10534, 9/11/70, USSDA 608; State #149953, 9/13/70, USSDA 684; Tenison, note to Private Secretary re Hijacking: German Position, 9/14/70, FCO 14/781; Idan, memo to Meroz re Plane Hijackings—Wischnewski's mission to Amman, 9/15/70, MFA 4464/3.
10. Cabinet meeting CM (70) 14th Conclusions, 9/10/70, CAB 128/47; Daunt, note to Gallagher, 9/11/70, FCO 14/779; Hooper, note to Trend re Miss Khaled, 9/11/70, CAB 164/795; note of meeting held at 10 Downing Street between Prime Minister Heath and selected ministers on 9/10/70 at 7:30 PM, 9/11/70, CAB 164/795; Gallagher, note to Private Secretary, 9/11/70, FCO 14/779; Graham, note to Sir Philip Adams, 9/11/70, FCO 14/779.
11. London #50 to MFA, 9/9/70, 091200, MFA 4464/1; Fried; Sara Raab interview.
12. Swinkels; Majer interview; Morse; "Freed US Citizens Tell of Their Fears," *New York Times,* 9/14/70, p. 1; Sara Raab interview; Freda, *Miami Herald.*
13. Amman telexcon with FCO, 9/11/70, PREM 15/201; FCO #2324 to Washington, 9/12/70, FCO 14/780; JAA Operations Log, items 29–30, 9/12/70, JAAMA; Amman telexcon with FCO, 9/11/70, PREM 15/201.
14. MER, p. 839; Gazit, "The Consolidation of Policy," p. 314, n. 1; FBIS, 9/14/70, p. H8; FBIS, 9/15/70, p. H2; *Haaretz,* 9/14/70, pp. 1–2; Ze'ev Schiff, *Haaretz,* 9/18/70; AP report in "Raids a Surprise," *New York Times,* 9/14/70, p. 1; "Guerrillas Warn of Reprisals," *New York Times,* 9/14/70, p. 24; "Israel Clears and Frees 75," *New York Times,* 9/15/70, p. 1.
15. *Haaretz,* 9/13/70, p. 2; Bern #2202, 9/11/70, NPMC NSC 330; Bern #2207, 9/12/70, USSDA 608; Amman telexcon with FCO 2030Z, 9/11/70, PREM 15/201; Sitrep as of 0800 12 September, 9/12/70, FCO 14/780; Transcript, telephone conversation between FCO Secretary and Mr. Rogers at 5 PM, 9/11/70, FCO 14/779; Washington #2667 to FCO, 9/11/70, FCO 14/779; Bern #293 to FCO, 9/18/70, FCO 14/783.
16. Geneva #3112, 9/11/70, USSDA 608; Bern #2215, 9/12/70, USSDA 306; Bern to FCO, 9/12/70, FCO 14/780; Bern #49 to MFA and MFA #415 to Washington, 9/12/70, MFA 4464/2; Situation report, 9/9/70, MFA 4464/1; MFA #201, 9/8/70, MFA 6603/19.

Explosions in the Desert

1. Freda, *Miami Herald;* Swinkels.
2. Amman #523 and Bern #251 to FCO, 9/12/70, FCO 14/780; Bern #2214, 9/12/70, USSDA 608; Bern #2217, 9/12/70, USSDA 306; Bern #2219, 9/12/70, NPMC NSC 330; Amman #4629, 9/12/70, USSDA 684; Bern #47 to MFA and Geneva #78 to MFA, 9/12/70, MFA 4464/2; Amman telexcon 1100Z, 9/12/70, PREM 15/202; Hanbury-Tenison, note re Hijacking, 9/12/70, PREM 15/202; Adams.

3. Sara Raab deposition, pp. 224–32, 241; "Free . . . Except for Oldest Son," *Rochester (NY) Democrat & Chronicle,* 9/13/70, pp. 1–2; "Released Hostages Tell of Their Ordeal," *New York Times,* 9/13/70, p. 1; Amman telexcon 1100Z, 9/12/70, PREM 15/202; *Haaretz,* 9/15/70, p. 2; *Haaretz,* 9/13/70, p. 2; BBC interview, video in author's possession; Amman #4638 and #4646, 9/12/70, USSDA 608; Amman #4635 and #4641, 9/12/70, USSDA 609; Amman #4647, 9/12/70, USSDA 684.
4. Cooper debrief, FCO 14/785; Barbara Mensch conversation.
5. JAA Operations Log, item 37, 9/12/70, JAAMA; Amman #558 to FCO, 9/14/70, FCO 14/781; Amman #4749, 9/14/70, USSDA 609; Bern #72 to MFA, 9/16/70, MFA 4464/3; "Arabs Blow Up 3 Jets," *New York Times,* 9/13/70, p. 1; "Front Is Adamant," *New York Times,* 9/14/70, p. 1; Bliner interview; Ajeilat interview; Cooper debrief, FCO 14/785; Nicosia #1710, 9/27/70, USSDA 307; Snow and Phillips, pp. 62, 65–67.
6. Amman #4652 and #4654, 9/12/70, USSDA 609; Amman #4666, 9/13/70, USSDA 609; Bern #56 to MFA, 9/13/70, MFA 4464/3; Amman #534 to FCO and FCO #158 to Bern, 9/12/70, FCO 14/780; Amman telexcon 1600Z, 9/12/70, PREM 15/202.
7. Amman #4683, 9/13/70, USSDA 2415; Amman #4744, 9/14/70, USSDA 609; FBIS, 9/14/70, pp. A2–4; FBIS, 9/15/70, p. A1.
8. Amman telexcon 1600Z, 9/12/70, PREM 15/202; FBIS, 9/14/70, p. A6; Amman #4663, 9/12/70, USSDA 609.
9. *Haaretz,* 9/14/70, p. 1; Amman #4800, 9/15/70, NPMC NSC 331; Amman #4803, 9/15/70, USSDA 609; Amman #557 to FCO, 9/14/70, FCO 14/781; Bern #265 to FCO, 9/15/70, FCO 14/781; Bern #62 to MFA, 9/14/70, MFA 4464/3.
10. Amman #4646 and #4662, 9/12/70, USSDA 608; Amman #4663, 9/12/70, USSDA 609; Nicosia #1587, 9/12/70, USSDA 306.
11. Cabinet meeting CM (70) 15th Conclusions, 9/12/70, CAB 128/47; London #7326, 9/12/70, USSDA 608.
12. "Eban Doubtful on Jordan," *New York Times,* 9/15/70; State #149919, 9/12/70, USSDA 684.
13. FCO #162 to Bern, 9/12/70, FCO 14/780; Bern #253 to FCO, 9/13/70, FCO 14/780; Gillmore, note to Private Secretary, 9/13/70, PREM 15/202; Bern #2235, 9/13/70, USSDA 306.
14. Tel Aviv #5015, 9/13/70, USSDA 609; MFA #437 to Washington, 9/13/70, MFA 4464/3; Gilmore, Note to Private Secretary, 9/13/70, PREM 15/202; FCO to Tel Aviv, 9/13/70, PREM 15/202; Tel Aviv #824 to FCO, 9/13/70, FCO 14/780; Rafael, pp. 243–44.
15. State #149923, 9/12/70, USSDA 684; Horan.

My Family Is Freed

1. "Front Is Adamant," *New York Times,* 9/14/70, p. 1; FBIS, 9/15/70, p. A3; Amman #4663, 9/12/70, USSDA 609; Amman # 4667, 9/13/70, USSDA 609; Amman #4671, 9/13/70, USSDA 665; Cooper debrief, FCO 14/785; Godber,

note re Mrs. Potts, 9/14/70, PREM 15/202 and FCO 14/780; Sara Raab deposition, p. 249.

2. FBIS, 9/16/70, p. A1; Kissinger Memorandum for the President re Hijacking situation report—10:30 AM, Sunday morning, 9/13/70, NPMC NSC 331; Idan, note to Meroz re plane hijackings—Wischnewski mission to Amman, 9/15/70, MFA 4464/3.
3. MFA #431 to Bonn, 9/13/70, MFA 4464/3; Amman #4694, 9/13/70, USSDA 609; "Bonn Rejects Arab Offer," *New York Times,* 9/14/70; FCO #164 to Bern, 9/13/70, FCO 14/780; Bern #2 to Amman, 9/14/70, FCO 14/781; Amman telexcon with FCO 1115Z, 9/13/70, PREM 15/202 and FCO 14/780.
4. FBIS, 9/15/70, p. A1.
5. Swinkels; Morse; Majer interview.
6. Berkowitz interview.
7. FCO #165 to Bern, 9/12/70, FCO 14/780; Gillmore, note to Private Secretary, 9/13/70, PREM 15/202; "Bonn Rejects Arab Offer," *New York Times,* 9/14/70; Bonn #10586, 9/14/70, USSDA 609.
8. FBIS, 9/14/70, p. D4; MER, p. 842.
9. MFA #414 to Geneva, 9/12/70, MFA 3216/11; Bern #2215, 9/12/70, USSDA 306; Tel Aviv #5012 and Geneva #3133, 9/12/70, USSDA 608; Tel Aviv #5015, 9/13/70, USSDA 609; Bern to FCO, 9/12/70, FCO 14/780.
10. Bern #2244, 9/13/70, USSDA 306; State #149946, 9/13/70, USSDA 684; Bern #2246, 9/14/70, USSDA 306; Bern #2248, 9/14/70, NPMC NSC 330; Amman #4676, #4679, and #4684, 9/13/70, USSDA 609; Bern #260 to FCO, 9/14/70, FCO 14/781; Amman #549 to FCO, 9/14/70, FCO 14/781; "Specter of Impasse Rises," *New York Times,* 9/14/70, p. 1.
11. Swinkels; Majer interview; Amman #4685, 9/13/70, USSDA 684; Amman #4706, 9/14/70, USSDA 684; Amman 551 to FCO, 9/14/70, PREM 15/202; "Front Is Adamant," *New York Times,* 9/14/70, p. 1; FBIS, 9/14/70, p. A1.
12. Amman telexcon with FCO 1530Z, 9/13/70, PREM 15/202; Amman #4684, #4688, and #4691, 9/13/70, USSDA 609; Tel Aviv 839 to FCO, 9/14/70, FCO 14/781; Powell, Note for the Record, 9/13/70, FCO 14/780; "Rogers and Aides Meet on Hostages," "Front Is Adamant," "Pilot Held by Arabs," all, *New York Times,* 9/14/70; FBIS, 9/15/70, p. A1; "Arabs Will Treat All US Hostages Like the Israelis," *New York Times,* 9/15/70, p. 1; *Haaretz,* 9/15/70, p. 1.
13. Cabinet Meeting CM (70) 16th Conclusions, 9/14/70, CAB 128/47; "Specter of Impasse Rises," *New York Times,* 9/14/70, p. 1; Hanbury-Tenison, Memo to Private Secretary re Move of Miss Leila Khaled, 9/13/70, FCO 14/780; Gillmore, note to Private Secretary, 9/14/70, FCO 14/780; Waddell, memo re Detention of Leila Khaled, 9/10/70, CAB 164/795; Amman telexcon with FCO 1115Z and telexcon with FCO 1530Z, 9/13/70, PREM 15/202; FCO #2029, #2031, and #2032 to Washington and Washington #2678 to FCO, 9/13/70, FCO 14/780; Washington #2679 to FCO, 9/14/70, FCO 14/780; Washington #2681 to FCO, 9/14/70, FCO 14/781; State #149954, 9/13/70, USSDA 684.
14. Swinkels.

15. MFA #486 to Washington, 9/15/70, MFA 4464/3; Bern #2248, 9/14/70, NPMC NSC 330; Bern #2247 and #2249, 9/14/70, USSDA 306; Bern #257 and #260 to FCO, 9/14/70, FCO 14/781; Long, note to Hanbury-Tenison re: German attitude, 9/14/70, FCO 14/781.

Negotiations at a Standstill

1. Majer interview; Swinkels.
2. Geneva #93 and #98 to MFA, 9/14/70, MFA 4464/3; Geneva #3142, 9/14/70, USSDA 684; Amman #4731, 9/14/70, NPMC NSC 615; Tel Aviv #4871, 9/7/70, NPMC NSC 330; Tel Aviv #5059 and #5063, 9/15/70, USSDA 306; State #155257, 9/22/70, USSDA 307; "US Aide Assails Guerrilla Action," *New York Times,* 9/15/70, p. 1.
3. MER, pp. 824, 842; *Haaretz,* 9/15/70, p. 1; FBIS, 9/15/70, pp. D2–4; Kissinger, Memorandum for the President re Midafternoon Report on the hijacking situation #21984, 9/14/70, NPMC NSC 331; Note re Hijacking: Summary of Latest Events, 9/14/70, PREM 15/202; Pargai, note re Vatican emissary—Hostages in Jordan, 9/14/70, MFA 4464/3; MFA #470, 9/14/70, MFA 4464/3.
4. *Haaretz,* 9/15/70, pp. 1–2; FBIS, 9/15/70, p. A1; FBIS, 9/16/70, p. A5; "Arabs Will Treat All US Hostages Like the Israelis," "At the Front's Amman Office," *New York Times,* 9/15/70, p. 1; Amman #560 to FCO, 9/14/70, FCO 14/781.
5. Swinkels; Berkowitz interview; "Arabs Will Treat All US Hostages Like the Israelis," *New York Times,* 9/15/70, p. 1; Amman #4750, 9/14/70, USSDA 684; Amman #4807, 9/15/70, USSDA 609; Amman #5 to The Hague, 9/14/70, FCO 14/781.
6. London #7374, 9/14/70, USSDA 609; Bern #2266, 9/15/70, USSDA 306; Bern #2319, 9/16/70, USSDA 2415; Bern #265 to FCO, 9/15/70, FCO 14/781; Bern #62 to MFA, 9/14/70, MFA 4464/3; Kissinger, Memorandum for the President re Hijacking Situation—Tuesday Morning, 9/15/70, NPMC NSC 331.

"I Just Want To Be Near My Daughter"

1. FBIS, 9/15/70, p. D1; Abu-Odeh, p. 3.
2. Amman #570, #573, and #579 to FCO, 9/15/70, FCO 14/781 and PREM 15/202; Cabinet meeting at 10 AM CM (70) 18th Conclusions, 9/16/70, CAB 128/47; Amman #4806 and #4815, 9/15/70, USSDA 609; FBIS, 9/15/70, p. A1; FBIS, 9/16/70, pp. A4–5; "Guerrillas Raise Their Price," *New York Times,* 9/16/70; *Haaretz,* 9/16/70, p. 2; Amman #2 to Bern, 9/15/70, FCO 14/781.
3. MFA #490 to Washington, MFA #170 to Bonn, and Bonn #81, #83, and #84 to MFA, 9/15/70, MFA 4464/3; Macan, note to Hanbury-Tenison, and Ibbott, Note to Tripp, 9/15/70, FCO 14/781.
4. London #110 to MFA, 9/15/70, MFA 4464/3; London #7404 and #7405 and State #150859, 9/15/70, USSDA 609; Graham, note to Chamberlain re

Hijacking: Extradition and Chamberlain, note to Graham, 9/15/70, FCO 14/781.

5. Amman #581 to FCO, 9/15/70, FCO 14/781; Beirut #7850, 9/17/70, USSDA 306.
6. MER, p. 842; FBIS, 9/15/70, p. D3; FBIS, 9/16/70; Amman #4795, 9/15/70, USSDA 2415; NEA Situation Report 19, 9/15/70, NSC330; Amman telexcon with FCO 1400Z, 9/14/70, PREM 15/202; Amman #2 to Bern, 9/15/70, FCO 14/781.
7. Geneva #3171, 9/14/70, USSDA 609; Geneva #3170, 9/15/70, USSDA 609; State #150884 and Bern #2288, 9/15/70, USSDA 306; Bern #272 to FCO, 9/15/70, FCO 14/781.
8. Nicosia #1609, 9/14/70, NPMC NSC 330; State #150121 and #150658 and Beirut #7719, 9/14/70, USSDA 338; Amman #4801, 9/15/70, USSDA 338; Beirut #7850, 9/17/70, USSDA 306; Amman #5038, 9/22/70, USSDA 338; Mensch interview; Girard interview.
9. FBIS, 9/15/70, p. D1; FBIS, 9/16/70, pp. D4 and D11; Olaimat interview; Abu-Odeh interview; Amman #4837, 9/16/70, USSDA 2415; Sitrep, 0800 BST, 9/16/70, PREM 15/124; MER pp. 843–44; El-Edroos, pp. 447–48; Amman #4808, #4809, #4810, and #4814, 9/15/70, USSDA 2415; Bern #2319, 9/16/70, USSDA 2415; Kissinger-Davies telecon, 9/15/70 5:50 PM, NPMC Kissinger Telecons 30; Kissinger, Memorandum for the President re Evening Report on the Hijacking Situation, 9/15/70, NPMC NSC 331; Amman, telexcon with FCO 0100BST, 9/16/70, FCO 14/782; Quandt, *Peace Process,* p. 78. According to Abu-Odeh, Hussein's meeting started in the afternoon and lasted until the early hours of the morning.
10. Kissinger, pp. 610–11; Kissinger memo to Bob Haldeman, undated but presumably written 9/16/70, NPMC Haig 971; Kissinger-Marvin Kalb telecon, 9/16/70 morning, NPMC Kissinger Telecons 6; Kissinger-Haldeman telecon, 9/17/70 8:53 AM, NPMC Kissinger Telecons 30; Saunders and Kennedy, Memorandum for Dr. Kissinger re WSAG meeting on Jordan and attachment "Arguments against military intervention in Jordan," 9/15/70, NPMC NSC H77; London #7467, 9/16/70, NPMC NSC 331; Memcon, telephone discussion between Greenhill, Kissinger, and Sisco at 0345, 9/16/70, PREM 15/202; MFA #233, 9/16/70, MFA 6603/19; Quandt, *Peace Process,* p. 77; Garfinkle, pp. 234–38; Goldstein and Zhukov; Dowty, pp. 143, 149, and 156.

The Eve of War

1. FBIS, 9/16/70, pp. D1, D3, D6–D7; FBIS, 9/17/70, pp. D8, D9, and D17; MER. P. 845; Sitrep 0700, 9/17/70, PREM 15/202; Kissinger, Memorandum for the President re Jordan/Hijacking Situation, 9/16/70, NPMC NSC 331; Bulloch, p. 63; Amman #4821, 9/16/70, USSDA 2415.
2. Cabinet meeting at 10 AM CM (70) 18th Conclusions, 9/16/70, CAB 128/47; FCO #172 to Bern, 9/16/70, FCO 14/782; Bout de papier, attached to Tripp memo to Private Secretary re Leila Khaled, 9/16/70, PREM 15/202 and FCO 14/782; MFA #530 to London and #524 to Bern, 9/16/70, MFA 4464/3.

3. Amman #4821 and #4832, 9/16/70, USSDA 2415; FBIS, 9/17/70, p. D5; Abu-Odeh interview; FBIS, 9/17/70, pp. D5–6; Abu-Odeh, p. 182.
4. Beirut #7802, 9/16/70, USSDA 2415; Beirut #7591, 9/11/70, USSDA 2415; Goldstein and Zhukov; Kissinger, Memorandum to the President re Overnight Development on Hijacking, 9/11/70, NPMC NSC 331; Kissinger, Memorandum for the President re Options in Jordan #22057, undated, NPMC NSC 615.
5. Bern #277 and #278 to FCO, 9/16/70, FCO 14/782; Bern #2319 and Amman #4831, 9/16/70, USSDA 2415; Note to file re Jordan: Internal Situation, Makins memo to Adams re Hijacking: Bern Group Meeting, and Adams note to Private Secretary, 9/16/70, PREM 15/202; MFA #530 to London and Bern #77 to MFA, 9/16/70, MFA 4464/3 and 6603/19.
6. Berkowitz interview; Freda; Majer interview.
7. *The Times,* 9/26/70, MFA 5898/11; Snow and Phillips, p. 89; Author site visit, 7/13/04; Majer interview; Morse.
8. MER, p. 845; FBIS, 9/14/70, p. A11; FBIS, 9/17/70, p. D13; Amman #4835 and #4836, 9/16/70, USSDA 2415.
9. FBIS, 9/17/70, p. H1; State #152282, 9/16/70, USSDA 609; Bern #2320, 9/17/70, USSDA 609; Bern #78 to MFA, 9/17/70, MFA 4464/3.

"A Little Excitement"

1. Amman #4849, #4850, #4853, #4856, #4860, #4865, #4875, and #4876, 9/17/70, USSDA 2415; Amman #4906, 9/18/70, USSDA 2415; Sitrep 0700, 9/17/70, PREM 15/202 and PREM 15/124; note, PREM 15/124; *Haaretz,* 9/18/70, p. 3; El-Edroos, pp. 448–52; Brown, p. 41; Haig, Memorandum for Kissinger re Jordanian Situation Report, 9/17/70, NPMC Haig 971; De Atkine, "Ambassador Dean Brown"; Shemesh, p. 132; author observation and analysis. Ma'aita, a commander in the area, claimed in an interview with the author that there were multiple thrusts, not just along the main road.
2. Amman #4867, 9/17/70, USSDA 609; Makins, note to Private Secretary re Hijacked Hostages, 9/17/70, FCO 14/782 and PREM 15/202; Washington #2731 to FCO, 9/17/70, FCO 14/782; *Haaretz,* 9/18/70, p. 1; CBS News, 9/27/70, VUTNA; Sufeig al-Jazi, who commanded all the Jordanian forces in Amman, claimed in an interview with the author that he had specifically ruled out cutting the water or electricity. He suggested that the *fedayeen*—who would later stop other supplies from reaching the populace—may have done so to turn the people against Hussein.
3. FBIS, 9/17/70, pp. F1–2; FBIS, 9/21/70, pp. F2–3.
4. Abu-Odeh interview; Abu-Rashed; Sayigh, p. 262; Adams; Amman telexcon 0630Z, 9/18/70, FCO 14/783; Amman #4853, #4856, #4858, #4860, #4863, #4865, #4873, #4876, and #4877, 9/17/70, USSDA 2415.
5. El-Edroos, pp. 449–52; Sayigh, p. 264; MER, pp. 846, 849–50; *Haaretz,* 9/18/70, p. 1; FBIS, 9/18/70, p. D1; Amman #4859 and #4871, 9/17/70, USSDA 2415; Haig, Memorandum for Kissinger re Jordanian Situation Report, 9/17/70, NPMC Haig 971.

6. Tel Aviv #5120 and Bonn #10771, 9/17/70, USSDA 609; *Haaretz,* 9/18/70, p. 2; London #121 to MFA, 9/17/70, MFA 4464/3; Telcon, telephone conversation between Greenhill and Sisco at 1 PM, 9/17/70, PREM 15/202 and PREM 15/124; Kissinger, telecon with Greenhill and Sisco, 9/17/70 8 AM, NPMC Kissinger Telecons 30; Kissinger, Memorandum for the President re The Situation in Jordan, 9/18/70, USSDA 615; Makins, note to Tripp re Hijacking, 9/17/70, FCO 14/782; FCO #175 to Bern and Tel Aviv #860 to FCO, 9/17/70, FCO 14/782.
7. *Haaretz,* 9/18/70, p. 3; FBIS, 9/17/70, p. D25; Amman #4849, #4861, #4868, #4871, #4876, and #4877, 9/17/70, USSDA 2415; Amman #4895 and #4906, 9/18/70, USSDA 2415; sitrep, 9/18/70 0600Z, PREM 15/124; Shemesh, pp. 141, 143; Sufeig al-Jazi interview; Olaimat interview; Lunt, p. 129; Sayigh, pp. 258–59, 262–64; Abu Iyad, pp. 77, 81–82; Ajami, p. 144; Brown, p. 42; De Atkine, "Amman 1970"; El-Edroos, pp. 437, 442, 445, 449–52; Zak, p. 123; Hart, pp. 304–5; author observation and analysis; "Guerrilla Radio Messages" and "Hussein's Tanks Clearing Guerrillas from Amman," *New York Times,* 9/18/70.
8. Bern #2337, 9/17/70, USSDA 306; Bern #285 to FCO, 9/17/70, FCO 14/782.
9. Amman #4878, #4880, #4881, and #4889, 9/17/70, USSDA 2415; MER, p. 845; Amman telexcon 1800Z, 9/17/70, PREM 15/203; *Haaretz,* 9/18/70, p. 3; FBIS, 9/17/70, p. D25.
10. Kissinger-Rogers telecon 9:20 AM, Kissinger-Nixon telecons 9:45 AM, 2:40 PM, and 9:30 PM, Kissinger-Frank Shakespeare telecon 6:55 PM, and Kissinger-Laird telecon 9:35 PM, 9/17/70, NPMC Kissinger Telecons 6; Kissinger, p. 614; Haig, p. 244; Quandt, *Peace Process,* pp. 79, 102; Nixon, p. 483; Dowty, pp. 115–18; MER, p. 849; Goldstein and Zhukov; Jim Skinner e-mails to author, 12/13/04 to 2/24/05.

An Extremely Close Call

1. Amman #4895, #4897, #4901, #4904, #4905, and #4906, 9/18/70, USSDA 2415; Amman telexcon 0630Z, 9/18/70, FCO 14/783; sitrep, 9/18/70 0600Z, PREM 15/124; MER, p. 846; Adams.
2. MER, p. 846; Tel Aviv #5143, 9/18/70, USSDA 2415; Berkowitz e-mail to author, 12/4/03.
3. MER, pp. 846, 847, 850; FBIS, 9/21/70, p. C1; El-Edroos, p. 454.
4. Tel Aviv #858 to FCO, FCO 14/783; Amman telexcons 0630Z and 0900Z, 9/18/70, FCO 14/783; State #154300, 9/18/70, USSDA 609.
5. Amman #4843, 9/16/70, USSDA 609; Amman #4883, 9/17/70, USSDA 609; Tel Aviv #5142 and Jerusalem #439, 9/18/70, USSDA 609.
6. Memcon, President Nixon et al. and Prime Minister Golda Meir et al., 9/18/70, NPMC NSC 134; State #154257, 9/18/70, USSDA 2385; State #154300, 9/18/70, USSDA 609; Quandt, *Peace Process,* p. 80; Rafael, p. 245.
7. Bern #2358, 9/18/70, USSDA 306; Tel Aviv #861 to FCO, 9/17/70, FCO 14/782; Bern #295 to FCO, 9/18/70, FCO 14/783; Bern #86 to MFA, 9/18/70,

MFA 4464/5; Beckett, memo to Tripp re The Meeting in Berne on 17 September, 9/17/70, FCO 14/782.

8. Amman telexcon with FCO 1230Z, 9/18/70, PREM 15/203; Sitrep, 9/19/70 0700BST, PREM 15/124; El-Edroos, p. 452.
9. Nicosia #1710, 9/27/70, USSDA 307; Morse. Freda. Freda added that "we were unconvinced" that the guerrillas would protect us.
10. Moscow #5445, 9/19/70, USSDA 2415; MER, p. 849; Sitrep, 9/19/70 0700BST, PREM 15/124; Kissinger, p. 616.
11. Seale, pp. 154–62; Cooley, p. 116; Hersh, p. 240; Garfinkle, p. 270; Dowty, pp. 115–18, 153; MER, p. 1150; Lawson, p. 68; Abu-Odeh interview; Neumark, pp. 345–348. Neumark's ground-breaking PhD thesis relies on newly available diplomatic cable traffic between Syria and East Germany, which had very close relations with Syria and whose STASI secret service was deeply entrenched in Syria during that period. On pp. 348 and 352 he claims that the Soviets hoped to bring down Hussein and to both weaken the Syrian army—so that it would require more assistance from the USSR—and Assad, who was not as close to the USSR as Atasi.
12. London #7528, 9/18/70, USSDA 2415; Quandt et al., *Politics,* p. 126; MER, p. 846, 850; El Edroos, p. 454.

Hussein's Momentary Edge

1. Amman #4926, #4927, #4928, and #4933, 9/19/70, USSDA 2415; Amman telexcon with FCO 0815 BST, 9/19/70, PREM 15/124.
2. Tel Aviv to MOD D14 191000Z, 9/19/70, PREM 15/124; MER, p. 859; Amman telexcon with FCO 0815 BST, 9/19/70, PREM 15/124; Amman telexcon with FCO 1600Z, 9/19/70, PREM 15/203; Kissinger-Rockefeller telecon 8:20 AM, 9/19/70, NPMC Kissinger Telecons 30; Amman #4929, #4930, #4937 and Tel Aviv #5165, 9/19/70, USSDA 2415; *Haaretz,* 9/20/70, p. 2; MER, p. 859; Olaimat interview; Freda; Majer interview.
3. Beirut #7901 and #7915, 9/18/70, USSDA 306; Beirut #7937, 9/20/70, USSDA 307.
4. MER, p. 850; Tel Aviv #5165 and Amman #4937, 9/19/70, USSDA 2415; Sitrep, 9/19/70 0700BST, PREM 15/124; Tel Aviv to MOD D14 191000Z, 9/19/70, PREM 15/124, which also claims that as of 1200Z, the tanks had not yet attacked.
5. Amman #4937, 9/19/70, USSDA 2415; Moon, Note to Mr. Armstrong, 9/19/70, PREM 15/124; Amman telexcon with FCO 1200BST, 9/19/70, FCO 14/783; Amman telexcon at 1830Z, 9/24/70, FCO 14/785; Amman telexcon with FCO 1600Z, 9/19/70, PREM 15/203; Tel Aviv to MOD D14 191200Z, 9/19/70, PREM 15/124.
6. Bern #2369 and #2371, 9/19/70, USSDA 306; Text of statement released for broadcast, PREM 15/124; Bern #299 to FCO, 9/19/70, FCO 14/783.
7. Amman #4941, 9/19/70, USSDA 2415; MER, p. 859; Amman to FCO, 9/20/70, FCO 14/783.
8. MER, p. 850.

Our Fate in the Balance

1. MER, pp. 850–53; Cooley, p. 116; El-Edroos, pp. 453–56; Brown; Salloukh; Apthan-Echraisha interview; Seale, pp. 154–62; Neumark, p. 348; Zak, p. 121, footnote 58; Tel Aviv at 1700Z and at 1930Z and Washington #2773 to FCO, 9/20/70, FCO 17/1065; Sitrep, 9/20/70 0700 BST, PREM 15/124; Record of conversation between Douglas-Home and King Hussein, 10/1/70, PREM 15/125; Kissinger, Memo to Nixon re Jordanian Request for Assistance, 9/20/70, NPMC 615; State #156646, 9/23/70, NPMC NSC 607; Amman #4945 and #4951 and Tel Aviv #5171, 9/20/70, USSDA 2415. The latter document estimates 14 to 17 tanks destroyed by 11 AM; Tel Aviv #5198, 9/21/70, USSDA 2415; MFA #496 from Foreign Minister's Office to Eban, 9/20/70, MFA 4464/5.
2. MER, pp. 851–853; Quandt et al., *Politics,* p. 126; FCO #803 to Moscow, 9/20/70, FCO 17/1065.
3. Zak, p. 125; Dobson, p. 36; Rafael, p. 247; Tel Aviv #878 to FCO, 9/20/70, FCO 17/1065; MER, pp. 854–55; FBIS, 9/21/70, pp. H6, H7, and H8; *Haaretz,* 9/10/70, p. 5; *Maariv,* 9/18/70; *Yediot Aharonot,* 9/19/70; *Haaretz,* 9/21/70, pp. 1–2; Summary notes from Eban-Home meeting, MFA 4567/45; Sitreps, 9/23/70 0700 BST and 9/24/70 0700, PREM 15/125. Britain estimated the Israeli buildup was equivalent to four brigades.
4. Amman #4965 and #4969, 9/20/70, USSDA 2415; Freda; MER, p. 859; El-Edroos, p. 453.
5. Beirut #7937, 9/20/70, USSDA 307; Bern #2372, #2376, and #2396, 9/21/70, USSDA 307; Bern #301 and #302 to FCO, 9/21/70, FCO 14/783; Bern #92 and #95 to MFA, 9/21/70, MFA 4464/5.
6. Amman telexcon with FCO 1600Z, 9/19/70, PREM 15/203; Bern #2376, 9/21/70, USSDA 307; cable to MFA at 1330, 9/21/70, MFA 6603/19; *Haaretz,* 9/23/70, p. 2.
7. Freda.
8. Gillmore, note to Tripp, 9/20/70, PREM 15/124; Amman #4951 and State #154415 and #154417, 9/20/70, USSDA 2415; Kissinger-Nixon telecon, morning, 9/20/70, NPMC Kissinger Telecons 29; Kissinger, pp. 618–19.
9. Amman #4983, 9/20/70, USSDA 2415; Amman to FCO 201000Z, cited in sitrep, 9/21/70 0700 BST, PREM 15/124; FCO #2101 and #2102 to Washington, 9/20/70, FCO 17/1065.
10. Kissinger, pp. 598–99, 620–24; Dowty, p. 169, footnote 95; Isaacson, p. 303; State #154419, 9/20/70, USSDA 2415; London #7572, 9/21/70, USSDA 2415; "Air Strikes Against Syrian Forces in Jordan," Pro and Con paper, NPMC NSC 615; Haig memo to Kissinger, 9/20/70, NPMC Haig 972; Haig, pp. 248–50; Action item list, in WSAG meeting folder for 8:30 AM, 9/21/70, NPMC NSC H77; Amman #627 and #628 to FCO and Amman #1 to UKMIS, 9/21/70, FCO 17/1065; Transcript of phone conversation between Greenhill and member of Kissinger's staff (Haig), 9/21/70 0200 BST, PREM 15/124; handwritten note (Commander Howe?), 9/21/70, PREM 15/124; Memo from A. Ibbott to Tripp, 9/21/70, FCO 14/783 and PREM 15/124;

Cabinet meeting, CM (70) 20th Conclusions, 9/21/70, CAB 128/47; Garfinkle, p. 271; *Haaretz,* 9/21/70, p. 1; Rafael, p. 247; Joseph Alsop, *International Herald Tribune,* 9/26–27/70.

A Desperate Situation

1. Tel Aviv #5198 and #5210 and State #154557, 9/21/70, USSDA 2415; sitrep, 9/22/70 0700 BST, PREM 15/124; Zak, p. 121, footnote 58; Rabin, p. 186; Gharaibeh interview; Apthan-Echraisha interview; Sayigh, p. 265.
2. *Haaretz,* 9/23/70, p. 2; Bern #2395, 9/21/70, USSDA 609; Bern #2377, 9/21/70, USSDA 307; Bern #301 to FCO, 9/21/70, FCO 14/783; Bern #91 and #96 to MFA, 9/21/70, MFA 4464/5.
3. Nicosia #1737, 9/30/70, USSDA 338; Amman #5426 and #5427, 9/29/70, USSDA 307; Amman #5475, 9/30/70, NPMC NSC 615; Berkowitz e-mail to author, 11/24/03.
4. Cabinet meeting CM (70) 20th Conclusions, 9/21/70, CAB 128/47; Tripp, memo re British Interests, 9/21/70, PREM 15/124; Sitrep, 9/23/70 0700 BST, PREM 15/125.
5. Haig, p. 249; Kissinger, pp. 625–26; State #155203, 9/21/70, NPMC NSC 615; Note headed "Rabin's Message—Monday, September 21, 1970—5:15 AM," NPMC 134 HAK-Rabin; Kissinger-Haig telecon 5 AM and Kissinger-Rogers telecon 7:15 AM, 9/21/70, NPMC Kissinger Telecons 29.
6. State #154587, 9/21/70, USSDA 338; Amman #5006, 9/21/70, USSDA 2415; Amman #4997, 9/21/70, NPMC NSC 615; Washington #2783 to FCO, PREM 15/124; *Haaretz,* 9/22/70, pp. 1–2; MER, p. 860; Saunders Memorandum for Dr. Kissinger re Background Perspective for WSAG (situation this afternoon), 9/21/70, NPMC NSC H77.
7. Amman telexcon with FCO 1630Z, 9/21/70, FCO 14/783; Saunders Memorandum for Dr. Kissinger re Background Perspective for WSAG (situation this afternoon), 9/21/70, NPMC NSC H77; El-Edroos, p. 456; State #154557, 9/21/70, USSDA 2415; Sitrep, 9/22/70 0700 BST, PREM 15/124.
8. Bliner interview; Nicosia #1710, 9/27/70, USSDA 307.
9. Bern #2399, 9/22/70, USSDA 307; Bern #314 to FCO, 9/22/70, FCO 14/783; Bern #306 to FCO, 9/22/70, FCO 14/784; Bern #100 to MFA, 9/22/70, MFA 4464/5.
10. State #155203, 9/21/70, NPMC NSC 615.

Poised To Intervene

1. *Haaretz,* 9/23/70, p. 1; El-Edroos, pp. 454, 456, suggests that the attacks started on Sept. 21, not Sept. 22; Apthan-Echraisha interview; Nashat Majali interview; Dowty, p. 173, footnote 109; De Atkine, "Amman 1970"; Salloukh; Brown; Cooley, p. 117; Amman telexcon with FCO 0630Z, 9/22/70, PREM 15/124; Sitrep, 9/23/70 0700 BST, 9/22/70, PREM 15/125; Sitrep, 9/23/70 0700 BST, 9/22/70, PREM 15/125; Haig, memoranda for Henry Kissinger re Conversation with Ambassador Rabin and re Israeli matter, 9/22/70, NPMC

NSC 607; Kissinger Memorandum for the President re Meeting on Jordan, 9/22/70, NPMC NSC 615.

2. *International Herald Tribune,* 9/28/70.
3. Khaled letter to mother, 9/22/70, PREM 15/203; Noyes, letter to Tesh, 9/22/70, CAB 164/795.
4. Robinson Memorandum for Dr. Kissinger re US Military Actions to Deter Soviet Intervention in the Middle East, 9/22/70, NPMC NSC H76; Saunders and Kennedy Memorandum for Dr. Kissinger re WSAG Meeting-Jordan-22 September 1970, 9/22/70, NPMC NSC H76; Kissinger Memorandum for the President re Meeting on Jordan, 9/22/70, NPMC NSC 615; Garfinkle, pp. 284–86; Goldstein and Zhukov; Zumwalt, p. 298.
5. Bern #2410 and State #155256, 9/22/70, USSDA 307; Sitrep, 9/23/70 0700 BST, PREM 15/125; Bern #307 and #308 to FCO, FCO #186 and #188 to Bern, and UNMIS #2003 to FCO, 9/22/70, FCO 14/784; Bern #309 to FCO, 9/23/70, FCO 14/784; Bern #103 and #104 to MFA, 9/22/70, MFA 4464/5; Bern #110 to MFA, 9/23/70, MFA 4464/5.
6. El-Edroos, p. 456; Salloukh; MER, p. 853: Many sources claim that the withdrawal began on Sept. 23; De Atkine, "Amman 1970"; Neumark, p. 350; Amman telexcon with FCO 1630Z, 9/22/70, PREM 15/124; Moon, memo to Heath re Middle East, 9/22/70, PREM 15/124.
7. MER, p. 860; Mensch interview; Amman #5054, 9/22/70, USSDA 307.
8. Heath, draft message to Nasser and FCO #1215 and #1216 to UKMIS, 9/22/70, PREM 15/124; Cairo # 1054, 9/23/70, PREM 15/125; FCO #194, 9/25/70, FCO 14/785; Sitrep, 9/24/70 0700, PREM 15/125; *Haaretz,* 9/22/70, p. 1; *Egyptian Gazette,* 9/22/70, p. 1; *Haaretz,* 9/23/70, p. 1; El-Edroos, p. 457; Cabinet meeting CM (70) 23rd Conclusions, 9/28/70, CAB 128/47.
9. Berkowitz interview; Berkowitz e-mail to author, 12/4/03; Nicosia #1737, 9/30/70, USSDA 338 claims that the men were relocated on Sept. 23.
10. Tel Aviv #5248, 9/22/70, NPMC NSC 607; Memorandum of Conversation, Rabin, Kissinger, et al., 9/22/70, NPMC NSC 134; *Haaretz,* 9/23/70, p. 2; Kissinger Memorandum for the President re The Situation in Jordan, 9/23/70, NPMC NSC H76; Quandt, *Peace Process,* p. 82.

Switzerland and Germany Cave

1. Saunders, Memorandum for Dr. Kissinger re The Situation In Jordan, 9/23/70, NPMC NSC H76; Kissinger Memorandum for the President re The Situation in Jordan, 9/23/70, NPMC NSC H76; MER, p. 861; FBIS, 9/23/70, pp. D2–3; Sayigh, p. 266; Cobban, p. 207; Hart, p. 321; Olaimat interview. Some historians report that the Jordanian forces had fired on Nimeiry's entourage. Olaimat, his Jordanian army escort, recalled that they were fired on by Palestinians.
2. Kissinger Memorandum for the President re The Situation in Jordan, 9/23/70, NPMC NSC H76; Kissinger, p. 629.

3. Beirut #8090 and Bern #2423, 9/23/70, USSDA 307; Bern #310, 9/23/70, FCO 14/784; Bern #110 to MFA, 9/23/70, MFA 4464/5. One version of the conversation indicates that the PFLP had the hostages' passports in their possession *in Beirut.*
4. El-Edroos, pp. 452, 456; Salloukh; Brown; Sayigh, pp. 264–65; including footnote 32; Hart, pp. 318–19; Shemesh, p. 111; Abu Iyad, p. 85; Cooley, p. 115; Seale, pp. 154–62; Abu-Odeh interview; Bengio interview; Baghdad #635 to FCO, 9/19/70, FCO 14/783; See MER, pp. 853–54. Many sources claim that the Syrian withdrawal started Sept. 23. Ghasib interview, claimed that Syria had lost 135 tanks and 1,500 dead and wounded. Apthan-Echraisha interview; Schoenbaum, pp. 171–77; Summary notes from meeting, MFA 4567/45; Amman telexcon with FCO, 9/23/70 1400Z, PREM 15/125; Tel Aviv #231610Z, 9/23/70, PREM 15/125. Syria never actually fully withdrew. The border that commandos from Syria had physically moved on Sept. 18 beyond Tura was shifted back months later after a citizen rebellion, but not returned all the way. Only in October 2004 did the two countries establish a joint commission to resolve the disputed 125 square kilometers. Petra news service, 11/20/04, www.petra.gov.jo/nepras/2004/Nov/20/22400000.htm.
5. Bern #111 and #113 to MFA, 9/23/70, MFA 4464/5; Bern #114 to MFA, 9/24/70, MFA 4464/5; Bern #2425 and #2427, 9/23/70, USSDA 307; Bern #311 through #314, 9/23/70, FCO 14/784; handwritten note, 10 Downing Street 2150, 9/23/70, PREM 15/203; note re Jordan hostages, 9/24/70, PREM 15/203; Moon, memo to Heath re The Middle East, 9/23/70, PREM 15/125.

What About the Hostages?

1. Kissinger, p. 630; Dowty, p. 179; Amman telexcon at 1830Z, 9/24/70, FCO 14/785; Paris #12857, 9/23/70, USSDA 609; Sitrep, 9/24/70 0700, PREM 15/125.
2. Amman #5135, 9/24/70, NPMC NSC H76; Amman #241240Z, 9/24/70, FCO 14/784; Amman telexcon at 1830Z, 9/24/70, FCO 14/785; Amman telexcon with FCO, 9/23/70 1400Z, PREM 15/125; *International Herald Tribune,* 9/23/70; *Le Monde,* 9/24/70.
3. Morse; Beirut #8168, 9/24/70, USSDA 307; Bern #323 to FCO, 9/25/70, FCO 14/785; Bern #120 to MFA, 9/25/70, MFA 4464/5.
4. Note to Moon, 9/24/70, PREM 15/125; Amman telexcon at 1830Z, 9/24/70, FCO 14/785.
5. State #157107, 9/24/70, USSDA 307; Bern #2450 and #2451, 9/25/70, USSDA 307; Bern #320, #321, and #322 to FCO, 9/25/70, FCO 14/785; FCO #190 to Bern, 9/24/70, FCO 14/785; Summary notes from meeting, MFA 4567/45; New York #425 to MFA, 9/24/70, MFA 4464/5; Bern #119 to MFA, 9/25/70, MFA 4464/5.
6. FBIS, 9/25/70, p. D3.
7. Washington #223 to MFA, 9/23/70, MFA 4464/5; Menachem Raab conversations; New York #433 to MFA, 9/24/70, MFA 4464/5.

European Hostages Rescued

1. Amman, telecon at 0630Z, 9/25/70, FCO 14/784; *International Herald Tribune,* 9/30/70; Freda.
2. FBIS, 9/25/70, p. D4; *The Times,* 9/26/70, MFA 5898/11; Amman telexcon 1600Z, 9/25/70, PREM 15/125; Amman #654 to FCO, 9/25/70, FCO 14/785; Amman #5226 and Beirut #8243, 9/26/70, USSDA 307; Snow and Phillips, pp. 151–52.
3. FBIS, 9/25/70, p. D1; Sufeig al-Jazi interview; Abu-Odeh interview; Bulloch, p. 67; Abu-Odeh, p. 184; Abu-Iyad, p. 89; Aburish, p. 113; Cooley, pp. 118, 120; Sitrep, 9/29/70 0700, PREM 15/125; Haig, Memorandum for the President re The Situation in Jordan #22416, 9/26/70, NPMC NSC 615; Kissinger, Memorandum for the President re Afternoon Situation Report on Jordan #22417, 9/25/70, NPMC NSC 615.
4. Bern #329 to FCO, 9/25/70, FCO 14/785; Bern #2461, 9/25/70, USSDA 307; Beirut #8187, 9/25/70, USSDA 609.
5. FBIS, 9/25/70, p. D4; Amman #5176 and #5183, 9/25/70, USSDA 307; Amman telexcon 1600Z, 9/25/70, PREM 15/125; Amman #654 to FCO, 9/25/70, FCO 14/784; Amman #656 to FCO and Bern #329 to FCO, 9/25/70, FCO 14/785; Kidron, memo to MFA re Hostages in Amman, 9/22/70, MFA 4464/5.
6. Tel Aviv #909 to FCO, Amman #660, and Beirut #509 to FCO, 9/25/70, FCO 14/785; Amman telexcon 1600Z, 9/26/70, FCO 14/785; Gillmore, memo to Cromartie and FCO #399 to Amman, 9/25/70, FCO 14/785; Amman telexcon 1600Z, 9/25/70, PREM 15/125; Moon, note to Farrow, 9/25/70, PREM 15/203; Bern #354 to FCO, 9/30/70, FCO 14/786.
7. Amman telexcon 1600Z, 9/25/70, PREM 15/125; Sayigh, pp. 266–67; Sitrep 0700, 9/27/70, FCO 14/785; Haig, Memorandum for the President re The Situation in Jordan #22416, 9/26/70, NPMC NSC 615.

Our Perilous Walk to Freedom

1. CBS News, 9/27/70, VUTNA.
2. Sitrep, 9/26/70 0700, FCO 14/785; Sitrep 0700, 9/27/70, FCO 14/785; Beirut #65 to FCO and Nicosia #261355Z, 9/26/70, FCO 14/785; Moon, note to Prime Minister, 9/26/70, PREM 15/203; MFA #740, 9/26/70, MFA 4464/5; *The Times,* 9/26/70, MFA 5898/11; Bern #2473 and Beirut #8231, 9/26/70, USSDA 307; Haig, Memorandum for the President re The Situation in Jordan #22416, 9/26/70, NPMC NSC 615.
3. Moon, note to Prime Minister, 9/26/70, PREM 15/203; Bern #128 to MFA, 9/26/70, MFA 4464/5; Bern #2473, 9/26/70, USSDA 307; Bern #334 to FCO, 9/26/70, FCO 14/785.
4. Cairo #1073 to FCO, 9/26/70, PREM 15/203; Amman #675 through #677 to FCO, 9/26/70, FCO 14/785; State #159075 and Amman #5219 and #5226, 9/26/70, USSDA 307.
5. CBS News, 9/27/70, VUTNA; Majer; Freda; Bliner; Note to Prime Minister, 9/27/70, PREM 15/203; Beckett, note to Adams re The Release of the Thirty-Two,

9/27/70, FCO 14/785; Baker Majali; official cables (e.g., Washington #2900 to FCO, 9/30/70, FCO 14/786) mistakenly refer to Azziz el-Dien as a second secretary at the Egyptian embassy in Amman. Egyptian Foreign Ministry archives indicate no diplomat that year by that name, and the embassy denied that any of its staff was involved (Amman telexcon 1600Z, 9/26/70, FCO 14/785).

6. Washington #2862 and Bonn #1133 to FCO and FCO #951 and #2177, 9/26/70, FCO 14/785; Moon, note to Prime Minister, 9/26/70, PREM 15/203; Tripp, memo to Greenhill re Hostages, 9/27/70, PREM 15/203; State #159075 and Amman #5221, 9/26/70, USSDA 307; Haig, Memorandum for the President, 9/26/70, NPMC Haig 972.
7. Cairo #2213, 9/26/70, USSDA 609; Cairo #1074 to FCO, 9/26/70, FCO 14/785; FCO #955, 9/27/70, FCO 14/785.
8. CBS News, 9/27/70, VUTNA; Muashir interview.

Six Missing Hostages

1. Amman #5254, 9/27/70, USSDA 307; Majer interview; Bliner interview; Tripp, note to Greenhill re Move of Leila Khaled to Cairo, 9/27/70, CAB 164/795.
2. Amman #5252, #5257, #5260, and #5261, 9/27/70, USSDA 307; Note to Prime Minister, 9/27/70, PREM 15/125; Amman #682 and #684 to FCO and Cairo #1077 to FCO, 9/27/70, FCO 14/785; Amman #5259, 9/27/70, USSDA 338; Amman telexcon 0600Z, 9/27/70, FCO 14/785.
3. Tripp, note to Greenhill re Move of Leila Khaled to Cairo, 9/27/70, CAB 164/795; Nicosia #1703 and #1706, 9/27/70, USSDA 338; Nicosia #1708, 9/27/70, USSDA 307; Nicosia #1711, 9/28/70, USSDA 338.
4. London #7748, 9/24/70, NPMC NSC H76; Kissinger, Memorandum for the President re The Situation in Jordan—1700 GMT, 9/28/70, NPMC NSC 615; Amman telexcon 0930Z, 9/24/70, PREM 15/125; Cairo #1081 to FCO, 9/28/70, PREM 15/125; Amman telexcon 1640Z and its continuation, 9/29/70, PREM 15/203; Cooley, p. 119.
5. Amman #5267, #5272, #5274, #5280, and #5285, 9/27/70, USSDA 307; Beckett, note to Adams re The Six Hostages, 9/27/70, FCO 14/785; Washington #2864 to FCO, 9/27/70, FCO 14/784; Amman #687 to FCO, 9/27/70, FCO 14/785.
6. Cabinet meeting CM (70) 23rd Conclusions, 9/28/70, CAB 128/47; Sitrep, 9/28/70 0700, PREM 15/125; Tripp, note to Greenhill re Move of Leila Khaled to Cairo, 9/27/70, CAB 164/795; Bern #337 to FCO and Bonn #1134 to FCO, 9/27/70, FCO 14/785; Bern #2489 and State #159169, 9/28/70, USSDA 307.
7. MFA #746, 9/27/70, MFA 4464/5; Bern #2479, 9/27/70, USSDA 307; FCO #202 to Bern, 9/29/70, FCO 14/786; Bern #358 to FCO, 10/1/70, FCO 14/786.

Nixon and Home

1. Rome #5484, 9/28/70, USSDA 338; CBS Evening News, 9/27/70, VUTNA; CBS Evening News, 9/28/70, VUTNA; NBC Nightly News, 9/28/70, VUTNA;

author's distinct recollection varies somewhat with Nixon comments to hostages, 1970_0305, 1970, NLB.

2. Daunt, note to Greenhill re Hostages: Khaled, 9/28/70, CAB 164/795; London #115 to MFA, 9/28/70, MFA 4464/5; Budgen, note to Tripp, and Simpson, note to Graham re Khaled, 9/28/70, FCO 14/785; Makins, memo to Tripp re Khaled and El Al, 9/29/70, FCO 14/786; Cairo #1107 to FCO, 9/30/70, FCO 14/786; Chamberlain, note to Tripp re Khaled, 9/30/70, FCO 14/786; London #7835, 9/28/70, USSDA 609; Sitrep, 9/28/70 0700, PREM 15/125.
3. Sitrep, 9/28/70 0700, PREM 15/125; Amman telexcon 1430Z, 9/28/70, PREM 15/125; Sitrep, 9/29/70 0700, PREM 15/125; Moon, note to Prime Minister re Middle East at 7:45 PM September 28, 9/28/70, PREM 15/125; Amman #704 to FCO, PREM 15/125; Amman telexcon 1100Z, 9/29/70, FCO 14/786; Amman #698 to FCO, Bern #347 to FCO, Cairo #1083 to FCO, and FCO #965 and #968 to Cairo, 9/28/70, FCO 14/785; Tel Aviv #925 to FCO, 9/29/70, FCO 14/786; Amman #5377 and Bern #2505, 9/29/70, USSDA 609; Amman #5322, 9/27/70, USSDA 307; Kissinger, Memorandum for the President re Jordan situation report, 9/28/70, NPMC NSC 615.
4. Sitrep, 9/29/70 0700, PREM 15/125; Salibi, p. 239.
5. Berkowitz interview; Berkowitz e-mail to author, 12/4/03.

Last Six Finally Free

1. Sitrep, 9/29/70 0700, PREM 15/125; Amman telexcon 0700Z, 9/29/70, FCO 14/786.
2. Amman telexcons 0700Z and 1100Z, 9/29/70, FCO 14/786.
3. FCO #442 to Tel Aviv, 9/29/70, FCO 14/786; London #178 to MFA, 9/29/70, MFA 4464/5.
4. Amman #5425, 9/29/70, USSDA 338; Amman #5412, #5414, #5426, and #5427, 9/29/70, USSDA 307; Berkowitz interview; Berkowitz e-mail to author, 11/24/03; Kissinger, Memorandum for the President re The Situation in Jordan—1800 GMT, September 29, 9/29/70, NPMC NSC 615; Amman #716 to FCO and Washington #2892 to FCO, 9/29/70, FCO 14/786.

European Capitulation and Culmination

1. FCO #271 and Amman #718 to FCO, 9/30/70, FCO 14/786; Amman telexcon, 9/30/70, FCO 14/786; Beirut #8391, Athens #5422, and Nicosia #1734, 9/30/70, USSDA 338; Beirut #8392, 9/30/70, USSDA 307; Berkowitz interview.
2. Amman #5465 and London #7975, 9/30/70, USSDA 609; State #160839, 9/30/70, USSDA 338; Amman #723 to FCO, 9/30/70, FCO 14/786; Tel Aviv #952 to FCO, 10/7/70, FCO 14/786; London #186 to MFA, 9/30/70, MFA 4464/5.
3. Cabinet meeting CM (70) 25th Conclusions, 10/1/70, CAB 128/47; Sitrep 0700, 9/30/70, PREM 15/125; Sitrep 0700, 10/1/70, PREM 15/125; Cairo #1116 to FCO, 10/1/70, FCO 14/786; Cairo #1158 to FCO, 10/7/70, FCO 14/786; London #7977, 9/30/70, USSDA 609. Israel would file a formal protest

over Khaled's release; after a British response about a month later, the issue would be dropped. Tel Aviv #939 and #943 to FCO, 10/4–5/70, FCO 14/786; Evans, note to Adams re Leila Khaled: Israeli Protest, 10/28/70, FCO 14/786; London #19 and #21 to MFA, 10/6–7/70, MFA 4464/4; London #83 to MFA, 11/16/70, MFA 4464/4 and 6603/20; Meron cable to Comay, 11/5/70, MFA 6603/20.

Epilogue

1. Shemesh, p. 148; Quandt et al., *Politics,* footnote on p. 128; Sayigh, p. 267; Susser, pp.132–42; Salibi pp. 239–41; El-Edroos, pp. 458, 460; MER, p. 855; Summary notes from Eban-Home meeting, MFA 4567/45; Seale, p. 162; Aburish, p. 115; Rabinovich, *Yom Kippur War,* p. 50; Rabin, p. 189; Kissinger-Argov telecon 6 PM, 9/23/70, NPMC Kissinger Telecons 6.

BIBLIOGRAPHY AND SOURCES

Archives

CAB, PREM, FCO	Cabinet, Premier, and Foreign Office Archives, British National Archives, London
JAAMA	Jordanian Arab Army Military Archives, Amman, Jordan
MFA	Ministry of Foreign Affairs Archives, Israel State Archives, Jerusalem
NPMC	Richard M. Nixon Presidential Materials Collection, College Park, Md
NLB	Nixon Papers, Richard M. Nixon Library & Birthplace, Yorba Linda, Ca
TWAHC	TWA historical collection, courtesy of Zana Allen, St. Louis, Mo
USSDA	State Department Archives, U.S. National Archives and Records Administration (NARA), College Park, Md
VUTNA	Vanderbilt University Television News Archive (VUTNA), Nashville, Tn

Articles

Brandon, Henry. "Jordan: The Forgotten Crisis (1)," *Foreign Policy,* 10 (Spring 1973b), pp. 158–70.

Brown, Neville. "Jordanian Civil War," *Military Review* 51, no. 9, Sept. 1971.

Goldstein, Lyle J. and Yuri M. Zhukov. "A Tale of Two Fleets: A Russian Perspective on the 1973 Naval Standoff in the Mediterranean," *Naval War College Review,* Spring 2004 (http://www.nwc.navy.mil/press/Review/2004/Spring/art2-sp04.htm).

Lesch, Ann. "Israeli Deportation of Palestinians from the West Bank and the Gaza Strip," *Journal of Palestine Studies* VIII, no. 2, Winter 1979, pp. 101–31.

Salloukh, Bassel F. "State Strength, Permeability, And Foreign Policy Behavior: Jordan In Theoretical Perspective," *Arab Studies Quarterly* 18, no. 2, Spring 1996.

Schoenbaum, David. "Jordan: The Forgotten Crisis (2)," *Foreign Policy* 10, Spring 1973, pp. 171–81.

Books

Abou Daoud and Gilles de Jonchay. *Palestine: De Jerusalem a Munich.* Paris: Editions Anne Carriere, 1999.

Abu Iyad: See Khalaf, Salah below.

Abu-Odeh, Adnan. *Jordanians, Palestinians, and the Hashemite Kingdom in the Middle East Peace Process.* Washington, DC: United States Institute of Peace, 1998.

Aburish, Said K. *Arafat: From Defender to Dictator.* New York and London: Bloomsbury Publishing, 1998.

Abu-Sharif, Bassam and Uzi Mahnaimi. *Best of Enemies.* Little Brown, 1995.

Ajami, Fuad. *The Arab Predicament: Arab Political Thought And Practice Since 1967.* Cambridge: Cambridge University Press, 1981.

Bailey, Clinton. *Jordan's Palestinian Challenge, 1948–1983: A Political History.* Boulder, Col.: Westview, 1984.

Becker, Jillian. *The PLO: The Rise and Fall of the Palestine Liberation Organization.* New York: St. Martin's Press, 1984.

Bulloch, John. *The Making of a War: The Middle East from 1967 to 1973.* London: Longman Group, 1974.

Cobban, Helena. *The Palestinian Liberation Organization.* Cambridge: Cambridge University Press, 1983.

Cohen, Yeruham. *The Allon Plan [*Hebrew: *Tokhnit Allon].* Hakibutz Hameuhad, 1972.

Cooley, John. *Green March, Black September: The Story of the Palestinian Arabs.* London: Frank Cass, 1973.

Dayan, Moshe. *Story of My Life.* New York: William Morrow, 1976.

Dishon, Daniel, ed. *Middle East Record, Volume Five: 1969–1970.* Jerusalem: Israel Universities Press, 1977.

Dobson, Christopher. *Black September: Its Short, Violent History.* New York: Macmillan, 1974.

Dowty, Alan. *Middle East Crisis: U.S. Decision-Making in 1958, 1970 and 1973.* Berkeley: University of California Press, 1984.

Eban, Abba. *Abba Eban: An Autobiography.* New York: Random House, 1977.

El-Edroos, Syed A. *The Hashemite Arab Army 1908–1979: An Appreciation and Analysis of Military Operations.* Amman, Jordan: Publishing Committee, 1980.

Garfinkle, Adam M. *United States Foreign Policy and the Jordan Crisis of 1970: A Cognitive Approach.* Doctoral diss., University of Pennsylvania, 1979.

Gazit, Shlomo. *Trapped Fools: Thirty Years of Israeli Policy in the Territories.* London: Frank Cass, 2003.

———. "The Consolidation of Policy and Organization Patterns in the Administered Territories (Emphasis on Judea and Samaria, 1967–1968)." MA thesis, Tel Aviv University, 1980.

Haig, Alexander. *Inner Circles: How America Changed the World: A Memoir.* Warner Books, 1992.

Hart, Alan. *Arafat: A Political Biography.* Bloomington, Ill.: Indiana University Press, 1989.

Hersh, Seymour M. *The Price of Power: Kissinger in the Nixon White House.* New York: Summit Books, 1983.

Herzog, Chaim. *The Arab-Israeli Wars.* New York: Vintage Books, 1984.

Indyk, Martin. *The Politics of Patronage: Israel and Egypt Between the Superpowers, 1962–1973.* Doctoral diss., Australian National University, 1977.

Isaacson, Walter. *Kissinger: A Biography.* New York: Touchstone/Simon & Schuster, 1992.

Kalb, Marvin and Bernard Kalb. *Kissinger.* New York: Dell, 1975.

Katz, Shmuel. *Battleground: Fact and Fantasy in Palestine.* New York: Taylor Productions, 2002.

Kazziha, Walid. *Revolutionary Transformation in the Arab World: Habash and His Comrades from Nationalism to Marxism.* New York: St. Martin's Press, 1975.

Khalaf, Salah (Abu Iyad). *My Home, My Land: A Narrative of the Palestinian Struggle.* New York: Time Books, 1981.

Khaled, Leila. *My People Shall Live.* London: Hodder & Stoughton, 1973.

Kissinger, Henry. *White House Years.* Brown & Company, 1979.

Lalor, Paul. *Black September 1970: The Palestinian Resistance Movement in Jordan, 1967–1971.* Doctoral diss., Oxford University, 1992.

Lawson, Fred H. *Why Syria Goes to War: Thirty Years of Confrontation.* Ithaca, NY: Cornell University Press, 1968.

Lunt, James. *Hussein of Jordan.* New York: William Morrow, 1989.

Morris, Benny. *The Birth of the Palestinian Refugee Problem.* Cambridge: Cambridge University Press, 1988.

Neumark, Aaron. *The Neo-Ba'ath Regime in Syria, 1966–1970* [Hebrew: *Mishtar Ha-Neo-Ba'ath B'Suria*]. Doctoral diss., Bar Ilan University, Ramat Gan, Israel, 2002.

Nixon, Richard. *RN: The Memoirs of Richard Nixon.* New York: Grosset & Dunlap, 1978.

Oren, Michael. *Six Days of War.* Oxford University Press, 2002.

Quandt, William B. *Peace Process: American Diplomacy and the Arab-Israeli Conflict Since 1967.* Washington, DC: Brookings Institute, 1993.

———. *Decade of Decisions: American Policy Toward the Arab-Israeli Conflict, 1967–1976.* Berkeley: University of California Press, 1977.

Quandt, William B., Fuad Jabber, and Ann Mosley Lesch. *The Politics of Palestinian Nationalism.* Berkeley: University of California Press, 1973.

Rabin, Yitzhak. *The Rabin Memoirs.* Berkeley: University of California Press, 1996.

Rabinovich, Abraham. *The Yom Kippur War: The Epic Encounter That Transformed the Middle East.* New York: Schocken Books, 2004.

Rabinovitch, Itamar and Haim Shaked, eds. *From June to October: The Middle East Between 1967 and 1973.* New Brunswick, NJ: Transaction, 1978.

Rafael, Gideon. *Destination Peace: Three Decades of Israeli Foreign Policy.* New York: Stein & Day, 1981.

Robins, Philip. *A History of Jordan.* Cambridge, UK: Cambridge University Press, 2004.

Rochat, André. *L'Homme à la Croix.* Éditions de l'Aire, 2005.

Ro'i, Yaacov. *From Encroachment to Involvement: A Documentary Study of Soviet Foreign Policy in the Middle East, 1945–1973.* New York: Wiley, 1974.

Rubin, Barry and Judith Colp Rubin. *Yasir Arafat: A Political Biography.* Oxford University Press, 2003.

Salibi, Kamal. *The Modern History of Jordan.* New York: St. Martin's Press, 1998.
Sayigh, Yezid. *The Armed Struggle and the Search for State: The Palestinian National Movement, 1949–1993.* Oxford University Press, 1997.
Seale, Patrick: *Asad of Syria: The Struggle for the Middle East.* London: Taurus, 1988.
Shemesh, Moshe. *The Palestinian Entity 1959–1974: Arab Politics and the PLO.* London: Frank Cass, 1989.
Snow, Peter. *Hussein: A Biography.* Washington, DC: Robert B. Luce, Inc., 1972.
Snow, Peter and David Phillips. *The Arab Hijack War.* New York: Ballantine Books, 1970.
Susser, Asher. *On Both Banks of the Jordan: A Political Biography of Wasfi Al-Tall.* Essex: Frank Cass, 1994.
———. *Jordan: Case Study of a Pivotal State.* Washington, DC: Washington Institute for Near East Policy, 2000.
Wilson, Harold. *The Chariot of Israel: Britain, America, and the State of Israel.* New York: Norton, 1981.
Yaari, Ehud. *Strike Terror: The Story of Fatah.* New York: Sabra Books, 1970.
Zak, Moshe. *Hussein Makes Peace: Thirty-plus Years on the Road to Peace* (Hebrew: *Hussein Oseh Shalom*). Ramat Gan, Israel: Bar Ilan University Press, 1996.
Zumwalt, Elmo. *On Watch: A Memoir.* New York: Quadrangle Books, 1976.

Bound Collection of Documents and Transcripts

HBY	Hamatsav B'Yarden, transcription of Arab broadcasts, September 1970
MER	Middle East Record, Israel Universities Press, Jerusalem
RAW	Record of the Arab World, September, Jebran Chamieh, ed., Beirut, Lebanon
FBIS	US Foreign Broadcast Information Service Daily Report

Diaries and Testimonials

Adams, Michael. Diary, EUL MS 241/1 box 2, Exeter University Library (Special Collections).
De Atkine, Norvell. Assistant U.S. Defense Attaché. "Amman 1970: A memoir," *Middle East Review of International Affairs* 6, no. 4, Dec. 2002.
———. "Ambassador Dean Brown and the Jordanian Crisis of 1970: A Study in Leadership," *American Diplomacy,* 2001.
Ferruggio, John. Pan Am Flight Director. Account in Peter Gelzinis, "1970 Hijacking Survivor Has Watched Terror Grow," *Boston Herald,* Sept. 30, 2001, p. 10.
Freda, George. Hostage. "Survival Was Day-by-Day for Victims of Hijackings," *Miami Herald,* Sept. 29, 1970.
———. "Hostage Tells It As It Was," *National Observer,* Oct. 5, 1970.
Fried, Millie (Leser). Hostage. Reflection on the Hijacking—30 Years Later, Reunion Journal, Sept. 2000.
Horan, Hume. U.S. Embassy official in Amman. Extract from oral history to the Foreign Service Institute, Oct. 2000—Jan. 2001, *American Diplomacy,* Jan. 2, 2002.
Leser, Menachem (Manny). Hostage. "Thirty Years After the Hijacking of September 1970—Perspectives," Reunion Journal, Sept. 2000.

Morse, Richard. Hostage. "Hijacked Victim's Own Story," *Boston Globe,* Oct. 4 and 5, 1970.

Raab, David. Hostage. Diary, Dec. 7, 1970.

Raab, Sara. Hostage. Taped interviews with journalists week of Sept. 13, 1970; deposition Aug. 16 and 22, 1972.

Raab, Tikva. Deposition, June 4, 1970.

Rosenrauch, Susan (Hirsch). Hostage. "Resilience and Coping in the Face of Trauma: A Retrospective Account Thirty Years After a Skyjacking," Reunion Journal, Sept. 2000.

Al-Sirhan, Mufadi abd Al-Musleh. Brigadier in Jordanian Army. Recollection communicated verbally July 2004, trans. Baker al-Majali in e-mails to author, Dec. 2004 and Jan. 2005.

Swinkels, Rudolf J. TWA purser. Debrief to TWA and CIA, week of Sept. 20, 1970.

Woods, Carroll D. TWA captain. CBS television interview, Sept. 27, 1970.

Interviews

Crew

Uri Bar-Lev, El Al pilot
Jim Majer, TWA copilot

Passengers

Gerald (Jerry) and Rivke Berkowitz
Sarah (Malka) Bliner
Sara Raab
Conversations with Yaakov Drillman, Barbara Mensch, Susan (Hirsch) Rosenrauch, and author's family members

Jordanians

Col. Yahya Abu-Farraj, Jordan Arab Army brigade commander
Adnan Abu-Odeh, then information minister in the Military Cabinet
Gen. (Ret.) Mansour Abu-Rashid, then intelligence officer in the 1st Division
Maj. Gen. (Ret.) Shafic Ajeilat, then major Jordan Arab Army
Col. (Ret.) Khaled Apthan-Echraisha, then brigade commander in the northern front
Brig. Gen. (Ret.) Abdul Mun'em Baker Al-Jariri, then head of royal garages
Col. Hussein Muhammad Gharaibeh, Jordan Arab Army chief of staff of the Northern Jordan Brigade
Maj. Gen. (Ret.) Mohammad Kassab al-Majali, then chief of body guards
Musa Keilani, editor, *El-Urdun*
Maj. Gen. (Ret.) Salman Maaita, then commander of *fedayeen* detention center
Dr. Baker Kh. Al-Majali, Jordanian researcher and historian
Gen. (Ret) Nashat Majali, then intelligence officer of the 2nd Division

Gen. Fahed Makboul, then colonel, deputy military commander of the Zarqa governorate
Dr. Muashir, head of Muashir Hospital
Maj. Gen. (Ret.) Mohammad Alian Olaimat, then commander of a forward unit in Amman
Sister Janet Simonian, nurse at Muashir Hospital
Senator Brig. (Ret.) Kaseb Sufeig al-Jazi, then Military Commander of Amman and commander of all Jordan Arab Army forces in Amman

Other

Bassam Abu-Sharif, then spokesperson for the PFLP
Robert Anderson, then PFC, C Company, 1st Battalion, 325th Airborne Infantry Regiment, 2nd Brigade, 82nd Airborne Division
Dr. Ofra Bengio, Moshe Dayan Center, Tel Aviv University
Norvell De Atkine, then assistant U.S. defense attaché, Amman
Claude Girard, then TWA director of International Flight Operations sent to Amman
Martin Mensch, father of hostage Barbara Mensch
Jim Skinner, then combat engineer, 82nd Airborne Division
Dr. Asher Susser, director, Moshe Dayan Center, Tel Aviv University

Other Media

100 Years of Terror, Israel Television, 2001.
Days That Shook the World, BBC, Nov. 14, 2003.
Hijacked, PBS American Experience, retrieved Oct. 19, 2006.
UK Confidential, BBC, Jan. 1, 2001. "The Guerrilla's Story," //http:news.bbc.co.uk/.
Walter Cronkite, "Profile: Remembering the Terrorist Hijackings of September 1970," *All Things Considered,* NPR, Sept. 9, 2003 (transcript in author's hands).

INDEX

Entries in *italics* refer to figures and illustrations.

Abu-Khalid, 24, 72
Abu-Mehanna, Mazen, 24–5
Abu-Nadir, 132
Abu-Nidal, 50, 59, 80, 99
Abu-Odeh, Adnan, 138
Abu-Omar, 35–6
Abu-Sharif, Bassam, 4–5, 55, 121, 134, 136–7, 233
Action Group for the Liberation of Palestine, 32
Adams, Michael, 121
Adgham, Bahi al-, 220
Agudas Harabonim, 68
Ajeilat, Maj. Shafic, 26–7
Ajluni, Mazin al-, 138
Algerian diplomats, 11, 37, 120, 158, 194, 205, 224, 231
Ali, Ali As-Sayed, 23
Allen, Frank, 10, 120, 123–4
American hostages, 35, 38–9, 53, 102, 108, 112, 117, 121, 127, 213–31, 234
American Jewish community, 69, 148
Amman
  cease-fires in, 56, 75–6, 81–2, 95, 208–9, 212–3, 227
  fighting in, 5–8, 33, 44, 50, 66, 69–70, 75–6, 78, 91, 117, 128, 134–7, 149–54, 156–9, 161–2, 164–5, 168, 170–3, 177–80, 187–8, 198, 203–6, 210–1
  hostages in, 39–40, 53, 110, 121–2, 145–57, 162, 184–5, 218–9. *See also* Ashrafiyeh apartment; Intercontinental Hotel; Philadelphia Hotel; Wahdat refugee camp.
  humanitarian situation in, 204
  layout of, 149–50, *151*
Annenberg, Walter, 113
Arab League, 137
Arab Liberation Front (ALF), 52
Arab summit in Cairo (1970), 194–5, 220
Arab Truce Supervision Team, 227
Arafat, Yasser, 4–8, 70, 82, 85, 110, 117, 138, 143–4, 158, 169–70, 185, 195, 198, 206, 208–9, 220, 223, 233
Arguello, Oscar, 22
Arguello, Patrick Joseph, 17–9, 22–3, 223
Asch, Shimon, 20
Ashrafiyeh apartment
  fighting near, 143, 150, 152–3, 156, 161, 164–5, 168–9, 171–3, 177, 179–80, 184–5, 192, 201, 203–5, 207, 211
  hostages in, 110, 112–3, 134, *147*, 179, 188–9, 192, 203–4, 207, 209, 211–2, 214–7
  interrogations in, 188–9
  in 2004, 189
Assad, Hafez, 165–6, 174, 194, 200, 234
As-Saiqa, 52
Atasi, Nurredin, 153, 166, 176, 195, 234
Austrian airliner bombing, 32
Azziz el-Dien, Youssef, 214–6, 220, 224, 227–8, 231

Badri, Fahik al-, 137
Bar-Lev, Uri, 18–21, 23
Bar-Levav, Motti, 19–20
Barnes, John, 56, 113–5
BBC, 83, 118, 142, 204
Beam, Jacob, 165
Beaumont, Sir Richard, 213, 216, 220–1, 224
Beeber, Mimi, 50, 108, 152, 217
Beirut
  BOAC hijacked plane in, 71–2
  negotiations in, 164, 169–70, 204–5
  Pan Am hijacked plane in, 23–4
Beirut Star, 83
Ben-Horin, Eliashiv, 133
Berkowitz, Gerald (Jerry), 45–7, 52, 82, 118–9, 129, 146, 162, 196, 224–5, 228, 231

Berkowitz, Rivke, 45–6, 129
Berkowitz, Talia, 45
Bern Group, 44–5, 57, 73, 85, 88–9, 96–7, 102–3, 114, 120, 124, 129–30, 142–3, 156, 158–9, 164, 172, 178, 185–6, 189–90, 193–5, 199, 201–2, 204–5, 209, 213, 215–6, 221
Besner, Dr. Julius, 30
Black September, 233–4
BOAC Flight 775
  hijacking, 70–3
  hostages, 79, 80, 83–5, 97, 105, 107–9, 112, 116, 121, 134, 173
  plane blown up, 109
  threats to hostages, 84–5
Boisard, Marcel, 130, 135, 164, 169–70, 172, 178
Boissier, Pierre, 135, 158, 164, 169–70, 172, 178, 185, 189, 194, 199, 201–2, 204–5, 209, 213
Brandt, Willy, 54, 98, 119, 133
Britain. *See* United Kingdom (UK)
Brown, Dean, 135, 138–9, 168, 181–2, 187, 196
Brubeck, William, 113, 121, 127
Burmeister, William, 129
Burton, Peter, 22–3

Cain, Lennett, 118
Cairo Agreement (1970), 220
Cairo International Airport, 24–5, 32
Catholics, 69
Ceylonese hostages, 105
Chesler, Fran (Foozie), 108, 165, 222
Chicago Sun-Times, 159
China, 4
cholera, 51, 52, 81, 97, 132, 219
Christian Church (Disciples of Christ), 69
Columbo, Emilio, 222
Comay, Michael, 21, 223, 228
Conference of Presidents of Major Jewish Organizations, 133
Cooke, Terrence Cardinal, 69
Cooper, Trevor, 71–3, 83–5, 108–10
counterhostages, 102
Cronkite, Walter, 25
Cuba, 11, 31

Daoud, Mohammad, 138, 144
David, Bruriah, 108, 113
David, Rabbi Jonathan, 90, 99, 113, 146, 172
Davies, Rodger, 139
Davis, Shelby, 89, 124, 130, 144, 148, 156, 185, 201–2, 205, 213
Dawson, Sir Walter, 15
Dawson Field. *See also* BOAC Flight 775; Swissair Flight 100; TWA Flight 741
  ICRC and, 26, 51
  last hostages moved from, 106–10
  planes blown up at, 16, 94, 109, 112, 118–9
  planes land at, 14–8, 25–30, 72
  press conference at, 55–6
  renamed Revolution Airport, 28
Dayan, Moshe, 50
Degani, Nachum, 20
Demerjian, Janet, 18, 20
Dobson, Christopher, 176–7
Douglas-Home, Sir Alec, 64, 73, 122, 180–1, 194–5, 228
Dowty, Alan, 203
Drillman, Yaakov, 55, 90, 172, 173, 184
"dual nationals," 35–7, 41–2, 46, 54, 56, 61, 102, 127, 201
  with "Israeli military status," 86, 93, 102–3, 110, 121
Dubois, Charles-Albert, 117, 121
Dunn, Richard, 134
Dutch hostages, 112, 121, 127, 129

East Bank, 3, 6
Eban, Abba, 64, 102, 115, 156, 228
Egypt, 3, 7, 24–5, 148, 158, 167, 182, 233–4
  European prisoners released to, 232
  hostage release and, 209, 221, 212–6, 224–5, 227
Egyptian embassy, Amman, 212–6, 227
Eisenberg, Avraham, 18
El Al
  attacks on planes, 20, 31–2, 32, 34
  security measures, 23
El Al Flight 219
  hijacking attempt thwarted, 18–23, 35, 129
electricity outages, 152, 172–3, 178, 187, 192
European-held prisoners, 17, 31–6, 40, 85–6, 88, 110, 132, 144–5, 205, 210, 213, 215–6, 221, 223, 231–2
European hostages, 108, 110, 146, 150, 207–16. *See also specific nationalities*

Fatah, 4–6, 26, 56, 119, 177, 233
FBI, 22, 61
fedayeen, defined, 4. *See also* Palestinian resistance movement; *and specific organizations*
Fehse, Louise, 17
Feinstein, Ben, 89–90, 123, 173, 184
Feinstein, Rabbi Moses, 68–9
Fenton, Bob, 219
Ferruggio, John, 23–5
Five Member Committee (Committee of Five), 137, 144
France, 200
Frank, Paul, 53–4, 98
Frascani, Dr., 94
Freda, George, 67, 104–5, 145, 165, 177, 179, 207, 215

Freeman, John, 42–3, 122–3, 181
Freymond, Jacques, 34, 103, 110–1, 113, 120, 124
Fund, Meyer, 90, 172–3, 184, 222

Gaza Strip, 101–2, 233
Gazit, Shlomo, 102
German hostages, 35, 37–8, 112–3, 117, 127, 210
German Social Democratic Party, 98
Germany (West Germany), 11, 31, 40, 42–4, 53–4, 60–1, 67, 89, 96, 98, 117, 119, 124, 129–30, 133, 148, 154–5, 158–9, 164, 201–2, 205, 210, 215, 221
Girard, Claude, 121, 129, 172
Godber, Joseph, 116
Golan Heights, 74, 177
Goldstein, Lyle, 193
Goren, Nava, 36
Goulborn, Cyril, 71
Graber, Pierre, 114, 185–6
Graham, John, 134
Greece, 32, 160
Greenhill, Denis, 43, 53, 113, 139, 141, 155–6, 181–2, 223, 228
Guam, USS (helicoper carrier), 160

Habash, Dr. George, 4, 7, 31, 56, 102
Hadassah, 58
Haddad, Dr. Wadia (Wadi), 4, 31
Haditha, Mashhur, 6, 37–9, 56, 69, 70, 75, 82
Haig, Alexander, 43, 137, 139, 141, 186–7, 196
Hajji (Wahdat guard), 106, 110–1, 132, 146
Halacha (Jewish law), 99, 132
Hamas, 233
Harari-Raful, Rabbi Abraham, 46, 82–3, 127, 186, 230
Harari-Raful, Rabbi Joseph, 46, 82–3, 127, 145, 186, 230
Harari-Raful, Rachel, 99
Hart, Alan, 6
Hasim, Ben, 145
Heath, Edward, 139, 154, 186, 194–5, 205, 210, 213
Heikal, Muhammad Hassanein, 213, 215–6, 219, 224
Helms, Richard, 61, 187
Helou, Charles, 24
hijackings. *See also specific planes*
  BOAC Flight 775, 70–3
  El Al Flight 219 attempt, 17–23, 35, 129
  history of, 31–2
  Pan Am Flight 93, 22–5
  Swissair Flight 100, 16–7
  TWA flight 741, 9–17
Hirsch, Howie, 12–3, 48
Hirsch, Robert, 12–3, 22
Hirsch, Susan (Susie), 12–3, 30, 39, 45, 48, 50, 68, 91

Hitler, Adolf, 53
Hodes, Kathy, 54
Hodes, Martha, 54
Holland, 129. *See also* Dutch hostages
Hollingsworth, John, 46, 82, 225, 228–30
Holocaust, 38–9, 60, 99, 133
Hoover, J. Edgar, 61
Horan, Hume, 115
hostages. *See specific detention areas; flights; individuals; nationalities; and parties negotiating*
Hubler, Ken, 113, 146, 214
Hussein, King of Jordan
  aftermath of civil war and, 233–4
  Arab summit in Cairo and, 220
  Arafat's departure and, 209
  assassination attempt on, 7–8
  autograph of, for Raab, 223
  civil war and, 78, 131, 137–43, 148, 150, 152–3, 157–9, 161, 163, 166, 170, 172, 175–7, 188, 191, 194–5, 198, 200, 220
  hijacking and hostages and, 32–3, 113
  military aid requested from US, UK, and Israel by, 138–40, 159, 176–7, 180–3, 186–7, 190, 194, 196–7, 200, 205, 234
  Palestinian resistance and, 3–8, 44, 53, 70, 76, 82, 95, 137–8
Hussein Refugee Camp, 149, 150, 168, 170, 177, 211
Hutner, Rabbi Isaac, 54, 69, 100, 105, 113, 129, 163, 215

Ibrahim, Samir Abdul Majid, 23
Independence, USS (aircraft carrier), 62, 85, 160
Indian hostages, 105
Intercontinental Hotel, 43–4, 53, 66, 69–70, 75–6, 78, 80, 86, 96–7, 105, 107, 110, 117, 129, 137, 150, 153, 161, 172–3, 195, 213–4
International Committee of the Red Cross (ICRC), 26, 32, 34, 38, 43–6, 50–4, 57, 60–1, 66–7, 76, 81–8, 94, 96, 102–16, 120, 124, 129–35, 145, 148, 158, 164, 169, 178, 185, 189, 194, 203–4, 214–7, 220, 224, 228
International Court of Justice, 134, 223
International Herald Tribune, 219, 222–3
Iraq, 4, 7, 26, 47, 61, 85–6, 141, 148, 159–60, 162, 167, 175, 177, 200, 234
  Ba'ath party, 162
Irbid
  fighting in, 52, 56, 66, 70, 75, 128, 135, 148, 154, 162, 170, 175, 182–3, 185, 195–6, 199–200
  hostages in, 47, 51–2, 61, 82–3, 87, 93, 103, 112, 115, 118–9, 121, 145–6, 162, 186, 195–6, 216, 224–5
  last six hostages in, released, 227–31

Israel
  Air Force, 18, 45, 177, 182
  Arab war vs., 3–5, 7, 36, 154–5, 233–4
  Cabinet, 56, 88
  Defense Forces, 26, 55, 115, 121, 127, 175–7, 200
  demands on, for release of prisoners, 36–7, 55–6, 85, 89, 103, 115, 128–9, 132, 141, 164, 178, 199, 205, 213, 215, 224, 231
  Egypt and, 225
  Foreign Ministry, 56, 73, 119–20, 145, 156
  hijackings as weapon vs., 17, 31, 50
  General Security Service, 19, 224
  Government Operations in the Occupied Territories, 102
  hostages' families and, 206
  importance of, for hostages, 185, 234
  items made in, confiscated, 49–50, 80–1
  Jordanian civil war and Hussein's request for aid, 139, 159, 176–7, 180–3, 186–7, 190, 194, 196–7, 200, 205, 234
  Khaled extradition and, 21, 41, 64, 134, 143, 221, 223, 228
  lack of Israeli hostages and, 127
  map of, in Irbid, 52
  Munich Olympic athletes murder and, 234
  negotiations and, 40–4, 50–6, 68–9, 73, 85–9, 102–3, 113–5, 119–20, 122–4, 129–30, 133–4, 141, 143–5, 148, 154–6, 158–9, 163, 172, 178, 185–6, 193–4, 201–2, 205, 210
  Rogers Plan and, 7, 148
  roundup of 450 Palestinians by, 101–2, 122
  Syria and, 166
  Tokyo International Convention and, 31
  War of Independence (1948), 3
Israeli "nationals," 35–7, 41–2, 55–6, 61, 110, 117, 121, 127, 155–6
  search for Israeli passports and, 33, 55
  "with military status or capacity," 50, 86, 93, 102–3, 110, 121
Italy, 200, 222
Iyad, Abu (Salakh Khalaf), 4, 158, 169, 198

Jacquinet, Louis, 44, 51, 120, 124, 127, 129, 132, 135
Jadid, Gen. Salah, 166
Jankelovitz, Erna, 39
Jenkins, Loren, 34, 37
Jensen, Linda, 76
Jerosch, Horst, 117
Jeschke, Klaus, 37–8, 113, 117
Jewish hostages, 12, 33, 36–42, 48–9, 52, 55, 57–9, 66, 82, 87–8, 93, 96–100, 102, 107–9, 126–7, 133, 186, 193–4, 201–2, 230–1. *See also* religious observances
  Orthodox, 57–8, 68–9, 82, 222, 230–1
John F. Kennedy, USS (carrier), 160
Johnson, Alexis, 200
Jordan. *See also* Jordanian Arab Army; Hussein, King; *and specific areas*
  aftermath and, 233–4
  Cabinet, 95, 138, 142–4
  cease-fire ending civil war and, 201, 208–13
  Foreign Ministry, 117
  Intelligence, 6
  hijacked planes and hostages and, 13–4, 32–3, 43–4, 113–4
  history of, 3–8, 31
  map of, *171*
Jordanian Air Force, 175, 191, 194, 200
Jordanian Arab Army (JAA)
  1st Infantry Division, 150, 164
  4th Mechanized Division, 150, 164
  40th Armored Brigade, 162, 175
  60th Armored Brigade, 150, 157, 175
  fight with *fedayeen*, 5–8, 52, 53, 56, 66, 69–70, 75–6, 88, 95, 119, 127–8, 149–54, 157–9, 163–5, 168–76, 185, 191, 200, 204, 209, 211, 227
  hostages and, 26–7, 30, 32, 35, 36, 42, 94, 100, 109, 116, 121, 207–8, 210, 219, 228
Jordanian Red Crescent, 179
Joseph, Halla, 29, 50, 100, 118
Jost, Walter, 210, 213

Kahane, Meir, 225
Kamal, Dr. Ahmed, 51, 65–6, 94, 112, 118, 120, 125–6, 129, 131–2
Kennedy, John F., 185
Khalaf, Salakh. *See*, Iyad, Abu
Khaled, Leila, 17–23, 32, 36, 40–1, 52–3, 64, 96, 98, 123, 129, 134, 143, 192, 215–6, 221, 223, 228, 231–2
Kiburis, Al, 10–2, 14, 50, 64, 100, 120, 124, 152, 172, 179, 184, 192, 215, 223
Kidron, M.R., 120
Kissinger, Henry, 61, 97, 139–41, 144, 156, 159–60, 165–6, 180, 182, 187, 196, 198–9, 203, 234
Kol, Avihu, 19–20
Koning, G.H.W. de, 121

Laghi, Monsignor Pio, 128
Laird, Melvin, 61
Lebanon, 24, 72–3, 144, 169–70, 233
  soldiers held in Israel, 132, 231
Leser, Manny, 60
Leser, Millie, 39, 60, 76, 99
Leser, Miriam, 60
Levavi, Arie, 73, 85, 88–9, 102, 130, 144–5, 148, 158–9, 194, 201–2, 205

Maher, Abu, 55, 121
Majali, Habis, 138, 153, 159, 161, 172, 176, 187–8, 199
Majer, James (Jim), 1–2, 10–2, 14, 16, 30, 64, 72, 76, 79, 89, 120, 123–4, 126, 152, 169, 215, 218–9
Malka, Sarah, 49, 59, 108–9, 184, 188–9, 218
Marti, Dr. Roland, 44, 51
McCarthy, Bettie, 9–13, 45
Meir, Golda, 75, 113, 148, 156, 163–4, 181–2, 234
Meltzer, Mitchell, 90, 123
Mensch, Barbara, 108, 136–7, 195
Mensch, Martin, 135–7, 172, 195
Metzner, Rosemarie, 10
Midgley, Eric, 87, 113–4, 144, 194
Miller, David, 90, 93, 127
Mitchell, John, 61
Mokhidinov, Nurradin, 166
Moorer, Adm. Thomas, 140
Moraine, Zipporah, 54–5
Morse, Richard (Dick), 10
Muashir Hospital, 216–7, 224, 229
Munich Airport assault (1970), 32
Munich Olympics murders (1972), 234

Nasser, Gamal Abdel, 24, 158, 195, 205, 209, 213, 215, 220–1, 224–5, 227, 233–4
National Association of Evangelicals, 69
National Council of Churches, 69
National Security Council, 140
Naville, Marcel, 164, 213
Newsweek, 34, 37, 83
Newton, Jeffrey, 49, 90, 123, 126, 184
New York Times, 133, 206
Nicosia, Cyprus, 97, 116–7, 136, 219–20, 222, 230
Nimeiry, Jaafar, 195, 198, 206, 208–9, 214
Nixon, Richard, 54, 61–2, 69, 75, 113, 144, 159, 160, 163, 165–6, 180, 182, 186–7, 198–9, 204, 222–5, 234
Northern Jordan, 45, 119, 127–8, 145, 148, 154, 162, 166–7, 170, 173–7, 182–3, 185, 188, 191, 194

Odell, Jerry, 76
Oesterreicher, Monsignor John, 69
Olaimat, Mohammad, 169
Olympic Airways hijacking, 17, 32, 44, 50
Orthodox Jewish American leaders, 68–9

Packard, David, 140
Palagonia, Bob, 67, 90, 93, 111, 123, 132, 192
Palestine Liberation Army (PLA), 166–7, 174, 176, 200
Palestine Liberation Organization (PLO)
- Central Committee, 5, 8, 76, 85, 111, 143, 154
- forced out of Jordan, 233
- history of, 5–8
- fighting and, 56, 66, 75–6, 81–2, 88, 95, 119, 128, 138–9, 144, 148–50, 158–9, 162, 167, 169–70, 172, 195, 198
- negotiations and, 86, 88, 97, 101–3, 110–1, 132, 206, 208–9, 214, 231
- Planning Council, 44

Palestinian Red Crescent Society (PRCS), 26, 95–6, 98, 119, 121, 129, 157
Palestinian resistance movement (*fedayeen*), 3–8, 42, 44, 61–2, 69–70, 233. *See also specific groups*
Pan Am Flight 93, hijacked and blown up, 22–5
Paul VI, Pope, 69
Peres, Shimon, 41
Perry, Major Bob, 6
Philadelphia Hotel, 107–8, 177
Phillips, John, 36, 69, 95, 117, 153, 161–2, 164, 168, 170, 180, 183, 200, 203–5, 214, 224
Pitparo, Connie, 76
Popper, David, 136
Popular Front for the Liberation of Palestine (PFLP)
- aftermath and, 233–4
- dissension within, 4, 35, 101, 122
- hijackings and terrorist acts by, 11–7, 22–4, 31–2, 50, 71–3
- history of, 4–5
- negotiations and treatment of hostages by, 26, 30, 32–7, 40–6, 53–6, 58, 60–1, 64, 69–70, 76, 80–1, 83, 85–8, 93, 95–8, 101–3, 106, 108–13, 115, 117–8, 120–1, 124, 127–9, 132–4, 136–7, 141, 143–6, 152–3, 158, 164, 170, 178, 185–6, 188–90, 193–4, 199, 201–5, 208, 210, 213–4, 224, 228, 231
- PLO and, 86, 97, 101–3, 110–1

Popular Liberation Forces (PLF), 52
Porter, Dwight, 24
Potts, Major Fawkes, 208
Potts, Mrs., 116
Potts, Suzy, 83–5
press, 37, 55–6, 107, 111–2, 120–1, 153–4, 172, 179, 194–5, 213–4, 219, 225, 231
Priddy, Jack, 23
Purdy, Sister Donna, 69

Raab, Menachem (father), 2, 9, 77, 115–7, 137, 206, 225, 234
Raab, Moshe (brother), 2, 9, 80, 90
Raab, Noam (brother), 2, 9, 68, 76, 95

Raab, Sara (mother), 2, 9, 33, 57, 65, 68, 76, 80, 89–90, 99, 105–8, 116–7, 126, 137, 225, 234
  interrogations of, 58–9, 74–5
Raab, Tikva (sister), 2, 9, 12, 65–6
Raab, Yaron (brother), 2, 9, 76, 107
Rabin, Yitzhak, 42–3, 69, 133, 141, 162, 182–3, 185–7, 190, 196, 234
Rafael, Gideon, 56, 114–5, 119, 156
Rahamim, Mordechai, 20, 32
Ramtha, 145, 154, 162, 166–7, 170, 174–6, 185, 191, 200
Rawlinson, Peter, 41, 98
refugee camps, 3, 5. *See also specific camps*
religious observance
  articles confiscated and, 49–50
  Kiddush, 98, 99
  kosher, 29, 42, 52, 57–60, 66, 126, 162–3, 180, 184, 186, 189, 192
  prayer, 65, 79, 99
  Psalms, 65, 79–80, 126
  Rosh Hashanah, 82, 152, 229–31
  Sabbath, 98–100, 107, 164–5, 172, 214
  Shema, 79, 90
  slichot, 82, 217
  tefillin, 79, 230
  yarmulke, 49, 79, 171
Revolution Airport. *See* Dawson Field
Riad, Mohamed, 216
Rifai, Abdul Moneim, 6, 82, 113
Rifai, Zeid, 196, 210, 219
Rochat, André, 32, 44, 50–1, 53, 55, 60–1, 66, 70, 73, 76, 83, 85–8, 94, 96–8, 103, 105–6, 110, 113, 120
Rogers, William, 7, 42, 61, 114, 121–3, 148, 159, 162–4, 180, 182, 187, 203, 205, 221–2
Rogers Plan, 7, 148, 158
Ryan, Kathleen, 22

Sadat, Anwar, 224–5, 234
Saratoga, USS (carrier), 160
Saudi, Ghazi al-, 26, 129
Sayigh, Yusuf, 44
Scheel, Walter, 133
Schreiber, Fries, 207
Schwartz, Robert, 46, 82, 103, 162, 225, 230–1
Shaker, Zeid bin-, 157
Shane, Mark, 90
Sharaf, Abdul Hamir, 114
Sisco, Joseph, 56, 97, 133, 141, 155–6, 180–2, 187
Six-Day War (1967), 3–5, 29
Soloveitchik, Rabbi Joseph B., 69
Southern Baptist Convention, 69
Southern Jordan, 127, 138
Soviet Union, 61, 140, 160, 176
  Fifth Eskadra, 144, 193
  Syrian invasion of Jordan and, 165–6, 174, 180–2, 187, 191, 193–4
Spain, 200
Spanish Embassy, Amman, 154
Springfield, USS (guided missile cruiser), 160
Sudan, 195
Suttles, Derrell, 145
Swinkels, Rudi, 10, 13, 29, 35, 51, 120, 123–4, 129
Swissair
  plane blown up (February 21, 1970), 32
  threats vs., 210
Swissair Flight 100
  crew, 55, 107–8, 184
  hijacking of, 16–7, 59
  hostages, 30, 34, 39–40, 87, 96, 107, 112–3, 116–7, 185
  lands at Dawson, 72–3
  plane blown up, 109, 112
Swiss hostages, 35, 44, 112, 127, 208, 210
Switzerland, 31, 33–5, 40, 42–5, 50, 53, 67, 73, 89, 96, 97, 114, 117, 124, 130, 135, 148, 185–6, 201–2, 205, 210, 215, 221, 231–2
Syria, 3, 7, 18, 50, 52, 61, 141, 153–4, 158–60, 162, 165–6, 234
  air force, 175, 177, 194, 200
  Ba'ath Party, 166, 194
  Jordan invaded by, 165–7, 170, 173–7, 180–3, 185–8, 190–1, 194, 198–200, 203
  Soviets and, 165–6, 174

Tall, Wasfi, 138, 219, 220, 233
  assassination of, 234
terrorism, 6–7, 42–3, 233–4. *See also specific acts*
Thailand, 46
Thering, Sister Rose Albert, 69
Tokyo International Convention (1936), 31
Trans World Airlines (TWA), 13, 55, 60, 77, 121, 228–9
  earlier hijackings and, 20, 32, 130, 158
TWA Flight 741
  blown up, 16, 94, 109, 118–9
  BOAC landing and, 72
  crew of, 9–12, 14, 29, 55, 59, 63–4, 67–8, 99–100, 120–1, 123–4
  discomfort and sleep on, 28–9, 65, 76–9
  first days on ground, 25–9, 45–50
  food and water on, 9, 12, 26, 29, 32, 41–2, 49, 51–2, 57–60, 66–8, 73, 79, 81, 95, 99
  hijacked, 1–2, 9–18, 22
  hostages moved from, 99–101, 106–12, 116–7
  interrogations and, 1–2, 36–7, 45–7, 50, 55, 58–9, 74–5, 89–90

TWA Flight 741—*continued*
lands at Dawson, 13–6
luggage searches and, 48–50, 80–1, 94, 106
medical help and supplies for, 25–6, 44, 51, 54, 65–8
passing time on, 45, 65–8, 79–80
rumor of baby born on, 87
sandstorm and, 94–5
sanitary conditions on, 29, 35, 55, 57, 63–4, 68, 79, 81, 105
Shabbat on, 98–9
Swissair landing and, 17
temperatures on, 34–5, 45, 49, 55, 76–7, 94–5
threats to hostages, 50, 55
women and children on, 10, 35, 41–2, 65, 79–80, 112
Tripp, Peter, 215, 221
Tunisia, 220
Turkey, 62, 200

United Arab Republic (UAR), 220, 223–4
United Church of Christ, 69
United Jewish Appeal, 206
United Kingdom (UK, Britain)
Aliens Order, 64, 98, 123
Criminal Investigations Division (CID), 21
Foreign and Commonwealth Office (FCO), 36, 41, 43, 115, 116, 139, 155, 156, 161, 205, 231
Jordanian civil war and Hussein's request for military aid, 180–3, 186, 194, 200
Khaled and, 21–2, 35, 40–1, 52–3, 64, 98, 134, 143, 192, 223, 228
negotiations and, 21, 31, 36, 40–1, 43, 60–1, 67, 73, 85–6, 89, 96, 114–5, 117, 121–4, 129–30, 133–4, 139, 141, 143–5, 148, 154–6, 164, 185, 194–5, 201–3, 205, 210, 212–3, 215–6, 220–1, 224
Security Services, 21, 71
UK embassies
Amman, 66, 113, 152, 161, 168, 170, 173, 183, 210–1, 218, 231
Beirut, 210
UK hostages, 35–6, 112, 127, 208, 210
United Nations, 120, 133
Security Council, 88, 190
United States, 4
82nd Airborne Division, 160, 182
aftermath and, 234
Defense Department, 46, 82
Jordanian civil war and Hussein's request for aid, 138–41, 181–3, 186–7, 190, 196–200, 203
military preparations of, 55, 62, 85, 160, 182–3, 193
negotiations and, 31, 40–3, 50, 53–4, 56, 59–62, 67, 89, 97–8, 113–4, 119–20, 122–4, 127, 133–5, 141, 144–5, 148, 153–6, 163, 193–4, 201–2, 210, 215, 220–1
Sixth Fleet, 62, 97, 140, 144, 160, 182, 185, 193
State Department, 13, 46, 54–5, 77, 115–6, 127, 136, 206, 216, 231
U.S. embassies
Amman, 8, 33, 35, 44, 53–5, 66, 70, 113, 117–8, 120–1, 138, 150–2, 156, 161, 163, 168, 170, 187, 210, 218–9, 225
Bangkok, 46
Cairo, 216

Van Lierop, Robert, 136–7
Vider, Shlomo, 18–9, 21
Vorontsov, Yuli, 180

Wahdat refugee camp
fighting in, 128, 150, 164, 168, 170, 177, 204, 207, 211
hostages in, 91–3, 99, 106, 110–3, 117–8, 121, 123–7, 129, 131–2, 142, 146–7, 150, 184
Wallace, Mrs., 116
Washington Special Action Group, 140, 181, 193
water shortages, 35, 68, 152, 178–9, 187–8, 192, 207, 211
Weizman, Ezer, 177
West, David, 85
West Bank, 3, 6, 101–2, 233
Wilson, Richard, 55, 60, 87, 97, 107, 121, 129, 172
Winteler, Guy, 26
Wischnewski, Hans, 98, 117, 119
Woods, Capt. Carroll D. (TWA pilot), 10–1, 15, 55, 64, 120–1, 123–4, 212
Woods, James (hostage), 46, 82, 119, 162, 225, 228, 230–1

Yanco, Vassil, 26

Zach, Uri, 18
Zarqa
fighting in, 8, 134–5, 148
hostages in "Country Club," 47, 100–1, 104–5, 112, 118, 120–1, 123–4, 126, 145, 147–8
Zauner, Franz, 15
Zayn, Mustafa, 134, 169–70, 172, 178, 185, 189, 194, 199, 204–5, 209
Zhukov, Yuri, 193
Zionism, 4, 7, 58
Zu'ayyin, Yusuf, 166
Zurhellen, J. Owen, 119, 148
Zweifel, David Eugene, 35–6